ALOHA AMERICA

Adria L. Imada

ALOHA AMERICA

HULA CIRCUITS THROUGH THE U.S. EMPIRE

Duke University Press   Durham and London   2012

© 2012 Duke University Press

Printed in the United States of America on acid-free paper ∞

Designed by Heather Hensley

Typeset in Warnock Pro by Copperline Book Services, Inc.

Library of Congress Cataloging-in-Publication Data appear
on the last printed page of this book.

An earlier version of chapter 4 was published as "Hawaiians on Tour: Hula Circuits through the American Empire"
in *American Quarterly* 56, no. 1 (March 2004). Portions of
chapter 5 were previously published as "The Army Learns
to Luau: Imperial Hospitality and Military Photography in
Hawai'i" in *The Contemporary Pacific* 20, no. 2 (2008).

Many times I have watched the ships sail in and out
of the port of Honolulu, and many times the question
came to my mind. Who made this great world? Why are
people different? Why are there different ways of talking?
What does the world look like away from here, far away?

Victoria Nalani Kneubuhl, *The Conversion of Ka'ahumanu*

CONTENTS

NOTE ON LANGUAGE

Following modern Hawaiian orthography, I use diacritical marks—the ʻokina (marking a glottal stop) and the kahakō (a macron indicating a long vowel)—for Hawaiian-language terms (e.g., Hawaiʻi). Since ʻōlelo Hawaiʻi (Hawaiian language) and its Native epistemology are critical and foundational to this study, I do not italicize Hawaiian words, in order to avoid marking an indigenous language foreign. Words such as "Hawaiian" are English words and therefore do not require diacritical marks. Nineteenth-century and early twentieth-century Hawaiian-language sources did not employ diacritical marks, therefore I have preserved the original spelling of names and words in these documents, with the exception of prominent names that follow contemporary spelling conventions (e.g., Liliʻuokalani; Kapahukulaokamāmalu).

Additionally, I use "Hawaiians" and "Native Hawaiians" to refer to Kanaka Maoli, or the indigenous people of the Hawaiian archipelago. Signifying indigeneity, these terms do not reference Hawaiʻi as a place of residence and therefore are not equivalent to a term like "Californian."

ACKNOWLEDGMENTS

This book is the product of an island culture, as am I—a small part of a larger whole. "Aunties" and "uncles"—the hula dancers and their 'ohana who animate this study—sustained me with stories and food from Connecticut to Hawai'i: the late, beloved Aunty Betty Puanani Makia; the late Leonard "Sonny" and Janet Kalolo; Leonard "Spike" and Lynn Makia; Uncle Kulani Purdy of New Jersey and Moloka'i; Lloyd and Marilee "Mimi" Gilliom of Maui ('ohana of the late Tūtū Jennie Napua Woodd); Aunties Lei Becker Furtado, Manu Kanemura, Te Moana Makolo, and Tutasi Wilson of Honolulu; and the late Raylani Kinney Akau, Rayner Kinney, and Teela Hailele on the island of Hawai'i. Many generously lent their personal collections and photographs. Aunty Carol Mae Kuuleinani Vanderford and the late and much-missed Uncle Mervyn Thompson on O'ahu tirelessly accompanied me on research trips and field outings, saved every useful story and photograph, shared their mana'o, and unexpectedly made me their hānai. They have been my makana.

In the contemporary hula world, I owe many thanks to kumu hula Uncle Ed Collier and Hālau o Nā Pua Kukui, especially Sean Nakayama, Kamele Collier, Kili Valmoja, Kekai Valmoja, Landon Patoc, Travis Dang, Devynne Sue, Dalton Sue, Ellarene Sue, and family, and cousin Ross Yamamoto for welcoming a newcomer to the hālau during its most intensive and sensitive training before the Merrie Monarch Festival competition. Uncle Ed willingly shared his wisdom with me, another youngster 'ono for knowledge. I also thank nā kumu hula Kekaimoku Yoshikawa and Vicky Holt Takamine for their aloha. My hula sister Gena Dutro and hula brother Blaine Ikaika Dutro have supported me from my early hemahema steps in hula for many years. While I tended to approach hula through language (asking at practice, "How low should the kaʻō go? Are our hands at a forty-five degree angle?"), they always move with feeling.

Far from the Pacific, my undergraduate advisers at Yale American Studies, Michael Denning and Laura Wexler, encouraged my first research project on Hawaiʻi. New York University's American Studies Program was an engaging place to develop as a scholar. Lisa Duggan, Faye Ginsburg, and Robin D. G. Kelley have been exceptional, passionate mentors. Alondra Nelson, Thuy Linh Nguyen Tu, and Tanya Erzen taught me much through their own interests, always with élan, style, and good humor. Jack Kuo Wei Tchen, Risa Morimoto, and the NYU Asian/Pacific/ American Studies Program provided a collegial environment in which to work, develop collaborative research, and teach. Faye Ginsburg and my cohort in the NYU Program in Culture and Media enabled me to think deeply about visuality and produce a documentary about Aunty Betty Makia. My adviser Andrew Ross asked the hardest and most generous questions that pushed me to refine my ideas and thinking at every stage. I am enormously grateful for his capacious intellect, unflagging dedication, and friendship.

The NYU Graduate School of Arts and Sciences, the Hawaiʻi Council for the Humanities, the Smithsonian Institution National Museum of American History and National Museum of Natural History Predoctoral Fellowship, the NYU Dean's Dissertation Fellowship, and the American Association of University Women Dissertation Fellowship supported my graduate education and dissertation research. Grants from the University of Oregon's Center for the Study of Women in Society, the UC San Diego Academic Senate, and the Hellman Fellowship provided me with critical time and resources to continue fieldwork in Hawaiʻi. A University of California President's Postdoctoral Fellowship at the University of California, Los Angeles, in the Asian American studies and history departments and the Huntington Library's Barbara Thom Postdoctoral Fellowship gave me space and time to refine my research. Henry Yu at UCLA; Rayna Green and Adrienne Kaeppler at the Smithsonian; and Roy Ritchie at the Huntington Library were invaluable interlocutors during fellowships at their institutions.

Dedicated archivists and librarians at the Hawaiʻi State Archives, Bishop Museum, the University of Hawaiʻi, Mānoa, and the Smithsonian Institution's National Museum of American History Archives Center made many years of archival research enjoyable and rewarding. I am especially grateful to James Cartwright of University of Hawai'i, Mānoa, and Charles Myers of Bishop Museum for facilitating the use of their institutions' important photograph collections.

The Center for Pacific Islands Studies and the Center for Hawaiian Studies at the University of Hawai'i, Mānoa; Harvard University's symposium on imperialism and capitalism in U.S. history; the Department of American Studies and Humanities Institute at the University of California, Davis; and the University of Southern California's Department of American Studies and Ethnicity gave me opportunities to present my work in progress. The ladies of Hui Ko'ae Kea, especially Aunty Hale Rowland, organized a public lecture in Honolulu that serendipitously reunited many former dancers from the U.S. hula circuit.

Ethnic studies departments at the University of Oregon and the University of California, San Diego, have been rewarding intellectual spaces in which to teach and learn. In particular, I thank Brian Klopotek, Shari Huhndorf, Lamia Karim, and the late Peggy Pascoe at the University of Oregon. Yen Le Espiritu, Ross Frank, Roberto Alvarez, Lisa Lowe, Curtis Marez, Natalia Molina, K. Wayne Yang, and David Serlin at UC San Diego encouraged the development of this book. George Lipsitz and I have not had the opportunity to work at the same institution, but his exceptional generosity, challenging but caring feedback, and timely advice have improved this book—and my survival in this sometimes prickly profession—immeasurably.

For their friendship and intellectual engagement, I thank J. Kēhaulani Kauanui, Teresia K. Teaiwa, Vicente M. Diaz, Terence Wesley-Smith, Julie Y. Chu, Grace Wang, and Isaac Moriwake. Kaleikoa Ka'eo, organic intellectual extraordinaire, and classmates in our papa 'ōlelo Hawai'i at University of Hawai'i, Mānoa's night school, have inspired through their mana'o and example. Lisa Sun-Hee Park, David Naguib Pellow, Kim Gilmore, and Julie Sze have pulled me through with laughter and care from points near and far. Cynthia Tolentino, brilliant friend and coconspirator, offered many meticulous readings of the manuscript over dumplings and cake, and encouraged me to think deeply and broadly. Loren Petrowski, Natalie Choi, Beth Derby, Sunyoung Lee, Jen Sung, Kathy Farkas, Steph Christensen, and the late Gordon Kato have been an unflagging network of support and goodwill. I am especially grateful to Matthew Uiagalelei who has always gone beyond the bounds of friendship, pushing me to write about the place where we both grew up. In many ways, this book was inspired by our conversations.

Suzanna Reiss, Mireille Miller-Young, Priya Srinivasan, Rachel St. John, Laura Harris, Rachel Mattson, Betsy Esch, John Troutman, Letitia Hickson, Noelani Arista, Puakea Nogelmeier, Ralph Lalepa Koga, Naomi Losch, and the late Natalie Bimel lent their enthusiasm to this research. Aunty Pat Namaka Bacon answered crucial inquiries about hula in the twentieth century. Victoria Nalani Kneubuhl graciously allowed the use of her evocative play, *The Conversion of Ka'ahumanu*, for the epigraph. In the latter stages of the project, Traci Voyles provided careful microfilm research assistance. I also wish to acknowledge Amy Ku'uleialoha Stillman and her generative research on hula, which has paved the way for my research and that of other scholars. I am further grateful to two readers who provided thoughtful and detailed suggestions that strengthened the book in innumerable ways. Ken Wissoker and Jade Brooks at Duke University Press expertly shepherded my manuscript from start to finish; mahalo for your care.

Though I chose a path that led me both closer to and further from home, my family has supported me without reservation. My parents, Warren and Dorothy Imada, welcomed me back to Honolulu during frequent and disruptive research trips, provided transportation, collected news articles, and sent care packages. With enthusiasm, they have shared my progress along the way. My extended family in Hawai'i, especially Aunty Jeanette Yamanaka, nourished me with stories and all manner of local delicacies during each trip back home. My grandparents Harry Setsuo and Lillian Kiyoka Eto passed away before I finished graduate school. As second-generation immigrants on Hawai'i plantations, their education came to a halt in elementary school. Remembering their meticulous penmanship, I credit them for supporting my schooling. My sister, Marcy Imada; my brother-in-law, Stacy Toyama; and Kenneth and Terue Mimura in Los Angeles have stepped in with meals, extra hands, and advice when I have most needed it.

Above all, I am luckiest to share a life with the sharpest mind and wit, Glen Mimura. He has read every word I've written and influenced the theoretical interventions of this book, while making me laugh every day. Naia came dancing into our lives late in the writing of this book. She is already a better dancer than her mother; may she become a better writer.

Many hula dancers say that it is their lifelong dream to appear in the Merrie Monarch Hula Festival or, better yet, to win a trophy at the world-renowned hula competition named in honor of King David Kalākaua, the nineteenth-century patron of traditional Hawaiian arts. Since 1971, this prestigious hula showcase has taken place at the Edith Kanaka'ole Stadium in the town of Hilo, Hawai'i. I accompanied the hula troupe Hālau o Nā Pua Kukui and its kumu hula (hula master), Ed Collier, as they prepared for the competition in 2006. Several months of intensive practice culminates in three nights of hula before a panel of judges, cheering sellout crowds, and live television cameras. Hālau hula (hula troupes) must be invited to participate, and each year twenty or more vie for recognition as the best in competitive hula.

During the week of competition, I bunked with the hālau's women dancers in a cabin a few miles away from Kīlauea Volcano. The backstage rhythms and preparations—the ironing of costumes, gossiping, the making of flower lei—were familiar to me because I had danced in smaller Honolulu competitions in the 1990s. While setting their hair in braids and curlers for that evening's performances, the dancers, whose ages ranged from midteens to midthirties, turned on the MTV reality show *My Super Sweet Sixteen*. In each episode, a girl and her family spend fortunes on sixteenth-birthday celebrations. The Merrie Monarch hula competition is a more modest and culturally specific version of this rite of passage, but many dancers and their families approach the contest with similar once-in-a-lifetime fervor, investing time and resources in this public display.[1]

Watching the TV birthday girl squeal as she received a new Lexus,

Fig. 1 Kamele Collier on stage at Merrie Monarch Festival, 2006.
PHOTOGRAPH BY DALTON SUE.

Kamele Collier, the senior member of the troupe, remarked, "This reminds me of the Princess of Brunei. Janet Jackson did a concert for her birthday." I asked Kamele where she had seen the princess's birthday party and she replied casually, "Oh, I danced hula for her in Brunei. We did a show right before Janet Jackson." As Kamele explained, the princess had invited her and nineteen other dancers from Hawai'i to give a half-hour performance in 1998. They were flown first class into the oil-rich sultanate, chauffeured in Mercedes limousines for two weeks, paid handsomely, and each given a diamond and sapphire–encrusted watch as a token of gratitude. Although Kamele intended to emphasize the Brunei princess's access to extraordinary wealth, she also revealed her own worldly experience afforded by hula. During and shortly after high school, Kamele danced hula in several U.S. states, New Zealand, Samoa, Tahiti, Germany, Wales, Switzerland, and France. She later joined two large shows in Waikīkī as a professional dancer, where she was responsible for choreographing hula and Polynesian dances, and performed as a solo dancer at a four-star resort. A mother of two, Kamele now serves as one of the leaders of her father's hālau (see figure 1).[2]

Fig. 2. Hālau o Nā Pua Kukui's Miss Aloha Hula contestant, Aisha Kilikina Kanoelani Valmoja with kumu hula Ed Collier, Merrie Monarch Festival, 2006. PHOTOGRAPH BY DALTON SUE.

Kamele's younger hula sisters in the troupe have also benefited from the soaring global interest in hula.[3] They perform abroad frequently in Japan, where hula has become a passionate avocation and multimillion-dollar industry. While sharing a bathroom with the girls, I noticed how the counters were lined with new beauty products—moisturizers, hair creams, makeup removers—sold only in Japan. They had purchased these modest luxuries while dancing on all-expense-paid trips. On the strength of their teacher's reputation and appearances in the Merrie Monarch festival, the young dancers of Hālau o Nā Pua Kukui fly to Japan a few times a year to perform hula at festivals and workshops and are treated as VIPS.[4]

Winners at this prestigious festival do not receive cash prizes but status and public validation, which usually result in increased student enrollment for a hālau and invitations to participate in hula festivals abroad. The hālau's Miss Aloha Hula contestant for 2006 in the female soloist category, Aisha Kilikina Kanoelani Valmoja (see figure 2), was featured on the cover of the Japanese magazine *Hula Heaven* during her competition preparation. *Hula Heaven* is but one of several glossy, photograph-rich publications in Japan dedicated to "hula and Hawaiian style." Kumu hula, whose hālau have consistently placed at the Merrie Monarch festival, have opened up profitable affiliate schools in Japan. Dancers whisper that a handful of kumu hula can earn $300 an hour teaching hula and up to $20,000 for a few weeks of work there; some return to Hawai'i with stacks of yen in their suitcases. These glimpses reveal the occasional material enhancements that young Kanaka Maoli (Native Hawaiian) and islander women gain via globalized hula circuits.[5] Hula is a potent cultural and economic opportunity structure in which women earn cultural capital and, occasionally, even a living wage, while charting their own desires for fashion, beauty, and travel.[6] Some dancers are able to turn hula into full- or part-time professions, without a college education or other formal credentials.[7]

Hula and Hawai'i have become nearly synonymous in the global cultural imaginary, bringing opportunity and challenges to Hawaiian women such as Kamele Collier. United Airlines has advertised its Hawai'i airfares as a "Honolulu Hula Sale" with an illustration of a dancer in a lā'ī (ti leaf) skirt.[8] Tourists are greeted in airports and hotel lobbies with photographs of hula dancers on luau brochures. From nineteenth-century descriptions of blasphemous hula dancers to present-day advertisements published by the Hawai'i Visitors and Convention Bureau that regularly include silhouettes of hula dancers, Hawai'i has been personified through the figure of the female dancer during more than a century of American colonization. More so than any other cultural or ethnographic artifact, the gendered hula dancer—or as she is known more familiarly in Americana, the "hula girl"—has come to represent Hawai'i. How and why hula performers have become such material and symbolic embodiments of Hawai'i are the focus of this book.

Like Kamele Collier and her hula sisters, previous generations of hula practitioners have had to negotiate the commodification of their bodies and art as hula took them in unexpected directions outside of the islands. Over a century ago, the first organized hula tour of Hawaiian po'e hula (hula practitioners) crossed the Pacific and Atlantic. A woman named Kini Kapahukulaokamāmalu (later known as Mrs. Jennie Wilson), one of the central historical figures of this study, left Hawai'i to tour North America and Europe shortly before the American-backed overthrow of the Hawaiian kingdom in 1893. Po'e hula, such as Kini, became highly visible, commodified objects for Euro-American audiences at world's fairs, vaudeville theaters, commercial nightclubs, and military bases. As Hawai'i's political and economic entanglements with the United States intensified during and after the overthrow of the Hawaiian government, so did the exhibition of Hawaiian cultural practices in the U.S. empire. Tours of hula outside the islands proliferated as the United States established political control over Hawai'i.

Aloha America examines U.S. imperial interests in Hawai'i through the circulation of hula. Hawaiians became legible and largely desirable to Americans through what I term "hula circuits"—popular tours of hula performers that crisscrossed both the Atlantic and Pacific, performing for largely Euro-American audiences in Western metropolitan centers, rural outposts, and small towns. Beginning in the late nineteenth century and peaking in the late 1950s, these hula circuits brought scores of Hawaiian men and women to the continental United States and Europe, but primarily staged the bodies and performances of Hawaiian women.[9] Hawai'i became familiar and assimilable to American audiences through the alluring female bodies those spectators saw circulating on the continent. Commodified Hawaiian culture—the "luau," the "hula girl," and "aloha"—became part of the American vernacular and everyday life.

The United States emerged as a colonial power with insular colonies and territories in the wake of the Spanish-American War in 1898. Hawai'i was the only overseas territory to become a U.S. state. Guam, Puerto Rico, Samoa, and the Philippines remained unincorporated territories and Cuba a semi-independent protectorate, all lacking the legal possibility of incorporation.[10] Yet it was by no means a foregone conclusion that Hawai'i would achieve annexation in 1898, status as an incorporated territory in 1900, and statehood in 1959.[11] Annexation was fiercely debated in the U.S. Senate and popular press after the U.S.-backed overthrow of the Hawaiian kingdom. The debate largely centered on whether the islands and their racially suspect inhabitants were worthy of the privileges of American citizenship. Who and what were Hawaiians? Stoked by fears of racially suspect "mongrel" and "Asiatic" populations, Americans were deeply divided about whether to admit Hawai'i to the United States.

Those who opposed and those who favored annexation issued opinions that took on a decidedly racist valence. A Chicago newspaper advocating annexation wanted universal suffrage withheld from Hawai'i on account of its racial character. The newspaper editorialized, "It would not do to admit Hawaii as a State, unless the character of the population underwent radical change."[12] These suspicions erupted throughout the twentieth century; in the 1930s questions arose about whether Hawai'i even deserved territorial status, and after World War II, Southern senators argued that Hawai'i harbored too many Asians.[13] Given this ambivalence, how did Hawai'i become legible and domesticated enough to be admitted into the union in 1959 by overwhelming congressional majority? Why did Hawai'i become a politically and culturally integral part of the United States? What assured Americans that Hawai'i would likely become "an American community" after annexation, as one writer confidently proclaimed?[14]

In practical terms, the United States enjoyed informal influence via white settlement in Hawai'i for nearly a century before it effected formal colonization. The existence of a haole (white) ruling class and extensive capital investment prior to American political interventions made Hawai'i distinct from other U.S. colonies and quasiprotectorates. Since their arrival in 1820, American missionaries had been increasing their political and economic control, reforming traditional land tenure, assuming power in kingdom cabinets, and industrializing agriculture. Descendants of these missionaries orchestrated the overthrow of the Hawaiian kingdom and ruled Hawai'i through large corporate trusts.

While long-standing settler colonialism and Hawai'i's military and strategic importance in the North Pacific cannot be underestimated, this book begins with a different premise: the popular cultural phenomenon of hula also helped to broker this process of incorporation and integration. I seek to reveal how the colonial relationship between the United States and Hawai'i has been constituted and intensified by cultural displays of hula since the U.S.-backed overthrow of the Hawaiian kingdom. For although colonialism has been understood and analyzed as a series of related political and economic processes and as the consolidation of political and economic interests, they are also deeply cultural projects.[15] As Nicholas Thomas writes, "Colonial cultures are not simply ideologies that mask, mystify or rationalize forms of oppression that are external to them; they are also expressive and constitutive of colonial relationships in themselves."[16]

Although this is not a study of the colonization of Hawai'i by the United States, I bring American imperialism and Hawaiian popular cultural practices into the same arena to deliberate on hula within a larger context of the political and economic incorporation of Hawai'i. Hula did not win uniform praise—indeed, it was excoriated at times as a barbaric practice—but live hula performances in the continental United States began a process of marking Hawai'i as an eroticized and feminized space, a space disposed to political, military, and tourist penetration. The staged hula in embodied, mediated, and discursive forms, I suggest, has made islander bodies available for the labor of leisure and translated Hawai'i into a safe sanctuary for the nation.

Hawai'i's colonial incorporation into the United States—the transformation of the islands from quasicolony, to U.S.-oriented republic, to territory, to the fiftieth state—has been a fraught and contested process. Occasionally Hawai'i becomes unfamiliar or jarring in the American imaginary. It can be treated as a "foreign, exotic place," as occurred in 2008, when Cokie Roberts, a National Public Radio senior news analyst, criticized Barack Obama, then a candidate for the presidency, for vacationing in Hawai'i, his birthplace and childhood home.[17] However, while Roberts was not alone in her assessment of the fiftieth state as an alien outpost, she was roundly berated for her ignorance by journalists, political pundits, and bloggers who claimed Hawai'i was a legitimate, albeit tropical, state.[18]

Hawai'i has indeed become a familiar domestic destination for Americans, with nearly 4.5 million tourists arriving each year from the continent.[19] Jet airlines made travel more affordable and accessible to Americans by the mid-twentieth century. Since then, the hallmark of middle-class status in the United States has been the honeymoon or family vacation to Hawai'i. Whereas the highbrow variant of American tourist consumption may have been Paris or Europe in the twentieth century, Hawai'i is a decidedly middlebrow, banal destination for outsiders. This was represented perhaps most emblematically by the quintessential American family, the Brady Bunch, exploring the islands during three television episodes broadcast in 1972.[20] How did Hawai'i enter this American orbit of leisure and repose to become a taken-for-granted domestic experience?

Aloha as Imperial Metaphor

In a little more than seventy years, American interventions transformed Hawai'i from an independent kingdom to the fiftieth state of the union. In the nineteenth century a succession of Native chiefly monarchs ruled Hawai'i but increasingly found their authority eroded by American missionaries and foreign businessmen in the islands. As early as 1854, the Hawaiian government began negotiating a reciprocity treaty with the United States that would permit Hawaiian sugar duty-free into U.S. markets. In exchange, the United States sought exclusive use of Pearl Harbor, the only natural harbor in the North Pacific, for a naval and fueling station, which the Hawaiian monarchy conceded in 1887 under threat of force by a militia of white settler businessmen.[21] The kingdom of Hawai'i ultimately paid an enormous price for this economic dispensation: loss of autonomy and eventual incorporation into America's Pacific empire.

By the 1880s, Western settlers and sugar planters in the islands sought Hawai'i's annexation to the United States in order to obtain favorable domestic status. For its own part, the United States was interested in obtaining a secure and permanent commercial and military foothold in the Pacific. In 1893, a group of haole businessmen and missionary descendants in the islands conspired to overthrow the Hawaiian kingdom with the help of U.S. marines. American marines landed in Honolulu Harbor, took control of government buildings, and effectively held Queen Lili'uokalani and her cabinet hostage. The queen at first refused to surrender to the conspirators, but to avoid bloodshed Lili'uokalani temporarily relinquished her crown under protest to the U.S. minister in Hawai'i on January 17, 1893.[22]

In the midst of its lengthy sugar tariff negotiations with the United States in the 1870s, the Kingdom of Hawai'i made its first appearance at a U.S. world's fair. During the Philadelphia Centennial Exposition in 1876, the reciprocity treaty was signed, making Hawai'i a virtual protectorate of the United States. A large sign reading "Aloha America" hung above Hawai'i's exhibit. Hula was not staged at this international exposition as it would be fewer than twenty years later, but the sentiment behind this greeting suggests Hawai'i's position as supplicant to its future colonizer.[23] "Aloha America" may be translated simply as "Hello, America" or "Greetings, America." It also serves as a summation of the colonial experience in Hawai'i. "Aloha America" manages to communicate the ambivalent yet intimate relationship Hawai'i has had with the United States over the last century. Consider the meaning of "aloha," possibly the most overdetermined Hawaiian word that has entered the English lexicon. "Aloha" is commonly used to say hello and good-bye, but it is also a highly contextual expression that may encompass love, sympathy, pity, joy, compassion, affection, veneration, and mercy.[24]

Hawaiians past and present have defined themselves through aloha, sustaining intimate bonds with family, friends (pili aloha), land (aloha 'āina), and guests with what Reverend Akaiko Akaka called "the very kernel of Hawaiian ethics, the very core of the Hawaiian life."[25] Another kupuna (elder) and mānaleo (native speaker of Hawaiian), Ralph Ka'ōnohiokalā Alapa'i explained in the 1980s, "Aloha is the spiritual essence of the tangible self, that gave you and me the breath of life."[26] The contemporary Kanaka Maoli educator and philosopher Manulani Aluli

Meyer declares aloha "our intelligence," borrowing from kumu hula Olana Ai.[27] Meyer elaborates, "Aloha is the life force found in our [Native Hawaiian] na'au [gut], the place where intelligence thrives."[28]

Yet, while aloha nourished Hawaiian self-regard and vitality, particular aspects of aloha were crudely instrumentalized and appropriated in colonial relations and discourse. Imagined and deployed as mutuality, intimacy, and hospitality, aloha has managed to mask U.S. imperial expansion in Hawai'i, providing an illuminating metaphor for U.S.-Hawai'i relations over the past century. Rather than being seen as violent and aggressive, colonial encounters between Hawaiians and Americans were frequently imagined as points of intimate contact, with Hawaiians freely giving aloha to Americans, and Americans eagerly accepting these gifts of hospitality. In one emblematic example, the celebratory illustrated book *Our Islands and Their People* introduced America's new acquisitions following its victory in 1898 in the Spanish-American War. It was one of dozens of popular illustrated books produced about the "new possessions" of the United States.[29] This passage describes Hawai'i's "boundless hospitality," a hospitality so frequently invoked that it became a common refrain: "The very words which a native uses in addressing a stranger indicate the character of the race—*Aloha nei*, the first meaning 'great gratification' and the latter, 'my country, myself, everything that I have is yours.' And they meant it, for it was their custom while in a state of paganism to surrender their grass huts and even their wives to the full and free gratification of strangers who visited them."[30]

In this florid narrative, the writer conjures an imperial fantasy of aloha in which Hawaiians, here gendered as male, naturally gave away everything they esteemed. The typical Hawaiians who emerged in these American accounts were "ideal communists" who shared and "can not do too much to manifest their good-will and desire for your comfort."[31] Figured as the inevitable outcome of Hawaiian hospitality toward outsiders, the American colonization of Hawai'i's land and people assumed a benign cast.

Unlike the massive armed military takeover of the Philippines by the United States, which prompted protracted battles between Filipino and American forces at the turn of the century, or the U.S. military conquest over Native America, Americans perceived the colonization of Hawai'i as relatively peaceful.[32] Hawaiians did not mount military uprisings, with the exception of an armed rebellion in 1895.[33] Their organized resistance to colonization and annexation materialized in the form of petition campaigns that defeated a U.S. annexation treaty in 1897. Historiography produced in the islands and the metropole further reified this passive narrative and naturalized Hawai'i's colonial status within the U.S. nation-state. In these narratives, colonization and military occupation was achieved with the tacit, if not willing, consent of Native Hawaiian and local populations.[34] Indeed the violence of U.S. imperial relations—the decimation and dispossession of the Native population, relentless suppression of Hawaiian language and cultural practices, imposition of a racist social and economic order, disfranchisement of Asian immigrants in the colony—was largely disguised until the emergence of the Hawaiian cultural renaissance and sovereignty movements in the 1960s and 1970s.

Empire as a "way of life" in the islands remains visible yet nearly unspeakable even today, manifesting itself as the most "militouristic" zone of the United States.[35] As described by Teresia K. Teaiwa, militourism is a "phenomenon by which military or paramilitary force ensures the smooth running of a tourist industry, and that same tourist industry masks the military force behind it."[36] Tourism and the military are inextricable and symbiotic forces in the islands: tourism is the state's largest industry, followed closely by U.S. Department of Defense spending.[37] What makes American empire in the islands so difficult to assess and repudiate is that it was and continues to be interpreted as a consequence of aloha. Aloha functions as a shorthand and brand for the islands today. "The Islands of Aloha" is an advertising slogan and registered trademark of the Hawai'i state tourist bureau.[38] Tourists and military personnel are exhorted to "discover aloha" during their "R & R" in the islands, and islanders are encouraged to contribute aloha to this hospitality industry.[39]

While aloha is a commodified product and service—the hospitality and love of Hawaiian people packaged and sold by a multinational, state-sponsored tourist industry—it is nevertheless insistently referred to as something elusive and noncorporeal: a "spirit," a "warmth," an "unseen force."[40] Hawai'i, like other tourist destinations, has been crippled by the global economic recession. The tourist industry hit a "crisis mode" in 2009, with visitor arrivals declining for nearly a year and hotel occupancy scraping record lows.[41] With its centrality to the wavering tourist economy in the islands, Native Hawaiian culture and its stewards—living Kanaka Maoli—remain a nexus of anxiety in the islands. More than ever, Hawai'i tourism must rely on the literal and performative aloha of Hawaiian cultural practitioners, especially hula performers, to compete as a "special and unique visitor destination."[42] For their part, hula performers must also rely to an uncomfortable degree on state tourism. This uneasy yet mutually dependent relationship between hula and tourism has developed over a century.

Aloha has been incorporated into an imperial repertoire, naturalizing colonization as benign, mutual, and consensual. Hula practitioners have performed and staged imperial scripts of aloha since the nineteenth century. For Americans consuming these performances, hula was neither an outgrowth of American expansionism nor a form of colonial labor, but a gift of aloha freely proffered, with no expectation of return. Live hula circuits established what I call an "imagined intimacy" between the United States and Hawai'i, a potent fantasy that enabled Americans to possess their island colony physically and figuratively. In this imperial fantasy, the United States and Hawai'i were figured as inseparable companions: Hawaiians as supplicants and Americans as guests. This interpretation allowed Americans to cast their relationship with the colony as benevolent and affectionate, without disrupting a colonial hierarchy. Hula performances dangled the promise of intimacy between Hawaiians and Americans, animating an imperial metaphor of aloha or love.[43] By metaphors of aloha, I mean that interactions between U.S. colonial institutions and Hawaiian subjects were not framed as a conflict with foreign bodies, but were experienced through affective metaphors of integration, assimilation, and submission. The stagecraft of imperial hospitality eroded the distinction between conquest and consent as it insisted on affective bonds between colonizer and colonized.

Encompassing chanted poetry and bodily movements, hula has provided a kinesthetic repertoire of Kanaka Maoli history, politics, and social life. Prior to Western contact and continuing through the late nineteenth century, hula was a highly venerated, selective, and restricted form of religious and political praxis. Its practitioners were guardians of Native historiography, cosmogony, and genealogies, undergoing ritualized training to reproduce and transmit knowledge for high-ranking chiefs. Some religious forms of hula honored akua (gods), having survived the repression of Christian missionaries who arrived in 1820. Spanning the sacred and secular, hula also provided entertainment for both chiefs and commoners. As late as the 1880s, hula was resurrected and enshrined by the Hawaiian monarchy as an anti-imperial, state-sponsored form of national revival in defiance of haole missionary settlers.

The earliest hula practitioners to perform abroad had been trained within this ritualized hula system. However, hula became imperial tableaux on Euro-American tourist circuits as po'e hula—particularly women— were recruited and cast as passive and subordinate fetishes. Sensational- ized as a transgressive dance performed by sexualized Hawaiian women, hula became visible on American stages around the time of the U.S.- backed overthrow in 1893. The same year of the overthrow, journalists de- scribed the practice as "the seductive hula hula passion dance," one whose "motive [was] grossly sensual."[44] Although most Hawaiians regarded hula as an embodied practice animating the genealogies of gods and chiefs, new American audiences came to associate the kinesthetic movements of Hawaiian bodies with the erotic pleasures of a new colony.

An Empire and Its Women

Imperial conquest has been complicated and secured by gendered and sexual subjugation. In *Orientalism*, Edward Said forcefully established the relationship between sexualized discursive formations and imperial dominion. Through its invention of a feminized and indolent "Orient," Europe was able to establish control over this new knowable object. The eroticization of Pacific women and the imperial possession of Oceania during the age of European discovery have been astutely connected by Bernard Smith.[45] The Pacific was made "pacific" through the aestheticiza- tion of its women, who were exposed quite literally in Western portrai- ture as beautiful and sexually available. Smith suggests that the image of the tempting Pacific woman made the entire Pacific "young, feminine, desirable and vulnerable, an ocean of desire."[46] In another settler-colonial context, that of the U.S. Southwest, the metonymic, enduring image of the "olla" maiden, a Pueblo woman carrying a pot on her head, personified the region. These picturesque images, Barbara A. Babcock has suggested, turned these Native women into "vessels of desire" and enabled gendered control over the region.[47]

Hawai'i was also subjected to gendered and sexualized conquest through regimes of representation. Within the imperial knowledge- production of the developing U.S. empire, Hawaiian women bore much symbolic weight. As ambassadors of aloha, Hawaiian women have been susceptible to the eroticization of their bodies and the insistent commod- ification of their aloha. If the imagined Orient was feminine and sexually alluring, the putatively primitive Hawai'i was similarly feminine and sen- sual, but also simpler and less civilized.[48] From their first appearance in the Western historical record, Hawaiian women have been represented as eagerly offering their sexual gifts, as Captain James Cook and his officers portrayed them enticing British sailors during his 1778 and 1779 landings in Hawai'i.[49] In the late nineteenth century, when the United States was preparing to administer its new imperial archipelago, representations of women and, to a lesser extent, children from Puerto Rico, the Philippines, Cuba, and Hawai'i were analyzed and compared by administrators in order to establish protocols and strategies for rule, as Lanny Thompson has examined. In the case of Hawai'i, narrative and visual representations of "exotic, beautiful" Hawaiian women residing in a civilized paradise produced material effects: a "logic of imperial rule" that swayed toward territorial government, as opposed to imperial government or protectorate status.[50]

These alluring Hawaiian women were often conflated with hula dancers in fin de siècle print culture, depicted with signifiers of hula such as flower lei and leaf skirts. Both men and women performed hula, but Hawaiian women were spectacularized on colonial stages and became metonyms for the nation of Hawai'i. Hawaiian women thus bore the responsibility of reproducing national knowledge for their people as they were commodified within U.S. tourist economies. As Partha Chatterjee discusses, during colonial struggles women are expected to be sanctuaries for the nation and receive protection from the perversion of the colonizing culture.[51] Like other colonized or postcolonial women, Hawaiian women can be both potential contaminants *and* virtuous refuges, signifying the moral corruption or rapturous beauty of Kanaka Maoli. Po'e hula have the privilege and burden of serving as the spiritual essence of their nation while representing the islands to outsiders.

Because it was and continues to be associated closely with Hawaiian women and their bodies, hula has met with both vitriolic criticism and passionate approval by missionaries, colonial settlers, tourists, and Hawaiian nationalists. Hula practitioners have danced on the fringes of respectability and been criticized for commodifying their bodies and cultural practices. Historically, the distinction between sex work and Hawaiian cultural performance has been very porous, with hula often being used as a proxy in popular and juridical discourses about sexual commerce and tourist commerce. Hula has been conflated with literal forms of prostitution—the performance of sexual acts in exchange for money—and metaphorical cultural prostitution, such as the sale of cultural patrimony to tourists. Indeed, soon after their arrival in 1820, Calvinist missionaries pressured ali'i (chiefs) to ban hula performances, with some alleging that prostitutes practiced hula.[52] These prohibitions forced hula underground and to remote areas of the islands.[53] Almost a century after the first missionary-led interdictions, hula retained its lascivious reputation. A Hawaiian woman identified only as "Madame Puahi" ignited scandal when she sought a license to give commercial hula performances in her Waikīkī home in 1913. The city sheriff, civic groups, and building inspectors alike tried to deny her the license, on the grounds that "lewd women" frequented the site.[54]

Women performing acculturated forms of hula for tourists—that is, hula performed with Western instrumentation—frequently receive harsh scrutiny and suspicion. Nathaniel B. Emerson, the Hawaiʻi-born ethnographer and missionary son, undertook a salvage ethnography of the ancient religious dances and poetry he fretted were being defiled by the tourist trade. The resulting study, *Unwritten Literature of Hawaii: The Sacred Songs of the Hula* (1909), became the definitive, edifying treatment of hula in the greater part of the twentieth century.[55] In it, Emerson opined about the regression of hula: "An institution of divine, that is, religious, origin, the hula in modern times has wandered so far and fallen so low that foreign and critical esteem has come to associate it with the riotous and passionate ebullitions of Polynesian kings and the amorous posturings of their voluptuaries."[56]

Not surprisingly, dancers performing on the tourist hula circuit were roundly rebuked by some members of their own communities. One of the central actors in this book, Kini Kapahukulaokamāmalu, returned to Hawaiʻi in 1896 after performing in Europe and North America. Hawaiians shunned her, saying, "You go to mainland and dance the hula—you disgrace the Hawaiians. You disgrace yourself. I don't want to talk with you."[57] In the 1950s, dancer Teela Hailele Holt received similar treatment. She remembered, "I wouldn't dance at home. People would be too critical, saying we used to dance for haoles. When I came home, I was embarrassed."[58] More recently, some who teach hula to nonislanders have been accused of corrupting the practice. The hula matriarch Paulie Jennings endured criticism for "selling hula out to foreigners" when she founded the hula competition E Hoʻi Mai Ka Piko (Return to the Source), also known as the World Invitational Hula Festival. Seeking to share hula, the nonprofit festival invites dancers from outside Hawaiʻi, including ones from Latin America and Asia, to learn and perform in Hawaiʻi. This has led some Hawaiʻi-based hālau hula (hula troupes) to boycott the festival.[59]

With the rise of decolonization and Native rights movements, hula performers can be seen as anathema to these political goals. Haunani-

Kay Trask, a scholar and Hawaiian sovereignty activist, has argued that Hawaiians who perform for tourists are prostituting their culture. They allow themselves to be exploited because they have been colonized: "Tourism is viewed as providing jobs, not as a form of cultural prostitution. Even those who have some glimmer of critical consciousness do not generally agree that the tourist industry prostitutes Hawaiian culture. This is a measure of our own mental oppression. . . . As colonized people, we are colonized to the extent that we are unaware of our oppression."[60] As a tourist commodity, hula seems inauthentic and fake, conveniently serving the needs of the neocolonial, multinational corporate tourist industry. Trask allegorizes Hawaiian dancers in order to draw attention to the material exploitation of Hawaiians by a neocolonial state. In her structural critique of tourism, performers remain shadowy abstractions, shorthands for exploitation suffered under colonialism.

In keeping with this skepticism of commodified bodies and knowledge, the movement for Hawaiian sovereignty and self-determination usually cites its origins in 1970s struggles over land development and evictions in such communities as Kalama Valley, Halawa, Ota Camp, Waimānalo, Waikāne-Waiāhole, Niumalu-Nāwiliwili, Mokauea, and Sand Island.[61] The reclamation of the island of Kahoʻolawe, which had been used for U.S. naval testing since 1941, also spurred Hawaiian anticolonial political formations.[62] Hula—and tourist hula in particular—is not considered an essential element of the movement's genealogy. While I concur that more visible and lauded aspects of land struggles were significant developments for the twentieth-century Hawaiian nationalist movement, I also weave hula and cultural practices into this genealogy in order to historicize lesser-known but vital connections between a range of commodified and noncommodified cultural knowledge and political practices. I attempt to analyze how hula, in multiple modalities and locations over the last century, produces "counter-memories" that contest sedimented histories of settler colonialism and sustain decolonizing processes.[63]

Discrepant Desires

As Trask asserts, Native bodies can become commodified objects and imperial fetishes. In tableaux of tourist hula, it would seem that Hawaiians are objects who "cannot represent themselves, they must be represented."[64] Hula performers were not only central to the colonial imaginary of Hawaiʻi, but were at times instrumentalized for U.S. empire building. In the twentieth century the Hawaiian "hula girl," as she became known in popular Americana—whether as an embodied or mediated figure—assisted in domesticating the Pacific for U.S. political, military, tourist, and economic interests. Only a year after Hawai'i's annexation by the United States, the hula dancer emerged as a sexualized hostess to American soldiers fighting in the Philippines. Honolulu became an essential fueling stop for U.S. military vessels headed to quell Filipinos who were waging anticolonial guerrilla warfare against American occupation. Aboard a transport vessel in Honolulu, American troops sang this song, "Sweet Mionomai":

> The nautch girls I have seen
> And the ballet's a fairy queen
> The pretty little oriental geisha—
> All the qualities and shades
> Of charming dancing maids
> I've seen in Europe, Africa and Asia
>
> Circassian dancers, too,
> Zoamacuecas in Peru,
> The Kafir dance, the Hottentot and Zulu.
> She who bears the wreath away
> Is the sweet Mionomai,
> The prettiest hula girl in Honolulu.[65]

The soldier-narrator encounters a panoply of eroticized dancing women during his militarized tours, but deems Hawaiian women by far the most desirable. There is no evidence to suggest that "Mionomai" became an enduring musical standard, but the imagined figure of the hula dancer motivated men moving from one stage in the Pacific empire to another during this segment of the Philippine-American War. The hula girl, then, might facilitate not only the integration of Hawai'i, but other tropical colonies into an American empire.

In their critiques of colonialism and neocolonialism, feminist scholars of the Pacific have discussed how female bodies have been deployed for colonial and neocolonial ends. Teresia K. Teaiwa has made the compelling argument that the iconography of the bikini, named after a U.S. nuclear test site in the Marshall Islands, exposes an eroticized female body that depoliticizes the violence of American colonialism and nuclear testing in Micronesia. Margaret Jolly, responding to Teaiwa, has proposed that sexual possession—imagined or otherwise—of beautiful Polynesian female bodies may be connected to military and colonial possession of the region.[66] Turning to Hawai'i, I consider how the positioning of hula bodies helps to conceal an illusory peace over a continuing military occupation. Throughout the twentieth century, particularly during World War II and the Vietnam War, Hawaiian women have performed important symbolic and material roles in American empire-building in Asia and the Pacific Islands, as I discuss in chapter 5.

But does their influence mean hula performers were locked within ideologies of empire as agents and collaborators? Louis Althusser maintains that ideology cannot be seen, but can hail its subjects nonetheless.[67] While hula performers were interpellated into imperial ideologies and scripts, I do not mean to suggest they were stable mediators of aloha. They did not always transmit imperial messages as they were intended. Hawaiian women and men have been largely subordinated on colonial stages, but they also inserted and created discrepant scenarios for themselves in hula circuits, at times usurping them. I remain interested in performers as more than allegorical figures and representations. My interest is in how they managed to seize their time on and off the stage for their own discrepant practices and desires. These unpredictable and occasionally insurgent disruptions—while not necessarily oppositional to colonialism—nonetheless disorganize empire. For as we know, colonialism is never complete. Although producing violence over the longue durée, empires are not as stable as they may appear, but shift according to the participation of both colonial and indigenous actors. Colonization was not a "fatal impact" dooming Hawaiians.[68] More than abused objects operating under false consciousness, this cohort of mobile dancers negotiated with colonization and tourist commodification as self-aware agents, brokers, and political actors. I seek to highlight the oscillation of power between colonial institutions, agents, and performers who were often the most direct mediators of Hawai'i's fantasy image.

Although empire and colonization may appear to be abstract processes, this is not a disembodied treatment—I turn my focus to the corporeal movements and experiences of Hawaiian performers and cultural brokers, both women and men, on the ground. I track how their countercolonial politics and desires at times weakened and pressured American hegemony in the islands, focusing on discrepant forms of participation, collusion, and political opposition by Hawaiian performers. I contend these subjects produced "counter-colonial" rather than "anticolonial" scenarios and critiques. Analyzing Chamorro converts to Christianity in

Guam, Vicente M. Diaz argues that they did not demonstrate explicit opposition to colonial institutions in an intentional and legible manner, but that their latent critiques may be better understood as counter-colonial.[69] Hula performers, too, were not simply "converted" objects, but responded to colonization with counter-colonial desires that were neither clearly oppositional nor accommodating.

Beyond coercion or resistance, a more useful analysis focuses on the "alternative," rather than "oppositional," politics of this cohort of Hawaiians, to employ Raymond Williams's productive distinction.[70] Men and women on the hula circuit did not appear to directly contribute to an anticolonial resistance movement, unlike Kanaka Maoli patriots who organized petition drives in Hawai'i that defeated an attempt at U.S. annexation.[71] However, po'e hula cannot simply be framed as "cultural" performers, for their labor and their productive activities—music, chant, and dance—were cultural *and* political. Refining Marxist evaluations that privilege the economic "base," Williams argues for the materiality of all struggles, including those relegated to putatively "superstructural" or cultural fields. Cultural activities are deeply material and productive— "elements of a whole material social process," he writes.[72] The practice of hula is not merely "aesthetic" or epiphenomenal to political life or labor; it and other cultural and religious performances ground Hawaiian political sovereignty. Jonathan Kamakawiwoʻole Osorio describes cultural activities undertaken in the late nineteenth century, including hula and the publication of chiefly genealogies, as "highly assertive of the glory and vitality of Hawaiian traditions." They enabled Hawaiians to distinguish themselves from acquisitive foreigners and constitute themselves as a nation as Western powers threatened their sovereignty.[73] This also speaks true of hula on the road, as I attempt to demonstrate.

In James C. Scott's analysis, the "hidden transcripts" of subordinated groups critique and rebel against public transcripts of domination.[74] This theory can be brought into productive conversation with the Hawaiian epistemology and practice of kaona, "veiled language" or hidden meanings.[75] Hawaiian poetry and song contain innuendoes, allusions, and metaphors purposely meant to conceal and reveal. The kaona of a song may reference clandestine lovers and activities in the guise of descriptions of flowers or landscapes only meant to be understood by select audiences. Kaona, as a tactic of enclosure and revelation, demarcated those who could interpret and those not meant to know. Hawaiian performers, I suggest, deployed kaona as a cultural and political resource in their colonial performances and travels; it served as a productive disguise for subtle and more dramatic political critiques and struggles against colonial incorporation.

Their "infrapolitics," what Scott describes as the often invisible "circumspect struggle waged daily by subordinate groups," can be detected in extraordinary and mundane aspects of life, sexuality, food, and fashion.[76] Within and beyond their stage performances, these dancers were political and cultural actors who wanted to have fun, dress up, and play. By examining these performers and their lives in full frame, I hope to demonstrate that Hawaiian performers were not merely passive objects in Euro-American tourist economies, but resisted and negotiated with colonization through their own "traveling cultures" and consumer practices.[77] They carved out their own homes, political expressions, and diasporic networks in view and out of view of foreign audiences.

In a rare, candid photograph I found of Hawaiian entertainers at the turn of the century, a group huddles together in Omaha, Nebraska. Their coats and hats appear splotched with snow, as if they had emerged from a snowball fight. Native American settlements outside tribal lands led to the phenomenon Philip J. Deloria has aptly called, in the case of Indian Country, "Indians in unexpected places"—the incongruous sight of an Indian in a modern landscape, whether it was Geronimo in a Cadillac, an Osage Indian driving an expensive automobile, or a Wild West performer playing ping pong.[78] Hawaiians' authenticity as an autochthonous people was and is often tied to their relationship to land and ocean. However, Hawaiians appeared in unexpected locations, such as snowbound streets, restricted military bases, diners in the deep South, Harlem nightclubs, and New York City taxicabs. Moving through the U.S. empire, they modeled a kind of Native modernity—a Hawaiian cosmopolitanism, if you will.

Hawaiian women on the hula circuit, especially, danced through uncharted territory. They unsettled preconceptions of Hawaiians as premodern, indolent "Kanakas" sitting on a faraway rock—"so pleasure-loving, so happy-go-lucky," as the *New York Times* described them.[79] But more important, they produced novel ideas of what Hawaiian women could be and do. Asserting autonomy from male authority with varying degrees of success, they traveled, smoked cigarettes, went to nightclubs, and created businesses. An important question I ask is, what did these performers want for themselves? What do they desire as they seek employment and self-fulfillment in places like Brunei, Japan, and New York?

What are the lived experiences of women and men who are potential agents of empire and a nascent decolonization movement?

The Aunties and the Archives

Born in 1933, Raylani Nihoa Pilialoha Kinney grew up on the U.S. hula circuit. Since the age of four to fifteen, she had lived in buses and hotels with a troupe of hula dancers and musicians. Led by her father, famed Hawaiian bandleader Ray Kinney, this troupe performed in hospitals, hotels, and military bases in almost every American state in the 1930s and 1940s. One memory of Raylani's extraordinary childhood delighted her: "Fireflies were beautiful in the South." And yet, her own grandchildren knew nothing about her cosmopolitan, peripatetic past and saw her only as a childcare provider from the sleepy town of Waimea, Hawai'i. They asked her, "What have you done, Grandma? You just take care of children." Raylani insisted, "But I've done all of these things and have seen things."[80] Her protest is emblematic of the gendered neglect and amnesia surrounding this history of hula and Hawaiian mobility. When I first began talking to Hawaiian and islander dancers who had headlined and performed on the professional circuit, most were surprised. They asked, "Why do you want to know my story?" Some demurred, "I'm not important." But when they began sharing their stories about fame, glamour, and occasional notoriety in their youth, it became clear many felt forgotten as they reached their seventies and eighties.

Indeed, when I began this research in the late 1990s, I was spurred by deep gaps in the history of hula. I discovered a newspaper clipping about famed Hawaiian dancers on tour in the 1930s and failed to recognize any of their names, though I grew up in Hawai'i and was an active member of a hālau hula. Despite the ubiquity of hula in present-day Hawai'i, people who dance hula today do not often talk about commercialized, tourist hula, particularly the kind of hapa haole (meaning "part foreign" or acculturated) hula that became popular in the twentieth century. One reason for this period's absence in historical and popular discourse is that hula associated with pre-European performance forms—glossed as hula kahiko (literally "old hula")—has become highly valorized for its more ostensibly "authentic" connection to indigenous Hawaiian values and practices. Acculturated hula, in contrast, is seen as tainted by tourist markets and removed from Native self-determination and nationalist causes. From this perspective, dancers who performed this "hapa haole" hula are far too colonized or "haole." While there is a growing body of scholarship emphasizing the connection between Kanaka Maoli sovereignty and cultural activism, there is little literature on tourist hula practices in the last century.[81]

The bodies of hula performers present a curious problem: they are hypervisible in popular culture while leaving only the faintest traces in archives. I am keenly aware that subordinated subjects and their live, often ephemeral, performances are often absent in official, state-oriented archives. To reconstruct hula circuits over the past century, I have depended on a range of primary and secondary sources in American and Hawai'i archives: English-language newspapers from the islands and the United States, Hawaiian-language newspapers, military films and photographs, oral histories, and guidebooks.[82] Colonial archives—what Ann Stoler has described as "intricate technologies of rule"—included intercultural tourist performers most often as archetypes (the hula girl, South Seas maidens), but rarely individuated.[83]

The appearance of intercultural hula performers and their travels abroad in Hawaiian-language newspapers is also attenuated, possibly because their travails were eclipsed by political turmoil. English-language newspapers published in Hawai'i and the United States provide more details, though not necessarily accurate, of hula tours and performances abroad. In the Hawai'i state (formerly territorial) archives, most of the visual materials on hula are grouped together as "Hula Dancers, Musicians, Groups."[84] Therefore, we only know a fraction of the names of female performers from the late nineteenth century and the early twentieth.[85] The movements of Hawaiian women from colony to metropole further complicate their documentation. As fourth-world women in the first world, tourist performers, and itinerant colonial laborers, po'e hula were, with few exceptions, anonymous and linger on the margins of territorial archives and U.S. national archives.

Because of the limitations of American and Hawaiian textual and visual archives, I found myself working in the interstices of archive and field, reconstituting and creating new archives with insights gained from hula performance and ethnographic research in hula communities. My lived participation in Hawai'i enabled a methodology that traffics freely between past and present, connecting colonization in the past and ongoing neocolonial pressures in a not-yet-decolonized fieldsite.[86] Foucault presses for the "insurrection of subjugated knowledges" in criticism.[87] He suggests that "it is through the re-appearance of . . . these local popular knowledges, these disqualified knowledges, that criticism performs its work."[88] I further propose to examine the "low-ranking knowledges" of (neo)colonial subjects and women, whose lives have been particularly illegible in colonial repositories and have seemed marginal to the practice of history.

To do so, my method has required a reliance on two overlapping systems of knowledge: archives of written texts and repertoires of live and mediated performances. Repertoire, as Diana Taylor theorizes it, is "embodied practice/knowledge" that enacts memory through live action.[89] In paying attention to the repertoire, Taylor suggests analyzing "scenarios" instead of texts and narratives. Scenarios enable the study of the "social construction of bodies in particular contexts" as well as embodied behaviors such as "gestures, attitudes, and tones not reducible to language."[90] Hula is an embodied practice that deploys what Joseph Roach has called "kinesthetic imagination," a principle and practice that enables a "way of thinking through movements."[91]

My first research tactic to bring these subjugated knowledges and movements into view has been to create alternative archives and repertoires of oral histories, photographs, personal memorabilia, performances, and films. I identified and found surviving dancers and their families, conducting open-ended interviews and relying on their extensive personal collections to interpret their life histories. As it is impossible to confine a study of hula and colonization to the past, my participation extended into intersecting arenas of contemporary Hawaiian sovereignty and hula, in other words, the ongoing, living repertoire of hula.

Most of the women maintained an active relationship to hula, whether directly or indirectly through their kin, and had varying connections to Kanaka Maoli cultural nationalism. I attended sovereignty marches, assisted with 'ohana (family) newsletters, and attended family reunions, hula rehearsals, hula competitions, informal performances, and fundraisers for Native Hawaiian rights. I also spent a year producing a video documentary of the dancer Betty Puanani Makia, her family, and her performing history centered around New York City.[92] In short, I was documenting and creating archives, as well as a repertoire, of the present.

At first the performers eluded me: they existed only as an inert list of names culled from a local newspaper archive, fittingly called a morgue. However, local kinship connections allowed me to track down a dancer from the hula circuit of the 1930s, animating my research. Meymo Ululani Holt had attended the same high school I had in Honolulu. When I stopped at the school library to look up her photograph in the 1930 annual, the archivist mentioned that another much younger "Meymo" was an alumna. Might they be related? I called her namesake, a grand-niece, and a few phone calls later was in touch with two nerve centers and kūpuna (elders) of the extended Holt clan. Though Meymo Ululani Holt had passed away a few years earlier, I was put in touch with Meymo's older daughter, who shared photographs and the Holt family genealogy with me. Her cousin and I visited Meymo's gravesite in the valley where my family lives. From here on, there was no such thing as simply gleaning the biographies of hula performers from newspaper clippings.

A few women proudly displayed glamorous framed portraits in their living rooms, while nearly all had compiled and tucked away elaborate albums and scrapbooks of their performing careers. Even if they did not intend their personal effects to be entered into official archives, they were prolific collectors and archivists in their own right. Though one professional dancer already had advanced Alzheimer's disease when I met her, she had stored a lifetime of newspaper clippings and photographs in several army trunks. Many dancers had already passed away or were in fragile health when I began this search. But even when they had passed away years before, their lineaments came into focus through the stories and faces of their descendants.

My second tactic is to offer what I call discrepant readings of official and unofficial archives and performance repertoire; that is, finding "hidden transcripts" within imperial scripts, scenarios, and tableaux.[93] Recognizing that a totalizing reconstruction of these women's experiences is impossible, I attempt to read archives against the grain or, as Saidiya Hartman has demonstrated in her critical reexamination of slave performances, to reclaim archives for "contrary purposes."[94] I rely on fragments and the ephemeral—those often gendered traces of women's desires, such as souvenirs, fashions, songs, photographs, and embodied gestures— that suggest daily acts of critique, contestation, survival, and pleasure during colonization.

My lived relationship to Hawai'i, a place I call home, has meant that my role as a researcher is simultaneously more fraught and intense. I am both insider and outsider in Hawai'i. Though born and raised in the islands, I am not Kanaka Maoli. I have access to community-based knowledge through my local kin networks, but I am also a non-Native researcher in a Kanaka Maoli community that is engaged in a long-standing decolonizing struggle and has been ethnographically overdetermined by Western scholarship. A non-Native scholar must be keenly aware of the complex ethics and politics of conducting research in a Native community and the potential epistemic violence that this relationship may produce. Many postcolonial studies have come to take as self-evident the analytical framework of Native and Other.[95] Marking the epistemological and political differences between Native and Other subjects has also been vital for indigenous movement politics in Hawai'i and other settler-colonial sites, cohering in the 1980s and 1990s.

However, while postcolonial anthropology and movement politics are animated by the distinction between Natives and Others, the assumption that a non-Native researcher is a problematic interpreter of Native histories, experiences, and values is neither universally nor consistently held. This framework does not obtain in the social values and everyday practices of my informants, predominantly Hawaiian women who came of age between the 1930s and the 1950s, and who predate the sovereignty and Native rights activism I discuss in the epilogue. The more significant values and concrete relations that organize these women's everyday lives are shared interactions via cultural training, place, gender, and local kin. They distinguish less between those who are Native and non-Native, but make judgments based on whether one is from Hawai'i and has community or family-based cultural knowledge of the islands. I became involved with these Hawaiian women as someone whose multigenerational family lived in the same neighborhoods, attended the same schools, and moved along similar circuits outside the islands. My research subjects and so-called informants recognized that I was not Hawaiian, but they treated me as someone more like them than not. I was a neighbor from one valley over, a hula sister, a hānai (adopted) niece.

For each individual dancer I encountered, I met extended families, grandchildren, and childhood friends, and whenever possible learned their hula genealogies and mo'o kū'auhau (kin genealogies). They became my "aunties," "aunty" being an island term of endearment and affection for an older woman, blood-related or not. My fieldnotes name them as Aunty X, Aunty Y, Aunty Z, although in this book I have abided by the convention of referring to my subjects by first name. However, this access was both a gift and a burden that brought its own challenges: the attendant obligations, confidences, and silences that come with intimate access to local knowledge. Many revealed sensitive disagreements, secrets, and traumas, relying on me to protect their privacy while narrating their experiences and passing them into the public domain. My decisions about how much to transmit of the women's lives in this book were shaped by their own conscious choices to unveil and protect particular aspects of sacred knowledge on hula circuits.

Producing scholarly work about hula has also come into productive tension with established modalities of authority, rank, and training in the hālau hula system, amplifying differences between writing and dancing. The kumu hula, who has earned his or her credentials through authorizing living bodies and the blessings of akua and ancestors, is the ultimate authority of a hālau; the word of the kumu is final. Haumāna (students) like me are expected to faithfully reproduce every movement taught by a kumu, particularly the chanted poetry and dances that make up a hula tradition.[96] Only with express permission are students allowed to creatively adapt movements, alter the repertoire, or rechoreograph chants; but dancers have certainly transformed repertoire, as evidenced by great shifts in performance styles over several decades.[97] In order to write about hula, I had to also unwork this fundamental dictate, as do dancers: I was not simply recording what I was taught, but interpreting and assembling a shifting repertoire with its contradictions and ellipses.

Embracing these challenges of the fragmented colonial and postcolonial archive, I have made a deliberate choice not to pursue a linear chronology. Rather than presenting a comprehensive history of hula or a compendium of Hawaiian performers and their itineraries, *Aloha America* frames performers as actors operating within U.S. colonizing processes. While proceeding roughly chronologically, the book places emphasis on particular performers and performance sites—embodiments of aloha that mediated Hawaiian hospitality.

The first two chapters of this book examine performers on fin de siècle hula circuits before and during the American overthrow of the monarchy. Over the last century and a half, hula practitioners performed in diverse venues for Euro-American audiences, but one of the earliest sites was the transnational royal court of Honolulu. Chapter 1 traces the origins of the hula circuit to late nineteenth-century transnational Honolulu. I introduce Kini Kapahukulaokamāmalu and her contemporaries, commoner (i.e., nonchiefly) women who received formal hula training and sponsorship in King David Kalākaua's royal court. Kalākaua, the ribald bon vivant known as the "Merrie Monarch," elevated hula and Native genealogical arts to a central stage of his reign, while battling hostile missionary and planter elements and U.S. economic pressure. Hula achieved notoriety because of its association with Hawaiian sexuality, but also materialized as a nationalist practice and opportunity structure for Hawaiian women during informal and formal U.S. colonization. By virtue of institutionalized hula training and their encounters with foreign people and ideas in the port town of Honolulu, commoner women emerged as transgressive, intercultural figures prior to their departure from Hawai'i. Their expertise in hula made them more valuable as protectors of Hawaiian genealogical knowledge, but also exposed them to criticism from Christian observers.

Chapter 2 takes a closer view of the counter-colonial tactics of these dancers during the first major hula tour of the continental United States and Europe. With the American colonial acquisition of overseas territories, Hawaiian women were interpellated as erotic collectibles in imperial entertainments such as the Chicago World's Columbian Exposition, dime museums, and vaudeville theaters. However, they were not simply reducible to imperial objects; they followed their own diversions as cosmopolitan tourists and consumers in contravention of nationality, gender, and rank. Peeking behind the theatrical curtain, I deliberate on how Hawaiian performers pursued their own idiosyncratic, gendered collecting and touristic practices in the age of Victoria, appropriating modern technologies such as studio photography and fashion. As they developed unexpected friendships and alliances backstage, their discrepant and modern desires at times ran counter to both Hawaiian anticolonial nationalism and American imperialist logics.

Although Hawaiian women performers have commanded the tourist spotlight over the last century because of the gendered hierarchies of colonial entertainments, chapter 3 of this book turns toward Hawaiian men who were influential brokers of hula and Hawaiian culture during the early territorial period. Organizing and presenting living Hawaiian villages at U.S. world's fairs, entrepreneurial and cosmopolitan men managed to convert their work in cultural performance into anticolonial political capital. These Hawaiian brokers—indeed, impresarios—circumvented and challenged the haole oligarchy of the islands by "playing Hawaiian" in commodified entertainment venues away from the colony.[98] Representing Hawai'i and Hawaiians directly to American audiences, these mobile actors merged culture and politics on the hula circuit and defied U.S. annexation in diasporic sites. Traveling far from the islands under conditions of political exile, they wrote and performed music and asserted their autonomy from the territorial government. With men serving as public brokers, hula circuits also produced internal gendered hierarchies.

Chapter 4 looks closely at hula circuits across the U.S. continent as Hawaiian women became ambassadors of aloha for the territory of Hawai'i.

Performing in popular Hawaiian showrooms in New York City, Chicago, and other metropolitan areas, they were heralded as "hula queens," celebrities, and success stories. Their commercial performances produced what I discuss as an imagined intimacy between Hawai'i and the United States, enabling American audiences to experience a fantasy of Hawai'i as a different but welcoming place. Live hula performances, while elevating Hawaiians to the principal brokers of Hawaiian culture, simultaneously helped to erase the presence of large numbers of immigrant Asians who lived in Hawai'i. Yet, hula also led island women to lives and careers both inside and outside entertainment during a time when many women were limited to racially and gender-stratified plantation and service industries. They created "traveling cultures" and gendered diasporas in often hostile and unfamiliar new cities, and they supported each other as "sisters" and fictive kin.

The final chapter of this book turns toward an enduring staging of aloha and hospitality: the luau. An extended performance of feasting in which hula played a central role, the tourist luau emerged at world's fairs in the United States at the beginning of the twentieth century. However, during World War II, volunteer hula troupes staged luaus in the islands for arriving American soldiers. Analyzing military films and photography taken by military combat photography units, I suggest how tourist luaus engendered an "imperial hospitality" that helped to restabilize intimacy between Hawaiian colonial subjects and the military. This highly gendered and racialized imperial hospitality produces an alchemy of "rest and relaxation" for tourists. While the sexuality of the Hawaiian population was regulated through this militouristic visual economy, islanders who performed in this "Pacific theater" developed counter-memories of their experiences that I disclose through dancers' alternative archives.

The epilogue of this book leads both backward and forward to the future of hula. By this, I mean to suggest one provenance of Hawai'i's present-day self-determination movement may be found in an unexpected site—the tourist hula circuit that sustained cultural reproduction and political contestation during American colonization. Challenged by a globalized economy, hula also provides energy for an ongoing Kanaka Maoli decolonization movement. Contemporary performers, like their forebears, cross into multiple realms of tourist performance, Native rights activism, and cultural competitions. There are few clear victories to be earned over U.S. empire, as the experiences of nineteenth-century kūpuna reveal, but new generations of po'e hula may look toward their tactics for sustenance and guidance.

CHAPTER 1

LADY JANE AT THE BOATHOUSE
The Intercultural World of Hula

One afternoon in 1889, eight young Hawaiian women dressed in long white holokū (gowns) and pinned up their long hair. They were to dance hula that afternoon at King David Kalākaua's boathouse, Healani, a few blocks from the royal palace. Due to the vigilant intercessions of Congregationalist missionaries who had arrived in Hawai'i from New England in 1820, po'e hula (hula practitioners) did not dare perform hula outdoors for their own enjoyment. During his reign from 1874 to 1891, Kalākaua famously defied abstemious missionaries and revived Hawaiian religious and cultural practices. With his support, hula began to make its way out of the shadows. The king's coronation and fiftieth-birthday jubilee celebrations showcased hula on the palace grounds in 1883 and 1886, much to the chagrin of missionary descendants. One found the performances so obscene that he pressed charges against the printers of the corona- tion program.[1] The women who were to dance at the king's boat- house did not perform at those events, but belonged to another group of court hula dancers called Hui Lei Mamo. According to one of its members, Kini Kapahukulaokamāmalu, Hui Lei Mamo was a "glee club" that Kalākaua had assembled in 1886.[2] Hui Lei Mamo performed hybrid forms of hula as well as choral music. All eight members were Hawaiian girls and women under the age of twenty.

At least once a week, from the hours of 2 PM to 5 PM, Hui Lei Mamo performed for the king's friends and foreign guests at Healani, his royal boathouse. On this occasion, they gathered to welcome the

Scottish writer Robert Louis Stevenson, who had sailed his yacht into Honolulu two days prior. The performers draped Stevenson and his stepson with leis and entertained them with hula performances.[3] The girls danced to mele (songs) in Hawaiian accompanied by Western instrumentation.[4] After the hula, the women excused themselves while the men played a game of whist and the champagne flowed.

Only three years later, three of the young women of Hui Lei Mamo found themselves performing on North American and European stages. Shortly before the U.S.-backed overthrow of the kingdom in 1893, they joined a hula troupe that made the first extensive tour of the United States and Europe. From 1892 to 1896, their circuits took them to an international exposition, vaudeville theaters, dime museums, and European royal courts. This group was the first of many other hula troupes to perform during the American colonization of the islands. Instead of wearing long gowns and mingling with foreign ambassadors, the women stood outside a theater at the Chicago World's Columbian Exposition's Midway Plaisance, beckoning audiences into a five-cent show of the "naughty naughty hula dance." Hula became an eroticized commodity in the global colonial marketplace, and the women who were trained protectors of this art traveled widely along these performance circuits.

The cosmopolitan boathouse in Honolulu where this group began its royal sponsorship is emblematic of the contradictions and opportunities during this transnational period in Hawaiian history, as the nation experienced extreme scrutiny and economic and political pressure prior to its formal colonization by the United States. It also prefigures the political and cultural stages on which hula would be exposed while on tour. Affording commoner Hawaiian women cultural training and advancement within a national institution, the boathouse also opened Hawaiians up to foreign criticism. It became notorious in Hawai'i and beyond as a space of irresponsible indulgence. Haole (white) settlers affiliated with the pro-American missionary party condemned hula and other boathouse entertainment as Hawaiian debauchery.

Culture was the terrain on which politics were argued, for Americans sympathetic to the U.S. annexationist cause treated Hawaiian cultural practices as indisputable empirical evidence of the political failures and inherent deficiency of Hawaiians. Sensational reports about the monarchy circulated on the continent for at least a decade after the king's death in 1891. Lucien Young, a lieutenant of the uss *Boston*, the warship that helped to overthrow the Hawaiian kingdom in 1893, wrote in his nationally published memoir that Kalākaua built the boathouse to accommodate "gambling, lewd practices, immoral exhibitions, drunken carousals, and the abominations of the hula dance." Young protested that the "scenes enacted there beggar description." American writers of travelogues like *Hawaiian America* (1899) argued that the profligacy of the king justified the Anglo-Saxon takeover of islands: Kalākaua had squandered his birthright and government revenues, displayed "loose morals," and gave white people little choice but to intercede and manage the islands' bountiful resources.[5]

Despite denunciations of the boathouse and hula performance, the women of Hui Lei Mamo were able to undertake intensive hula training even after Kalākaua's death, thanks to state-sponsored support. Kini Kapahukulaokamāmalu was one of these dancers. Fourteen years old when Kalākaua handpicked her for the hula troupe in 1886, Kini became his particular favorite.[6] He called her "Lady Jane," although she was a commoner and not of ali'i (chiefly) birth and rank. As maka'āinana (commoner) women with access to ali'i nui (high-ranking chiefs), foreign residents, and sojourners, hula performers in Kalākaua's court occupied multiple statuses and unsettled hierarchies based on class, occupation, gender, and rank. Within the Hawaiian court, they negotiated the interface of old and new, tradition and innovation, foreign and Native, propriety and daring—negotiations that anticipated ones they would face during their off-island circuits.

In this chapter, I follow Kini Kapahu and her contemporaries from the margins of Hawaiian life into roles as state-supported performers with ambiguous standing in the intercultural world of Honolulu. Hula was a gendered cultural opportunity structure that opened up for Hawaiian women in the years preceding the U.S.-backed overthrow of the Hawaiian kingdom in 1893. Emerging as a national practice in late nineteenth-century Honolulu, hula reinserted sacred and secular genealogical practices into public life and elevated commoner women like Kini. Hula simultaneously advanced and challenged Hawaiian women. It offered them intensive training in Hawaiian history, traditional arts, as well as savoir faire in a transnational court. Hula was an intercultural strategy and a way for women practitioners to navigate between multiple worlds and positions. I discuss hula in late nineteenth-century Hawai'i and the transnational world of the boathouse in order to illuminate the ways dancers were already hybrid, intercultural figures before they embarked on their world tours. They served as the foundation of a modern Hawaiian nation and as reproducers of political and cultural knowledge, while also performing as new kinds of Hawaiian subjects. But their engagement with hula also made them more visible and susceptible to scrutiny and criticism from Native and non-Native quarters, as we shall see.

Colonial Suppression and Hula Revival

Before examining how hula was received and transformed along its transnational circuits, we must first attend to the meaning of hula and its resurgence in the intercultural milieu of late nineteenth-century Honolulu. A single category of dance did not exist in Hawai'i. According to ethnomusicologist Adrienne L. Kaeppler, prior to Western contact Hawaiians performed ha'a, ritual movements in offerings to a god at a heiau (temple). Ha'a was distinct from hula, dance movements performed for humans in a nonsacred, informal context. Calvinist missionaries discouraged Hawaiian chiefs from allowing public displays of "dancing," whether for gods or humans. In response to this prohibition, ha'a was adapted into the semisacred form of hula pahu (hula performed with the sharkskin drum).[7]

More than dance, hula can be thought of as an embodied form of history. There is a strong organic connection between historiography, politics, and hula. Within this broad category of sacred and secular performance, bodily movements were less critical than the chanted poetry that communicated the births and achievements of chiefs, recorded the genealogies of high chiefs back to the akua (gods), and relayed Hawaiian epics.[8] In these performances, gesticulation was appreciated, but not necessary.[9] Some po'e hula joined the households of chiefs, with each ali'i sponsoring its own hula retinue.[10] Hawai'i's most esteemed twentieth-century ethnographer, Mary Kawena Pukui, observes, "A good hula master was always found in the court of his chief."[11] Enjoying chiefly patronage, po'e hula were historians and the "biographers" of the chiefs.[12] They scripted the ali'i's political and divine right to rule by venerating them in chant and performing their connections to godly ancestors.

Hula has often been discussed as a "traditional" repository—an archive containing a fixed body of knowledge that is passed down relatively intact from generation to generation. Yet hula is more of a *living* repertoire than a repository securing official state history. Hula, as a form of embodied and kinesthetic historical knowledge, accommodated flexibility, change, and innovation as its practitioners and political patrons shifted. Dependent on orality, hula chants were not committed to writing until the latter half of the nineteenth century.

While hula communicated serious political scripts, it also provided entertainment and release for chiefs and commoners alike. Pukui contends, "The people loved dancers because they were so much fun and because they gave so much happiness."[13] Early European visitors observed dancers amusing crowds of people. William Ellis, a missionary from the London Missionary Society, described a particularly joyous performance in Kailua, Hawai'i, in 1823. A large entourage accompanied five "strolling musicians and dancers" as they performed for several hours in front of one of Governor Kuakini's houses. A male soloist dressed in a magnificent yellow pā'ū kapa (bark-cloth skirt) chanted "the achievements of former kings of Hawaii," much pleasing Kuakini.[14]

Congregationalist missionaries from New England began settling in the Hawaiian Islands in the 1820s. Equipped with a Calvinist work ethic, they associated hula with Hawaiian debauchery, idleness, and sexuality, qualities that made Hawaiians unproductive workers in the emerging capitalist economies of Hawai'i.[15] These missionaries rightly suspected, though did not fully comprehend, the sexual and spiritual potency of hula, and they objected to the practice on those grounds, for hula was indeed embedded in a culture of sexual arousal. The usual conclusion to a formal courtly performance of dances was the athletic hula ma'i, hula honoring the genitals of a chief.[16] Hula ma'i encouraged procreation and the continuation of a chiefly line.

The influential American missionary Hiram Bingham surveyed the "heathen song and dance" in Liholiho's (also known as King Kamehameha II) court in 1820. He wrote, "The whole arrangement and process of their old hulas are designed to promote lasciviousness, and of course the practice could not flourish in modest communities."[17] Bingham and his contemporaries pressured the Hawaiian government to ban the practice.[18] As early as 1823, some ali'i nui stopped hula performances in their courts. Hula was strictly regulated by civil codes passed by the Hawaiian legislature in 1851 and 1859. In 1859, any public exhibition of hula that charged admission was forbidden without a prohibitive ten-dollar license issued by the ministry of the interior. Those who danced unlicensed risked imprisonment or fines. Furthermore, licenses were only valid for performances in the port city of Honolulu. Although some ali'i continued to support hula, these laws effectively erased hula from urban areas and the public sphere.[19] Pukui observed, "After they [the missionaries] gained control, it was only the small and out-of-the-way areas that dance continued to flourish, for people were sometimes arrested for dancing."[20]

Missionaries and their descendants were not the only ones who censured the hula; some Christian Hawaiians also objected. One Hawaiian wrote to the Hawaiian newspaper *Nupepa Kuokoa* to criticize the hula performed during the mourning of ali'i Victoria Kamāmalu Ka'ahumanu in 1866. Titled "Pau ole no hoi ka hana kahiko o Hawaii nei" (The old practices of Hawaii are not over), the letter reads, in part:

> [Hula was not] the right thing to do because it was done with real joy as though a great benefit would be derived. It was the mourning of a pagan people. It is not wrong to lament, to chant his kahea inoa [name chant] if done as a regret for the separation but to dance to and fro, that is not affectionate mourning. It is like saying there is gladness over the death of the high chief . . . so let us do things to please the great ruler, that is, the Loving God.[21]

Other reproachful letters from Hawaiians were printed around the same time.[22]

As Hawaiian cultural autonomy was assailed, so, too, was Hawaiian governance undermined by interlocking missionary and sugar-planter interests in the 1880s. These industries were controlled by haole of foreign and Hawaiian birth. Formal colonization by the United States was a decade away, but the kingdom had "a foundering independence" by the middle of King Kalākaua's reign due to haole assaults on the king and efforts to terminate the monarchy, as Jonathan Kay Kamakawiwo'ole Osorio contends.[23] Noenoe K. Silva also astutely observes that Kalākaua had the "misfortune" to reign during a period when the sons of haole missionaries came of age; unlike their fathers, they were unsupervised by an outside foreign mission.[24] Thus, even prior to formal colonization in 1898, Hawai'i was a nation subordinated to the interests of the United States and settler-missionary businessmen, and Hawaiians were increasingly subjugated, colonial subjects.

In 1887 a secret organization called the "Hawaiian League," composed of "mission boys," sugar planters, and businessmen, used the threat of an all-white militia to force Kalākaua to appoint a new cabinet made up of the militia's members and to accept a new constitution.[25] The constitution of 1887—nicknamed the "Bayonet Constitution" because of the coercive circumstances of its adoption—reduced the king to a constitutional monarch with severely limited powers. The House of Nobles in the legislature was no longer appointed by the king, but elected, and Kalākaua did not retain the authority to remove his ministers.

Fig. 3 King David
Kalākaua. COURTESY
OF HAWAI'I STATE ARCHIVES.

That same year, Hawaiian independence was further compromised when the king's new "reform" cabinet renewed a reciprocity treaty with the United States that allowed sugar planters in Hawai'i to reap great profits. In exchange for renewal of a treaty that permitted Hawaiian sugar duty-free into the United States, the United States sought exclusive use of Pearl Harbor, the only natural harbor in the north Pacific, for a naval and commercial port.[26] Kalākaua had refused, but weakened by the Bayonet Constitution, he was unable to prevent the renewal of the reciprocity treaty. Thus the United States secured Pearl Harbor and an official military foothold in Hawai'i in 1887.

Increasingly constrained by internal and external pressures, the king instituted cultural policies to reinvigorate the Hawaiian nation. Born in 1836, David La'amea Kalākaua believed that the lāhui (Hawaiian nation) and his people would prosper with the rebirth of traditional cultural practices (see figure 3). He supported the public performance of hula and established two societies that cultivated Native history and genealogy: Ka Papa Kū'auhau o Nā Ali'i (Board of Genealogy of Chiefs) and Hale Nāua. The first organization, Ka Papa Kū'auhau, researched and published the

Fig. 4 Hula at Kalākaua's birthday jubilee, 1886. COURTESY OF HAWAI'I STATE ARCHIVES.

Kumulipo, the central genealogical, cosmogonic text linking the ali'i to the gods, which Silva describes as "a narrative of the lāhui from the beginning of time."[27]

At his poni mō'ī (coronation) in 1883 and his birthday jubilee in 1886, the king incorporated performances of sacred hula and important historical tableaux into these official state ceremonies (see figure 4).[28] Po'e hula from his court chanted and performed ancient temple hula and composed new mele in Kalākaua's honor, reinforcing the king's chiefly genealogy back to the gods.[29] As many as sixty dancers at a time may have performed at the jubilee, with subsequent line changes of similar numbers.[30] Pukui writes of the jubilee, "Dancers and musicians gathered from end to end of the group. Many rare dances were seen then as well as the commoner ones."[31]

Noenoe K. Silva argues these displays did more than fortify the king's individual right to rule, but legitimated the nation and constituted a national narrative for Hawai'i.[32] The reinsertion of Native history and cultural texts into the public sphere on these important state occasions "forever ended the missionary prohibition of such activities" while resisting colonization and the degradation of Hawaiian epistemology.[33] In the historiography of hula and as remembered by a current anticolonial

Hawaiian movement, Kalākaua's late nineteenth-century celebrations constitute a key moment in the nation's history, a symbolic return to Native practices. These memories are activated today, as Kalākaua—known affectionately as the "Merrie Monarch"—is venerated at hula festivals in the islands and overseas. The Merrie Monarch Festival in Hilo, Hawai'i, the islands' preeminent hula competition, has been staged annually since 1964. Portraits of the king and his consort are prominently displayed next to the hula stage, and Hawaiian men and women are chosen to represent the Kalākaua court during the festivities.

As with more quotidian displays of hula, haole and Kanaka opinion was sharply divided over the value of a Native cultural renaissance. While significant to Hawaiians, the king's galas were interpreted by haole in the islands as profligacy and frivolity. Americans in attendance reported to U.S. newspapers that the coronation was "a most uncalled for and absurd affair, and a sinful expenditure of money."[34] This critical inspection of Hawaiian behavior extended to women dancers at the royal boathouse and their forays into new Western markets.

Gendered Opportunities

Due to Kalākaua's support, hula became formally institutionalized within the Westernized constitutional monarchy. In anticipation of his coronation in 1883, Kalākaua brought kumu hula (hula teachers) and their hālau (troupes) from the countryside and neighboring islands to his court.[35] The po'e hula became court retainers, living in their own hale pili (grass huts) on the palace grounds for several months while preparing for the coronation performances.[36] As they had prior to Western colonial settlement, the po'e hula confirmed the ali'i's sacred genealogy; this time, however, they did so within a hybrid nation-state asserting itself against Euro-American hegemony.

After the royal festivities concluded, some kumu hula remained in the capital city. Perhaps the most lasting outcome of the state sponsorship of hula was the training of a younger generation of dancers. The Kalākaua period initiated wider cultural reproduction via a new cohort of hula practitioners. Kalākaua's slogan, "Ho'oulu Lāhui" (increase, or "grow," the nation), points to the potential he saw in the nation's youth. Similar to W. E. B. Du Bois's model of the "Talented Tenth," which championed the higher education of the best and brightest of African American youth in the postemancipation era, Kalākaua also invested in exceptional students who would be valuable to the longevity of the lāhui.

In the 1880s, Kalākaua initiated a state-sponsored study abroad program for talented Hawaiians. Eighteen youth were handpicked by Kalākaua to study in Japan, China, England, Scotland, Italy, and the United States. Many of the students were of ali'i birth or belonged to socially prominent families; Kalākaua likely hoped that they would become future leaders for his government and the lāhui.[37] Funded by the national legislature, they studied a diverse range of subjects, including medicine, art, military science, and law. Of the eighteen participants, only one was a woman, and she was to study art and music.[38] Formal opportunities for educational and professional advancement were therefore almost entirely limited to Hawaiian men through kingdom programs.

In contrast to the Hawaiians Abroad program, Kalākaua's sponsorship of hula invested in women, many of them of maka'āinana background. While few Hawaiian women of commoner status attended Western missionary schools, some were able to undertake apprenticeships in hula through the court or through hālau hula. We do not know how many benefited from this revival, for hula troupes did not keep written records of their members, and unlike participants in government programs, kingdom records did not document court and hālau dancers.[39] However, Nathaniel B. Emerson, a physician, missionary son, and folklorist, interviewed several practitioners at the turn of the century who had either performed hula in Kalākaua's court or learned from po'e hula affiliated with the court.[40] His field diaries from 1898 to 1906, during his research in many island districts, also suggest hula was vibrant and widespread at this time.

Hālau hula, some of which received monarchical support, became the institution through which a critical subset of Hawaiian women received rigorous training in performance, history, religion, and protocol. Kalākaua's other Hawaiian cultural organizations, Hale Nāua and Ka Papa Kū'auhau, restricted membership to men and women of ali'i rank, but one did not need chiefly status to join a hālau hula.[41] Hula became a gendered cultural opportunity structure, as nonchiefly women were able to advance during the resignification and institutionalization of hula as a national practice. While both men and women performed hula, female po'e hula enjoyed increased stature and acquired cultural capital under Kalākaua. They became repositories of historical knowledge, and their talents enabled them to enter the hierarchical court as well as seek employment and travel outside of the islands.

Yet we cannot assume that hula provided a natural sanctuary for Hawaiian women at the turn of the century, for the role of gender in hula practice was ambiguous. The ethnomusicologist Dorothy B. Barrère concludes that there is no historical evidence that hula was danced solely by men prior to European contact; in fact, Hawaiian legends and mele reveal women as some of the earliest hula practitioners.[42] Diverse gender practices were accepted in the realm of hula as māhū, transgendered or effeminate men who embodied both genders, became advanced practitioners.[43]

Nevertheless, hula was stratified by gender. Mary Kawena Pukui explains: "In the olden days the musicians or hoopaa were men and never women, but the dancers were both men and women. To become a hoopaa it was necessary to learn not only the meles but also the innumerable prayers. It was the hoopaas who eventually became kumus or teachers of the hula."[44] Thus men, including māhū, occupied the highest echelons of hula; they comprised the teachers as well as the elite class of hoʻopaʻa, the chanters and musicians who may receive further training and advance to kumu hula. Women, on the other hand, occupied an elementary order of hula—they were certainly skilled as dancers, but ordinarily did not undergo secondary and tertiary stages of training as hoʻopaʻa and kumu hula. Women were not considered the cultural reproducers of hula; men and māhū instead became the favored inheritors of hula genealogies. Pukui herself had to fight to become trained as hoʻopaʻa in the 1930s.[45]

Yet while men were entitled to privileged positions within hula, women took the initiative to cultivate and sustain the practice, especially during and after the Kalākaua period. The influential hula teacher Keahi Luahine (1887–1937) is but one exemplar of this gendered cultural reproduction. As part of her own contribution to the national revival, Queen Kapiʻolani, Kalākaua's consort, went to Kauaʻi around 1885 and suggested that the eight-year-old Keahi be reared on Oʻahu with her older sister. Keahi later undertook training in a hālau hula toward the end of Kalākaua's reign. As a girl, she was restricted from becoming a hoʻopaʻa, while three male relatives were trained to become hoʻopaʻa in a hālau.[46]

Keahi may not have received formal kumu hula (master teacher) status, but she nevertheless passed down her well-honed hula knowledge to three women who were and are arguably some of the most influential hula specialists in the twentieth century: ethnographer Mary Kawena Pukui (1895–1986); Pukui's hānai (adopted, literally meaning "feeding") daughter Patience Namakauahoaokawenaʻulaokalaniikiikikalaninui Wiggin Bacon (b. 1920) who remains an irreplaceable kumu (source) in her own right;

and Keahi's grand-niece and hānai daughter ʻIolani Luahine (1915–1978), a famed and audacious female hula soloist.[47] Pukui paid homage to Keahi and the efforts of other overlooked women: "When men did not care to learn the old dances any more, it was the women who learned and saved them for us. Innumerable were those dances and meles now lost to us, but for the remaining fragments we are deeply grateful to those who preserved them. To the women who learned the dances that the men were forgetting, I also give my mahalo nui [thank you]."[48] This matrilineage has enabled the endurance of hula practices until the present. Women were very visible guardians of hula traditions, but also made careful decisions "behind the scenes, out of casual sight lines," as Amy Kuʻuleialoha Stillman has described them, about how to safeguard and selectively reproduce the deep cultural knowledge with which they had been entrusted.[49]

Hula Schools and Repertoire

Kini Kapahu was a makaʻāinana woman of modest origins who learned hula during the Kalākaua renaissance. Her full name was Ana Kini Kapahukulaokamāmalu Kuululani McColgan Huhu. I focus on Kini, as she is the sole female performer from the late nineteenth century whose biography was documented, primarily because she became an influential public figure later in Hawaiʻi—as a cultural authority in her own right and the wife of the first Democratic mayor of Honolulu.[50] Born in 1872 to a Hawaiian mother and an Irish immigrant to Hawaiʻi named John N. McColgan, Kini was the fourteenth of sixteen children (see figure 5). She was adopted and raised by a Hawaiian woman named Kapahukulaokamāmalu and her husband through the common Hawaiian practice of sharing children through hānai. Kapahukulaokamāmalu was a friend of Queen Kapiʻolani, as well as a dancer and chanter who performed on state occasions for Kalākaua, although she was not a court retainer. Growing up next door to Kalākaua's estate, Kini was fascinated by hula performed by the king's retainers. She and her mother would walk to the king's property to watch them practice, and Kini would attempt to copy what she had seen.[51] These were her first forays into hula.

In her teens, Kini became a member of Hui Lei Mamo, but after Kalākaua's death in 1891, she and two of her cohort acquired hula training from teachers associated with Kalākaua's renaissance. The kumu hula Namakeʻelua (sometimes recorded as Nama-elua) claimed to have been "the chief royal hula-master" during the king's birthday jubilee. He had decided to remain in Honolulu instead of returning to his home on the

Fig. 5 Kini Kapahukulaokamāmalu, age eighteen, ca. 1890.
COURTESY OF HAWAI'I STATE ARCHIVES.

island of Kauaʻi.[52] Kini's mother asked him to teach her daughter at his pā hula (hula school), also known as a hālau hula.

Four Hawaiian women entered this pā hula. Three of them—Kini, Pauahi Pinao, and Annie (or Ani) Grube—had been Hui Lei Mamo dancers.[53] The fourth was a woman named Nakai, who did not appear to have a prior relationship to Kalākaua's court.[54] Their intensive training commenced in 1892, with the young women taking residence in the teacher's home. For about six weeks, the dancers dedicated themselves to the female goddess Laka, the patron of hula, and erected a hula kuahu (hula altar), imploring Laka to give them knowledge. Kini claimed to never have forgotten any of the hula she learned during this time because she carefully adhered to strict rules, including ones that required dancers to abstain from sexual intercourse and particular foods. They danced for about six hours a day, taking swims in the ocean and meals in between practices.

Hula practice was a part of a sacred realm and governed by strict rules, because hula performances manifested the gods' and aliʻi's mana (sacred power) and rank.[55] While undergoing training, dancers were kapu (sacred or consecrated) and under the protection of Laka. They observed hula kuahu rituals and performed prayers for Laka.[56] Dancers made sure they were clean while kapu. They also avoided līpepepeʻe seaweed and heʻe (squid), foods whose names were inauspiciously linked to hiding (peʻe) and fleeing, or heʻe (also the word for squid), and therefore might encourage the dissipation of knowledge.[57] On the day of the ʻūniki (ritual graduation), graduates of other hula schools came to watch the four women dance.[58] Only after undergoing ʻūniki were they released from sacredness to become noa (free). The following day, they celebrated their release with a feast and public performance for friends and family.[59] With the ending of their hula training, these four women became full-fledged ʻōlohe hula (hula masters), but they did not have court patronage.

They undertook training in hula genres associated with indigenous pre-European contact traditions, very different from the hula kuʻi (hybrid hula) of the court that freely blended Western and Hawaiian dance vocabularies. Kini described the hālau repertoire she learned as "very religious." She learned hula and chants in honor of gods and aliʻi; she likely also learned mele maʻi, as was the case with other training from this period.[60] They also trained in hula pahu and hula ālaʻapapa, distinct but sacred genres.[61] Performed with a sharkskin drum, hula pahu was associated with ancient temple rituals, while hula ālaʻapapa was performed with an ipu heke (double gourd) and often dedicated to the gods.[62] Kini had seen these dances performed by her mother and other older dancers. Kini explained, "I went to the hālau because I want to learn the old fashioned [hula]."[63]

Although Kini glossed this style as "old fashioned," she was actually learning ancient repertoire, as well as other hula that spanned the secular to the sacred. The genealogical mele they practiced meant that they were learning history and genealogy—mele that placed them in "an unbroken chain" from the present to "the primeval life forces."[64] Poʻe hula were training to become living archives of history and the nation. The dancers embodied history as they practiced genealogical oli (chants) and mele.

While archives secure official state history, prioritizing order, classification, and standardization, hula is a different kind of corporeal archive. It was and continues to be an oral and embodied practice transmitted through chant and kinesthetic movements. Not committed to written record until the late nineteenth century, it was a flexible, living repertoire capable of adjusting to the vicissitudes of chiefly patrons and outside influences, as it was with the hula kuʻi's keen application of Western musical tempos and vocabularies.[65] Hula is able to encompass multiple genealogies simultaneously, as reflected in the proverb "Aʻohe pau ka ʻike i ka hālau hoʻokahi" (Not all knowledge is found in one hālau).[66] Because it favors flexibility and creativity, it is less a fixed repository than a historical process.

As Noenoe K. Silva and Lilikalā Kameʻeleihiwa, Kanaka Maoli scholars, have emphasized, genealogy encourages those in the present to see themselves connected to the past as well as to future generations. The dancers contributed implicitly to a nationalist project by learning and performing cosmogonic genealogies; this was anticolonial and subversive in the face of impending cultural and economic domination by the West. As Kameʻeleihiwa writes, "The hundreds of generations recounted in Hawaiian genealogies were especially important to Hawaiians after Western contact because by the 1870s, many people, especially foreigners, cruelly predicted the complete demise of the Hawaiian race as inevitable."[67]

Although the Hui Lei Mamo and its members would appear to be associated with frivolity and entertainment, they assumed cultural and political authority that endured after the death of its founder, King Kalākaua. When the princess Victoria Poomaikalani, sister-in-law of Kalākaua, died in 1895, the Hui Lei Mamo commemorated her passing and took on official bereavement duties, chanting the kanikau (mourning chant) at her services.[68] As performed by a group of former court attendants, the funerary lament extolled the aliʻi and her genealogical relations, but also glorified the Hawaiian nation.[69]

On the Waterfront

As a public form of entertainment and amusement, hula was also useful for entertaining foreigners. Ruling chiefs in the early nineteenth century entertained Western visitors with performances of hula, though these were eventually curtailed because of missionary interventions.[70] King Kalākaua, however, reintroduced hula into court hospitality. David Kalākaua embodied the heterodoxy of late nineteenth-century Hawaiʻi.

Speaking British-inflected English and fluent in Hawaiian, the king had received a missionary-influenced education at the Royal School but was schooled in Hawaiian practices by his kahu (caregivers). A thirty-second-degree Mason and a Christian, he also became the first monarch to circumnavigate the globe in 1881. In the transnational court of Kalākaua, one would find oio, uhu, and moi, delectable local fishes, served with mashed potatoes and preceded by mulligatawny soup.[71] Inspired by the European courts he had visited during his world tour, he placed a jewel-encrusted crown upon his head at his European-styled coronation in 1883, but also prominently displayed the sacred kāhili (feathered standard) of the aliʻi. The king insisted on equipping his homes with modern amenities; Healani boathouse and ʻIolani Palace each boasted newly invented telephones, and the palace enjoyed electric lights four years before the White House.

When Kalākaua formed Hui Lei Mamo, his singing and hula group, in 1886, the eight girls became immersed in this cosmopolitan world. Fourteen years old when she joined Kalākaua's court, Kini Kapahu named Pauahi Pinao, Annie Grube, Malie Kaleikoa, Aiala, and Namakokahai as other members of the group (see figure 6).[72] All were daughters of court retainers except for Kini. During their time with the court, they learned to represent the king and lāhui Hawaiʻi (nation of Hawaiʻi) through their bodies, manners, and self-presentation, but also utilized their time in the court for their own discrepant purposes.

Although they performed hula with indigenous movements, instrumentation, and chanting in the hālau hula, the young women of Hui Lei Mamo performed only the hula kuʻi in court, or what Kini termed "the modern hula."[73] "Kuʻi" means "to join, stitch, sew" and hula kuʻi is literally a "joined hula" of indigenous and Western performance vocabularies.[74] In Amy Kuʻuleialoha Stillman's analysis, the hula kuʻi was the invention of "practitioners [who] sought to combine components of the indigenous Hawaiian music and dance traditions with elements of Western music and dance that had become popular, especially in urban Honolulu."[75] Performed in Hawaiian language and accompanied by Western instruments such as the guitar, ʻukulele, and piano, as well as Hawaiian percussive instruments, this hula kuʻi incorporated polka or waltz tempos and couplet verses. Hawaiian poetry remained central, but it was sung to Western music.

The hula kuʻi emerged during Kalākaua's cultural revival, and Kini Kapahu even claimed that Kalākaua was the one who invented the genre.

Fig. 6 King Kalākaua's Hui Lei Mamo dancers, ca. 1886. Front row, left to right: Namahana, possibly Aiala, Pauahi Pinao, Kalua, Pinao. Back row, left to right: possibly Annie Grube, Kini Kapahukulaokamāmalu, unidentified. COURTESY OF HAWAIʻI STATE ARCHIVES.

Kini explained that the king "took some steps out of the old-fashioned and put them into the modern [hula] with guitar. He was the first one to start this."[76] While there was likely no single innovator, the mixing of traditional hula experts and skilled Hawaiian and foreign musicians trained in Western music undoubtedly spurred creativity and invention in Kalākaua's cosmopolitan court.[77] Quartets and quintets of Hawaiian male musicians affiliated with the king's Royal Hawaiian Band played music, while the young girls of Hui Lei Mamo danced this hybrid hula. Rather than wearing costuming associated with indigenous performance genres, including items such as the pāʻū kapa, the girls performed in tailored attire that similarly reflected a hybrid European-Hawaiian sensibility: white, floor-length holokū and shoes.

Hula kuʻi serves as an apt metaphor for the imaginative responses to change by Hawaiian performers. They were not passive recipients of Western ideas and products, but were flexible innovators who appropriated what they desired from the outside and blended it with the familiar to arrive at something novel and unexpected. In the face of vast cultural and political dislocation, they were actively shaping a Native Hawaiian modernity that would help them adapt to and survive formal colonization in the next decade. A mark of their modernity was an ability to reinvent themselves, to peruse everything available to them and adopt what was most useful. Ever resourceful, the women who performed the hula kuʻi in the interior of a boathouse would continue to stitch together strategies for self-preservation and autonomy along their wide-ranging North American and European tours. Through the boathouse, a microcosm of the shifting intercultural society of nineteenth-century Honolulu, they became disquietingly modern subjects.

The boathouse was an interstitial space between genteel palace life, elite island society, and the working classes of Honolulu, both foreign and Hawaiian. Located about a mile away from the royal palace grounds, the Honolulu pier was the portal to a highly disorderly waterfront known for racial and class mixing, illicit sexual assignations, and riotous barrooms, dancehalls, and theaters.[78] The port city of Honolulu had earned the moniker "The Cesspit of the Pacific" by the 1850s, as much for its moral pollution as its open sewers.[79] And yet, perhaps because of its proximity to illicit urban excitements, Kalākaua favored the waterfront. The grand ʻIolani Palace hosted official state business, but the two-story boathouse, built over the harbor using stilts, was where the king could relax. Here, on the margins of the court, he played cards, gambled, and drank prodigiously.

Kalākaua earned the sobriquet "Merrie Monarch" for his love of amusement and revelry. Robert Louis Stevenson, during his sojourn in the islands, admired Kalākaua, calling him "a very fine, intelligent fellow."[80] But he also bemoaned the sovereign's immense appetite for champagne, saying, "A bottle of fizz is like a glass of sherry to him; he thinks nothing of five or six in an afternoon as a whet for dinner."[81] Healani, the boathouse, hosted gentile entertainments by the light of day, such as canoe regattas, performances by the king's hula troupe, and choral music by his siblings' glee clubs. But in the evenings, the boathouse became a ribald space for the king and other men to enjoy all-night games of poker and free-flowing alcohol. As one American travel writer lamented, the boathouse was "where the cares of state were dissipated during Kalakaua's reign."[82]

The Honolulu waterfront's unsavory reputation arose because it literally and symbolically marked a boundary between the indigenous and the foreign. Through this portal, bodies, germs, and ideas flowed into and out of the islands, a flow that had changed Hawaiʻi dramatically over the last seventy years of contact. Greg Dening has theorized cultural contact and

Fig. 7 Healani boathouse, Honolulu. COURTESY OF BISHOP MUSEUM.

transformation in the Marquesas using beaches as a metaphor for permeable cultural boundaries: "Beaches must be crossed to enter them [islands] or leave them, to make them or change them." Each group—Native and European—transmitted their own cultural signs across beaches.[83] In the process of crossing these beaches—in this case the Te Enata (Marquesans) meeting the Te Aoe (the strangers, or Europeans)—islands were remade and cultures transformed.

On another Pacific beach, Healani was a liminal space where partial cultural worlds met and at times collided. Hovering over the water, neither on land nor entirely on the sea, the indeterminate structure of Healani symbolized the monarchy's bold but precarious position (see figure 7). On the edge of the familiar and the new, the boathouse operated as an informal meeting ground where heterogeneous ranks of foreigners, islanders, and figures in-between mingled and learned about each other (see figure 8). As such, the boathouse was an intensified version of the changing cultural and social milieu of the islands.

Circumventing conventions of polite society, Kalākaua hosted foreign dignitaries, naval officers, sugar barons, European royalty, musicians, writers, and actors. One of the king's regular poker games reputedly included a cabinet minister, banker, lawyer, and butcher.[84] Nationality, social class, status, and occupation did not seem to matter as much as

Fig. 8 Robert Louis Stevenson is entertained by King Kalākaua at Healani boathouse, 1889. Kalākaua is seated at the far left; Stevenson is next to him. The boathouse musicians are standing. COURTESY OF BISHOP MUSEUM.

novelty. Foreigners passing through Honolulu on their way to Australia or back from California might have expected an invitation to the boathouse for a lūʻau or hula performance (see figure 9). Katie Putnam, American opera singer, and the prince and princess of Bourbon were among the personages who partook of the king's hospitality.[85]

The blurring of status and class differences at the boathouse recalls Mikhail Bakhtin's description of the temporary social leveling enacted during carnival: "The suspension of all hierarchical precedence during carnival time was of particular significance. Rank was especially evident during official feasts; everyone was expected to appear in the full regalia of his calling . . . and to take the place corresponding to his position. It was a consecration of inequality. On the contrary, all were considered equal during carnival. Here, in the town square, a special form of free and familiar contact reigned among people who were usually divided by the barriers of caste, property, profession, and age."[86] On the unruly waterfront away from the court, the Healani boathouse also upended hierarchies. As a participant, Kini Kapahu experienced a restrained, yet carnivalesque, world where boundaries were relaxed and roles reversed, at least momentarily.

Fig. 9 Lūʻau at Healani boathouse, ca. 1883. On this occasion, Kalākaua hosted guests from London. Hawaiian and haole guests dine side by side, with Kalākaua and his consort seated at the far end of the table. COURTESY OF HAWAIIAN HISTORICAL SOCIETY.

Outsiders were confounded in this transnational salon; Euro-Americans may have owned their superiority, but could not assert it consistently. Young Hawaiian boys and girls of common birth observed how foreigners ate and danced, while foreigners learned that even a king with "copper color" skin had a white chamberlain, displayed impeccable decorum, and spoke flawless British-inflected English.[87] The gaze flowed in multiple directions: Hawaiians scrutinized foreigners who were out of place while clumsily performing Hawaiian protocol. Haole did not know how to eat poi with their fingers and stumbled while retreating backward from the king and queen according to Hawaiian custom.

Rank, the bedrock of Hawaiʻi's religious, social, and political system, was unsettled in the space of the boathouse and by the social leveling produced by performance. With few exceptions, Hawaiian society was highly stratified, with birth determining commoner or chiefly rank. As Martha Beckwith writes, "Position in old Hawaii, both social and political, depended in the first instance upon rank, and rank upon blood descent—hence the importance of genealogy as proof of high ancestry."[88] Davida Malo, the early nineteenth-century Hawaiian historian, described the distinct separation between the aliʻi and men: "O ke aliʻi no ka mea maluna o na kanaka a pau" (The ali'i was the one person above all the people).[89] In some exceptional circumstances, male warriors were able to move up in rank by demonstrating heroism in battle.[90]

At the boathouse, however, commoners interacted with royalty, and young Hawaiian performers were chosen on the basis of their ability, not rank. Henry Berger, a talented Prussian army musician recruited to Hawai'i by Lota Kapuāiwa (King Kamehameha V), led the kingdom's Royal Hawaiian Band and brought in young Hawaiian men, many from reformatory institutions.[91] Under Berger's direction, these men honed their mandolin, banjo, violin, and bass playing for the king and his guests. Neither were the Hawaiian girls and women of Hui Lei Mamo of royal birth, but they learned a valuable cultural art under the sponsorship of their sovereign.

The king himself did not simply patronize hula and music, but was an active choreographer, composer, and musician. Kini describes Kalākaua's taking a stick and counting out the tempo for the hula ku'i, and he played the 'ukulele, one of the new Western instruments he championed.[92] Unlike commercial entertainment venues that strictly divide the performer and consumer from the backstage and stage, the boathouse blurred these distinctions. The king took great interest in his productions and personally supervised his dancers and musicians.[93] He could be roundly criticized for having blurred the boundary between ruling and performing. An American newspaper sniped erroneously, "It was not so very many years ago that his Majesty of the Cannibal Islands . . . was earning a modest livelihood by picking a banjo in the disreputable dives along the water front of Honolulu."[94]

Kini Kapahu was usually called by her English given name "Jennie," or "Kini," which is the Hawaiian transliteration of "Jennie." However, the king arrived at his own nickname for her, "Lady Jane." The invented title "Lady Jane" further suggests the irreverent atmosphere of this particular place and time. Kini was a commoner, but within the boathouse she could become a lady. Kini's transformation into a lady was all the more remarkable considering that she and the other Hawaiian girls traversed a site inappropriate for proper young women. Gavan Daws notes, "It was generally understood that the [Honolulu] harbor was no place for a lady."[95] In the early 1800s, nonchiefly women engaged in sexual trade with foreigners on Pacific Island beachfronts; these interactions ranged from coercive to self-motivated and are not simply reducible to prostitution, as David A. Chappell observes.[96] However, the port of Honolulu became

internationally infamous as a depraved harbor, and American missionaries targeted supposed "orgies" held aboard ships.[97] The waterfront of
Kalākaua's era was populated by the socially marginal: the indigent, the
poor, prostitutes, and sailors. Even the king indulged in excesses of liquor
and no-limit card games there.

The hula dancers also inhabited the margins of respectability because
of their transgressive vocation and gender. They were introduced to the
kind of scrutiny they would face during their hula tours a few years later.
They learned that their bodies and moral character, far more than their
art, would be exposed via their performances. Objectified by primitivist discourse in the islands and abroad, hula dancers were articulated as
sexually and racially other. Most Euro-American observers treated hula
as part of the demimonde and its practitioners indecorous figures. The
erotic "hula-hula dances" revived by Kalākaua were characterized by
American newspapers as "highly improper" relics of "primitive Hawaii"
and the "forbidden pleasure of the Sandwich Islanders."[98] A metonymic
relationship between hula and the Hawaiian Islands was already in formation in tourist discourse preceding the U.S. takeover, a productive system of knowledge that would be strengthened in future decades.

One of the king's American guests, the manager of an opera singer, attended a party at the boathouse in 1890 along with European officials and
their wives. In a U.S. newspaper travelogue, he described "the koula-koula
[his gloss on the hula] danced by fourteen native girls with bare limbs and
grass anklets." While generally approving of the performance, the writer
cautioned that it may not be appropriate for some audiences: "The dancers were very graceful and the dance beautiful, but so amorous that the
ladies turned aside their heads."[99] Rendered into beautiful yet promiscu-
ous savages through the scopophilic gaze of Euro-Americans, Hawaiian
women knew before leaving the islands that they would have to negotiate
between propriety and innovation.

The young women paid the steepest price for their unorthodox decisions. In the islands, Hawaiians and haole, friends and strangers alike,
censured the dancers for performing hula. Kini lamented the mockery of
her childhood friends, recalling, "How they hate the hula. Oh, shame."[100]
Kini cried and did her best to ignore their taunts. This hostility was inter-
nalized by many Hawaiians and precipitated a broad containment of hula
well until the first decades of the twentieth century. Alarmed that many
dances were disappearing, Mary Kawena Pukui undertook the systematic
study of hula with her daughter Patience Nāmaka Wiggin in the 1930s

and 1940s. Pukui remarked that although the late nineteenth-century monarchs Queen Emma and King Kalākaua supported hula, "for many years, hula was looked down upon and no respectable boy or girl was ever permitted to watch one, much less dance it."[101]

Other dancers at the beginning of the twentieth century struggled to reconcile their Christian faith with a practice associated with sexuality and sin. Kauhai Likua, a court dancer from the Kalākaua period, stopped dancing hula after she became a church minister. Likua decided to teach hula secretly to a single pupil on Maui, Emma Kapiolani Farden Sharpe. Sharpe persuaded Likua by saying, "[We are] both children of God and when she [Likua] died she would take all her knowledge with her."[102] Sharpe's own father had forbidden her to learn hula because he associated it with "what was being danced on Lahaina Street" (in the port town of Lahaina). But under Likua's tutelage, Sharpe later became an influential hula teacher herself.

Despite public antagonism, the boathouse proved a productive intercultural world for poʻe hula. They were entrusted with a formal responsibility to learn new dances and perform the hula kuʻi for the king's guests. Beyond that, they could take advantage of the court to pursue their own interests. Kini had only a few years of formal schooling but was intellectually curious. The transnational court served as her education and encouraged her to defy gendered conventions. She became friends with the young Hawaiian boys who played Western instruments at the boathouse. Kini had grown up with an adoptive Hawaiian mother who was an expert in oli and had watched the king's poʻe hula perform since she was a child. However, Kini grew fascinated by new Western music and instruments. When the king's quintet took a break at the boathouse, she picked up one of their ʻukulele and tried to teach herself how to play. The king noticed and asked, "Oh, Lady Jane, you want to play like me?" He urged her to keep practicing, and even gave her an ʻukulele of her own.[103]

Hawaiian girls from "decent" homes were discouraged from playing music in public, but spurred by the example of the skilled boathouse musicians, Kini practiced the ʻukulele and banjo at home. She said, "All Hawaiians think I'm crazy girl to do that thing in the street. In Hawaiian, they talk loud so I can hear [what they're saying about me]." Their criticism made her more defiant: "I play more, stand by the window. I play more. I play loud, very loud."[104] She was not content to merely listen to the developing new music, but wanted to compose and direct. She later performed the 'ukulele on the U.S. continent; her willingness to improvise and seize the stage were talents that would serve her well in unfamiliar American environments.

Furthermore, the performers enjoyed regular contact with royalty and foreigners, as well as other Hawaiian commoners. When they were not performing, the hula dancers learned to ballroom dance from a foreign sailor with red hair who was the king's barber.[105] The girls' first language was Hawaiian, but they also practiced speaking English with British and American visitors. The court inspired Kini to see the world. She said, "I wanted to go to the Mainland [U.S. continent] so much . . . and I kept telling my Mama, 'You, me, we work, Mama, until we have money to see the Mainland.'"[106] These encounters with outsiders may not have been sustained interactions, but they sparked the women's curiosity and inspired them to seek and experience the world outside of Hawai'i.

In the court the young women took early lessons in self-presentation and Western dress and deportment. They were developing strategies that would help them contest their indecent reputations in future travels. An equally critical part of their performance was the performance of femininity: to appear as proper ladies for the king's guests and to represent the kingdom. They knew how to curtsy when other royalty and dignitaries arrived at the court. To perform the hula ku'i, they wore long Western gowns.[107] This courtly etiquette proved useful when they encountered royalty in Europe during their travels.

In the one extant photograph of Hui Lei Mamo, the young women are dressed as schoolgirls: they posed wearing boots and white sailor uniforms trimmed with ribbons (see figure 6). Their hairstyles—carefully coiffed, waved, and pinned back—are most suggestive of their attention to modern fashion. In the islands, the women were already representing themselves as hybrid subjects and performing as "ex-primitives."[108] In other words, they were eagerly learning how to become cosmopolitan by outfitting themselves as modern Hawaiian women. A few years later when they adopted the legible dress of Hawaiian dancers—grass skirts and lei—on stage at the Chicago World's Columbian Exposition in 1893, they did so self-consciously and with more than a touch of irony. They were playing Hawaiian for the foreign audience, performing their "Hawaiianness" as expected.

Well-versed in both courtly decorum and sacred arts, some of the women of Kalākaua's court would soon be recruited to perform in North

America. They were the living historical archive of the nation as they un-settled gendered boundaries and birthrights. The boathouse was just the beginning of their journey; they would cross many more beaches.

Foreign Crossings

Whether in Chicago or Honolulu, whether in the presence of kings, tourists, or journalists, Kini Kapahu insisted on defining her own terms whenever possible and refused to be maligned. If necessary, she fought back physically, but most often she defended herself with witty and acid retorts. Her repartee allowed her to temporarily occupy a position of power and destabilize her opponent's secure vantage point. Kini took ad-vantage of momentary opportunities to assert her parity, and that of her nation, with Americans.

When her hula troupe arrived in the United States for the first time in 1892, they were confronted immediately with the bureaucratic authority of the U.S. nation-state—personified by immigration gatekeepers that rel-egated Hawaiians to members of a lesser nation. Immigration policies had begun to stem the flow of nonwhites. Whereas individual states had been delegated to oversee immigration prior to 1891, the federal government established the Bureau of Immigration that year to more carefully moni-tor immigration, as Southern and Eastern Europeans increased signifi-cantly relative to arrivals from Northern and Western Europe. The first federal law that restricted immigration on the basis of race, the Chinese Exclusion Act, had been passed a decade earlier and was renewed in 1892 for another ten years. Fears of the decline of white civilization stirred as the birth rates for native-born whites declined and nonwhite immi-gration soared. Theodore Roosevelt expressed this anxiety by writing at the turn of the century that whites faced "race suicide."[109] Non-European immigrants petitioning for naturalized citizenship—including a Chinese immigrant, a Syrian, an Arab, and a Hawaiian—were also denied on racial grounds in state and federal courts in the late nineteenth century and the early twentieth.[110]

Processing the six Hawaiian performers in San Francisco, the customs agent examined their Hawaiian kingdom passports and recorded the Ha-waiians as "immigrants," rather than tourists with Hawaiian citizenship. Their classification as immigrants may have occurred since Hawaiians' racial categorization was considered ambiguous yet unquestionably in-ferior to that of Caucasians. In 1889, a Utah court described a Hawai-ian petitioner known only as "Kanaka Nian" as "of Malayan or Mongolian complexion" and denied him naturalized U.S. citizenship on the grounds that Hawaiians could not be classed with Caucasians.[111] While nineteenth-century scientific research on the Hawaiian "race" classified Hawaiians as "Polynesian," Hawaiians were well aware that the Western world viewed them most popularly as savages and cannibals.[112] In 1867 Samuel Mānaiakalani Kamakau, the Hawaiian historian, wrote that the Western world insisted on seeing Hawaiians as a "race of maneaters."[113] The king of Hawai'i himself could not escape such inflammatory portrayals in the United States. Upon Kalākaua's election as head of state in 1874, he became known as a "king of cannibals." One Philadelphia newspaper asserted that the king's blood had been "enriched by many cannibal feasts."[114] Other regional newspapers, while generally noting his regal bearing, continued to mock him as a cannibal king during his tour of the United States in 1874.[115]

Furthermore, popular and political discourse often conflated Hawaiians with the more familiar racial figures of Africans and African Americans. To mark Hawaiians as subordinate, American journalists and cartoonists relied upon existing language and visual codes for blacks and slaves, describing King Kalākaua as a "big darkey" and a "dusky highness."[116] Cartoonists drew Kalākaua's successor and sister Queen Lili'uokalani with large lips and kinky hair, infantilizing her through tropes of the enslaved African, such as the "mammy," a matronly domestic servant, and the "pickaninny," a slave child.[117] After Lili'uokalani was deposed by white missionary descendants, the American press, regardless of their positions on annexation, ridiculed her rightful political claims to the kingdom. For why should a "cannibal island queen," a "crafty barbarian," or a "black" queen whose political affairs were worthy of a "Negro song and dance" be restored to the throne?[118]

A white customs agent processing arrivals at the San Francisco port, even if not immediately familiar with the popular or scientific racial taxonomy marking Hawaiians as savage, would have looked at the Hawaiian performers' brown skin and categorized them as racially distinct, if not subordinate. Kini recognized the existing American antipathy to the category of immigrant.[119] She confronted the agent: "I tell him Hawaiians never been immigrants. We have immigrants in Hawai'i . . . and they have white skin like you."[120] With this clever retort, she was able to take the freighted term "immigrant"—racialized at the time to encompass nearly anyone other than the native-born "Anglo-Saxon"—and shift its burden to those privileged within the overlapping categories of "white,"

"American," and "citizen." Challenging the racist logic that poised white Americans above Hawaiians and others, she subverted whiteness by making it into a marked category and shrewdly turned whites into racial and cultural outsiders. Appropriating the racialized language of the state, she critiqued the uneven terms of her own entrance into the United States as a Hawaiian woman, a citizen of a weaker nation.

Kini would continue to confound the categorization of Hawaiians as racially and sexually other. Although adopted and raised by Hawaiians, Kini was born to a Hawaiian woman and an Irish immigrant to Hawai'i and kept in contact with her birth family, as was customary in the islands. She acknowledged her Irish parentage matter-of-factly, but considered herself Hawaiian and avoided quantitative terms such as "half-Hawaiian," "part-Hawaiian," or "hapa haole" (part-white), terms that privilege blood-quantum classification in the determination of Hawaiian belonging and cultural identity. Blood logic would soon become an effective means of racial management in the Hawaiian territory, as the federal government in the early twentieth century defined "native Hawaiians" as those with at least one-half blood quantum. As J. Kēhaulani Kauanui has incisively observed, this restrictive blood criteria encouraged the dilution and disappearance of Hawaiians and ultimately worked to extinguish Hawaiian claims to land and sovereignty.[121]

While the United States would delimit Hawaiian identity via restrictive blood criteria, Hawaiians emphasized their relatedness through inclusive genealogical, kinship, and cultural practices.[122] Being half European and having lighter skin did not exclude Kini from Hawaiian cultural training, nor did it offer her more privileged access to these circles. Within the court hula troupes or the hula school, racial phenotype did not accord with rank or treatment; rather the performance of cultural knowledge and proficiency was paramount in hula.

However, Kini strategically deployed her racially mixed background in the United States to contest racialized exclusion. To generate publicity for hula performances, American vaudeville managers would arrange for newspaper reporters to interview the women. Reporters were accustomed to writing sensational stories about Hawaiians as uncivilized savages, but Hawaiians remained an uncommon sight on the continent. During at least one session, incredulous reporters asked the women if they were indeed Hawaiian. Kini declined to give a straightforward answer. Instead, she pointed to her friend and fellow court dancer Pauahi Pinao, who was darker-skinned and more legibly Hawaiian than she. Kini stated simply,

"I'm only part of her. My other part is like you." When the puzzled reporters queried, "What is your other half?" she simply replied, "Irish." They could only respond in surprise, "Is that so?" Kini giggled when retelling this anecdote in 1962, pleased that she had managed to befuddle the white Americans.[123]

By saying, "I am like you," Kini was insisting on a commensurate status with her American inquisitors. She used a hereditary claim to whiteness to subvert the dominant racial lens. She tricked the Americans into seeing themselves as racially marked and thus reversed the gaze of her examiners. Yet by briefly claiming her Irish background, she was not conceding Hawaiians were inferior to whites but asserting her equality with whites. By implying Irish was white, she was also unwittingly playing with the category of "white," which in a nineteenth-century North American context also had an unstable relationship to "Irish."

Although Kini and her troupe gained entry as "immigrants" and would later become subject to U.S. territorial rule, she was quick to display defiance during her travels. One might even speculate that Kini acquired an imperious hauteur from observing how Hawaiian ali'i and European nobility behaved at court. This attitude served her well when she had to defend herself and her subordinated nation. A Hawaiian friend described her later in life: "[Kini] carried herself with such a degree of arrogance that it was both hateful and wonderful to see. . . . And she didn't acknowledge anybody, but she acknowledged everybody in total when she came with this and you look at our aliis from Europe and they do the same thing."[124] As they moved along American and European transnational hula circuits, Kini and her peers continued to make the dominant order "function in another register" and subvert their colonized status.[125]

CHAPTER 2

MODERN DESIRES AND COUNTER-COLONIAL TACTICS
Gender, Performance, and the Erotics of Empire

When King David Kalākaua died in 1891, hula performers affiliated with his court no longer enjoyed his patronage. But an opportunity presented itself to his dancers through an American visitor a year later. On a walk through Honolulu, a haole tourist named Harry W. Foster heard the sounds of pahu (sharkskin drums) and ipu (gourd instruments) coming from the dancer Kini Kapahukulaokamāmalu's home. He and his wife returned to watch the hālau hula (hula troupe) perform hula another day, and he immediately asked the group to tour the United States.[1] Foster was not a professional showman, but a jeweler from San Francisco vacationing in Hawaiʻi, and hula became his new venture.[2]

On first impulse Kini declined because she was scared of such a long journey. However, she had dreamed of visiting the United States and decided to request passports from the current monarch, Queen Liliʻuokalani. Kini asked Liliʻuokalani in Hawaiian: "You know, your majesty, I want to go to the mainland." The queen replied, "Aren't you afraid to go?" Kini insisted, "Not me, I want to go." The queen gave her permission, calling Kini an "akamai" (smart) girl.[3] Kini returned and asked her fellow dancers, "Don't you want to go? You don't have to go but I'm going to go."[4] Eventually the remaining three women in the hālau signed onto the tour. Foster also hired two men, brothers named Kanuku and Kamuku.[5] They were hoʻopaʻa, chanters who provided essential poetry and drumming.[6] With the addition of these men, the troupe totaled six. Foster was in the right place at the right time: he was able to capitalize on the availability of extremely skilled dancers who only two years prior were in the personal entourage of the king.[7] The four women were 'ōlohe hula, or graduates of a hālau hula.[8]

While hula had been available as a tourist amusement in the port cities of Hawai'i or at private gatherings, this fledging venture took hula away from the islands and into mass commercial entertainment in Euro-American cities. Bringing colonial curiosities to new publics, this fin de siècle tour represents a shift in attention to Hawai'i that accompanied the American and settler-missionary usurpation of Hawaiian sovereignty in 1893. Promoters like Foster were able to take advantage of a trained pool of laborer-performers who were no longer patronized within a state infrastructure. Euro-American agents, promoters, and spectators became the new patrons of hula, replacing chiefs and broadening the scale of hula as Hawai'i became part of the U.S. imperial ambit.

Hula performers, particularly young women of maka'āinana (commoner) rank, took advantage of the opportunity to travel and represent their country away from the islands. Beginning in 1892, the troupe toured a wide swath of North American and European mass-entertainment venues for four years.[9] Kini was twenty years old at the time, and the other three women were around the same age. The only extant photograph of the troupe was taken shortly after their arrival in San Francisco (see figure 10).[10] After California, Kini and the other five members of the troupe toured the western U.S. states and British Columbia.[11] They reached Chicago in April 1893 for the opening of the World's Columbian Exposition. After living and working at the Chicago exposition for six months, the dancers joined a vaudeville circuit that crossed the American South. In the spring of 1894, they departed for European capitals such as Paris, London, and Munich, where they performed in commercial working-class theaters and royal palaces. They returned to the Northeast United States a year later, and then made their way through the vaudeville theater and dime museum circuit.

Presented as authentic novelties from the Sandwich Islands, they shared the stage with the likes of African American "Creole" minstrels, Bedouin Arab acrobats, and bearded ladies.[12] Along the journey, two performers—the ho'opa'a Kanuku and the 'ōlapa (dancer) Nakai—left the troupe for Samoa, while the ho'opa'a Kamuku stayed behind in Germany. The remainder of the original hula troupe returned to Honolulu in the spring of 1896.

This was the first major translocal, if not global, tour of the hula.[13]

Fig. 10 Hula troupe in San Francisco, ca. 1892. Back row standing, left to right: possibly Nakai, Pauahi Pinao, Kini Kapahukulaokamāmalu, possibly Annie Grube. Front row: brothers Kamuku and Kanuku. COURTESY OF HAWAI'I STATE ARCHIVES.

They were one of the first troupes to receive sustained attention outside the islands, to be chronicled by regional and national reviews, guidebooks, and newspapers. The U.S.-backed overthrow in 1893 laid the foundation for the formal colonization of Hawai'i and prompted heightened curiosity about the archipelago and its Native people. The troupe learned of the overthrow of the constitutional monarchy in January 1893 while thousands of miles away from home. With the sovereignty of their nation jeopardized by the American intervention, the performers became, in effect, potential colonial subjects of interest to the United States.

Although Hawai'i was not a formal political territory of the United States until its annexation in 1898, Hawaiians were increasingly subjugated, imperial subjects during the last three decades of the nineteenth century. A colonial class made up of missionary-business settlers controlled Hawai'i's Western-oriented export industries, and the economy became debt-ridden and dependent on U.S. sugar markets. These American missionary descendants, many of whom were sugar planters and brokers, also had assumed authority and positions in the Hawaiian government after the imposition of the Bayonet Constitution in 1887.[14] Empowered by their relationship to export markets and their influence on Congress, these missionary sons managed to pressure Kalākaua to accept the constitution and reciprocity treaty that further undermined the political and economic autonomy of the monarchy, pushing it toward insolvency.

Kalākaua's sister Lili'uokalani inherited the throne after his death in 1891. She planned to unveil another constitution to replace the Bayonet Constitution that had abrogated the rights of Hawaiians and the monarchy.[15] Threatened by a more assertive Hawaiian throne, the missionary sons and businessmen who had curtailed Kalākaua's powers organized a group called the "Annexation Club." While they had been secretly working to secure American support for annexation, the proposed constitution became the club's excuse to depose the queen in January 1893. That month, the Annexation Club formed the Committee of Safety, which orchestrated the unlawful overthrow of the Hawaiian kingdom with the help of the U.S. minister to Hawai'i, John L. Stevens. American marines landed in Honolulu Harbor, took control of government buildings, and effectively held the queen and her cabinet hostage. The queen at first refused to surrender to the conspirators, but to avoid bloodshed Lili'uokalani temporarily relinquished her crown to Minister Stevens under extreme protest on 17 January 1893. The new provisional government (PG) violated international law and treaties held between the United States and the kingdom, but Stevens recognized the PG and proclaimed Hawai'i an American protectorate.[16]

Kini said she was "stunned and sick at heart" to hear about the overthrow while on tour. Deeply distressed by this news, the hula troupe decided not to return home.[17] The upheaval in the islands likely contributed to the troupe's extension of their tour beyond their initial six-month contract. With their government usurped by pro-U.S. annexationists, the performers who had left holding kingdom passports were unmoored in the United States. They encountered unfamiliar and thrilling worlds, knowing they might return to a homeland irrevocably altered in their absence.

Hula operated both as colonial commodity and counter-colonial tactic during the critical period following the overthrow. Resignified as a national, anti-imperialist practice in the Kalākaua period, hula was appropriated for tourist export and marketed as a commodity in a developing mass-culture industry. While hula had been a political script in the islands, hula performers were unwittingly catapulted into being cultural ambassadors for their nation. Their entrance into a transnational marketplace brought hula practitioners further opportunities and complications. American imperial interest enabled trained cadres of hula dancers to develop new paths through entertainment circuits while their bodies were interpellated as signs of Hawaiians' uncivilized nature. Women's bodily movements on stage provided an occasion for American audiences to indulge in scopophilic pleasure from Hawaiian bodies and ascribe Hawaiians to a lower order of humanity. The dancers I discuss were the first of many who entered the colonial pipeline to the U.S. continent after the overthrow in 1893 and annexation in 1898. Hula became both a more expansive and restrictive structure through which Native Hawaiian women were able to travel abroad, seek adventure, and gain cultural capital.

Fin de siècle colonial scripts wrote Hawaiian women and their bodies into the consciousnesses of Euro-Americans, but what I call countercolonial tactics and performances helped to unravel those scripts. Michel de Certeau describes tactics as "the ingenious ways in which the weak make use of the strong."[18] He argues that consumption is neither passive nor docile; users adapt, manipulate, and reappropriate products, space, and time according to "their own interests and their own rules."[19] Indians subjugated by Spanish colonization practiced this creative manipulation: "[They] often used the laws, practices, and representations that were imposed on them by force or by fascination to ends other than those of their conquerors; they made something else out of them; they subverted them from within—not by rejecting them or by transforming them . . . but by many different ways of using them in the service of rules, customs or convictions foreign to the colonization which they could not escape." Those operating from a position of relative weakness do not have the advantage of what Certeau delineates as *strategies*—actions that control space and master time. In contrast, "a tactic is an art of the weak," operating in between, accepting "the chance offerings of the moment," and mobilized by trickery.[20]

Hawaiian women, though frequently displayed as imperial objects, were not passive commodities in the constraining order of empire; they improvised tactics to subvert colonial scripts that insisted on primitivist eroticized roles, asserted hula as a legitimate practice, and presented themselves as modern Native women and cosmopolitan tourists. Hawaiian women landed in metropolitan centers and engaged with modes of tourist consumption for their own discrepant purposes. They pursued gendered collecting and touristic practices, appropriating technologies such as studio photography and urbane fashion for their own desires. In a cultural economy dominated by rules they could not escape, how did they produce a poetics of resistance or diversion?

Because they were pursuing self-fashioning for their own purposes, their modern desires—for travel, adventure, and style—ran aground of both anticolonial nationalism and U.S. imperialist logics. Their self-presentation and performances were not necessarily *anticolonial* in an organized or intentional manner. For this reason, Hawaiian women responded with *counter-colonial* tactics and desires. Here I borrow from Vicente M. Diaz's use of "counter-colonial" to describe Chamorro practices and desires that are not easily categorized as anticolonial but nevertheless contain latent critiques of imperial influence.[21]

While these dancers were on tour, Hawaiian women patriots in the islands were organizing protests against the overthrow of their queen and the abrogation of their sovereignty, as Noenoe K. Silva illuminates in her study *Aloha Betrayed: Native Hawaiian Resistance to American Colonialism.*[22] Dancing hula away from the lāhui (nation), women dancers, unlike their contemporaries, can be seen as doubly removed from the center of politics, with only an attenuated relationship to an anticolonial resistance movement. Hula, however, was a critical part of the political and cultural survival of Hawaiians. Silva writes, "The old religion, dance, moʻolelo, mele, and moʻokūʻauhau were like the iwikuamoʻo (spine) for the lāhui; without their own traditions they could not stand up to the colonial onslaught."[23] Poʻe hula, throughout their wide-ranging travels and negotiations with commodity culture, continued to reproduce Native historiography and genealogies as they had been trained to do.

Analyzing a different subordinated group, working-class African Americans, Robin D. G. Kelley argues that culture is neither ancillary to politics nor epiphenomenal to labor, but is in fact constitutive of political consciousness. He writes, "I am rejecting the tendency to dichotomize people's lives, to assume that clear-cut 'political' motivations exist separately from issues of economic well-being, safety, pleasure, cultural expression, sexuality, freedom of mobility and other facets of daily life. Politics is not separate from lived experience or the imaginary world of what is possible; to the contrary, politics is about these things."[24] Culture, pleasure, and politics mingle messily, and everyday engagements with cultural forms and expressions are integral to the way people interpret and struggle with power relations.

In a Hawaiian context, cultural performances were a terrain in which colonial politics unfolded and were contested by practitioners. Colonization was not a "fatal impact" for those in its grip. Nicholas Thomas reminds us that colonial projects "are often projected rather than realized."[25] There were few transparent instances of resistance and triumph over colonialism; there were, rather, uneven oscillations of power and traces of the women's dialogic negotiations with colonization and autonomy. The stories of hula performers are of the retreats, small challenges, and frequent sorrows that comprise, as well as unsettle, processes of colonialism and subjugation. Although this group of Hawaiians rarely registered outright victories, they often evaded and deflected forces that sought to define and rule them.[26] For they were not only constrained by American imperialism and tourist economies, but by rank, class, and patriarchal hierarchies within the islands. Poʻe hula did not invent their counter-colonial tactics; these tactics were based on skills they had begun acquiring in the transnational court of Honolulu before their departure.

I purposely do not follow a linear chronology of Hawaiian performers on tour.[27] To reveal the oscillations of colonial power that at once restrained and liberated Hawaiian performers, I move between spectacularized performances and the women's tactics of consumption and diversion. This is a compensatory approach, aimed to shift attention away from the hypervisible, eroticized bodies of subaltern subjects toward their more clandestine practices. However, despite the overexposure of their bodies, these performers and their fin de siècle tours left but faint traces in Hawaiian and American archives, traces that are difficult to pursue a century later.[28] The reasons for this are abundant—these performers were makaʻāinana women and marginalized intercultural figures, and individual biographies were obscured by the archetypal categorization of the women as "hula dancers." With one known exception, the dancers appear to have died young and did not have children.[29] They moved between multiple locales while on tour, making it difficult for island newspapers to track them when the political turmoil of the American overthrow and attempts to restore the kingdom took precedence. However, they and numerous contemporaries are the "native informants" whose knowledge underwrote twentieth-century ethnography and ethnomusicology of Hawaiʻi, while remaining largely anonymous or undocumented.[30]

When subjects are obscured within the extant archive, how might we disclose their tactics? In order to make their hidden transcripts more visible—the often overlooked gestures and desires theorized by James C. Scott—I look at alternative archives and repertoire that do not marshal the authority of the nation, whether an imperial nation or an emerging postcolonial nation.[31] The performer did not intend for their corporeal movements, souvenir photographs, jewelry, and ephemera such as silk ribbons and hairpins to become part of official state archives. Yet because these movements and objects are on the margins of these sites of knowledge-production, they are revealing of, to use Certeau's words, "the clandestine forms taken by the dispersed, tactical, and makeshift creativity of groups already caught in the nets of discipline."[32] As advanced by subaltern and feminist studies, this method also means looking for the partial, the fragment, and the hidden in these archives and ephemera.[33] Unedited, audiotaped interviews of Kini Kapahu conducted by ethnomusicologist Joann Kealiinohomoku remain the most extensive archival resource. For while the questions directed at Kini were centered largely on her biography and hula training, Kini's replies are not constrained by a strict narrative structure; they meander promiscuously into the seemingly tangential and anecdotal. However, these ruptures in her narration can yield valuable insight into the performers' stealthy and fleeting challenges to their subordinate status.

Colonial Objects

Imperial interest in Hawai'i intensified after the U.S. overthrow of the kingdom, and descriptions of amorous and sexually alluring Hawaiian women began circulating in the American press. Issued less than a month after the overthrow, a typical assessment concluded, "The young women have rich olive complexions, well developed forms, black, glossy hair, and large lustrous eyes."[34] These reports created an elemental archetype of Hawaiian womanhood as physically perfect, charming, and sexually available; Hawaiian women were "the most beautiful of all the dark skinned races," fell in love but once, and died of unrequited love. Writers expressed their fascination with women's anatomy with descriptions like, "Their eyes are glorious, their lips are rounded, but rarely too full. Their armes [sic] are absolutely matchless, with dainty wrists and biceps simply luxurious in their delicious curves. Their ankles are perfect, and their feet are small, with high arched insteps."[35]

Into these mythic representations, living hula dancers would breathe life. Hula's reputation preceded the arrival of the dancers in the United States. A month before the hula dancers arrived in Chicago, a Chicago daily newspaper provided this assessment: "The most beautiful Hawaiian girls are the Hula girls when dressed in their fantastic costumes for this interesting dance."[36] The Hawaiian women most visible in the continental United States after the overthrow were hula dancers. Conflated with Hawaiian women, dancers also became metonyms for the Hawaiian nation in the American cultural imagination. They circulated as salient living "ethnographic fragments" representing the whole of the islands in increasing numbers after 1893.[37] Hawaiian hula practitioners found their bodies scrutinized and fetishized on American and European stages and in complementary media.

Hawaiians were but recent indigenous trophies and souvenirs in a long chain of New World curiosities. Beginning in the seventeenth century, indigenous peoples were brought from the Americas and Pacific Islands to be presented to European courts. Pocahontas, the famed Powhatan Indian, became a celebrity in the court of King James I in 1616. During the Age of Exploration, the French explorer Bougainville ushered a young Tahitian man named Ahutoru to France in 1768 and brought him to the king. In 1774, Mai (or Omai) journeyed from Raiatea to England on Captain James Cook's second voyage. Omai lived in London for two years and became a celebrated personality. He learned English, attended the opera, and acquired genteel table manners that he displayed at aristocratic banquets.[38]

Lanny Thompson has argued persuasively that imperial narratives at the turn of the century provided a means of examining and evaluating the new archipelagic possessions of the United States after the Spanish-American War.[39] For Hawai'i, hula performance constituted another important type of imperial knowledge-production for the United States in the late nineteenth century—a pleasurable form of entertainment that enabled appraisal, assessment, and ultimately a managerial approach of territorial incorporation.[40] In these early tours, live hula performances enacted a relationship between the islands and the United States that I call an imagined intimacy. In this imagined relationship, the colonization of the islands is a natural, inevitable series of encounters, the joining of Hawai'i and America allegorized as Native women beckoning non-Native outsiders to the islands. Eroticized on commercial stages, hula and the young women who performed this art served as analogues for the Hawaiian Islands. Hawaiians who could be reviled as undesirable "primitives" in social and political discourse off-stage came to be imagined as largely assimilable and desirable through hula performances and the gendered bodies associated with hula.

Hula dancers became fetish objects of the developing U.S. empire. For the West, the hula dancer—and by extension, the colony of Hawai'i—was a figure onto which its forbidden sexual desires and anxieties could be projected. Hawai'i became part of the "porno-tropics," to utilize Anne McClintock's concept, offering sexual freedom, playfulness, and an association with the pleasure missing from modern civilization.[41] On the U.S. continent, hula was publicized as a proxy for sexual and geographic exploration—the best opportunity for white spectators to experience contact, however imaginary, with their new overseas subjects. In the "correlative constitution" of power and knowledge theorized by Foucault, a field of knowledge enacts material effects or power relations.[42] Ultimately these representational regimes of Hawai'i had very material dimensions. Imagined as feminine, passive, and full of sensual good will, Hawai'i came to be understood and treated as manageable: an attractive territory that could and should be integrated into the United States.

There were many accomplished performers who could have been chosen to perform on the continent, but Euro-American promoters made a deliberate choice to cast young women rather than older male and female dancers. The ho'opa'a, men expert at the aural aspects of hula (chanted poetry and instrumentation), nearly disappear in the coverage of hula performances at the turn of the century. The men were eclipsed by the bodies of the female dancers, whose movements intrigued Euro-American observers.

The sexual and racial difference of Hawaiian women was mutually constituted in the American imagination through hula. Put another way, the perceived gender and sexual difference of performers—their nakedness and promiscuity—became constituted as racial otherness. One observer of the women's hula performances at a vaudeville theater outside the Chicago world's fair likened the "hula-hula" to an orgasmic and orgiastic dance. The hula was "a wild barbaric affair, a whirl of lithe bodies and agile brown limbs, a flashing of flowery wreaths and black, savage eyes." This observer contended, "The dancers . . . writhe and twist till they nearly faint from exhaustion."[43] Deriving scopophilic pleasure watching these bodies, the writer expressed a release similar to sexual climax. The semiotics of the performances were not fixed; Hawaiian women could be read as menacing or gentle, but their eroticism and racial subordination remained constant.

The hula, as interpreted by outsiders in this "performative economy," unleashed primitive sexuality and could be a shocking distillation of Hawaiians' remove from civilization.[44] As one travel writer who observed hula in the islands reported to the *Washington Post*, the hula was a "highly-spiced form of social dissipation in the islands."[45] Upon witnessing a rehearsal of hula in Chicago, another reviewer for the *Chicago Daily Tribune* called the women "simple barbarians" who at least had the sense to be ashamed of their own bodies. He characterized them as "half a dozen semi-savages, whose color did not permit them to blush in the Caucasian fashion; but whose human instincts made them to cover themselves, and made them shrink from the excesses of their aboriginal exercises."[46] The appearance of Hawaiians at dime museums—amusement palaces that offered freak-show attractions, scientific exhibits, and live variety shows—alongside human oddities and animals like the "monster fat boy," bearded ladies, and singing roosters inserted them into an interpretive framework that rendered them subhuman.[47] Representations of primitive hula dancers tapered off by the late Hawaiian territorial period and were replaced by that of more docile, compliant women.

Fair Ladies

The women made their continental debut at the Chicago World's Columbian Exposition, where a panoply of colonial trophies was put on display. Ostensibly commemorating Columbus's arrival in the New World, the fair also celebrated the United States' own imperial ambitions as it began to expand its overseas reach. The Chicago exposition had an astounding number of attendees: over 27 million people out of a national population of 62 million.[48] World's fairs in Europe and the United States in the late nineteenth century featured "human showcases" of foreign and indigenous peoples that championed racial difference and the civilizational superiority of Euro-America.[49] Nearly a mile long, the Midway Plaisance of the Chicago World's Columbian Exposition was packed solid with amusements and living ethnographic villages considered improper for the main exposition or the "White City." The contrasting effect of the Midway and White City was instructive: nonwhites were barbaric and disorderly, while whites were capable of the highest technological achievements.

The Midway was organized loosely around a village schema.[50] Nonwhites were imported from foreign countries—or in the case of American Indians, from other parts of the continent—and erected their own housing on the midway grounds. Each village, whether Algerian, Brazilian, or "Esquimaux," was supposed to represent a specific ethnic group and "culture."[51] The layout of the exposition grounds followed a rough evolutionary scale and racial hierarchy: one could begin a survey of humanity in the Midway Plaisance with the most "savage" Dahomeyans, view a middle evolutionary ground of Chinese, American Indians, and Arabs, taper off into the highest echelons of Irish and Germans, before finally entering the true civilization of the White City.[52] These displays provided ideological weight for Western economic domination and colonization.

Timothy Mitchell analyzes how colonial exhibitions effectively organized the "world as a picture." The world became "an object on display, to be viewed, experienced, and investigated."[53] Egyptians visiting Paris in 1889 were amazed to see how museums, people, public parks, and their own bodies, were rendered into observable objects. Europeans re-created an Egyptian bazaar at the Exposition Universelle, even painting its façade to make it look dirty. Moreover, these representations centered the observer, giving him an isolated platform to take in the world as represented.[54]

A similar visual mechanism guided the organization of the Chicago World's Columbian Exposition. Guidebooks of the fair told visitors how to view exhibits from such a commanding vantage point. Buttressed with maps and diagrams, they instructed visitors to proceed step by step throughout the Midway Plaisance. One illustrated magazine, *The Cosmopolitan*, described what would unfold before their eyes in a single day: "For a matter of twenty-five cents you may take her to the top of the Swiss alps. Or down to the awful bottom of the giant crater of the sea of fire at Honolulu, or to other similar world wonders of landscape, while all along your route are samples of the architecture, inhabitants, manners and customs, home-life and characteristic products of the wild and civilized races of the world."[55] In sum, the fair was "the world as plaything."

Subject to this disciplinary display, Hawaiians were brought into view at this sensory feast in Chicago. Upon their arrival at the fair in 1893, the hula dancers realized they would have to be seen and play up their bodies and sexuality. They competed with scores of other erotic pleasures, like the Egyptian danse du ventre (belly dance) for audiences along the Midway. Their particular selling point was their novelty as living representatives of America's new Pacific satellite. Serving as her own barker at the "Hawaiian Village," Kini Kapahu played the 'ukulele and performed this "ballyhoo" to draw crowds into the ticket booth:

On the Midway, Midway, Midway Plaisance
Where the naughty girls from Honolulu do the naughty hula dance
The married men with their wives cast about a [longing] glance
At all the naughty naughty doings at the Midway Plaisance.[56]

Her provocative poem helped to fill the 300-seat theater five times a day. Like a peep show, the barker system plays with visibility; it promises sensual delights while deferring access. As a theatrical device, the ballyhoo operates by separating the visible from the hidden, offering only a glimpse of what is hidden behind the curtain. To sell tickets, Kini implied that unspeakable acts ("naughty naughty doings") could be witnessed behind the show curtain.

Kini claimed that she did not mind calling the hula "naughty"; she and the other dancers recognized that the popularity of the hula performance was not based on their proficiency and talent as ʻōlohe hula—as it had been in the royal court and hālau hula—but on the eroticism of their bodies. Made visually accessible, the women performers struggled to assert autonomy over their bodies and their decorum. Some American theater promoters demanded that the dancers reveal more of their bodies on stage, and audiences in turn insisted they expose their breasts as expected of erotic primitives. A friend of Kini's described the American expectation for them to be "naked, take everything off." When one American promoter of a hula show told the women to dance only with their skirts, Kini argued that they were not those "kind of people" and fought to keep her clothes on. Even when they were not performing, the women found it nearly impossible to escape the gaze and hands of white spectators. Kini recalled to her friend, "No matter where you went, people stared at you. . . . One [man] even pinched me." She tried to hit the offender and missed, but warned him in English, "Don't touch me."[57]

Counter-Colonial Performances

In Hawaiʻi, hula was a historical and political repertoire with some relationship to entertainment, but how did it change when it became categorized and marketed in the continental United States and Europe as vernacular entertainment? To be sure, hula had already entered the local cash economy in Hawaiʻi, with performers entertaining sailors from merchant and whaling ships at least as early as the 1830s, but Western mass entertainment commodified hula on a global scale. Commodity fetishism, as described by Marx, removes the production of a commodity from view and transforms relations between people into relations between things.[58] The alienation of hula performances obscured vital social and religious relations—the rigorous training, spiritual sustenance, and genealogical inheritances, for instance—that enabled their production. Dancers were no longer performing for themselves or in the service of aliʻi.

Hula became a tourist commodity with an attached price and time. Whereas in Hawaiʻi hula had no temporal limitations and could continue for hours, the brevity of a paid tourist performance—discrete and distilled to a period as short as ten minutes—was a convention adopted from Midway and vaudeville formulas.[59] Along tourist circuits, hula was necessarily transformed when removed from audiences knowledgeable in Hawaiian language and the hula's chanted poetry and genealogy. Its consumption by foreign viewers necessitated an interpretive framework to make the performance legible, whether that framework was put forth by a theater barker, written program, or narrator.

We know the most about hula performed at the Chicago fair, but the troupe likely performed a similar repertoire at venues along their vaudeville, café-concert, and dime-museum circuits. As described by Kini, the ten-minute show included hula ʻōlapa, hula ʻalaʻapapa (discussed below), hula ʻuliʻuli (feathered gourd hula), hula pūʻili (bamboo instrument hula), vocal arrangements, ʻukulele songs, as well as the hula kuʻi (hybrid hula) that they had learned in Kalākaua's court.[60] Heterogeneous genres were represented in the show, but the dancers conformed to the hula they had performed in court and in the hālau hula. The inclusion of the genres of hula ʻōlapa and hula ʻalaʻapapa, both performed to chanted poetic texts, suggests that the repertoire in Chicago was not entirely tourist-oriented.[61]

Hula ʻōlapa originated in the late monarchical period. Often honoring aliʻi, it is a nonsacred genre that has a standardized poetic pattern, often in couplets, and a concluding line, "Haina ʻia mai ana kapuana" (Let the story be told).[62] Hula ʻalaʻapapa are sacred and of "greater antiquity" than hula ʻōlapa, having being acquired while kapu (consecrated) and "bound by the observance of altar rituals honoring [the hula goddess] Laka."[63] Many hula ʻalaʻapapa are dedicated to the gods; others are mele maʻi that encourage procreation and fertility. It is likely that the troupe learned hula ʻalaʻapapa during training with the hālau hula, while they danced the sung form of hula ʻōlapa (otherwise known as hula kuʻi) at Kalākaua's court. They practiced hula and reproduced this repertoire as they had been taught.

Being vaudeville performers and ʻōlohe hula was not a contradiction.

The troupe made a distinction between performing for tourists and for Hawaiians, but did not eschew the tourist marketplace. They negotiated between the integrity of sacred knowledge and its commodity form. While the hula ku'i emphasized innovation, the performers were careful not to change the dances they learned during their hālau training. Some of the hula ku'i and the vocal pieces performed may have been adapted to Western tastes, but other repertoires like the hula 'ōlapa and 'āla'apapa were left intact. The performance of sacred and nonsacred hula had to meet exacting standards.

As hula entered commodity exchange, the dancers managed to control its visibility. Kini insisted: "We don't dance outside, on the street. We don't go down to the wharf and dance to everybody, to every Tom, Dick and Harry, oh no!" She maintained, whether performed in Hawai'i or the United States, "Hula's got to be in the house, not on the street . . . [or else] people [would] say, 'Look at that,' they make fun of it."[64] The theatrical stage and discursive framing of the hula—as a "naughty dance" along the Midway, for instance—rendered the women visually and aurally accessible, but they subverted their visibility by delineating private and public space. What mattered to the po'e hula was dancing inside an enclosed interior space, one marked off as private.

Ironically, the exposure of hula may have helped po'e hula dance with greater ease under the cover of tourist entertainment. The hula's affiliation with sensational dime-museum and vaudeville fare helped to camouflage the inherently political content of the dance: a hidden transcript or kaona (veiled meaning) of the public script. Performing sacred and secular hula in tourist venues may have been a productive outlet for po'e hula that had been under surveillance from missionary sons. It was only a decade prior that Kalākaua came under fire by haole for supporting the revival of hula and displaying it at his coronation and jubilee. Undoubtedly, the performers were familiar with the obscenity charges filed against the publisher of the coronation mele. They knew that many haole and Hawaiians in the islands reviled hula.[65] When the po'e hula performed hula ko'ihonua or mele ma'i in Europe or in North America, it is unlikely spectators would have been able to understand that they were venerating chiefly genitalia. Hidden in plain sight, hula framed as tourist enjoyment, whether salacious or benign, enabled cultural reproduction away from repressive forces within the colony. Hula not only survived its avid consumption, but thrived.

Hula circuits ran strikingly parallel to the circulation of sacred Indian dances outside reservations at contemporaneous Wild West shows, which were some of the most popular and successful U.S. commercial entertainments.[66] Jacqueline Shea Murphy argues that U.S. and Canadian governments encouraged Indian participation in stage representations of Indianness while restricting ceremonial dance practices in the late nineteenth century. This "theatricalization of dance" advanced political control of Native bodies, religion, culture, and ultimately, land.[67]

However, while this theatrical system commodified Native lifeways for non-Native spectators, it nonetheless provided important authorizing structures for Hawaiian and Indian performers. Vine Deloria Jr. contends that Show Indians on Buffalo Bill's Wild West circuit escaped the confines of government reservations. "Individuals otherwise regarded as dangerous characters" could leave and participate in tours without the interference of the Bureau of Indian Affairs. Deloria writes, "Touring with Buffalo Bill probably saved some of the [Oglala Sioux] chiefs from undue pressure and persecution by the government at home." Despite the racism of the dramatic performances, many Indians were able to gain freedom and education apart from the reservation and government programs and observe American society.[68] Shea Murphy further suggests that Indians saw continuities between their performances on stage and their own ways of life; thus, "their show dancing also continued to function as Native dancing."[69] Indians displayed culturally significant skills at Wild West shows, and, in a related vein, hula contributed a counter-colonial repertoire to the tourist marketplace.

While it is difficult to cleave the poetry from the bodily movements of the hula, the aurality of the hula may have taken on more significance in foreign lands. The poetic texts suggest a sly counter-colonial transcript within the tourist performance, or to use the Hawaiian concept of kaona, a hidden poetic meaning. Some hula ʻōlapa were mele aliʻi (songs in honor of chiefs), and because the poʻe hula had learned them during Kalākaua's reign, they likely performed chants and mele honoring Kalākaua's genealogy and his connections to high chiefs and the gods. Jonathan Kay Kamakawiwoʻole Osorio observes, "Hula was never just entertainment. It represented the very finest art of an ancient civilization and was itself political because many of the mele were praises of the Aliʻi genealogies and their relationships to the akua."[70]

Dancing hula for tourists did not mean hula practitioners consented to the ongoing American takeover of their country. These mele aliʻi took on added resonance on the U.S. continent during the turmoil of the American overthrow and annexation, which was being vigorously contested by friends and kin at home through organized petition campaigns and an armed but short-lived counterrevolution.[71] The chants in Hawaiian, unintelligible to foreign audiences, enabled discursive flexibility. Performing mele like "Kawika" or "O Kalākaua He Inoa" (Kalākaua is his name) exalted chiefs and kings under the noses of tourists who thought they were simply watching frivolous movements illustrating the quaint customs of Hawaiian life.[72] Spectators would not have known that poʻe hula were honoring their akua (gods) or the chiefly lines that had produced aliʻi nui (monarchs) like Kamehameha, Kalākaua, and their deposed queen Liliʻuokalani.[73] With the central poetic text incomprehensible to visitors, the aurality of hula was diminished in favor of kinesthetic movements, or in Kini's words, "hip shaking."[74] Indeed, descriptions of live hula on the continent—whether complementary or disdainful—were centered on embodied exhibits, never the implied or explicit meaning of mele.

Commodification and Wage Labor

Entering into commodity culture, hula became an extracted economic resource and a distinct form of colonial wage labor. On the face of it, the commodification of hula performances transformed poʻe hula into wage laborers who were hired and, to a large degree, exploited by theatrical managers who reaped most of the profits. A Honolulu newspaper reported that Harry W. Foster, their first manager, would pay the performers five dollars a week plus all of their expenses for six months.[75] If this figure was accurate, it was considerably lower than the wage of dime-museum performers at the turn of the century who earned from $25 to $500 a week. Lecture-room performers at dime museums could earn $25 to $35 a week.[76] Compared to contemporaneous plantation field laborers in Hawaiʻi, however, performers on the hula circuit earned nearly twice as much.[77]

Performers had little recourse to exploitation; unscrupulous managers could terminate contracts without notice and issue unreasonable demands. They were also vulnerable as a racialized workforce in a country where there were few other Hawaiians. Toward the end of their four-year vaudeville tour, the dancers became stranded in Logansport, Indiana, after Annie Grube, one of the dancers, was hospitalized. The troupe's American manager demanded that she dive from a forty-feet-high bridge as a publicity stunt. As Annie told a reporter for the *Chicago Tribune*, "I said I was afraid, but he declared he could have me arrested if I broke my contract. So one evening just before the performance I made the jump. The water was only two feet deep instead of twelve as the manager had said."[78] She broke her leg in two places. The manager fired the troupe and withheld five weeks' wages. They had no way to pay for their return to Hawai'i and ended up appealing to the Hawaiian consul in Chicago. In the end, the dancers had to work their way slowly back to the West Coast by performing in what a Honolulu newspaper described as "cheap museums."[79]

E. P. Thompson, in *The Making of the English Working Class*, discusses the imposition of time discipline on artisans and their transformation into wage laborers. Work was strictly segregated from leisure, and the everyday lives of factory workers became subject to the rhythms of labor.[80] Yet hula did not fully transform from a system of courtly patronage to capitalist wage labor; it could not be segregated from leisure and religious practice. Hula was not simply reducible to wage labor or surplus labor, nor was it commodified solely on the basis of time. This remains true of hula practitioners today in what is arguably a much more intensified global tourist marketplace. Even when performance is highly lucrative, people do not dance hula simply for monetary gain. In fact, having hula as an occupation meant that women were not shuttled into more regulated forms of wage labor; their expertise allowed them to bypass plantations and low-level service work.

When dancers were not performing, their time was unrestricted and their lives punctuated by other pleasures like travel, sightseeing, and fashion. Performing for tourists was not entirely drudgery, like factory work; it was an opportunity to be compensated for artistic expression and to gain a measure of recognition and autonomy in the process. As Jayna Brown has contended, black women performers during this same period blurred the boundaries between labor and play. She argues that these modern subjects "reclaimed their bodies *in*, as well as *from*, the world of work" as they moved their bodies and earned money.[81] Creativity and commercial exploitation became melded in complicated ways.

Po'e hula seemed to enjoy performing for tourists and at times found the task both challenging and amusing. Kini reprised her "naughty naughty hula dance" ballyhoo from the Chicago Midway in public life in Hawai'i. "Can't I sing that little ditty?" she cajoled interviewers nearly sixty years after her appearance at the exposition.[82] She sang the song whenever she wanted to flirt and draw attention to herself, well into her eighties.

The hula as a ritualized form of social, political, and religious performance imposed further inherent limits to its commodification. John Kahaʻi Topolinski, a contemporary kumu hula (hula teacher), writes that hula has three main functions: "To honor the gods; to remind Hawaiians of the greatness of their nobility (*aliʻi*), their race, and their epics; and to enforce perfectionism in the art of the dance." In a similar vein, Kini maintained, "Hula is very religious, it has to be just so. Songs belong to the aliʻi. You cannot give to another person. Someone will call out, 'That song belongs to king so and so!' It's very very strict."[83] Tickets to a particular performance could be "sold," but the hula repertoire was inalienable and could not be given away. To use Annette Weiner's concept, hula was an "inalienable possession."[84] Hula *genealogy* was an inalienable possession that could not be bought or sold, but could only be attained through strict training and adherence to cultural protocol.

The hula teacher Alice Kuʻuleialohapoinaʻole Kanakaoluna Nāmakelua, born twenty years after Kini Kapahu in 1892, explained the religious restrictions on hula reproduction and the dire consequences for careless transmission: "At the age of sixteen I was trained by my last hula instructor David Kahoʻaleawai Kaluhiakalani who served as a chanter for Prince Kūhiō. He advised me not to teach the ancient hula if I should venture out to teach. That is the reason why I've never taught the traditional hula. He warned me that if I forgot a single foot movement, hand motion, or word of a chant, I would be breaking a kapu [taboo] and either myself or my student would physically suffer for it."[85]

In contrast to hula repertoire, hula *performances* could be commodified and consumed as exoticized entertainment. Theatrical promoters could profit from hula performances and American audiences could purchase tickets for hula performances, but these publics could not acquire hula genealogy. By undergoing training, dancers inserted themselves in a genealogy: a specific repertoire of chants and movements transmitted from teacher to disciple, from generation to generation. A dancer could trace his or her genealogy through these performances: an expansive history crossing time and space that hailed the living, the dead, and akua. Cultural knowledge may have been repackaged for touristic consumption, but it was not easily reproduced. Chants or mele, particularly those acquired and transmitted while observing hula kuahu rituals, could not be rededicated or rechoreographed for another aliʻi or akua. Nor did the performance of a mele mean that it was alienated, bartered, or given to an audience member, regardless of whether money exchanged hands.

Contemporary kumu hula continue to impose restrictions on the reproduction and transmission of certain mele, including their public performances. The hula dancer, as an animating vessel of the aliʻi's or akua's mana (power), may perform the mele, but cannot give it away to an audience member or dedicate it to another aliʻi.

Colonial Visuality

Expositions and theatrical stages created a panoptic stage for viewers, while photographs functioned as another kind of visual mechanism, making Hawaiian women's bodies manifest. Photographs extended the gaze of spectators far beyond the space and time of live performance, allowing tourists to commemorate their encounters with the exotic and erotic. John Tagg, expanding on the relationship between discipline and visibility, argues that the photographic frame scrutinized bodies and instituted what he calls "a means of surveillance."[86]

Photographic postcards sent by French tourists, soldiers, and colonists in the early twentieth century animated the French colonial expedition in Algeria and spawned the Orientalist fantasy of the harem. Malek Alloula argues in *The Colonial Harem* that the postcard was "the fertilizer of the colonial vision."[87] Fixated on the Algerienne, the Orientalist gaze dissected the body of the Algerian woman. Analyzing the American imperial vision, Vicente L. Rafael has observed that rather than making Filipinos invisible, "colonialism instigated the proliferation of images of Filipino bodies."[88] Many of these images circulated during the Filipino insurgent war against American colonization; they were also distributed at the St. Louis World's Fair in 1904, where tribes from the Philippines were on display.

Photographs of Hawaiian women dressed as hula dancers also circulated via prolific memoirs and travelogues around the overthrow in 1893 and annexation of the Hawaiian Islands in 1898. Articulating the relationship between late nineteenth-century imperial representations and material power, Lanny Thompson has argued that these works were "not capricious fantasies about exotic peoples." Rather, they were "the means of study, evaluation, and legitimation with the expressed intent to rule."[89] These representational regimes of Hawaiʻi are punctuated by a persistent voyeurism; they closely scrutinize Hawaiian women's bodies and reveal them as simultaneously lewd, exotic, and desirable. The new territory of Hawaiʻi became imaginable, almost palpable, through the bodies of sexually alluring, eroticized hula dancers, and would gain further legibility when live dancers stepped onto American stages.

John R. Musick's *Hawaii: Our New Possessions*, as one example of these imperial narratives, worked intertextually with photographs to produce a scopophilic gaze. King Kalākaua's court dancers appear in two photographs: the young women Aiala and Pauahi Pinao from Hui Lei Mamo, and in another, the male hoʻopaʻa Kamuku and Kanuku. Accompanying them was this voyeuristic account of hula bodies: "Kalakaua, the last king, was very fond of hula dancing and all kinds of debauchery. The hula dance is a voluptuous movement of the body to a doleful music, the feet having little to do with it. Kalakaua's hula girls sometimes danced nude, but the usual costume is a skirt made of grass, coming to the knees, the body being naked or having a loose waist ornamented with flowers. The laws now prohibit nude dancing, tho such exhibitions are still given in private, for the amusement of tourists with depraved minds."[90] Similarly, a memoir by the U.S. naval lieutenant Lucien Young about Hawaiʻi disparaged the hula in 1899. But Young's lambasting of hula as "an exhibition of indecent pantomime" merely serves as an excuse to unveil the "hula girl": a full-page photograph of a woman with her breasts exposed.[91]

Visual media—photographs, stereographs, and cartes de visite—also became popular souvenirs for visitors to sideshows, world's fairs, and dime museums in the United States.[92] The rise of mass urban entertainment at the end of the nineteenth century intersected with an interest in photography as hobby and entertainment. Spectators collected photographs of the entertainments, and amateur photographers honed their skills. At the Chicago World's Columbian Exposition, photographs and stereographs of Midway performers were assembled as collections and sold as souvenirs like *The Chicago Times Portfolio of the Midway Types*.[93] These media enabled viewers to re-create and experience the fair in their own parlors.

A photographic portrait from Kini's collection was taken at a photography studio, likely during the Chicago World's Fair of 1893 (see figure 11). It is a cabinet card, similar to the smaller format carte de visite. Both were popular late nineteenth-century photographic styles that mounted a thin albumen print onto cardboard. Kini and Pauahi are dressed in costuming that mark them as hula dancers, and they are framed by props that signal Hawaiianness: dried grass skirts and flower leis adorning their ankles, hair, and necks. Photographs of hula dancers taken at the Chicago fair and other fin de siècle fairs in Buffalo and Omaha seem blandly inoffensive and humanizing in comparison to frenzied, rapturous narrative accounts. Nevertheless, like the other published photographs of "hula girls,"

Fig. 11 Cabinet card,
Pauahi Pinao and Kini
Kapahukulaokamāmalu.
Chicago, ca. 1893.
COURTESY OF HAWAI'I
STATE ARCHIVES.

they frame female dancers as ethnographic objects and living signs of Hawaiianness.[94]

It is likely that concessions where the dancers performed sold this portrait and similar ones as souvenirs.[95] Robert Bogdan refers to photography as the television of the Victorian age, due to its sheer popularity.[96] At the Chicago fair, some performers were able to directly negotiate a nominal snapshot fee with amateur photographers, but they did not personally receive a percentage of the scores of official photographic albums tightly controlled and sold by the fair's Department of Photography and other concessionaires.[97] Dime-museum and freak-show performers often commissioned their own exoticizing cartes de visite and supplemented their income through the sale of such items. Souvenir photographs proved an essential means of support for the Hawaiian dancers when they were abandoned by an unscrupulous manager in 1895. Stranded in Indiana for several weeks, the troupe raised money for their return passage to Hawai'i by selling photographs of themselves and giving hula performances.[98]

High Style

Given their transformation into spectacles on imperial stages, how did the performers intervene? The women responded in complex and creative ways to the objectifying imperial gaze of photography and the ethnographic stage. They were well aware of how they were being framed as Native women and colonial souvenirs, and undertook their own image-making and collecting practices. Their ambivalent relationship to photography extended into their uses of portraiture and snapshots, which offered them limited forms of self-expression and a chance to model modernity. From their alternative collections and ephemera, nascent critiques emerge of the ways their bodies were colonized and consumed.

The women dancers arrived by ship in San Francisco in 1892, dressed inappropriately for the inclement weather. Wearing brightly colored cotton holokū dresses and wide-brimmed straw hats, they found themselves gawked at by curious reporters.[99] Treated as live novelties at the pier, they also did their share of observing. Kini looked back at the white American women and was shocked to see them wearing fur. She recalled, "I looked over the rail of our ship and there were people staring up at us and the women had *animals* around their necks. . . . I thought they were lions or tigers or something until somebody told us about fur pieces."[100] Animal fur was particularly anathema to the climate and culture of Hawai'i, but Kini recognized it as a potent signifier of wealth and social status for Euro-Americans. Despite her surprise at this heretofore unfamiliar fashion, Kini herself modeled a fur-lined coat in a photography studio in Louisville, Kentucky, only a few years later (see figure 12).

This is a compelling illustration of her tactics of consumption, what Certeau describes as inventive uses of power by the weak. While Kini recognized that she and her friends were visual spectacles ("there were people staring up at us"), she was also a keen observer, the mistress of her own vista, deploying what bell hooks has theorized as "the oppositional gaze."[101] Staring back at middle-class white women, at their gestures and fashions, Kini reconstituted her image and struck her own self-conscious pose. The women's experiments with self-fashioning allowed them to express their own discrepant desires for style and beauty, and resist their interpellation as sexualized commodities. They quickly assimilated fashion codes to present themselves as cosmopolitan. Middle-class African Americans sat for similarly dignified photographic portraits around the same time; W. E. B. Du Bois collected and displayed a collection of these

Fig. 12 Kini Kapahukulaokamāmalu, photograph taken at Howell photography studio, Louisville, Kentucky, ca. 1896.
COURTESY OF HAWAI'I STATE ARCHIVES.

photographs at the Paris Exposition in 1900 as an antiracist, visual assertion of African American humanity.[102]

Kini's ability to learn quickly, adapt, and refigure signs of modernity had been acquired in the cosmopolitan court of Honolulu. She and the other court dancers dressed fashionably, assuming class-conscious roles as court "ladies." They donned demure dresses and learned to pin their waved hair. Hawaiian women were savvy consumers of Euro-American fashions not long after Western contact. They began carrying small mirrors after the arrival of Westerners and adapted their kapa (bark cloth) skirts to accommodate European cloth. Gifts from sailors brought adornments of Chinese silks and parasols.[103] In the 1870s and 1880s, numerous advertisements printed in Hawaiian newspapers suggest that ordinary, nonchiefly Hawaiians were avid consumers of Western fashion. One ad urged them to peruse new goods brought by ship to Honolulu from Philadelphia in 1876, items including women's "kamaa wahine ili-kao kiekie pihi" (buttoned kid-leather shoes), "wati pakeke wahine a me na kaula" (women's chained pocket watches), and "mikilima keokeo" (white gloves).[104] Similar enticements of delicate laces, corsets, parasols, shawls, and stockings from Paris, London, and New York were periodically sold at bazaars near the Honolulu waterfront.[105]

Ironically, even the cabinet card of Kini and Pauahi costumed as hula performers in Chicago, which was likely sold as a fair souvenir of "authentic hula girls," reveals signs of their hybridity (see figure 11). Their popularity in the West was based on their authenticity as real Hawaiian women. For example, during their engagement at a vaudeville theater in Chicago, they were promoted as a "decided novelty" brought "direct from the Sandwich Islands."[106] However, this photograph can be read as an unstable representation; it is not a fixed signifier of "Hawaiianness." The women hold Westernized instruments; their hair is carefully styled and curled, and they wear rings, lockets, and bracelets. Kini cradles an 'ukulele, an instrument adapted from a Portuguese string instrument, while the dancers' cotton skirts and blouses were imposed by the influence of Calvinist missionaries. Nor was the grass skirt indigenous to Hawai'i. Though it was becoming emblematic of "Hawai'i" in the twentieth century, it had been appropriated from the Gilbert Islands during Kalākaua's reign. The dancers' dried skirts were an invention born of necessity during foreign tours, since they were unable to obtain fresh lā'ī (ti leaves) outside Hawai'i. Later they fashioned skirts out of string dipped in green dye.[107] During Chicago's late fall, they substituted artificial flowers for fresh ones.

During the troupe's six-month engagement in Chicago, it also performed in a vaudeville show, sharing billing with an African American female burlesque revue at Sam T. Jack's Madison Opera House near the fairgrounds.[108] *The Creole Show* and the "hula hula" brought racialized women's bodies together in a single erotic spectacle. Kini posed for a portrait at the same Chicago photography studio during this period, styling herself in a dark, full-length mutton-sleeved gown and plumed hat (see figure 13).[109] Unlike the hula photograph that captured her body and Pauahi's in full, Kini is framed here in a three-quarter-length shot typi-

Fig. 13 Kini Kapahukulaokamāmalu, photograph taken at
J. B. Wilson photography studio, Chicago, ca. 1892–93.
COURTESY OF HAWAI'I STATE ARCHIVES.

cal of Western portraiture. There is little to indicate that she was a "hula girl," for no indigenous accoutrement is visible, and even her long hair, an essential part of the iconic "hula girl," was pulled back discreetly. Kini kept abreast of current fashion, for the leg-o-mutton sleeves, nipped waist, and full skirt were fashionable in the early 1890s.[110] The puffed sleeves, full skirt, and corset beneath created the idealized hourglass silhouette adopted by Victorian women, a shape distinct from that of the unfettered late nineteenth-century hula body, with its loose layers of cotton, dried pandanus, or ti leaves. The sleeve of Kini's gown suggests how au courant she was—it is very full but the drooping puff fitted below the elbow was the most stylish sleeve shape by 1893, the year the photograph was likely taken.[111]

While the dancers did not earn very much, they placed a priority on careful grooming and self-presentation. They were determined to pose as well-heeled, socially respectable, middle-class women. Their chosen garments were not inexpensive; nearly all dresses were custom-made in the 1890s—a woman either hired seamstresses or sewed her garments herself.[112] Though fashion was pleasurable for these Hawaiian women, it was also intimately related to the realm of labor. As Angela McRobbie has written about the fashion industry in the United Kingdom, sewing is a gendered skill often passed down between generations of black and Asian women.[113] Kini appears to have supported herself for a time by sewing and may have sewn some of her own gowns. After she returned to Hawai'i in 1896, she was listed in the Honolulu city directory as a seamstress doing "fancy needlework."[114] One of Kini's friends described her creativity and skill as a dressmaker: "She was very very handy with the needle. . . . She created a lot of her own clothes."[115] Dressmaking provided both a livelihood and attractive adornments that may have been difficult to purchase. Hawaiian women fashioned and modeled their own hula costumes and leisure dress, as would future generations of Pacific Islander women on the hula circuit.

Kathy Peiss writes of immigrant working-class women, "Dress became a cultural terrain of pleasure, expressiveness, romance, and autonomy."[116] Yearning for the stylish clothing of their wealthier counterparts, they read fashion columns and imitated the latest styles. One sixteen-year-old factory worker insisted, "A girl must have clothes if she is to go into high society at Ulmer Park or Coney Island or the theatre." The desires of the women from the colonies were no different, and perhaps even more acute than those of white immigrant women. We cannot dismiss their forays into Victorian fashion as a meaningless, insignificant act, nor can we reduce their pursuit of style to colonial mimicry. For Hawaiian women, presenting themselves as Victorian ladies was a potent act of criticism.

Colonized women faced different public expectations than white women, regardless of class. Nudity was anathema to late Victorian propriety, which required ladies to wrap themselves "in a mantle of proper reserve."[117] In contrast, maximum exposure was demanded of Hawaiian women. Expected to reveal their bodies while on stage, they took pains with their off-stage personae. They used clothing to defend themselves and dismantle their interpellation as shameless "barbarians" when they were off-stage. For Hawaiian women, particularly unmarried makaʻāinana women who had neither the privileges of wealth nor education, these self-possessed poses enabled them to critique their objectification. However, their efforts were not necessarily well received or successful. After receiving studio photographs of the hula dancers on tour, a Hawaiʻi newspaper owned by the annexationist and missionary son Lorrin A. Thurston sniped that the women were "dressed in gaudy European style."[118] This response suggests that missionary elites may have interpreted the women's stagings of civility as snobbish affectation or colonial mimicry.

Makaʻāinana women may have developed their strategies in concert with chiefly Hawaiian women, who strategically adopted Victorian postures of propriety and decorum as an anticolonial tactic. Queen Liliʻuokalani, for instance, in her autobiography *Hawaii's Story by Hawaii's Queen*, published during the aftermath of the U.S. overthrow, asserted her legitimacy as a modern ruler through her elegant manners and Christian bearing (see figure 14).[119] Other aliʻi Hawaiian women, such as Mrs. Emma Nawahi and Mrs. Abigail Campbell, attiring themselves in Victorian dress, negotiated between behaving publicly as proper Christian ladies and being outspoken opponents to U.S. annexation.[120] Yet women of common birth also contested their colonial subjugation while inserting an implicit critique of Hawaiian rank and class hierarchy.

These performers may appear to possess little agency or will to contest the American abrogation of Hawaiian sovereignty. The women are not legible as nationalists; they chose not to return home during the political crisis, nor did they belong to a political vanguard or organize a resistance movement against the U.S. annexation, as did other Hawaiian women. Indeed, their photographs do not easily fit into a teleology of political resistance. Rather they suggest that photography could be used by women for their own discrepant and idiosyncratic ends. Writing of portraits of bourgeois Filipinos in a similar time period, Vicente L. Rafael says that these photographs are "all the more compelling" because "they seem to escape instrumentalization and reduction into either colonial or anticolonial narratives."[121] This is also true of these Hawaiian countercolonial portraits.

In the harshest Marxist critiques, fashion is framed as a betrayal of "authentic" politics. Yet fashion and style are not merely manifestations of false consciousness or illusory distractions from authentic political work. Dick Hebdige and Angela McRobbie assert that consumption and fashion

Fig. 14 Queen
Lili'uokalani.
COURTESY OF HAWAI'I
STATE ARCHIVES.

are more than passive forms of political expression. Commodities do not simply reinscribe hegemonic relations, but, as Hebdige argues, can be "symbolically 'repossessed' in everyday life and endowed with implicitly oppositional meanings."[122] Style enables subcultures to challenge hegemony, albeit indirectly and "obliquely" via remixed signs, as did punks who ripped T-shirts and mods who cut up the Union Jack to create jackets. Akin to "noise" rather than "sound," the anarchic signs of style can be read as surrealist, yet opaque, critiques of Thatcherite neoconservatism.[123] Young girls who did not have the punks' access to the streets read fashion magazines and joined fan clubs from their bedrooms, encouraging alternative identity formations, as McRobbie has argued.[124] In another racialized historical context, Robin D. G. Kelley argues that working-class African Americans found pleasure dressing up and fleshing out a collective identity based on something besides a maid's or servant's uniform. Stylish clothing allowed them to use their bodies for their own desires rather than be instrumentalized for another's profit.[125]

In the portraits collected along her tours, Kini is figuring out what fits and suits her. On the same day Kini sat for her fur coat portrait in Louisville, Kentucky, she took at least one other photograph, as did one of her friends. It was taken during the troupe's vaudeville tour in 1896. Kini posed in a high-necked lace-trimmed dress, modeling adornments that immediately signified modernity and her facility with current fashion: jewelry, hairpins, earrings, and bracelets on each wrist (see figure 15). The other Hawaiian woman, who could be the dancer Nakai, posed in a crisp nautical gown with a waistband from which a heart-shaped charm dangles (see figure 16). These experiments with performance and public personae suggest a playfulness and self-consciousness. Kini's face betrays a slight, bemused smile while she wears her fur coat (see figure 12). It is as if she is saying, "I am trying out this haircomb. I am putting on a costume." Kini's forays into fashion and modes of self-presentation may have fueled her confidence as she navigated the empire. Throughout her long life, Kini was to display her flair for fashion and trend-spotting. She attended the National Democratic Convention in New York City as a delegate in 1924 and returned to Honolulu with her hair bobbed, a style not yet seen in Hawai'i.[126]

A mark of the women's modernity was their ability to adapt. As they did with the hula ku'i in Hawai'i, they perused what was available to them and adopted was most useful. Their poses are performances of reinvention. To paraphrase Certeau, tactics introduce play into the foundations of power.[127] These poses are, to be sure, clandestine gestures, perhaps without lasting consequences, but nevertheless reveal that Hawaiians were undefeated by racist disciplining and capable of bold interventions in the face of colonial power. Colonialism falters when people refuse to see themselves through the eyes of the colonizer. Kini's forceful posturing later in life—she imperiously declared herself an authority on Hawaiian protocol and opposed her husband's policies while he was mayor of Honolulu—and her ability to command a room may also owe a debt to these early expressions (see figure 17).

Fig. 15 Kini
Kapahukulaokamāmalu
wearing charm bracelet,
Louisville, Kentucky, ca. 1896.
COURTESY OF HAWAI'I STATE
ARCHIVES.

Fig. 16 The dancer Nakai
(last name unknown) posing
at Howell photography
studio, Louisville, Kentucky,
ca. 1896. COURTESY OF HAWAI'I
STATE ARCHIVES.

Fig. 17 Kini Kapahukulaokamāmalu looking at nineteenth-century photographs of hula in the Hawai'i territorial archives on her eighty-seventh birthday, 4 March 1959. COURTESY OF HAWAI'I STATE ARCHIVES.

Native Tourists

Kini's collection of photographs in the Hawai'i State Archives has been categorized via a taxonomy that disrupts the integrity and temporality of her collecting practices; they are combined with other photographs under the single category of "People—Wilson." Kini's collection was not meant to be public, but her "counterarchive" assembles photographic portraits and other souvenirs of her tours.[128] Kini collected photographs of her friends and fellow po'e hula wearing Western dresses and hula costumes along the hula circuits (see figures 18.1 and 18.2). The photographs suggest that they sat for portraits in places like Chicago, Berlin, Louisville, and Buffalo, and exchanged photographs as souvenirs of their time as tourists. The souvenirs are revealing of their off-stage lives and their mutual aloha. Kini continued to express affection for her troupe long after they had died: "I feel aloha for all those girls we went together, and the two men."[129]

"Natives" and "tourists" are thought to be incommensurable categories; they seem consigned to their own separate spaces and times—the tourist with modernity and the Native with the premodern and primi-

Fig. 18.1

Fig. 18.2

The dancers Mele, age nineteen, and Malie, last names unknown, were members of John H. Wilson's hula troupe. These photographs were taken during the Omaha Greater America Exposition, 1899. COURTESY OF HAWAI'I STATE ARCHIVES.

tive. Teresia K. Teaiwa, however, challenges the assumed incompatibility of "Natives" and "tourists," writing, "A tourist is assumed to be traveling. A Native is assumed to dwell, but Natives may also travel, and a tourist may also be a Native."[130] Philip J. Deloria also describes the discomfort and "category confusion" that results from American Indians appearing "in unexpected places": the ostensibly premodern Geronimo riding in a Cadillac, the Wild West show performer floating down Venice canals in a gondola, or the buckskin-clad woman sitting under a hairdryer.[131] Hawaiians were also thought to be strangers to modernity. However, fin de siècle hula dancers blurred this distinction, performing their Nativeness for tourists while also behaving as Native tourists. They possessed a modern sensibility, immersing themselves in urban and global worlds.

Traveling to the heart of the Western empire—Chicago, Paris, New York, London—hula performers collected souvenirs and went sightseeing. Their experiences as metropolitan tourists suggest that they were not only being collected on their travels; they were assembling their own collections from multiple vantage points. Kini's collection contains an informal snapshot from the Greater America Exposition in Omaha, Nebraska, in 1899. With the introduction of the hand-held Kodak camera to the American consumer market in 1888, the photograph was no longer confined to the interior of the photography studio, and amateurs were able to take their own informal snapshots.[132] Kini and her future husband John H. Wilson managed about twelve Hawaiian women and fourteen men at the fair's Hawaiian village.[133] In the photograph, a group of about twenty Hawaiians play in the snow in Omaha. Their heavy coats and hats are flecked with white patches, and some wear fur shawls and capes. Hats bedecked with flowers suggest an interest in fashion as well as a desire to sustain Hawaiian decorative practices in a wintry climate. One woman who closely resembles Kini is wearing an animal pelt around her neck. Captured by the camera, another young girl is dropping a handful of snow above her head. Snow was a novelty for Hawaiians, part of an anomalous encounter. Like other fairgoers in this period, the Hawaiians commemorated their experience of winter and the fair with a photograph. It stands in opposition to photographs taken of them as ethnographic spectacles, an example of what we might call Hawaiians appearing "in unexpected places," to borrow Deloria's phrase.

Other Pacific Islander women at this time were astute intercultural travelers and cultural brokers practicing selective tourist commodification. Makereti (also known as Maggie Papakura) was the daughter of a high-ranking Maori woman of the Te Arawa iwi in Aotearoa (New Zealand). Born in 1872, the same year as Kini Kapahu, Makereti also had a mixed cultural background and embarked on similar tourist paths. As discussed by Maori feminist scholar Ngahuia Te Awekotuku, Makereti was trained to be a Victorian lady by her English father, but was also taken to the forest by her Maori elders to learn and practice traditional knowledge. She later wrote an ethnography of Maori practices at Oxford University.[134] She managed to carve out her own space within Victorian New Zealand and England, becoming famous as a guide in the hot springs region of Whakarewarewa.

She guided the Duke and Duchess of Cornwall during their stay in 1901 and later organized a group of Maori entertainers called "The Arawa Warriors and Maori Maidens," which performed in Sydney, Melbourne, and London in 1910. Maori women like Makereti and Te Awekotuku's elders were tourist guides and cultural brokers with "complex native agendas" that were not limited to the dictates of the tourist industry. Teaiwa helpfully observes, "Te Awekotuku seems more interested in identifying the personalized politics of cultural commodification and negotiation rather than dismissing indigenous participation in the industry."[135] In other words, these performers are more than allegorical figures or shorthands for failed engagements with capitalism.

Gender further complicates the divide between Natives and tourists. Maka'āinana women were at a particular disadvantage as potential travelers and laborers outside of the islands. While not strictly sequestered in the domestic sphere, Native Hawaiian women had less access to employment and education channels outside the islands. They were not the preferred labor source for merchant ships; that was the purview of men. Alienated from the land since the Māhele (division) of 1848 that privatized land tenure, maka'āinana Hawaiian men and women were differently integrated into the global economy. Recruited for their facility on water, thousands of young Hawaiian men left the islands on merchant vessels and whaling ships and participated in the fur trade, gold rushes, and whaling in the 1840s and 1850s.[136] These early "maritime sojourners" sailed as far as China, Europe, Mexico, and North America.[137] Though vastly outnumbered by their male counterparts, some Hawaiian women seized the opportunity to voyage on foreign ships and whet their appetites for adventure. David A. Chappell contends that nineteenth-century Pacific Islander women could enhance their status by acting as "mediators between ship and shore" for their sexual partners and foreign husbands, doing invaluable work as cultural interpreters and negotiators.[138] On early voyages, women could "also travel as tourists, without burdensome expectations," as a Raiatean wife of a trader was able to experience Valparaiso and a Marquesan woman Salem, Massachusetts.[139]

But "seafaring ladies" who chose to holoholo—the Hawaiian phrase for "wander for pleasure"—risked social sanctions. Hawaiian women were often berated for dancing hula. However, they jeopardized their public virtue even further by choosing to perform abroad. Kini's mother, a skilled dancer who had encouraged her daughter to learn hula, drew the line at the idea of a tour. She hid Kini's clothes to prevent her from leaving for the United States, but Kini departed despite these objections.[140] When Kini returned to Hawai'i in 1896, Hawaiians and haole alike mocked her for performing in a foreign country where the hula was perceived as a "dirty dance."[141] Her reputation irrevocably damaged upon her return, Kini wept in the street.[142] She said, "The old ones frowned on dancing in public. Even my friends called me 'hilahila' (shameful) and on the street they would spit at me."[143]

Despite the sometimes painful consequences of their choices, this early generation of hula performers ushered in a new kind of modernity for commoner Hawaiian women in the twentieth century. The "New Woman" in America at the turn of the century was a protofeminist: independent, athletic, sexual, and modern.[144] These New Women expanded women's roles, taking advantage of educational and professional training.[145] The New Woman was most likely an educated white woman residing in an American city, not a woman from the colonies. However, like the New Woman, the dancers forged a space for Hawaiian women as sophisticated modern travelers who had reached the highest level of indigenous cultural training. Facing the colonization of their country, Kini and her contemporaries, cosmopolitan and self-possessed, boldly explored their social independence far from home. Hawaiian women skirted the bounds of respectability of both middle-class Hawaiian and American society by traveling and living away from their families for extended periods of time. White, single, working-class American women living apart from their families in urban rooming houses were called "women adrift" for their social and sexual transgressions. When ali'i women traveled, they were chaperoned by governesses or ladies-in-waiting. However, these Hawaiian performers not only lived on their own, they were constantly on the move, contravening conventions of class, sexuality, and nation.

Mae Ngai has argued convincingly for a shift from an analysis of world's fairs as "visions of empire" that objectify the "other" to a more complicated analysis of the role of the "other" as a social actor who pursued "his or her own agenda."[146] The experiences and reactions of fairgoers are well documented by scholars and contemporary newspapers and can be reconstructed through reviews, diaries, and souvenirs. However, rarely do we hear from those who were on display, and what their lives off-stage were like. Much of the literature on performance has concentrated on the gaze directed to people on stage, rather than what the performers saw and experienced.[147]

To be sure, precinematic attractions like the Midway and ethnographic entertainment isolated bodies and subjected them to an "unreturnable gaze."[148] However, behind the show curtains the gaze was not fixed, but worked in multiple directions. There was no single framing mechanism of the theater or museum, nor one set of observing eyes set apart from its objects. While guidebooks treat the ethnographic exhibitions as separate entities, a flow of languages, foods, and performances occurred backstage and in the performers' living quarters. Kini's observations and encounters disrupt the formulation of the fair as a site of imperial observation and collection.

Like other tourists, Hawaiian performers took in one of the Chicago Midway's most popular exhibits, the "Street of Cairo," the simulacrum that had confused Egyptian fairgoers in Paris. Kini said, "We went to this big building [with] everything Egypt. Land of Egypt. River running and all that. Stalls, the people, the camels, big, big, big."[149] But they were not simply spectators. The Hawaiians found they shared much in common with other colonial performers, such as Egyptians and Samoans. The Hawaiian troupe performed near a much larger Samoan village on the Midway Plaisance. A white merchant in Samoa had brought twenty-five Samoans, Tongans, and Wallis Islanders to Chicago for a concession featuring dancing and craft-making.[150] The Hawaiians and Samoans got along particularly well because their spoken language was similar enough to communicate. "We used to go over [to see them] from the back entrance. We talk all the time," Kini explained.[151] Hawaiians and other Polynesian entertainers commiserated in Chicago. After the fair, the dancer Nakai and the hoʻopaʻa Kanuku decided to go to Samoa with performers from this village before returning to Hawaiʻi.[152]

Kini and her group also mingled with the women dancers at the fair. "We like to make friends with girls from other countries," said Kini. Located in the Street of Cairo exhibit, the Middle Eastern and North African belly dance was another popular and scandalous Midway attraction.[153] Also known as the danse du ventre or, more disparagingly, "hootch cootch," the belly dance was likened to the hula. Both dances were considered risqué and astonished observers.[154] The Hawaiians, however, saw the ghawazi (Egyptian female belly dancers) as fellow artists; they observed the women closely and admired the way they skillfully manipulated their bodies—first their stomachs, their shoulders, and then their breasts.[155]

The poʻe hula and the ghawazi lived side by side on the fairgrounds for six months, and these encounters endured in the form of a gift. As a token of their friendship, the Egyptian dancers gave Kini twelve metal bracelets. These were no ordinary adornments—each metal bracelet was measured to fit her wrists and soldered on. One girl held each band while another laid torch to metal. Thus forged on her arms, these bracelets became inalienable. As Kini grew heavier later in life, she was unable to take them off. During an illness, doctors tried to make her cut off the bracelets. She refused, saying, "Do you want me to cut you? I satisfy myself, not you. Take it off? What for? Leave it there."[156] They relented after she said she would find new doctors. These bracelets remained a material reminder of friendships developed behind the Midway stage; Kini wore them for seventy years until her death in 1962. As suggested by their lasting construction and Kini's objections to their removal, the bracelets were more than attractive accoutrements. They were what Nicholas Thomas has called "prestige articles," gifts that accrue personal and wider social value for the recipient because they signify a relationship with the givers.[157] Associated with the group's circulations outside the islands, the bracelets vested the wearer with cosmopolitan status.

In pre-European Hawaiʻi, aliʻi displayed their rank through bodily adornments like lei niho palaoa, a carved whale tooth strung onto thick ropes of braided human hair. These and the brilliantly colored ʻahuʻula (feather capes) were reserved for aliʻi. As diplomatic and personal relationships were established with European nations in the nineteenth century, high chiefs exchanged ceremonial gifts with European monarchs. Queen Emma, the consort of King Kamehameha IV, traveled to England in 1865, where she was granted an audience with Queen Victoria, the ruler of the most powerful empire in the world at the time. After their meeting, Victoria gave Emma a bracelet. Emma described it as "a bracelet of gold and onix with her portrait & hair in it and a writing of ʻVictoria R. Nov. 27, 1865.'"[158] Queen Emma posed for a photographic portrait around 1870; she wore either this bracelet or another amethyst and pearl bracelet given

Fig. 19 Queen Emma, ca. 1870, wearing jewels given by British royalty. She stands next to the silver christening cup given by Queen Victoria to her son, Prince Albert Edward Kauikeaouli Leiopapa a Kamehameha. COURTESY OF HAWAI'I STATE ARCHIVES.

to her by the Duke of Edinburgh during his visit to Hawai'i in 1869. She also holds a bouquet brooch, another gift from the duke (see figure 19).[159] By flanking herself with gifts from the British throne, Emma was amplifying her connection to the British Empire in order to increase her prestige and establish herself as a credible successor to the Hawaiian monarchy.[160]

Kini encountered monarchs as a performer in Europe, but she built more lasting relationships with commoner women of other nations. Kini posed with Egyptian bracelets that appear to adorn her arms in her hula portrait taken in Chicago (see figure 11). This suggests that the performers were not simply aspiring to gendered Euro-American standards of style, but were appropriating Hawaiian chiefly practices of status accumulation and adornment. Kini would create a bracelet of her own—a unique status object—while on tour.

The Grand Tour

At Kalākaua's coronation ball in 1883, a kumu hula named Kaonowai and his troupe performed a hula kuʻi, "Ano ʻai ke aloha na laʻi a Ehu." Composed for Kalākaua, the mele celebrates his world tour that led him through Europe, Asia, and the United States in 1881. The mele follows the monarch on his American travels through locales such as Kikako (Chicago), Kanaluiki (St. Louis), Bokekona (Boston), Nu Hawena (New Haven), and Kaleponi (California).[161] The dancers trained in his court were to take a similar route of their own, though they were commoners. Through hula, performers gained access to routes previously available largely to wealthy and high-ranking aliʻi.[162] Beginning in early 1894, the hula troupe left the United States for Europe; their tours through belle-époque Europe brought them to private audiences with monarchs and to riotous urban theaters.[163] While on display, women were able to expand the opportunity structure of hula, becoming tourists and cultural ambassadors for the kingdom.

The hula performers began in the German Empire and ended in England. In Germany, the troupe performed at a Munich theater, where one of the guests was the king of Saxony. Enraptured by the hula performance, the king requested to meet the troupe and invited them to tour his palace the following day.[164] After Germany, the group moved on to Paris, where they danced hula at the Folies-Bergère and performed for the president of France at his residence. The Folies-Bergère was a new form of theater for the working and lower middle classes, a café-concert that mixed highbrow and lowbrow entertainment in variety "revues" similar to those of American vaudeville. Heretofore unknown in Europe, the poʻe hula provided an unusual spectacle for Parisians, sharing the stage with acts such as circus trainers, bearded ladies, trapeze artists, and boxing kangaroos. Proceeding to England, they made a wide circuit for two months through England's theaters and finally closed at London's Crystal Palace. Only a few years prior, William Cody (also known as Buffalo Bill) and his entourage of American Indians had become sensations in Europe. They staged special Wild West shows for Queen Victoria's Golden Jubilee in 1887 and toured France, Spain, Italy, Germany, and England in 1889–90.[165]

In Europe, the Hawaiian women were able to demonstrate the decorum and worldly sophistication that they developed during their apprenticeship in Kalākaua's court. In Berlin, the troupe performed at a private party for the German emperor, Kaiser Wilhelm II. During their presentation to the emperor, the Hawaiian women curtsied. Kini reminded him of his acquaintance with Dowager Queen Kapiʻolani of Hawaiʻi, the consort of the late mōʻī (monarch) Kalākaua. The emperor told them that he indeed had met Queen Kapiʻolani and her sister-in-law Liliʻuokalani, the future queen of Hawaiʻi, in 1887 at Queen Victoria's Golden Jubilee.[166] By mentioning the royal family, Kini presented herself as an envoy of the Hawaiian kingdom, despite the ascendance of Americans in the islands and her appearance as a court curiosity. In the wake of the overthrow and takeover by pro-American missionary sons, Kalākaua's project of fortifying Hawaiʻi's independence through diplomatic relationships and consulates came to an abrupt end. The poʻe hula instead became de facto cultural ambassadors for the islands as they traveled.

Placed on display through vernacular entertainment, they also took in the sights as tourists. Kini enjoyed touring Europe, finding much to be impressed by, including the extravagant regalia of European monarchs. In Berlin, they saw theatrical performances such as a Punch and Judy puppet show.[167] The performers treated their European tour like a grand tour, the edifying rite of passage enjoyed by upper-class British men and women. This was their chance to acquire a liberal education and cultural capital, as had the Hawaiian youths whose educations abroad were sponsored by the monarchy a decade prior. Most Hawaiian women of commoner status would not have had the opportunity to travel, but Kini was able to make claims that she had seen the world and developed connections, as she did throughout her life after she returned to the islands. She proudly asserted, when "people talk about going around to see places, they never saw places I have."[168] New contacts and global interactions opened up to commoner women apart from elite channels.

Sitting Bull, Red Shirt, and Rocky Bear were celebrity American Indian performers on Buffalo Bill's Wild West circuit who "strolled the streets of the world's cities" and "often received invitations to meet social and political elites wherever the show stopped."[169] However, while Indian men could become flâneurs in Paris, Indian women were not likely to be performers. As L. G. Moses observes, Indian women, if they traveled, accompanied male performers as companions or wives. Hawaiian women, however, became celebrities and headliners, without needing the aid of husbands, brothers, or fathers.

During her travels through Germany, Kini collected coins and engraved them with the names of the cities she stopped in, including Berlin, Chemnitz, Hamburg, and München. Along with the Egyptian bracelets, she wore them for much of her life on a charm bracelet as a souvenir of her adventure.[170] They are visible on her left wrist in two portraits taken in Louisville, Kentucky (see figures 12 and 15). Unlike the stereopticon and jewelry received by Queen Emma from Napoleon III and Queen Victoria, Kini's charms were not luxuries. She utilized inexpensive coins, such as the German ten-pfennig, coins worth but a few American cents. However, engraved with names, places, and dates, the charms became entangled with recollections and anecdotes of Kini's travels. The charms signified her relationship to a world outside of Hawai'i; they are analogous to the art, books, and cultural artifacts brought back by British men from grand tours that symbolized wealth and prestige.[171] Adorning her body, these charms signaled Kini's global encounters.

To take what is commonplace and transform it into a personal effect is a highly gendered collecting practice. Susan Stewart observes that the souvenir allows for an experience to be privatized and interiorized. "The souvenir reduces the public, the monumental, and the three-dimensional into the miniature, that which can be enveloped by the body, or into the two-dimensional representation, that which can be appropriated within the privatized view of the individual subject."[172] Kini incorporated these souvenirs into her body. But her particular choice of materials—the coin—was not accidental; it signals an attempt to humanize the coin of the realm. The currency that commodified the women could be made into a precious memento; the hardness of commodity exchange rendered personal and meaningful. Marx argued that commodity fetishism, the worship of objects that seem to be magical, "sensuous things," obscures the social relations upon which economic exchanges are based.[173] The women were turned into fetish objects through commodified entertainment. However, Kini performed a different kind of magic on these coins, reinserting the social and corporeal into an economic relationship and interrupting the commodity exchange. She transformed what was alienable—the coin—into an "inalienable possession" that became an extension of her body.[174]

On one tiny coin, a German twenty-pfennig, Kini had engraved the name of the man she loved and would marry years later, "Johnie Wilson, Honolulu, HI."[175] There is no date on the German empire coin, but she probably engraved it after she returned to the United States in 1896. Johnny Wilson's name is misspelled, but the misspelling works as a kind of personal claim bearing her own mark. Wilson was Kini's childhood friend and hailed from a different social class. His family was of ali'i birth and had elite social connections among Hawaiian royalty and haole missionaries. She had loved him for years, but she was unable to fulfill her attachment. This charm held Kini's private hope and unresolved longing for many years.

Aloha 'Oe

After their European tours, Kini and her hula troupe worked their way west along the dime-museum and vaudeville theater circuit in the United States. In Chicago in 1895, Kini's group crossed unexpectedly with a group of Hawaiian musicians who were also touring in the United States after the overthrow.[176] The young men from the anticolonial Bana Lahui, or Puali Puhiohe Lahui (Hawaiian National Band), saw Kini's photograph posted outside a vaudeville theater and entered the theater as the hula troupe was closing the show.[177] As Kini and her group sang the famous Hawaiian ballad "Aloha 'Oe" (Love to you), a song composed by the deposed queen Lili'uokalani, they heard men's voices join the chorus. Because the stage lights in the theater were bright, Kini could not see their faces, but both groups continued to sing spontaneously together. The impromptu performance finally ended after many encores, and about twenty "boys" from the Bana Lahui came backstage to the dressing room, where the men and women were reunited far from home.[178] I narrate this encounter not simply in order to recount an accidental reunion. This incident is a reminder of how nationalist expression and resistance can be entangled with the erotics of empire. The performance was a palimpsest of colonial and anticolonial meanings, containing multiple layers of desire for different actors.

On the one hand, the vaudeville hula show promised an imperial performance for American spectators. The hula show, advertised with the photograph of Kini, offered a firsthand opportunity to see the live bodies of hula girls. Audiences could partake of the erotics of empire in the form of "the seductive hula-hula passion dance," as one travel writer called it.[179] However, the spontaneous singing of "Aloha 'Oe" that day also contained a counter-colonial valence. When the Bana Lahui and the dancers were reunited in the summer of 1895, all were political exiles. The troupe had chosen not to return to Hawai'i after hearing of the overthrow, while the band had refused employment from the pro-American, annexationist Republic of Hawai'i and left the islands for the United States. By that summer, both the band and the hula troupe were acutely aware that the Republic of Hawai'i was holding the queen under house arrest. While imprisoned in her palace, Lili'uokalani had transcribed "Aloha 'Oe." Americans did not know the political genealogy of the song, but Hawaiians in attendance would have. Singing "Aloha ʻOe" in the empire honored the queen's memory and strengthened Hawaiians' resolve to support her restoration.[180]

There was, however, another kind of kaona—hidden meaning—in the performance, far more personal than this theatrical setting reveals. Kaona is the embedded meaning in Hawaiian poetry, an indigenous poetic device that resonates with James C. Scott's concept of hidden transcripts. The erotics of empire encompassed far more than the Western consumption of Hawaiian bodies. Backstage in Chicago, Kini Kapahu reunited with her own object of desire, John H. Wilson, her childhood playmate. "Aloha ʻOe" precipitated a new beginning for Kini and Johnny Wilson (also known as Keoni Wilisona), who was the national band's manager. They began a furtive love affair. It is Johnny's misspelled name that Kini engraved on one of her German coins, likely not long after this reunion in 1895. They were prevented from marrying by Johnny's mother's adamant objections to Kini. Like many other women of upperclass Hawaiian society, Eveline "Kitty" Melita Kilioulani Kaopaokalani Townsend Wilson found hula disgraceful and the women who practiced it even more so. After undertaking two more tours through the United States and a tumultuous relationship that endured through Johnny's brief marriage to a white American woman, Kini and Johnny would eventually marry in 1908.

The couple would join imperial hula circuits in the United States in order to live away from strictures of family and community. These performances offered them personal and political freedoms beyond Hawaiʻi. Their aloha and desire mingled promiscuously with the perils of commodified tourism and the exigencies of political dissent, pushing us to look beyond immediately legible expressions of political independence, defiance, or capitulation. We must approach the counter-colonial erotics of tourism, cultural production, and the performers' own bodies, for these tours embraced many things—politics, love, creative expression, adventure, and bodily desires—that are not easily disentangled.

CHAPTER 3

IMPRESARIOS ON THE MIDWAY
World's Fairs and Colonial Politics

The newly elected Democratic mayor of Honolulu, John Henry Wilson, awoke on his fifty-second birthday in 1923, to a serenade by the Royal Hawaiian Band. Directed by the mayor's longtime friend and traveling companion Mekia Kealakai, the municipal band began with "Nalanieha," a song Kealakai had composed for Wilson's political campaign. It also played music associated with Wilson's career as a Hawaiian showman.[1] As an early impresario of Hawaiian entertainment, Wilson led three tours of music and hula across the continental United States from 1895 to 1902.[2] He, along with his wife, Kini Kapahukulaokamāmalu, helped to create spectacular living attractions at international expositions that brought Hawaiians from the new territory to the heart of the U.S. empire. While Wilson's careers as a politician and showman may seem incongruous and unrelated, his political skills and influence in Hawai'i and Washington can be traced to his role as a cultural broker at the turn of the century. He learned to unsettle the haole (white) oligarchy, represent Hawaiians, and speak directly to Americans during his work as an independent cultural entrepreneur.

Returning to Hawai'i from American tours, Johnny, as he was affectionately known, began to build the islands' Democratic Party as a way to break the feudal plantation system. He made it his life's mission to thwart the Republican Party, the bastion of U.S. annexationists, and the nepotism bred by its corporate monopolies. Working his way up from building roads and organizing longshoremen,

Fig. 20 John H. Wilson as mayor of Honolulu.
COURTESY OF HAWAI'I STATE ARCHIVES.

he became one of the most influential politicians in the early territorial period. He served as mayor of Honolulu for multiple terms from 1920 to 1954 and as the chairperson of the territory's Democratic National Committee for more than thirty years, from 1912 to 1944 (see figure 20). As a Democratic leader, he oversaw the party slate for local elections, while his influence extended far beyond the territory to Washington, D.C. There, he lobbied Congress and issued recommendations for key federal appointments, including that of the territorial governor. By the time of his death in 1956, an interracial Democratic Party in Hawai'i—supported by a working-class and labor electorate—had eclipsed the Republicans.

Hawaiians like Johnny saw their chances for the restoration of the crown wither within a few years of the overthrow in 1893. In 1894, the annexationists declared a "Republic of Hawaii" that replaced the provisional government. In January 1895, an armed attempt to reinstate the monarchy by royalist supporters failed. The Republic of Hawai'i placed Queen Lili'uokalani on trial and convicted her of conspiracy and treason for her alleged knowledge of the revolt. She was forced to abdicate her throne and was imprisoned in the royal palace. To achieve American annexation and the goal of exporting tariff-free sugar to the U.S. continent, haole elites of the republic established an alliance with Washington. Although Congress failed to pass treaties of annexation for five years, it annexed the islands by joint resolution in 1898, during the Spanish-American War; this action required a simple majority of both houses rather than a two-thirds majority for a treaty.[3] Two years later, Congress passed the Organic Act of 1900, which made Hawai'i an incorporated U.S. territory and granted U.S. citizenship to all citizens of the republic.

Unlike in other U.S. quasiprotectorates, such as the Philippines and Puerto Rico, the United States did not have to install a new colonial apparatus in the Hawaiian archipelago, for Euro-Americans and their progeny had been strengthening their political and economic infrastructure since 1820, reforming traditional land tenure, assuming influential positions in kingdom cabinets, and industrializing agriculture. White settlers governed Hawai'i through large, nepotistic, corporate trusts and their coercive regime. The haole planter class pressed Hawaiians to accept the putative privileges of American citizenship. A new territorial government prepared high-ranking ali'i to become subordinate partners and commoners to become second-class citizens. But many Hawaiians also insisted on defining their own paths and challenging the annexationists within a newly established American system. After annexation, many royalists participated in party and electoral politics, establishing the Home Rule party in 1900 to increase Native Hawaiian governance.[4]

However, in this early period of American colonization, cultural performance was another important aspect of anticolonial political work. International expositions were fertile political and cultural terrains far outside the islands, with the ability to influence politics between the colony and metropole. Hawaiian brokers and performers did not treat their work at the expositions as separate from politics on the islands, but as productive opportunities for refining and disseminating political discourse before wider imperial audiences. As Hawaiians danced hula, weaved baskets, and brokered Hawaiian culture for Americans on the continent, they represented their country and asserted that they, not only white missionary sons, should determine the future of Hawai'i. The infrapolitics of exposition performances, the values and pragmatic forms of resistance, were forged through commodified performative realms.[5] Expositions were arenas of play and infrapolitical labor for Hawaiians. If public transcripts of hospitality and aloha were extracted from subordinated Hawaiians on colonial stages, where might we see their hidden transcripts of critique and resistance? Through subtle and dramatic performative acts of music, hula, chant, and conviviality, their veiled critiques and artful resistance pressed up against dominant imperial discourse.

At these early expositions, white settlers and Native cultural brokers wrestled over competing ideas of modernity. The oligarchy presented Hawai'i as a tropical frontier with accelerated industrial and agricultural development and the corporatist disciplining of indigenous and immigrant workers. However, Hawaiian cultural performers and brokers pursued discrepant modernities, presenting their own ideas of Hawaiian temporality, space, and bodily practices. They offered important countermemories to the oligarchy's insistent vision of Hawai'i's future as a U.S. territory. As they sang on tour, the children of Hawai'i would remain "ever loyal to the land" and nation.[6] They would rather eat stones than accept the republican government's money.

Several of these cultural brokers and performers—including the future political leaders Johnny Wilson and William Joseph Huelani Coelho— were bicultural and mixed-race Hawaiians who had seemingly embraced the precepts of Christianity and Western education. Yet these putatively assimilated men proved dangerous to the ruling elite and provoked deep antipathy, for they left the colony to represent their homeland to Americans. Highly entrepreneurial and cosmopolitan, they self-primitivized on the world stage while seeking to foreclose the authority of the haole oligarchy.

Scholars and observers of hula have long been suspicious of its engagement with tourism and capitalism, fearing the disappearance of authentic Hawaiian culture and people. However, selective commodification did not doom hula. Hawaiian performers, even during their initial incorporation into the U.S. nation-state, negotiated with colonization and tourist markets as self-aware agents, brokers, and political actors. They were not merely passive objects in Euro-American tourist economies, but managed to resist colonization through the strategic exhibition of Hawaiian cultural practices. They performed a complicated dance between the struggle for independence and the struggle to represent themselves as fully realized people with political will. By "playing Hawaiian" and commodifying Hawaiian cultural practices for American audiences, they challenged the territorial government in diasporic settings. Their sojourns in the United States presented them with an opportunity to perform outside the constricting ambit of the colony and relay directly to Americans their opposition to annexation. Via commodified entertainment, they sang and performed alternative political scenarios within the empire.

Although Americans and the federal government were complicit in the colonization of the islands, Hawaiians sought flexible alliances with mainland Americans to reconstitute local control over the islands. Hawaiian cultural brokers at these territorial world's fairs were committed to defying the white settler oligarchy. As highly mobile actors, hula and musical troupes constituted a flow of bodies and labor outside the control of the plantation system. Their movements and performances bypassed the territorial government, disrupting the imperial logic and hierarchies of patronage that linked the territory and the federal government. As Julian Go has theorized, U.S. colonial projects were constituted through a series of interlocking and evolving relationships between colony and metropole, what he calls translocal "chains of empire." These imperial chains "link colonial populations, colonial states, and metropolitan actors" and are accountable to multiple forces and shifting policies.[7] Hawaiian performers inserted themselves as vital links within this chain, loosening the hold of haole settlers. They were political and cultural leaders in their own right who would have to be reckoned with as active participants in the emergent colony.

Offering competing representations at U.S. world's fairs, Hawaiians frustrated members of the haole oligarchy who desired sole access to the brokering of Hawai'i. Hawaiian performers walked a fine line between deference and defiance: their very presence in the United States signaled their independence from the oligarchy of the islands. Hawaiian troupes crafted their own relationships with American capital and audiences, though they were required to display themselves as unthreatening primitives. At the same time, they traveled to the continent to train themselves for political work and pursue other desires for erotic fulfillment, creative expression, and adventure. The fairs—as highly gendered political and cultural stages—allowed some Kanaka men to rehearse and refine their roles as interlocutors with federal politicians, white business leaders, and Hawaiian constituencies. They took advantage of the growing market for racialized commercial entertainment to assert their independence from haole patrons, establish alternative alliances, and generate financial and cultural capital outside the islands.

White Settlement and Colonial Capitalism

During Hawai'i's republican and territorial periods, the kama'āina haole (Hawai'i-born white) oligarchy maintained an iron grip on the government and the island economy. Missionary families and their lineal descendants, with surnames such as Baldwin, Castle, Dillingham, and Alexander, had invested in interlocking corporations of plantations, banking, railways, shipping, and insurance known as the "Big Five."[8] Sugar, the largest Big Five industry, was extremely profitable, thanks to the sugar quota planters received after annexation. Planters exported sugar to the continental United States without paying the tariff of thirty-four dollars per ton. After 1898, the industry expanded further, with thirteen new plantations funded by $40 million more in capital investment.[9] Through a vertical monopoly on sugar, affiliated corporations grew, refined, marketed, and shipped the sugar.

The economy required an unyielding political structure to run smoothly. Lorrin A. Thurston, a key participant in the conspiracy to overthrow the monarchy, outlined the aristocratic, authoritarian regime sought by the postoverthrow regime: "What we desire is some form of territorial government which will give an effective Executive, which will not be subject to the whims, caprices and dishonesty of an irresponsible legislative body; as well as maintain stable gov't; make revolution impossible, encourage investment of capital and development of resources."[10]

After the United States made Hawai'i an incorporated territory in 1900, the ruling class was permitted internal control by Washington.[11] The plantation oligarchy continued to exert control over the territorial governor, the territorial delegate to Congress, and the local legislature.[12] Appointed by the president of the United States for a four-year term, the territorial governor was affiliated with and beholden to the sugar plantations and the Honolulu Chamber of Commerce. The island oligarchy, as it was pithily described by one scholar, believed "the business of government in the Islands was business."[13] The territory's first appointed governor was the missionary son Sanford B. Dole, who was also the Republic of Hawai'i's first president. The republic secured favorable trade, immigration, and subsidy policies from the federal government, as well as high-ranking judicial and executive appointments for their brethren and affiliates.

Island-born mission boys closed ranks through coercion and economic might. Nonpropertied Hawaiians and Asian immigrants became grossly marginalized. When the Republic of Hawai'i was established in 1894, it instituted property and income requirements for voting and an oath of loyalty to the new government, which disfranchised many Hawaiians.[14] Only 18 percent of voters registered in 1894 were Hawaiian, and haole became the majority of the electorate.[15] Nor could Asians vote in the republic; Asian plantation workers were largely rendered ineligible to vote because of English-language, citizenship, and property requirements.[16]

While the Big Five consolidated its hold on the Hawaiian Islands through industrial plantations, the federal government was acquiring and administering new overseas possessions. Fin de siècle expositions staged in the United States—including the Greater America Exposition (GAE) of 1899 in Omaha, Nebraska, and the Pan-American Exposition (PAE) of 1901 in Buffalo, New York—sought to show off America's colonial booty acquired in 1898 from the Spanish-American War, namely, the Philippines, Guam, Puerto Rico, and Hawai'i.[17] The American annexation of Hawai'i, although not a direct result of the war, was an extension of expansionism in this period. The needs of Hawai'i's plantation class coincided quite nicely with those of the federal government and exposition management. Following the overthrow, the haole oligarchy seized upon these world's fairs to showcase the islands' industrial and commercial potential. From 1894 to 1915, the republican and territorial governments sent ten official exhibits to international expositions (see the chronology).[18]

Concerned with strengthening economic relations between Hawai'i and the United States, the islands' Chamber of Commerce allocated $10,000 for the exhibit and sent a commission to the GAE in Omaha in 1899. The Chamber of Commerce of Honolulu, an auxiliary of the republican government, organized the first fair exhibits for the territory. Its members were haole businessmen or business boosters who closely represented the interests of the Big Five oligarchy. The president and the secretary of the commission, Edward Towse and Daniel Logan, respectively, were editors of the *Pacific Commercial Advertiser*, the oligarchy's mouthpiece, purchased by a leading annexationist, Lorrin A. Thurston, in 1895. No Hawaiians were members of the commission.

The exhibits advertised Hawai'i as a new American possession ripe for further U.S. settlement and capitalist investment. The chamber of commerce's 4,000-square-foot exhibit was housed with other colonial exhibits in a government building referred to as the "colonial building." Partly educational and mostly commercial, the exhibit displayed the islands' agricultural commodities, such as sugar, rice, coffee, and canned and preserved tropical fruits.[19] Some ethnographic "curios by natives," such as kapa (bark cloth) and a canoe were displayed, but the commission concentrated on showing Hawai'i's attractiveness, resources, and development.[20] These agricultural products were produced by contract labor and large-scale cultivation on industrial plantations. Many were also exported to United States under favorable tariffs granted to the colony after annexation. By sparking interest in the colony, the Hawai'i exhibit hoped to lure white settlers and investors from the continental United States. The oligarchy desired the settlement of white Anglo-Saxons who could expand the American frontier to Hawai'i, Americanize the islands, and reduce the influence of Hawaiian and Asian communities. The commissioners reported that they spoke to many potentially "desirable people" about investment possibilities in the islands.

The second major element of the colonial exhibit was the "handiwork" of Hawaiian boys and girls educated at Christian schools. The Kamehameha School for Boys contributed "specimens of workmanship" from their carpentry, blacksmithing, and tailoring courses, while Hawaiian girls educated in Christian seminaries sent their fancywork.[21] These samples served as tangible evidence of the progress of the Hawaiian people: with Christian conversion and trade education, Hawaiians were capable of contributing to the developing industrial economy. They appeared to have been transformed into industrious colonial charges under the influence of American institutions.

The colonial exhibit poised modernity in terms of capitalist progress: rapid industrial development, the conversion of land to centralized agricultural production, the pursuit of bourgeois cultural arts and leisure, and the exploitation of natural resources and labor. White civilizing agents stood at the center of this development, with Hawaiians serving as marginalized subordinates and Asians as necessary but reviled laborers. Kama'āina haole industrialists also visited the Omaha fair and publicized their support for annexation. Distinguished members of the Waterhouse and Dillingham families, who owned plantations and railways, made a grand entrance. One of them, the scion of a leader in the Republic of Hawai'i, championed U.S. annexation, telling the *Omaha World-Herald* that "the people of the islands as a class were delighted at annexation and were proud of the mother country."[22]

The commissioners also asserted the inevitability of Hawaiian conversion to the American political system, but had to suppress questions from Americans about Hawaiian unrest. Protesting their annexation and colonization, Hawaiians had been boycotting elections in the Republic of Hawai'i and refused to elect a legislature.[23] Although many Hawaiians remained unconvinced of the benefits of American rule, the exhibit suggested that white control of the islands had been achieved and that Kanaka Maoli had been brought under American stewardship. The commission argued that order and prosperity had been restored and that the islands were faring much better under the U.S. flag.

Unfortunately for the commissioners, the colonial exhibit was chronically short of products to display. For the first two months, they had no sugar to show and were still waiting for shipments of rice, coffee, and landscape paintings.[24] Even when fully stocked, it was a haphazard and uninspired display that ultimately proved a failure. The outcome was even worse for the Hawai'i Chamber of Commerce at the Buffalo exposition in 1901. Although business leaders wanted to send an exhibit to Buffalo, there were no territorial legislative funds available.[25]

The commissioners soon encountered an even bigger challenge in their midst—a group of sophisticated Hawaiian performers. Hawaiians organized independent ethnographic concessions at the Omaha Greater America Exposition in 1899 and the Buffalo Pan-American Exposition in 1901. In Omaha, the commissioners were surprised to learn they would be competing with a private concession, a Hawaiian village housed in the midway section of the fair.[26] The commission could not exercise direct control over the village but watched it very carefully, fearful that it would contradict their presentation of the islands as a civilized land worthy of American investment.[27] The commissioners found themselves in the uncomfortable position of being upstaged by Hawaiians in the village. The attractions of diving children, hula dancers, and entrancing music far surpassed their dull colonial exhibits. Unsanctioned by colonial and federal administrators, Hawaiian performers became de facto ambassadors for the islands.

Live Hawaiians

Aspiring to teach Americans about the nation's recent colonial acquisitions, imperial expositions displayed the products and "ethnological features" of the colonies.[28] As was the case at the Chicago World's Columbian Exposition in 1893, the ethnographic entertainments on the midways in Omaha and Buffalo were funded by private investors and separated from official governmental displays. The Hawaiian village was but one of many immersive experiences on the midway; fairgoers could also enter a Philippine village with one hundred imported Filipinos, an "Old Plantation" of fifty "genuine Negros" from the South, "Darkest Africa," a Street of Mexico, an Indian Congress, and Cuban, Inuit, and Japanese villages.[29] The Hawaiian villagers became associated with other racialized peoples and sideshow attractions at fin de siècle fairs. For example, the impresario E. W. McConnell advertised his Hawaiian village in Buffalo along with seven other concessions on his "Red Star Route," among them a baby incubator, a simulacrum of a Hawaiian volcano, and a Filipino village.[30]

The Hawaiian troupe at the Chicago World's Columbian Exposition in 1893 consisted of only six po'e hula (hula practitioners), while the living Hawaiian villages at the fairs in Omaha and Buffalo followed a more elaborate ethnographic entertainment formula. The Hawaiian villages at each fair had between twenty-six and forty-four performers—including entire families—living in reconstructed hale pili (grass huts) on the midway grounds.[31] Visitors paid a twenty-five-cent admission fee to enter the village building where they could see quotidian activities as well as staged performances. The villages provided an immersive and sensory experience. Visitors could watch diving, take in a concert of Hawaiian music and hula, and eat Hawaiian food and sample island coffee at an "Aloha restaurant." Live performances in the theaters were the pièce de résistance, but the women in the village also put their artistry to work for tourists, busily weaving hats and kapa mats, and sewing with machines. In Buffalo, the village also housed a separate attraction, the Kilauea Volcano Cyclorama, a lifelike replica of the famous Hawaiian landmark on the island of Hawai'i, complete with Hawaiian priests who appeased the volcano goddess. These villages were early prototypes for ethnographic villages and cultural attractions that are tourist standards today in places such as Hawai'i, Fiji, and Aotearoa (New Zealand).

Millions in the Midwest and upstate New York likely encountered Hawaiians for the first time at these exhibits.[32] In Omaha, the Hawaiian village was one of the "best patronized concessions on the grounds," and its hula and music show was praised as "one of the finest performances ever witnessed on an exposition grounds."[33] Overall attendance at the GAE was disappointing compared to the exposition that preceded it the year before.[34] However, its Aloha Theater had to be expanded to accommodate more patrons as Hawaiians became one of the most popular attractions along the Buffalo midway (see figure 21). Buffalo newspapers proposed that the best way to learn about this "new possession . . . much talked of at the present time" was by visiting firsthand the Hawaiian village on the midway.[35]

The village concessions had no connection—financial or otherwise—

Fig. 21 Fairgoers outside Hawaiian village at the Buffalo Pan-American Exposition, 1901.
COURTESY OF HAWAI'I STATE ARCHIVES.

with exhibits produced by the Honolulu Chamber of Commerce. Instead, exposition concessions like the Hawaiian village were funded by businessmen from Omaha and Buffalo who received a dividend if the ventures were profitable. American investors handed the management of midway concessions off to an experienced American showman, who then relied on Native brokers to organize the labor and sales. In this case, the Hawaiian middleman between the investment group, concessionaire, and troupe was Johnny H. Wilson, the future mayor of Honolulu. He handled daily management and lived on the fairgrounds with the troupe. As troupe manager, Johnny received a guarantee and percentage of the proceeds.

The Hawaiian performers that Johnny hired for Buffalo signed six-month contracts with salaries ranging from twelve to twenty-five dollars a month, for which they were to work every day of the week except Sunday.[36] The performers' salaries and contract terms were likely similar in Omaha. As a point of comparison, contract field laborers on Hawaiian plantations earned a monthly wage of approximately $17.50 in 1900.[37] Although they did not receive significantly more compensation, performers may have chosen this work because it was more pleasurable than back-breaking stoop labor in the cane fields or the other low-level service labor available then. If their contracts were structured similarly to those of previous Hawaiian performers in the United States, they probably had their steerage to and from the fair and daily living expenses covered as well. The midway contracts gave them a chance to earn a decent living, tour the powerful country that had colonized theirs, and increase their individual prestige and fame. During the same period, American Indian students were also mastering Western instruments and music. They played in Indian reservation school bands and performed for white audiences. Despite the disciplinary regime of music instruction that required them to perform their conversion to civilization, these youths often enjoyed playing and treated music as an opportunity to leave oppressive boarding schools and acquire a trade.[38]

Johnny hired Mekia Kealakai, a Hawaiian National Band flutist, to select musicians for both expositions.[39] Johnny's childhood friend Kini Kapahu, the ʻōlohe hula (hula expert) with a wealth of vaudeville experience, likely had a hand in choosing the hula performers. Johnny's maternal uncle, George H. Peck Monewa Townsend, was assistant manager. Most of the so-called villagers had experience as musicians, singers, chanters, or hula dancers. In Omaha, the group included a Quintette Club of expert musicians from the Hawaiian National Band, as well as several male and female poʻe hula and hoʻopaʻa (chanters). The English-Hawaiian James Shaw family and ʻukulele expert Ernest Kaai were notable members.[40]

In Buffalo, the eighteen women and twenty-six Hawaiian men similarly included musicians, artisans, and poʻe hula with a broad range of talents.[41] Members of the Hawaiian Glee Club—David Nape, Mekia Kealakai, Kimokeo, Opu, William Joseph Huelani Coelho, and Charles H. Baker—were part of the troupe. The musicians John "Jack" Paoakalani Heleluhe, Richard Reuter, William McComber, Anthony Zablan, James Kulolio, July Paka, Charles Baker, and William Alohikea also joined them (see figure 22).[42] We do not know all of the names of the women, but four of them were Mele, Abbie Clark, Annie Hilo, and Lilie Veiri. At least two young children performed hula with the troupe as well.

Several in the Omaha and Buffalo troupes were already extremely accomplished showmen. David Nape had been a member of the Hawaiian National Band since his youth. He also played oboe and composed hallmark ballads of the period, such as "Kuu Home" and "Pua Mohala." Mekia Kealakai, who played the flute, piano, and trombone, had toured the United States with the anticolonial Bana Lahui (Hawaiian National

Fig. 22 Hawaiian musicians of Wilson troupe, Buffalo Pan-American Exposition, 1901. Photograph by Beach (Buffalo, N.Y.). COURTESY OF BISHOP MUSEUM. Seated, left to right: Mekia Kealakai, William Alohikea, David Nape. Center row, left to right: Anthony Zablan, James Kulolio, July Paka, Charles Baker. Back row, left to right: John "Jack" Paoakalani Heleluhe, Richard Reuter, William McComber.

Band) in 1895–96. John Philip Sousa, the era's most prolific American bandmaster and "March King," heard Mekia playing flute with the Hawaiian band at the Pan-American Exposition in Buffalo in 1901 and called him the "greatest flutist" he had "ever heard." Sousa was so impressed with Mekia's triple-tongue playing that he asked him to join his own band that was performing in Buffalo at the time.[43]

The Stanford Showman

Johnny Wilson was by no means raised to become an impresario. Nor had he ever lived in a grass hut in the islands. Also known as Keoni Wilisona in the Hawaiian press, he was a light-skinned hapa haole (part-white) man who embodied the highly mixed and multinational nature of the upper echelons of Hawaiian society; he was Tahitian, Hawaiian, and haole.[44] Born in 1871, Johnny had ali'i (chiefly) status through his Hawaiian maternal great-grandmother, but perhaps more significantly, his family enjoyed access to rarified haole and Hawaiian circles.

His full name, John Henry Nalanieha Tuaorai Tamarii Wilson, reflects his Polynesian and European lineages.[45] His Hawaiian name, "Nalanieha," or the four heavens, honored four ali'i: David Kalākaua and his siblings Lili'uokalani, Leleiohoku, and Miriam Likelike, all gifted musicians and composers. Kalākaua and Lili'uokalani were close friends of Johnny's family. His maternal grandmother, Harriet Kapakulani Kekahililani Hawaiiloa Blanchard Townsend, was Queen Lili'uokalani's personal seamstress. His mother, Eveline "Kitty" Melita Kilioulani Kaopaokalani Townsend Wilson, served as the queen's lady-in-waiting from her youth until Kitty died.[46]

"Tuaorai Tamarii" are Johnny's Tahitian names; he was named after his father, Charles Burnette Tuaorai Wilson, and his paternal uncle, Richard E. Tamarii Wilson. Charles and Richard were born in Tahiti to a Scottish trader and a high-ranking Tahitian woman named Tetaria. After the sudden death of their father, Charles and Richard were sent to Honolulu. Although a blacksmith by trade, Charles ascended Hawai'i's social and political ladder through his association with King Kalākaua and the royal family.[47] Charles excelled in shooting, rowing, and boxing, and his dashing success endeared him to the bon vivant king. Kalākaua rewarded Charles by appointing him to positions as fire chief and waterworks superintendent. Through ambition and talent, this outsider was able to infiltrate the traditional rank system, later becoming Lili'uokalani's marshal and a member of her privy council. Charles Wilson was the last member of the queen's council to surrender his firearms after the overthrow on 17 January 1893.

Johnny's intimate relationship to the crown and his mixed-race status offered him mobility and important advantages relative to other Hawaiians. Although his future lover Kini Kapahu was also hapa haole, her adoptive Hawaiian parents were of modest means and far lower social standing than the Wilsons. The queen included Johnny in her official entourage, while his playmates were the princes Jonah Kūhiō Kalaniana'ole and David and Edward Kawānanakoa. With financial sponsorship from the queen, Johnny was able to join the founding class of Stanford University in 1891, where the future president Herbert Hoover was one of his classmates and friends. There he began studying engineering, but in the spring of 1894 he lost his funding due to the overthrow and had to withdraw from school.

A strong royalist, Johnny opposed U.S. annexation and may have even assisted with the purchase and shipping of arms from San Francisco for the rebellion against the Republic of Hawai'i in January 1895.[48] His uncle

George Monewa Townsend, who came to the Omaha exposition as co-manager, participated in the armed revolt and was tried for treason.[49] Regardless of Johnny's specific role in the affair, he found the overthrow unjust and experienced the downfall of the kingdom as a personal loss. Johnny embodied a kind of class- and status-conscious Native modernity. Through his maternal uncle George, he grew up conversant in Hawaiian cultural practices, but was anxious about keeping up with haole mission boys who were being groomed for Ivy League schools and the boards of their fathers' corporations.[50] Even when Johnny attended Stanford and excelled in engineering, his white classmates christened him "Kanaka Jack." "Kanaka," meaning man or person in Hawaiian, was often used by whites as a denigrating epithet for Hawaiians. Throughout his life, Johnny's choices revealed the tensions of his upbringing—having to fulfill his family's aspirations and his responsibility to Hawaiians as a whole.

Johnny was being groomed to become a leader in business or politics, but the overthrow and takeover of the islands threw him off course. He had two key meetings in his young adult life that influenced his turn toward showmanship. While at Stanford, he met an exposition showman named E. W. McConnell who was working for the Hawaiian village concession at the Midwinter Fair in San Francisco in 1894. It was McConnell who later invited Johnny to join his Hawaiian concessions in Omaha and Buffalo. A few months later, after he had withdrawn from Stanford, Johnny tried to secure an engineering job from the sugar baron Claus Spreckels on his California railroad line. Spreckels, a San Francisco sugar refiner, handled most of Hawai'i's sugar crop and had served as one of Johnny's guardians while he attended Stanford.[51] Instead of hiring him for the railroad, Spreckels handed Johnny his first entertainment job managing the Bana Lahui in 1895 (see figure 23). This experience sparked his interest in show business as an alternative to the plantation system. Johnny astutely recognized Hawaiian entertainment as a unique transnational political and business opportunity at a time when both political power and the means of production in Hawai'i were in the grasp of the oligarchy.

Like other Hawaiian leaders from this period, Johnny did not so much resent Americans on the continent for extinguishing the kingdom, but reserved his greatest contempt for Hawai'i-born Americans who had orchestrated the overthrow and extracted the islands' greatest resources for their own profit.[52] He saw them feasting while those below them starved. Determined to create an alternative to the missionary oligarchy and resist the feudal system of territorial Hawai'i, Johnny Wilson started with small en-

Fig. 23 John H. Wilson, ca. 1895. He wears a Hawaiian flag pin on his lapel and a national seal on his hat as a sign of loyalty to the deposed kingdom.
COURTESY OF HAWAI'I STATE ARCHIVES.

trepreneurial interventions. After returning home from managing the national band in 1896, he launched several business and engineering ventures, including the construction of the sewage system in Honolulu and major roads (see figure 24). His most ambitious and long-standing project was the blasting of the Pali Road, which opened up the previously remote windward side of the island of Oʻahu to the city of Honolulu. The Pali became one of Oʻahu's most vital transportation routes in the twentieth century.

Johnny's sympathies also lay with the small businessman and underdog. He saw that with the colonial government underwriting a monopolized economy, Hawaiians could not secure their own homesteads for small-scale production or subsistence farming, while large sugar plantations and railroads expropriated choice expanses of kingdom lands. Shipping companies were not concerned with small independent producers, but with managing the flow from their affiliated plantations of export commodities such as sugar. Since small farmers had no other means to

Fig. 24 John H. Wilson, age 26, ca. 1897.
COURTESY OF HAWAI'I STATE ARCHIVES.

do so, Johnny helped rural Hawaiians haul their rice and taro to Honolulu markets with a light steamship.[53] While different from road construction and taro shipping, entertainment in the continental United States was another way for Johnny to circumvent the power of missionary sons by creating new social and economic networks. He sought to further sharpen these skills at U.S. expositions.

Other Hawaiian entertainers at the fair brought a similar wealth of knowledge and commitments to these American ventures. Crossing into multiple fields of action, they belie categorization by vocation or political party. William Joseph Huelani Coelho, another Hawaiian cultural and political broker at the Buffalo fair, performed as one of the kahuna (Hawaiian priests) on the midway's Hawaiian volcano concession, which adjoined the village. Coelho helped manage the village and appeared to have performed oli (chants) and hula. Like Johnny Wilson, Coelho was a well-educated, mixed-race man. The son of a Hawaiian mother and a

Portuguese father, he had eclectic professions, talents, and avocations. Before leaving for the Buffalo fair, the seminary-trained Coelho had taken on civic and leadership responsibilities within or aligned with the administrations of the Republic and the Territory of Hawai'i. He clerked for the district court in 1897.[54] He cordoned off plague patients as a volunteer inspector for the board of health during the plague of 1899.[55] Coelho also served as a notary public under the territory's attorney general, and edited the establishment newspaper *Nupepa Kuokoa* in 1900.[56]

However, as a musician, singer, composer, and hula practitioner, Coelho obliquely criticized and worked against the missionary elite. He performed with the royalist Hawaiian National Band, directed the Hawaiian Glee Club, and helped to found the Young Hawaiians Institute. These were anticolonial musical groups that supported royalist causes and performed European choral music and Hawaiian mele in the aftermath of the overthrow and annexation. The Young Hawaiians Institute, for example, held Hawaiian music concerts that benefited the wives and children of men who had participated in the armed rebellion of 1895.[57]

Coelho worked in politics in order to empower Hawaiians within the new territorial government. Like Johnny Wilson, he was a committed royalist but chose to join the Republican Party as a path toward power-sharing with haole annexationists. He eventually became a leader of the local party.[58] The Republican Party was founded in the islands after the Organic Act of 1900 established a territorial form of government for Hawai'i. Although Coelho had decided to work within the colonial structure, he believed that the missionary and planter class—whom he called "missionary hypocrites"—were systematically destroying Hawaiians.[59] Coelho traveled to the PAE exposition in 1901, a Buffalo newspaper editorialized, to "study Americanisms for he realizes that the tide sets to that end in his own land."[60] However, this is an incomplete, if not inaccurate, interpretation of Coelho's desires. Rather than surrendering to an inexorable American tide, Coelho sought to increase Hawaiian participation in territorial politics and shift influence away from the haole oligarchy. To this end, he immersed himself in U.S. political culture, studied its people and institutions, and circulated widely among white Americans, African Americans, and foreign groups at the exposition.

The Village People

At a typical live performance at the Hawaiian theater in the villages, a band played orchestral numbers, followed by the glee club's English and

Fig. 25 Hawaiian musician Anthony Zablan with 'ukulele, Buffalo Pan-American Exposition, 1901. COURTESY OF HAWAI'I STATE ARCHIVES.

Hawaiian-language vocal music (see figure 25). The musical selections led in to the main feature, the "hula-hula dance" by Hawaiian women.[61] American audiences had neither seen nor heard an ensemble of banjo, violin, flute, 'ukulele, guitar, mandolin, and bass viol playing Western melodies with Hawaiian vocals.[62] When the Aloha Theater opened at the Omaha exposition, the novel Hawaiian performances became "the talk of all the music-loving public."[63] The performers also appealed to the crowd with familiar American hits like "When You Were Sweet Sixteen."

The polysemic nature of live Hawaiian performances put contradictory meanings into play, depending on the context and who was participating and observing. Hawaiian practices of feasting, dancing, and singing could be read, on the one hand, as exotic entertainment for mass American audiences. These scenarios often confirmed for white Americans that Hawaiians were sensual but indolent beings, subordinates who could not be trusted to govern themselves. Live performances produced highly voyeuristic and erotic pleasures for acquisitive and inquisitive Americans learning about their new imperial possession. They helped to establish an imagined intimacy between Americans and the territory—a hospitable place within arm's reach, animated by the bodies of seemingly amiable Hawaiians.

In contrast to their American counterparts, white annexationist settlers in the islands saw in these performances not docile Hawaiians, but recalcitrant Natives who disturbed their economic pathways, who would rather dance and sing for a few dollars than accept their roles as laborers or lower-tier managers in a plantation system. Hawaiians threatened capitalist investment by exhibiting the islands as a primitive, undeveloped outpost. At the expositions in Buffalo and Omaha, the Hawaiian villages eclipsed the official promotional exhibits sponsored by the territory. The haole elite in the islands were threatened not merely by the collective representation of Hawai'i as a morally backward colony, but by the realization they would have to develop a codependent relationship with Hawaiian subjects. Hawaiians were becoming formidable rivals in the marketing of the islands and could not simply be cordoned off.

At the same time, performances of hula and music were more than a cultural form of wage labor, allowing Hawaiians to express and enact individual and communal desires that defied annexationists. Many performers were deeply motivated to subvert the haole oligarchy, and as a result, their performances were often explicitly anticolonial in intent and effect. However, these diasporic performances are not only strictly reducible to the oppositional. As with Kini Kapahu and the poʻe hula who pursued modern fashions and Victorian respectability on the road, the layered desires, erotic play, and spiritual and community formations that underwrote and animated these public performances were alternative, counter-colonial contestations. These social and political actors also fulfilled personal ambitions for love, status, and modernity, tugged by discrepant desires on the margins of statist colonial politics.

Oli, hula, and mele were not merely "harmless catharsis" that protected the status quo, but in themselves constituted acts of resistance and rebellion.[64] Hawaiians composed and played mele that affirmed their cultural grounding in the islands and their collective aloha for their home and each other. George Lipsitz has described popular music as "an arena where memories of the past serve to critique and change the present."[65] Paralleling genealogies of performance in the circum-Atlantic world analyzed by Joseph Roach, Hawaiian performances at expositions publicly enacted counter-memories to settler impositions on Hawaiian space, time, land, bodies, and governance.[66] As collective memories enacted by bodies bearing the consequences of history, hula, chants, and mele provided alternative narratives and epistemologies to those offered by the ruling haole and Americans.[67] Performers relived Hawaiian cosmogony, genealogy, and glorified aliʻi and commoner achievements. The islands, while valued by planters and financiers for their commodified output, were revealed as much more in songs and chants: they were generative sites for political legacies, kinship, and aloha. The performances contained what Saidiya Hartman has called "utopian and transformative impulses that [were] unrealizable within the terms of the current order."[68]

Counter-colonial politics and kaona were embedded in the commodified songs, entertainment, hula, and musical performances at the fairs, even if American audiences were unable to fully grasp their meanings. A chant had two meanings: a literal meaning and the kaona, or inner meaning. Mary Kawena Pukui describes this inner meaning as "sometimes so veiled that only the people to whom the chant belonged understood it, and sometimes so obvious that anyone who knew the figurative speech of old Hawaii could see it very plainly."[69] Kaona is a poetic strategy of intimacy, concealment, and disclosure that relies on allusion and metaphor to communicate with select, privileged audiences.[70] The kaona, Pukui explains, told the "straight, consecutive story, although dressed in a garb of colors that did not seem to match. Persons were sometimes referred to as rain, winds, ferns, trees, birds, ships, and so on."[71] It suggests a kind of intimacy much different from the imagined intimacy produced through colonial regimes; it is an intimacy that demarcates an enclosed personal space or relationship (e.g., between lovers) rather than the imagined community of an imperial audience.

Kaona was a productive political tactic for Hawaiian tourist performers at the beginning of the century. They placed culturally encoded performances on full view for audiences while performing political critiques for privileged audiences. The purposeful choice of their repertoire, for instance, is kind of kaona or message. Poʻe hula and musicians deliberately performed chants and compositions written by or for aliʻi of the Kalākaua line, those who had been deposed through military force and annexation. The Hawaiian musicians performed songs that soon became popular with American audiences, such as "Aloha ʻOe," "Kuʻu Pua i Paoakalani," and "Lei Poni Moi." These mele were indelibly associated with the deposed queen Liliʻuokalani, who had composed them, while they activated ties between the performers and their sovereigns.[72] The lyrics to the love song "Lei Poni Moi" (Carnation Lei), for instance, were written by Lili'uokalani, but set to music by Coelho.[73] The village performers also honored their ali'i Kalākaua by choosing to perform his love songs "Akahi Hoi" and "Sweet Lei Lehua."[74]

The kaona of the mele "Ku'u Pua i Paoakalani," in particular, affirmed the group's affiliation and support for their deposed queen. "Ku'u Pua i Paoakalani" kept the ongoing political struggle of the kingdom alive, as the queen had composed this mele while imprisoned by the Republic of Hawai'i for eight months in 1895. It also may have honored the village's manager, Johnny Wilson. During the queen's eight-month imprisonment, she was allowed the company of one lady-in-waiting, Mrs. Kitty Wilson, and was restricted from receiving any outside literature.[75] According to one popular account, Kitty's son Johnny smuggled contraband newspapers to the queen by wrapping them around flowers from her garden.[76] To honor Johnny for his loyalty during her ordeal, the queen later composed this mele. Even if this narrative is apocryphal and Johnny was not the heroic smuggler, the queen indeed received "bits of news" disguised as wrapping paper during her confinement.[77]

This tactic of smuggling contraband under the unsuspecting noses of the annexationists also describes the subterranean political activities of Hawaiians at world's fairs. Johnny Wilson sold copies of sheet music for these compositions at the Hawaiian villages, along with photographs of Queen Lili'uokalani, suggesting that he intended to publicize the political upheaval in the islands. As manager of the Bana Lahui from 1895–96, Johnny sold similar sheet music during the band's U.S. tours. Versions of this sheet music featured a large photograph of Queen Lili'uokalani on her throne or in regalia, and proclaimed that the songs were written by "Her Majesty during her imprisonment by the Republican Gov't of Hawaii."

In the guise of soothing entertainment, Hawaiian cultural performances could take on a charged political valence. The songs used a Western melodic scale and tempos pleasing to American ears, but hewed to the structures, conventions, and themes of Hawaiian poetry. The nonrhyming poetry drew upon the imagery of natural locales, flowers, and lei to narrativize love affairs, the accomplishments of esteemed figures, and recent national events.[78] Hybridized forms of Hawaiian popular music after the overthrow were critical to public and hidden transcripts of resistance to U.S. colonization. Arguing that popular music can facilitate political critique in oblique forms, George Lipsitz writes, "Hegemony is not just imposed on society from the top; it is struggled for from below, and no terrain is a more important part of that struggle than popular culture."[79]

Many of the songs performed on the midway were mele hoʻoipoipo (love songs) that American audiences would not have been able to understand but were amply legible to those that performed them. Celebrating the erotic capacity and survival of Hawaiians, these mele registered that Hawaiians had not been fully disciplined by Christian moral proscriptions. Nor had they accepted the missionaries' austere mandate that sex was for procreation, not gratification. "Ahi Wela" (Hot Fire), a popular Hawaiian love song at American fairs, leaves little to the imagination in describing a couple's satisfying activities:

Ahi wela mai nei loko [Like a hot fire inside]
I ka hana a ke aloha [The action of love]
E lalawe nei kuʻu kino [Going through my entire body]
Konikoni lua i ka pō nei [Throbbing last night][80]

Performed frequently in Omaha and Buffalo, the mele is still sung and recorded today.

In addition to performing arts, Hawaiians represented the best of their cultural worlds to Americans and did so with care and pride, even as they were being paid to do so. They added their cooking and eating practices to the paid repertoire of live cultural performances, blurring the distinction between quotidian activities and performance. Their backstage lives and on-stage performances were equally on display. Delighted guests partook of the lūʻau, celebratory pig roasting and feasting, a first at U.S. expositions. Assistant manager George Monewa Townsend, Johnny's uncle, carefully introduced the process of dressing and baking the meat and pounding taro root into poi (a Hawaiian staple). Here in the Omaha village, the guests "had to sit on the ground in the native fashion and use their fingers instead of knives and forks."[81] They could watch "a sight seldom to be seen": how Hawaiians inserted hot rocks into pigs and baked them in an imu (underground oven with hot rocks).[82]

Yet these tourist luaus were not just for foreign consumption and spectacle; the delicacies of poi, sweet potatoes, and limu (seaweed) brought Hawaiians great pleasure far from home. While serving as exotic props in a tourist commodity, these staples were fully appreciated by Hawaiians. Their weekly lūʻau was an important way for the group to maintain familiar island routines and live together comfortably. In Omaha they kept a large reserve of poi in a cooler for their own consumption, some of which Johnny delivered to Queen Liliʻuokalani herself in Washington, D.C. The queen had been living in the capital while petitioning Congress to compensate Hawaiians for crown lands seized by the Republic of Hawaiʻi. It became apparent that these fair rituals could assert the memory of the kingdom and venerate their sovereign, for the Hawaiian musicians and dancers planned a lūʻau in honor of Queen Liliʻuokalani's birthday on 2 September 1899. Prince David Kawānanakoa, the queen's cousin and Johnny's childhood friend, shipped two boxes of frozen poi, fish, and seaweed weighing 1,200 pounds from Honolulu.[83] The poʻe hula were to travel from Omaha to furnish music and dancing for the celebration. Ethnographic work mingled with their backstage lives and political practices. The lūʻau was simultaneously a form of commodified labor, a political message, and a communal festivity, but this would shift in the twentieth century (see chapter 5).

Intimate Relations

Hawaiʻi, through its people, food, clothing, trees, music, and dance, was rendered legible and consumable in a single, discrete site. Performing scripts of aloha—love, affinity, and sharing—Hawaiian performers brokered the developing colonial relationship between the United States and Hawaiʻi. These scripts produced an imagined intimacy between Hawaiian hosts and American guests, transforming colonization into relations of hospitality and mutuality. After partaking of Hawaiian hospitality, "one will have very little trouble to imagine himself thousands of miles away on the Sandwich Islands," an Omaha newspaper asserted.[84] Fairgoers came away with what they considered an authentic and enriching experience of the charming colony.

As a point of contrast, Americans at fin de siècle fairs came away feeling superior to and fearful of loathsome Filipinos, their other colonial acquisitions. The Philippine village concessions at the St. Louis Exposition in 1904, the Lewis and Clark Exposition in 1905, and Alaska-Yukon-Pacific Exposition in 1909 became some of the most popular fair attractions. The Igorot, in particular, were described as members of "barbaric tribes" and primitive dog-eaters who required America's civilizing influence.[85]

However, hula performances mediated through the bodies of women captured the imagination of American audiences in a different modality. The sweet vocal music of Hawaiian men elicited delight and effusive praise, but hula was the most valuable, attention-grabbing, and easily

exploitable cultural commodity in the Hawaiian villages. Audiences insisted on interpreting Hawaiʻi through the sexualized female bodies of the
dancers. The published photographs of Hawaiians from the Omaha and
Buffalo fairs were nearly all of girls and young women, elaborated with
captions like "Hawaiian Dancing Girls," "Midway Beauties—Dancers,
Hawaiian village," and "Hawaiian Maiden."[86] One midway review made
this pronouncement: "The dancing girls form [the village's] most seductive enticement."[87] Although men performed on stage as ʻōlapa (dancers)
and hoʻopaʻa, they became almost invisible in public discourse about hula.

In an illustrated account of the Buffalo Pan-American Exposition, a
humorous fictional character "Uncle Hank" followed crowds into the
Hawaiian village. There he imitated the "sinuous hip wriggle of the Hula-
Hula dance, vociferously whistling the seductive music as an accompaniment."[88] The cartoon of the "hula hula dancer" reveals a woman in profile
who thrusts her hips outward. The hybrid Hawaiian music performed
by men, as Uncle Hank said, was merely an "accompaniment." It supplemented but could not supplant the experience.

Hula bodies were sensationalized for Western consumption on the
fairgrounds. With its appearance in a few cities and towns between 1892
and 1896 (see chapter 2), hula performance had just begun to circulate in
the United States. To draw ticket buyers to the show, the "spieler," a man
named "Professor" Maurice Tobin, the self-proclaimed "King of the Midway," ballyhooed outside the Hawaiian villages in Omaha and Buffalo.[89]
Relying on young women's bodies to draw ticket buyers inside, Tobin insisted that the Hawaiian women stand with him outside in scant costuming. In Buffalo, they wore such little clothing that they got sick when
the temperature dipped.[90] Tobin's spiel announced: "Walk right up, ladies
and gentlemen; walk up, and see the genuine Hawaiian beauties from the
sunny southern seas. They don't wear clothes in their native land, and I
call on you all to witness the ease and grace with which they conform to
the customs of civilization. Don't they look nice?"[91]

Photographs of two dancers identified by Kini Kapahu as Mele and
Malie were taken at the Omaha fair and belie Tobin's claim; both women
wore full pāʻū (skirts) and modest long-sleeved cotton tops, the standard
hula costume at this time (see figures 18.1 and 18.2).[92] Tobin also deliberately reported inaccuracies in his ballyhoo that Hawaiians walked about
barefoot and did not know any English. As was the case in Chicago, the
meanings of the dance and chants were nearly rendered irrelevant by the
physicality of the performers' bodies. As sexualized commodities, Ha-

waiian women were expected to share their aloha and give audiences a taste of the islands by baring their bodies. Their putative sexual openness became the public transcript of hula.

Despite the heightened visibility of hula, it remains difficult to identify hula repertoire at the early world's fairs, for Kini Kapahu did not discuss specific hula performances at these fairs in her oral accounts, nor did dancers leave archival traces elsewhere. However, since Kini had selected the po'e hula and produced the shows, it was extremely likely that the men and women performed sacred and semisacred hula repertoires similar to those on the Chicago Midway in 1893. Under Kini's watchful eye, the dancers at Omaha and Buffalo would have had to have been both highly trained in hula, perhaps even 'ōlohe hula (hula experts) who had graduated from a pā hula (hula academy) as she had. They would have been under strict orders to adhere to their training and spiritual protocol. Even later in life, Kini was extremely exacting. When she taught hula in the 1930s, she lashed out at her students with her cane if they did not perform correctly.[93] She also disliked seeing the hula reduced to "hip swinging" in commercial tourist contexts. In the 1950s, Kini had become a trusted hula authority who condemned tourist officials in Hawai'i for exploiting the sexuality of hula dancers and misusing sacred royal symbols during Aloha Week festivities. She found the tourist hula to be based too much on bodily movements; with its "shake shake shake," the hula was "too much show" for her.[94]

To reconstruct early twentieth-century fair performances, we are left to rely on incomplete descriptions written by Americans who had never seen hula previously. At Buffalo and likely in Omaha, the group reportedly performed hula 'āla'apapa, hula 'ōlapa, and hula pahu, genres that venerated akua (gods) and ali'i and could not be altered for tourist consumption.[95] A photograph published of the "olupa dancers" (meaning 'ōlapa) in a souvenir book from the Buffalo midway shows a group of young women standing outside the Hawaiian village, along with an older male ho'opa'a who holds an ipu heke (double gourd).[96] Although misspelled, the name of this group—"the 'ōlapa dancers"—suggests the inclusion of the genre of hula 'ōlapa that honored particular ali'i (see figure 26). A description of men playing ipu (gourd instruments) on the Buffalo midway offers additional corroboration for the inclusion of hula 'ōlapa and possibly hula 'āla'apapa: "The hula hula is the genuine expression of real feeling, accompanied by no tuneful harp or glib piano or resinous violin, but filtered through all the monotonous fall of the soft, bare feet of the brown women

Fig. 26 "The Olupa Dancers from the Royal Hula Hula House of Queen Liliuokalani, Hawaiian Village," printed in *Snap Shots on the Midway of the Pan-Am Expo*, 1901.

on pine boards is the crescendic thump of two silent male crouchers, who pound with rhythmic regularity on hollow gourds."[97]

Hawaiians also performed oli within the Hawaiian theater and its affiliated concession, the Kilauea Volcano Cyclorama. The cyclorama was a lifelike replica of the famous Hawaiian landmark on the island of Hawai'i, complete with Hawaiian kahuna (priests) who appeased Pele, the volcano goddess. While showman E. W. McConnell owned the cyclorama in Buffalo, it is not insignificant that the attraction was originally commissioned and built by the missionary son and annexationist Lorrin A. Thurston. Forming the Cyclorama Company with other kama'aina haole investors, Thurston brought the concession to the Chicago World's Columbian Exposition in 1893, around the same time he was lobbying the U.S. government for the annexation of Hawai'i.[98] He and his contemporaries reaped profits from the spectacularization of Hawaiian religious practices while denigrating them in public life.

In Hawaiian religion, Kīlauea is the natural form of the volcano goddess Pele. Worshipped in particular by women, Pele was both feared and celebrated for her sexual passion, distemper, and vengeful nature.[99] Pele destroyed her sister's best friend and turned her own lover into stone before settling in the firepit of Kīlauea. Hawaiians revered Pele for her ability to create and destroy at will, but she was domesticated for Euro-

American consumption at American expositions. Painted white and dressed in flowing robes by an American artist named Ellen Rankin Copp, the recalcitrant Pele was transformed into a twenty-five-feet-high Greek goddess.[100] She became a benign white woman holding an Olympian flame, the central character in "a romantic Hawaiian legend," as one exposition guidebook explained.[101]

Walking beneath this statue of Pele into the volcano, curious ticket-holders consumed an acutely gendered experience of Hawai'i. They strolled deeper into the metaphoric interior of a woman, following a passage simulating lava tubes to the center of the crater, where paintings, electrical lights, and mechanical effects created fire and a series of lava eruptions. They ended in a circle, with a full 360-degree view of the erupting crater. Gazing upward, one saw "bubbling and seething pools and lakes of fire; tall, jagged crags; toppling masses of rocks; outpourings of lava."[102] Yet the aural and visual effects simulated drama, never real heat or danger. The feminized islands, with their unruly eruptions and tendency toward natural disorder, were aestheticized and symbolically disciplined.

Hawaiian troubadours performed music and oli outside the Volcano Cyclorama. The oli were represented as calculated, exotic ballyhoos in American news reports. In Chicago a newspaper described the kahuna's chant as "a sort of advertising solicitor's talk to the start of Hawaiian mythology. It sounded somewhat like a 'sol-fa exercise' delivered by a man in great pain."[103] At the Pan-American Exposition, the *Buffalo Courier* provided an account of oli by an elderly kahuna who had come to Buffalo to perform on the midway stage. The article printed the kahuna's chants for the goddess Hi'iaka-i-ka-Poli-o-Pele, a significant figure in Hawaiian religion and hula, and the younger sister of the volcano goddess Pele. As quoted, the chants begins with, "Tuu hoa i ta ino, Tuu hoa i ta malie, Tuu hoa i na tai ewalu" (My friend in the storm; my friend in the calm; my friend in the eight oceans). It may well be an oli for Hi'iaka, but this chant was also part of standard mourning chants for ali'i.[104]

What can we make of the presence of such oli within midway tableaux that otherwise promoted and celebrated the capitalist conversion and settlement of Hawaiian bodies, land, and akua? Oli is an essential element of Hawaiian religious and cultural protocol. American accounts of kahuna chants like these, although likely exaggerated, indicate that pre-European forms of Hawaiian religious practices had been woven into midway performances in plain view. Poetry and chant are not empty words or merely symbolic; they contain the power to heal and even provoke death.[105] Pukui explains, "The kaona of a chant was believed to be potent enough to bring lovers together, to mend broken homes or to break up an undesirable union."[106] Viewed this way, the chants were forces opposing the symbolic and material control of haole elites. They threatened to disrupt the teleology and logic of colonialism, development, and tourism in Hawai'i that the cyclorama represented.

Lorrin A. Thurston and his investors intended not only to lure tourists inside the cyclorama, but for the attraction to promote the soon-to-be annexed islands on a national scale and bring tourists to Hawai'i. For most non-Hawaiian spectators, the chants' meaning was incomprehensible entertainment. Yet chants and dances that expressed reverence for Hawaiian 'āina and akua were Hawaiian political narratives that challenged the ideology of Hawai'i as virgin land waiting to be developed by colonial capitalism. Oli and hula about Pele and her sister Hi'iaka animate much of Hawaiian hula and mythology; in them, men are made cognizant of their feeble status in the face of engulfing lava flows and the mercurial temper of Pele. Frequently untamed, the land and Hawaiian women wielded awesome power and demanded supplication. Emerging from a commodified entertainment structure, these performances sustained a Hawaiian intimacy with land and spiritual patrons that could not be easily overwritten by settler colonialism.[107]

Disciplining Hawaiians

In Indian Country at the turn of the century, bicultural, assimilated Indians who chose to reject the reservation were referred to as "Blanket Indians." Although educated in Western schools and converted to Christianity, they chose to go back to wearing "the blanket."[108] Philip J. Deloria contends that these supposedly pacified Indians could be the most dangerous Natives of all; they threatened the reservation system by throwing away the "gifts" of civilization for savage Indian life. In Western eyes, they were potentially monstrous subjects who demonstrated how knowledge in the hands of a Native could be dangerous. Johnny Wilson and his troupe resembled these Blanket Indians in spirit; they had been given the privileges of haole education, social training, and access, but chose to "go Native."

Johnny Wilson, who was light-skinned enough to pass as white, had enjoyed elite status in Honolulu society, but refused a leadership role within the Republic of Hawai'i and the annexed territory. Straddling colonial capitalism and anticolonial self-representation, astute entrepreneurs placed precontact, "primitive" Hawai'i in full view before their overseers in the territory and the continental empire. To the chagrin of the haole elite, these performances asserted a counter-memory of Hawaiian life and political desires deeply at odds with the colonial Republic of Hawai'i.

Hawaiian performances provoked anxiety among influential haole in the territory. Scandalized by exhibits of hula at the fair, they tried to discredit the practice. Hula was not accepted in polite society in the islands; it was considered a potent sign of Hawaiian degeneracy. The Reverend Sereno Bishop, an American missionary in Hawai'i and frequent contributor to U.S. journals about Hawai'i, protested the exhibition of dances.[109] "Since Chicago and Omaha tens of thousands of people regard Hawaii as a place where semi-barbarians hold high revel and the limit of indecency is easily reached. The impression has no right to exist but it has been carefully inculcated with results which are detrimental, even in a business sense, to the welfare of these islands. We hope that, in the future, Government aid will be withheld from any Hawaiian exhibit abroad which at all savors, in the living, human sense, of aboriginal savagery."[110] Like his Calvinist predecessors, Reverend Bishop censured the hula, correctly recognizing that hula provided religious sustenance for Hawaiian people, even those who had converted to Christianity. Hula connected them to their ali'i, genealogies, and akua. Hula practitioners escaped missionary surveillance by performing on the continent, and many Americans indeed appreciated the hula rather than denigrated it, whether because of its perceived sexual expression or authentic pathway to Hawaiianness. While Bishop was mistaken—no government monies had been used to support the Hawaiian villages—other concerned parties in the business and missionary communities swiftly chimed in to assail the Hawaiian village and institute a ban from afar.

The *Buffalo Courier* reported shortly after the opening of the Buffalo fair that the *Pacific Commercial Advertiser* of Honolulu objected to live Hawaiian performances at the exposition. The latter newspaper had argued that the exhibit would harm the islands by presenting the "barbarian side of former Hawaiian life at $20 per week and try[ing] to create the impression that the residents of the islands are uncivilized and that Hawaii is an abode of heathenism." Settler-colonial business interests were anxious to tame indigenous people and their cultural practices, in order to prove Hawai'i was a place of "modern progress."[111]

This argument was reinforced more forcefully that same month by a scathing cartoon printed in the PCA, "Hawaii at Exposition, Our Civiliza-

Fig. 27 "Hawaii at Exposition," *Pacific Commercial Advertiser*, 14 May 1901.

tion on Parade" (see figure 27).[112] A barker hawks tickets for a Hawaiian village, pointing to a female hula dancer who is dressed in a lāʻī skirt but with her upper torso covered only by leis. A sign in front of the grass hut reads, "A continuous performance of the hula dancers on the inside: exhibition of Poi eating . . . and okolehao [moonshine] drinking." A few musicians—men wearing skirts and holding ʻukulele—sing behind the woman. Another sign behind the barker reads: "A member of the first legislature of Hawaii soon to arrive. Will be on exhibition. Don't fail to see it." This was likely a pointed swipe at William Huelani Coelho, one of the performers who also served as leader of the territory's Republican Party. The cartoon took aim at Hawaiians for revealing themselves as half-naked primitives and uncouth hula dancers. In the opinion of haole businessmen, Hawaiians' "playing Hawaiian" reflected poorly on the new territory, whose leaders were trying to secure equal footing within the nation and demonstrate how the colonial regime had effectively pacified and reformed its subjects.

The haole oligarchy feared Hawaiians outside their circle who spoke for the territory on national and world stages. To contain the threat, the oligarchy's strategic response was immediate. It began to reassert control over the image of Hawai'i by sending a compensatory educational exhibit to Buffalo and by planning a larger exhibit for the next major American exposition after Buffalo, the Louisiana Purchase Exposition in St. Louis, Missouri, in 1904. Alarmed by the popularity of the Hawaiian performances at the Buffalo fair, the territorial legislature of Hawai'i hastily authorized $3,500 for an educational exhibit. The *Pacific Commercial Advertiser* wrote: "Many fine pieces of [school] work will be exhibited which will surprise the American population which yet believes that Hawaii is a land of cannibals."[113]

A Hawaiian woman named Miss Rosalie "Rose" Compton Kahipuleokalaniahumanu Davison, who was assistant secretary of the territorial board of education, was chosen to assemble the exhibit and go to Buffalo as commissioner of the Hawai'i exhibit (see figure 28). All the larger Christian schools in the islands contributed the products of Hawaiian students, such as school assignments written in English, industrial products, and sewing.[114] Like the displays by the chamber of commerce at the Omaha fair, this work demonstrated that Hawaiians had progressed under an American educational system.[115] It suggested that Hawaiians were capable of acquiring the English language and could be trained as industrial workers.

Rose Davison traveled from Hawai'i to Buffalo, accompanied by at least two other Hawaiian women—a "half-native" schoolteacher Mapuana (inaccurately reported as Mapuena) Smith, who was also the daughter of the clerk of the territorial supreme court, and "a full-blooded native maid" identified as Miss Ordway.[116] Led by an impeccably educated, mixed-race Hawaiian woman, the retinue became an exhibit of Kanaka civility, as important as the sewing, lacework, and mathematics samples. The women were living displays whose dignified comportment was meant to offset hula dancers and chanting savages on the midway. These teachers, giving interviews to the American press, were to show Americans that not all Hawaiian women were practitioners of the hip-swinging hula.

A year after the Buffalo exposition in 1901, territorial officials and businessmen were still trying to recivilize the islands by organizing another exhibit. The commissioner general for the St. Louis Louisiana Purchase Exposition, a man named John Barrett, traveled to Hawai'i in 1902 to meet with territorial officials and businessmen. Barrett encouraged haole leaders to contribute an exhibition that would appropriately show off the islands' industries. An "industrial, economic, agricultural, educational,

Fig. 28 Rose Compton Kahipuleokalaniahumanu Davison.
COURTESY OF HAWAI'I STATE ARCHIVES.

geographical, ethnological and governmental exhibit" would instruct the people of the United States about the islands under American supervision. A display of America's possessions acquired in 1898 suited a fair commemorating the hundredth anniversary of the Louisiana Purchase in 1803. The Louisiana Purchase, which had removed to the west all Indians east of the Mississippi, had expanded U.S. borders and was an example of early U.S. empire building.[117]

Addressing the meeting, Barrett told haole leaders that St. Louis was their opportunity to repair the reputation of Hawai'i and stem the export of hula: "So many people in the United States know nothing of Hawaii, for instance, except what they have seen at Buffalo. There the feature which was impressed upon their mind was that the people sang and danced."[118] The St. Louis fair would enable Hawai'i "under the new regime of annexa-

Fig. 29 "What We Don't Want at St. Louis," *Pacific Commercial Advertiser*, 2 May 1902.

tion to show herself to the rest of the United States in her true light." If Hawai'i failed to contribute an official exhibit, it would risk being represented by unofficial midway concessions, such as the "hula hula," Barrett warned: "We [the Louisiana Purchase Exposition managers] want Hawaii to be seen, studied and admired at St. Louis in her legitimate exhibits, rather than made an agent for the theatrical amusement in the form of hula hula dances . . . Provided the business interests and the government of Hawaii will participate on a scale which will be creditable alike to the Islands and to the Exposition, the officials and citizens of this Territory can rest assured that Hawaii will not be disgraced by unwholesome Midway attractions."[119]

Barrett had accurately assessed the kama'āina haole's angst about hula. Next to the front-page article about Barrett's exhortations, the PCA featured a large cartoon, "What We Don't Want at St. Louis."[120] In it, white men lined up in front of a Hawaiian village to see "spicy—rich—sensational, the dancing girls in the famous Hawaiian hulas" (see figure 29). One "dancing girl" was shown topless on a large sign outside the village. The spieler cried, "Don't Go to Hawaii, Come here and see it all," while hawking ten-cent tickets for the hula show.

To counter previous mass displays of hula, the Honolulu Chamber of Commerce planned to install an exhibit that highlighted the evolution of the Hawaiian population under U.S. rule by tracing the "internal, moral and intellectual progress" of Hawaiians from their "primitive" beginnings. The educational department even considered bringing a class of children to St. Louis to "sing native songs" and demonstrate how the American school system produced fine pupils.[121] In many ways, these exhibits were intended to fulfill the mission of the educational exhibit started by Rose Davison in Buffalo. Despite their grand plans, the chamber of commerce and the territorial government received only a $30,000 appropriation from the legislature. In the end, the territory was only able to install a modest agricultural exhibit of tropical fruits and insects that was probably placed in the U.S. government building with exhibits of the rest of its overseas colonies.[122] Administrators and business leaders nevertheless saw the exhibit as a compensatory antidote to the damage wrought by hula. The *Los Angeles Times* reported, "Vigorous objections have been made to hula hula dancing and other similar displays. Preparations, have, therefore, been made for showing, in an attractive manner, the resources of the Hawaiian Islands [at the St. Louis exposition]."[123] At the same time, however, Hawaiian brokers were flexing their muscles, learning that their skills as cultural translators were becoming more valuable as ties deepened between the territory and the United States. They understood that cultural translation and representation were commodities as valuable as sugar and pineapple, and that their skills would be in demand.

Hawaiian Interventions

The future of the Hawaiian territory was fought over by competing constituencies at fin de siècle expositions. As Raymond Williams writes, a lived hegemony has "continually to be renewed, recreated, defended, and modified. It is also continually resisted, limited, altered, challenged by pressure not at all its own."[124] Despite the oligarchy's subjugation of the territory, it could not fully control the symbolic and discursive terrain of Hawaiian cultural productions. Hawaiians exerted their own alternative and, at times, counterhegemonic visions of their nation on the midway.

Hawaiian performers and activists contributed to what Michael Denning has described as a "cultural front"—the participation, reorganization, and mobilization of social actors into cultural institutions and long-term historic projects.[125] While the origins of Hawaiian opposition to the West through national institutions and practices may be traced to King Kalākaua's cultural renaissance a few decades earlier, these post-overthrow activists converged in a "structure of feeling," an inchoate site of ideological contestation.[126] They developed new cultural and political forms and transformed existing ones. Popular music, chant, storytelling, and sermons were part of their creative, transnational merging of labor, politics, and business.

As they performed, Hawaiians intervened in the objectification of their bodies and cultural practices, projecting alternate visions of their history, land, and future. They were not static objects receiving instruction on becoming industrial workers, charming performers, and infantilized colonial subjects. While on display, Hawaiians were determined to get the most they could out of the fair, absorbing knowledge about American institutions and refining their public platforms. Temporarily escaping colonial authority and supervision in Hawai'i, they pursued economic self-sufficiency and personal edification on the continent.

Philip J. Deloria describes American Indians performing on contemporaneous commodified circuits as "imagemakers" who "recognized that political and legal struggles are tightly linked to ideologies and images."[127] John W. Troutman has also examined professional Native musicians who performed "Indianness" on tour. Gaining new audiences, fame, and financial success through entertainment, they intervened in federal Indian policy and resisted assimilation, he argues.[128] Like their Indian counterparts, Hawaiian performers were pursuing similar agendas and intervening in the representation of Hawaiianness. Johnny Wilson and his fellow villagers served as cultural translators for white audiences while deploying sub rosa a range of personal and political agendas. Soon after their arrival in Omaha, Johnny discreetly dispatched his uncle George Monewa Townsend to purchase a schooner in Seattle.[129] They were planning a new shipping venture that would help Hawaiian farmers develop markets for their products. Johnny did not rely on the territorial legislature or the Honolulu Chamber of Commerce to conduct business on the continent: he circumvented the plantation class and created novel axes of power. He and his troupe worked directly with white American showmen, politicians, midway managers, and businessmen on the continent.

Although Johnny was technically hired by the American showman E. W. McConnell to manage the Hawaiian concessions, he did not think of himself as a subordinate. Instead, he referred to McConnell as "an old business partner of mine."[130] Johnny also summarized his position at these fairs as that of an "original advertising advance agent" for the islands, and he treated the show as one of several businesses that allowed him to work outside the plantation system.[131] Johnny operated essentially as an independent agent and cultural broker, making connections that he continued to tap even after he became a politician in Hawai'i. These same skills he acquired as a showman helped him succeed in territorial and federal politics.

During his stint at the Buffalo Exposition in 1901, Johnny became friends with a Democratic Party leader named Norman E. Mack.[132] Mack was the Democratic National Committeeman from New York and editor of the *Buffalo Times*. Over a decade later, Johnny was elected Hawai'i's representative to the Democratic National Committee and attended his first national convention in Baltimore in 1912. Mack remembered his old friend Johnny and introduced the novice politician to other party big-wigs; these introductions helped Johnny establish a reputation and authority within the national party. These networks outside the territory helped him shift political power away from the haole oligarchy toward labor, multiethnic, and working-class constituencies. Relying on alliances forged during his showman years, Johnny traveled nearly every year for thirty years to Washington in order to lobby U.S. senators, secretaries, and presidents on Hawai'i-related policies and appointments, which were critical to the eventual unhinging of the Republican Party in Hawai'i.

Like Johnny, William Joseph Huelani Coelho was an aspiring politician who opposed U.S. annexation, but he chose to work through the Republican Party. In his capacity as secretary of the territorial Republican Party, Coelho had corresponded frequently with prominent Republicans such as Senator Mark Hanna and President William McKinley prior to the exposition. Hanna was a wealthy industrialist from Ohio who had recently won a Senate seat. He had also served as McKinley's presidential campaign manager. On the occasion of Hanna's visit to the Buffalo fair, the Hawaiian village staged a special performance. After Hanna inquired about Coelho, the two men were introduced and "shook hands like brothers." Hanna was considerably impressed with this learned "Hawaiian Republican leader" after they conversed at length about political conditions in the islands.[133] Hawaiian performers, despite their sideshow reputation on the midway, demonstrated that they deserved courtesy from national leaders.

While we do not know whether this discussion yielded a lasting alliance, the brief in-person encounter undoubtedly enhanced Coelho's political stature. This meeting was deeply symbolic of the autonomous relationships Hawaiians cultivated with political leaders on the continent, prompting haole Republicans at home to fire away at the upstart Coelho. Even though they ostensibly belonged the same party, kamaʻāina haole did not appreciate Hawaiians' having direct access to the federal government. After annexation, haole leaders strategized to gain favorable trade and immigration policies in Washington for their plantations and businesses. To discredit Coelho, the *Pacific Commercial Advertiser* published a belittling caricature of the meeting between Coelho and Senator Hanna at the Hawaiian village called "Coelho's Interview, Self-Reported" (see figure 30).[134] Here Coelho is grossly exaggerated as a hula dancer. Holding an ʻukulele, he wears only a lāʻī skirt and flower lei and towers over Hanna. He reaches down to shake Hanna's hand, saying, "Yes, Mr. Hanna, I am that Brilliant Hawaiian leader." The cartoon mocked Coelho's outsized pretensions, intimating that he was a debased hula dancer who only imagined himself equal to an eminent American senator. Nevertheless, Coelho received some praise from newspapers in Buffalo for being a visiting dignitary and "man of affairs in Hawaii."[135]

Hawaiian brokers brilliantly displayed a bicultural dexterity that enabled them to forge coalitions and gain the admiration of American publics. Fluent in Hawaiian and the grammar of colonial politics, Johnny and Coelho seemed equally comfortable "playing Hawaiian" for tourists and negotiating with national politicians.[136] They understood that transnational politics shared a performative and communicative character with tourist tableaux like roasting pigs and dancing. Both required persuasion and deft alliances with multiple constituencies. They treated meetings with tourists and senators as performative stagings that influenced public discourse. Proving themselves as skillful as, if not better than, white men in business, politics, and public relations, these cultural brokers negotiated their images in U.S. newspapers. Coelho tried to sway public opinion to the advantage of Hawaiians by providing human-interest stories that would showcase their civility.

"Here among Strangers"

Putting his oratorical and poetic talents to work, William Huelani Coelho artfully merged Christian metaphors with political critique in a series of weekly, standing-room-only sermons on the midway that were reported in Buffalo papers. Wearing their Sunday best, starched dresses and suits, the

Fig. 30 "Coelho's Interview, Self-Reported," *Pacific Commercial Advertiser*, 10 June 1901.

villagers transformed the exterior of the Hawaiian village into a theatrical church, where they sang English and Hawaiian-language hymns, read biblical passages aloud, and listened to Coelho preach. Like the hymns they performed, the service blended Christian idioms with Hawaiian expressive practices. The novelty of putatively barbaric Hawaiians' worshipping as Christians on the midway attracted inquisitive fairgoers who lined up to see the unusual service. But Hawaiians seized this opportunity to argue for commensurate status with white Americans. These church performances were "charismatic act[s]" of dissent that ruptured the public transcript of domination. Charisma is not merely a physical quality or possession, but "a relationship in which engaged observers recognize (and may, in fact, help inspire) a quality they admire," as James C. Scott writes.[137]

One Sunday, Coelho delivered a charismatic sermon in Hawaiian called "The Actor and His Creator," in which he argued for an inclusive vision of Christianity that encompassed all who worshipped faithfully. He reminded the Hawaiian entertainers that the word of God was for everyone, even for those he had "destined to the life of a player." One did not need a church to worship God, because "he was as ready to hear their petitions from the door of a Midway theater as from the finest cathedral."[138] Performers were worthy of God's love. This sermon served as a subtle chastisement to those who demeaned Hawaiians on the basis of their race, colonized status, or cultural practices. It was an inspired appropriation of Christian rhetoric to assert Hawaiian equality, "using the cultural raw materials of the white man's religion" to undermine power.[139] The women dancers performed their civility by dressing in immaculate white dresses and offering individual testimonials of faith, such as, "I trust that I am on the road to heaven."[140]

The Hawaiian performers realized that they had the weighty responsibility to serve as envoys for their nation. Intervening in the oligarchy's representation of Hawaiian land and people as exploitable and expendable commodities, they sought to educate American observers about their own desires for political independence and equality. Recognizing the critical task at hand, Coelho urged his fellow Hawaiians to behave respectfully in the United States so that they might elevate their nation in distress. He spoke until tears ran down his face:

> We are here among strangers, yet by the law as man makes them they and we are of the one great country. Let us remember this. Be dignified, hear yourselves with pride and courtesy. Be thoughtful to make a good impression, so that the millions of new faces that greet yours will recognize you as true men and women. Remember the honor of our home, of dear Hawaii. Guard it and advance its glory. So act that all the Americans who see us shall say that they are glad to know us as true men and women. Above all, by no act of word bring shame or the unfortunate kind of notoriety on us. Do right and all will be right with us and Hawaii will be advanced as she deserves to be in the appreciation of the world.[141]

The Hawaiian congregation wept in response, and these services appeared to convince observers that Hawaiians were exemplary Christians. Impressed by their "evident sincerity and devotion," the *Buffalo Courier* declared, "The Hawaiians are a Godly race."[142] Even the notorious hula dancer, whose moral character came under constant scrutiny, scored a victory in the court of public opinion when the paper judged that her profession did not "detract from the sincerity of her Christian professions."[143] The hula was declared "an innocent expression of native grace to the Hawaiians."

Coelho—with his supporting cast of pious worshippers—successfully proposed and enacted an alternative modernity for Hawaiians: they were genteel and enlightened while continuing to hew to Native spiritual and cultural values. Asserting that they were more than savage attractions, they reframed themselves as complex political actors and civilized aesthetes. Negotiating between the press, mainland tourists, and midway management, Coelho honed rhetorical skills that later served him well as a legislator.

Like Johnny Wilson, who championed organized labor and the multiethnic poor during his political career, Coelho worked within electoral politics in Hawai'i to assist subordinated Hawaiians. After the exposition, he became active in establishing "home rule," Hawaiian independence from plantation owners that controlled the government. He supported his fellow Republican, Prince Jonah Kūhiō Kalaniana'ole, in Kūhiō's successful bids to become the territorial delegate to U.S. Congress that began in 1902. Kūhiō, although initially supported by the haole oligarchy, advocated policies that enfranchised Hawaiians, including the decentralization of the territorial government and a Hawaiian homesteading act. Coelho encouraged Kūhiō, writing, "Our cup [as Hawaiians] is bitter, but let's fight it to the bitter end."[144]

Coelho himself gained an elected position in the territorial government, representing his home island of Maui as a legislator and senator. He served in the territorial house in 1905 and 1923, and the senate from 1907 to 1909.[145] Though not much is known about his legislative career, one of his lasting legacies was the territory's public university system. As a Maui junior senator, he sponsored two legislative bills that established in 1907 the College of Agriculture and Mechanic Arts of the Territory of Hawaii. This land-grant school would later become the University of Hawai'i. At this time, only Hawai'i and Alaska had no institution of higher learning among all the nation's states and incorporated territories. The wealthy haole oligarchy regularly sent their children to Ivy League universities, while the growing working and middle classes of Hawai'i had nowhere to educate their children.[146] For his efforts to democratize education, Coelho Way in Nu'uanu Valley on the island of O'ahu was named in his honor and still exists today.[147]

Gendered Erasures

Transnational entertainment afforded some Hawaiians an oppositional venue, but it was by no means a utopian space. Besides suffering from homesickness, performers had to contend with extreme temperatures, illness, and serious disease. In Omaha's early fall, the radical shift in temperatures—from 57 to 99 degrees—as well as being overworked, sickened the performers enough to cause shows to be canceled.[148] In the spring, an unexpected late blast of cold weather in Buffalo felled Hawaiians, Mexicans, Indians, and "Esquimos" living on the midway.[149] Housed in a stockyard with no heat, the twenty Inuit performers suffered the most, and one was afflicted with consumption. Quartered in pens fit for cattle, racialized midway performers could be treated as livestock. Hawaiians shook "as though with the ague" and later that week, the Hawaiian women were taken to the hospital at the exposition to be examined. The Hawaiian village suffered an outbreak of mumps, while tuberculosis and measles spread through other midway villages.[150]

The internal and external organization of cultural labor in tourist markets also largely conformed to existing hierarchies of class, race, social status, and gender. As was the case with maka'āinana women abroad on earlier tours, birth and rank did not seem to limit access to U.S. mass-entertainment circuits, as commoners were able to take advantage of this expanding opportunity structure. Yet Native entrepreneurship produced and relied upon highly uneven gendered relationships and erasures. As Hawaiians gained mobility outside the tightly controlled colony, Hawaiian men proved the more privileged and favored subjects, particularly those who were educated and part-white. This preference was conditioned by the gendered and racialized hierarchy of American exposition management. Theatrical agents preferred to work with male Native managers, not Native women. Hawaiians were not a unique case—such was the case with Kwakwa̱ka'wakw, American Indians, Egyptians, and other ethnographic fair entertainers.

At the Omaha fair in 1899 and the Buffalo fair in 1901, the management of the Hawaiian village was starkly divided by gender: Kini Kapahu's job was managing the so-called hula girls, and Johnny Wilson the "singing boys."[151] Kini did not dance hula in Omaha or Buffalo—she seemed to have been an off-stage manager and producer there—but she had a weighty task before her. She had to determine how to adapt the hula for a non-Hawaiian audience who interpreted hula as erotic pantomime, rather than religious and political forms of embodied knowledge. Kini was arguably just as, if not more, experienced than Johnny in American show business, for she had already toured North America and Europe on a theatrical circuit. Yet even her lover Johnny did not appear to treat her as an equal partner; his show diary reveals that he doled out Kini's salary along with the rest of his Hawaiian troupe. Johnny was devoted to Kini, but spoke of men like the showman E. W. McConnell and the musician Mekia Kealakai, not Kini, as part of his show business fraternity.

Furthermore, not only did Kini fail to receive managerial credit for her abilities, she also shouldered the personal blame for exhibiting hula abroad. Many Hawaiian and haole Christians believed that hula was inappropriate for public exhibition, especially performances in the United States, its emerging colonial patron. Kini was publicly excoriated upon her homecomings to Hawai'i in 1896 and 1902. She reported that Hawaiians and haole made fun of her, called her names, and spat on her in the streets. Johnny's mother, Eveline "Kitty" Wilson, fiercely disapproved of Kini because she was a "hula girl," and the couple did not marry until 1908, a decade after Kitty's death.[152] Sensitive to this harsh reception, Kini taught hula to some Hawaiians discreetly but refrained from dancing hula in public until 1922.[153] Instead she retreated from the limelight and began farming and raising pigs and chickens in remote Pelekenu Valley on the island of Moloka'i. She lived largely without Johnny until he was elected mayor of Honolulu in 1920, when she moved to the state capitol to assume a more active role as first lady. Johnny, on the other hand, did not appear to receive any direct personal criticism for profiting from hula.

While Johnny Wilson and William Coelho were able to quite seamlessly move into political prominence after brokering tourist entertainment, Kini Kapahu and other female po'e hula received fewer rewards at greater personal cost. Little is known about the futures of the young girls who danced hula in Omaha and Buffalo, but the 'ōlohe hula who toured North America and Europe with Kini died young and had truncated careers as dancers.[154] We do know the distressing fate of a hula dancer from Kalākaua's court who was a contemporary of Kini's, the oft-photographed and beloved beauty Emalia Kaihumua, who performed hula at one contemporaneous international exposition, the San Francisco Midwinter Exposition in 1894 (see figure 31). Known affectionately as "Sweet Emalia," she was the namesake of the famous love song "Aia i Hilo One" and the composer of the mele "He Aloha Moku o Keawe" during her sojourn to San Francisco.[155] Emalia and other dancers had a much more difficult professional and personal trajectory than male glee club singers and concert

Fig. 31 Emalia Kaihumua, standing in center, ca. 1890. COURTESY OF HAWAI'I STATE ARCHIVES.

band musicians, who generally garnered fame over the next half century. Although we cannot be too quick to conclude that her transnational hula career was the reason for her demise, Sweet Emalia perhaps met the most ignominious end of all; only three years after her return to the islands in 1897, she was institutionalized in a "hale pupule," an insane asylum. Later she appears to have died alone of mental illness.[156]

Emalia's demise may be an extreme example, but none of the young fin de siècle female dancers appear to have had extensive public careers in the islands because of lingering antipathy to hula performance, whether performed for tourists or practiced among Hawaiians privately. Long into the twentieth century, hula was treated as an opprobrious practice unfit for ladies. Kini's contemporaries found themselves guarding their reputations against the disgraceful hula. In 1902, for example, Theresa Owana Kaohelelani Laanui Wilcox, the high-ranking ali'i and wife of Robert Wilcox, the Hawaiian delegate to Congress, defended herself against reports that she had danced hula on a ship returning to the islands. She insisted, "I am not so shortsighted as to forget my position as the wife of the Delegate to Congress from these Islands. I have always borne myself with the dignity which the position imposes upon one."[157]

Female hula bodies were made visible through live performance, postcards, photographs, and other tourist media, but hula did not begin to resurge and receive public approval until the 1920s and 1930s, when the same haole settlers who had vilified hula decided that it would usefully draw tourists to the islands. Seeking to centralize their control over the exhibition and commodification of Hawaiian cultural practices, they effectively cut Hawaiians out of the brokering process. Johnny Wilson and other Hawaiians tried to take more musical and dance troupes to expositions in the U.S. continent and Europe, but the territorial government assumed control over Hawaiian entertainment.[158] Even in the 1930s and 1940s, when hula began moving briskly along transnational circuits again, female hula dancers generally had shorter and far less prolific careers in entertainment than their male counterparts in music and management.

At world's fairs, Hawaiian representatives fell along a rough hierarchy— part-white Native Hawaiian men at the top, followed by Hawaiian men, and Hawaiian women at the bottom. Hawaiian women had to tread lightly while performing in public because they could be treated as vulgar trollops; yet their male counterparts enjoyed accolades as refined esthetes. Hawaiian women proved much more vulnerable as the primary spectacles, yet enjoyed far less latitude to control their bodies and terms of representation. Women had the most to lose, literally and figuratively, by performing hula on midway stages. Hawaiian and American men negotiated their contracts, the terms of their appearances, spoke for them in the press, and at certain key moments seized responsibility for brokering their bodies. Hawaiian women were less able to insert themselves as independent agents within chains of empire, and rarely did they serve as direct brokers of their bodies and desires. They were forced to rely upon male Hawaiian intermediaries and white, male American concessionaires.[159]

In Buffalo Hawaiian women, along with other dancing women on the midway, became caught in a power struggle over the exposure of their bodies. Along with concessions such as the "Beautiful Orient," "Around the World," and "Venice in America," the Hawaiian village utilized women, often meagerly dressed, as ballyhoo attractions. In order to elevate the reputation of the midway, the management of the exposition in Buffalo issued a policy in July 1901 that banned all women from their perches.[160] The "midway men," or male concessionaires like E. W. McConnell and Johnny Wilson, decided to defy the order, arguing, "No exposition can live without a Midway, and no Midway can live without a ballyhoo. We need the women and are going to have them."[161] They then ordered

their women, including those at the Hawaiian village, to be paraded outside and ballyhoo, which prompted exposition guards to remove them
forcefully on a busy Saturday night. It is unclear what the women themselves thought of the action, but they became pawns in a skirmish between different groups of men, rather than being able to control their own
exhibition. The Hawaiian women had complained earlier about being exposed to the bitter weather outside, so they may have preferred to remain
inside the theater. Perhaps others, like the Egyptian women riding on the
camels for their ballyhoo, did not mind. Upper management finally won
the pitched battle; some women were allowed outside, but were screened
from sight.

The Erotics of Diaspora and Other Futures

The opinions of Hawaiian women about their workplaces remain largely
oblique, while the agendas of Hawaiian men are more readily revealed
through their political legacies. The sole Hawaiian woman interviewed
by the Buffalo press was a young girl in the Hawaiian village—"the little
weaver," as she was called—who may have also danced hula. She had impeccable educational credentials as a graduate of the Kamehameha Girls'
Schools, a private academy for Hawaiian youth funded by an ali'i. This
girl had "accompanied McConnell's colony only because she saw in the
voyage a chance to enhance her knowledge of the states."[162] Her desire for
personal edification marked her as no different, at least at that moment,
from someone like Coelho, but she made that brief appearance in the
historical record and then disappeared from view. Kini Kapahu's political
beliefs and motivations were similarly obscured, although she resented
U.S. annexation as much as Johnny Wilson and the other royalists with
whom she toured. The day the United States annexed Hawai'i, 12 August
1898, Kini cried while watching the lowering of the Hawaiian flag at the
royal palace.[163]

The relative absence of Hawaiian women in media and political institutions, rather than suggesting that they were politically inert, urge us
to look beyond the most legible expressions of political independence,
defiance, or capitulation. Going on tour was a chance for Hawaiians to
take chances, explore the world, and activate a range of uncategorized
desires—for erotic fulfillment, adventure, creative production, and political and economic freedoms. Love and desire mingled with the pleasures
of adventure and the exigencies of political dissent. We must take seri-
ously the erotics of tourism—not simply the erotic charge that spectators

derived from watching colonial bodies dance and sing on stage, but the erotic possibilities for Hawaiian performers in diasporic locations.

For Johnny and Kini, joining the fairs brought both political and personal autonomy. Johnny had married a white American woman from California for a few months in 1899, prior to the Buffalo exposition. It was a brief but disastrous union, and Johnny fled to the continent with Kini. For Kini and Johnny, the village enterprises in Omaha and Buffalo meant being able to live together as lovers, while Johnny remained legally married.[164] They may have been seeking liberation from colonial authority and supervision, but they also escaped, at least temporarily, the strictures of a family and a community that disapproved of a "hula girl" who would marry a gentleman. Apart from anticolonial networks like those developed between U.S. senators and fledging politicians, these tours made possible forms of nonnormative communality and affinity among Hawaiians. Nationalist expression and resistance was messily entangled with the erotics of empire.

Let me end this chapter as I began it, with a song. This mele is a diasporic Hawaiian song rooted in the United States. On the troupe's journey across the continental United States to the Buffalo exposition, a train derailed in front of them, and the group had to wait for hours in the train station until the track was cleared. Johnny Wilson recalled:

> We went to the hotel for breakfast . . . and after eating, several of the girls in our party went out to gather flowers. It was springtime and the countryside was abloom. Coming back to our Pullman the girls sat down in the grass and commenced to weave leis. I got my camera and took a picture of the group. Kealakei [the band leader Mekia Kealakai] and two or three of the boys were absent. Hearing an occasional strain of music from within the Pullman I investigated and found the absentees busy on "Lei Awapuhi," which in English means "The Wreath of Ginger." They were so wrapped up in their composing that they refused to come outside to have a picture taken.[165]

In California, red poppies bloomed instead of wild ginger, but inspired by the scene of the women amidst the flowers, the musician Mekia Kealakai composed a melody for a love song. In the song, the speaker likens beautiful ginger buds to his or her lover, and strings a lei to bind him or her closer:

Naʻu e ke aloha e kui a lawa [My love, you are securely bound to me]
Me aʻu kou lei ʻawapuhi [Your ginger lei to me].[166]

"Lei ʻAwapuhi" was one of the few songs composed by a Hawaiian that became popular in the United States before it was ever heard in Hawaiʻi.[167]
Kealakai may have had a particular woman in mind as he wrote the song:
the hula dancer Mele Nawaaheihei, who was also a member of the troupe,
and whom Kealakai married that year. Kealakai applied a familiar Hawaiian poetic trope—intimacy with the landscape as an analogy for intimacy
with one's lover—to his new conditions on the U.S. continent.

This incident is at once an individual love story and a reminder of how
Hawaiians were translating their new colonial environment into terms
of their own. "Lei ʻAwapuhi" reveals a side of Hawaiians' relationship to
the United States that was not simply about colonial loss and dislocation,
but about new affiliations, anticipation, and survival. The fin de siècle expositions were arguably the beginning of a Hawaiian cultural diaspora—
performers launched entertainment careers and a host of cultural productions far and wide after the Omaha and Buffalo fairs. While many
returned home, several musicians and their families found success along
circuits across the continental United States.[168]

Johnny Wilson managed an extensive American vaudeville tour after
Buffalo. Sixteen entertainers—including the Hawaiian Glee Club and at
least two female hula dancers—were booked on the famous Keith-Albee
vaudeville circuit from late 1901 until the spring of 1902.[169] Johnny's
vaudeville diary reveals stops in Milwaukee, Cleveland, Lansing, and To-
ledo along Keith's Empire Vaudeville Circuit. The group then traveled
back east to New York, where the troupe became the head attraction at
the opening of new Orpheum Theater in Brooklyn.[170] After Brooklyn, the
troupe joined the Orpheum circuit in California, going between vaudeville theaters in San Francisco and Los Angeles every two weeks.[171] The
group received offers from the Moss Empire Circuit in London and the
Coney Island amusement park, but Johnny declined.

Kini and Johnny returned to Hawaiʻi in April 1902 after about five
months on the vaudeville circuit, while others divided into quartets and
quintets and headed east. The James Shaw family, veterans of the Omaha
fair, settled in Long Island, New York, and became professional vaude-
villians. The Shaw family daughter Winifred Leimomi Shaw, performing
as "Wini Shaw," became a Broadway and Hollywood star in the 1930s,
singing in Warner Bros. musicals. The troubadour Mekia Kealakai toured

Europe and the United States with his wife Mele for two decades, taking extended engagements in London, Paris, and New York.[172] He did not return home until 1920, when Mayor Johnny Wilson exhorted him to take over as bandmaster of the Royal Hawaiian Band. The musician July Paka married a part-Indian woman named Toots. Together they launched "Toots Paka's Hawaiians" in 1902. The group became a headlining vaudeville act, playing the Orpheum circuit in New York, Chicago, and other cities for over two decades.[173] William Alohikea toured the United States and settled in Spokane, Washington.[174] Writing in 1937, Johnny said that there were other original performers from his troupe still residing in and around New York City.[175]

As these dispersals suggest, Hawaiians were incorporated into an expanding U.S. empire, but insisted on crafting paths for themselves as metropolitan pioneers. The travels, adventures, and diasporic settlement of Hawaiian performers produced an expansive and expanding notion of land and home far beyond the islands. More songs like "Lei 'Awapuhi" would be composed as later generations of Hawaiian performers relocated to the United States in the twentieth century and adopted American cities as their homelands.

CHAPTER 4

"HULA QUEENS" AND "CINDERELLAS"
Imagined Intimacy in the Empire

At the New York World's Fair in 1939, a group of young hula dancers known as the Aloha Maids gave 5,000 flower leis to fairgoers and danced during an all-day celebration of the islands. In front of fair commissioners, military officials, and the mayor of New York City, these hula performers publicized the mutual benefits of increased trade between the United States and its Pacific territory. As had been outlined by Hawai'i's territorial governor that day, the continued importation of Hawaiian sugar to the continental United States would bolster the territory's military value while encouraging the consumption of American goods by the Hawaiian market.[1] This rhetoric of mutuality and affinity was staged through the "Native dances" of the Aloha Maids, women dancers from Hawai'i who headlined at the Hotel Lexington's Hawaiian Room, which had made its debut in Manhattan earlier that year. Hula dancers no longer ballyhooed on midway sideshows but became respectable headliners in New York City and ambassadors for the territory.

What happened to transform hula from ignominy to celebrated practice in the islands and the United States? Maligned in the early territorial period, by the 1930s hula had become essential to the growth of tourism and Hawai'i's economic development. The orientation of the territorial economy had shifted from agribusiness to new crops of tourists. Hawaiian bodies and culture—particularly Hawaiian music and hula—became valued commodities for the tourist industry, both inside and outside Hawai'i. As ambassadors of aloha, Hawaiian performers promoted Hawai'i's charms. Hula encouraged Hawai'i's integration into the U.S. empire during the late territorial period and helped to groom the islands for statehood by providing a benign cultural identity. Hawaiian cultural practices were highly politicized, for whoever brokered the presentation of Hawaiian culture influenced Hawai'i's political and economic future.

In the developing tourist economy, Hawaiian cultural practitioners labored to revive traditional forms of hula, but they also put themselves on display. By the 1930s, Hawaiians had managed to create self-sustaining enterprises as tourist entertainers in the islands, creating conditions for their export overseas. The Aloha Maids were part of a generation of Hawaiian women who left Hawai'i between the 1930s and 1950s for the continent. No longer confined to midway villages and vaudeville acts, as it had been since the late nineteenth century, hula was packaged by American nightclubs and showrooms as middlebrow American entertainment. Called "hula queens" and "Cinderellas" by the Hawai'i press, hula dancers joined popular entertainment circuits that routed them between Hawai'i and American cities. Hula dancers, traveling by airplane, bus, and train, traversed the continental United States for stretches of several months to several years (see figure 32). A potent form of colonial labor, hula was also a golden ticket out of Hawai'i for many women, promising fame and glamour. Although Hawaiian men continued to practice and teach hula in the islands, women were favored as dancers on American tourist circuits.

The federal government officially incorporated Hawai'i as a territory in 1900, but Americans on the continent did not come into close contact with Hawaiians on a broad scale until the 1930s. In the years prior to World War II, as the Pacific colony and Pacific fleet grew more important to national security, Americans needed to define Hawai'i and Hawaiians for their own interests. Concomitant with tourism, American military operations mounted in Hawai'i, where the United States required a foothold to assert itself against Japan. In an era before jet planes delivered Americans to the islands, Americans came to experience Hawai'i through live performances on the continent.

Imperial hula circuits in the twentieth century intensified an imagined intimacy between Hawai'i and the United States. A fantasy of reciprocal attachment, this imagined intimacy made it impossible, indeed unimaginable, for Americans to part from their colony. Hawaiian women produced a feminized version of Hawai'i on stage, offering their aloha—the promise of intimacy and affection—to the United States through live hula

Fig. 32 Ray Kinney and the Aloha Maids—Lillian Leimomi Woodd, Jennie Napua Woodd, and Pualani Mossman—catching a Manhattan taxicab. COURTESY OF GILLIOM FAMILY.

performances. The dreams spun out of hula made the distant territory familiar to those who had never visited the islands and obscured American military and tourist expansion.

Hawaiians, however, developed intimate attachments within the United States as they toured and settled. Often reimagining their relationship to Hawai'i and American imperial centers, performers created multiple homes away from "home." Hawaiian performance circuits, while often causing dislocation, enabled many Hawaiians in the islands and in American urban centers to secure a degree of independence and pleasure. Although these imperial hula circuits were not structures of their own choosing, within them Hawaiians sustained cultural reproduction, pursued employment and education, and created diasporic communities. While dancers participated in the colonial scripting of aloha and appeared to have been interpellated by state-oriented goals, they set out to accomplish their own discrepant agendas, which are not usually legible as oppositional to colonization, but nevertheless suggest alternative uses of their bodies, time, and space. These women were much more than the South Seas maidens, "hularinas," or Cinderellas they were purported to be.

In order to begin understanding how entertainment circuits in the United States operated during this period of tourist and military development, it is necessary to grasp the island scene and the conditions from which these performers emerged. To do so, we must begin in territorial Hawai'i and follow Hawaiian and islander women who moved from Hawai'i to the U.S. continent to take their chances as performers.

The New Plantations

More than 2,500 miles away from the California coast, Hawai'i was the jewel of the American colonial periphery. In "Song of the Islands," a twenty-minute promotional film produced by the Hawaii Tourist Bureau in 1934, white American tourists bid a bittersweet good-bye to Honolulu after a stay in the islands. Draped in long carnation leis on a steamship deck, they are serenaded by a group of strolling Hawaiian musicians. Shown in Fox movie theaters in the United States, such films necessarily obscured the social and political relations that enabled this leisurely experience.

Territorial Hawai'i of the 1920s and 1930s was firmly governed by a kama'āina haole (Hawai'i-born white) oligarchy and its five interlocking corporations, called the Big Five. Hawai'i had much in common with the plantation economies of other tropical possessions in the Caribbean: racialized class structures, the concentration of economic power in a few hands, an export imbalance to North America and Europe, and a strong American military presence. U.S. defense spending propped up the territory's economy; by 1940 the armed forces population was six times what it was in 1920.[2] Besides military bases, Hawai'i extended the promise of beaches and sun. In the 1920s, American and European tourists started to arrive in greater numbers on steamships. In 1921, a Honolulu writer predicted that tourists "without doubt" were "THE leading crop of the future."[3] Although tourism ranked a distant third to sugar and pineapple cultivation, the Big Five recognized the potential profits of the trade. Haole business and government leaders began to market Hawai'i and develop the territory's tourist infrastructure. In 1925 the Hawaii Tourist Bureau, which was part of the Hawaii Chamber of Commerce, allocated $125,000 a year for tourist promotion. Ten years later, even during the Great Depression, the tourist bureau spent $100,000 on a "comprehensive campaign" to "tell the world of Hawaii."[4]

Luxury hotels became the new plantations. In 1927, Matson Navigation Company, a Big Five company, opened the Royal Hawaiian Hotel in Waikīkī. The local elite, including former Hawaiian royalty, arrived in black tie for the opening of the elegant property. Matson—the shipping monopoly that controlled all routes between Hawai'i and North America—enjoyed a large market share of the early tourist industry.[5] After sailing on the S.S. *Lurline*, Matson's luxury ocean liner, visitors would stay in Hawai'i at a Matson-owned property. In the mid-1930s, Hollywood movie stars such as Shirley Temple, Mary Pickford, and Bing Crosby flocked to Waikīkī for vacations, as did the "great and new great of the world."[6] The tourist industry saw glimmers of success that were to be realized with mass tourism in the years after World War II.[7]

Hawaiian musicians and dancers proved themselves influential envoys of Hawai'i as they began circulating in world's fairs and expositions in the 1890s, although the haole oligarchy disapproved of Hawaiian hula performance and sought to clamp down on fin de siècle Hawaiian brokers like Johnny H. Wilson, who brought hula to the continental United States. Haole leaders feared that the disreputable hula would eclipse their own efforts to Americanize the islands and encourage capitalist investment (see chapter 3). They effectively cordoned hula from official territorial functions for over a decade until they saw that Hawaiian culture could be packaged as an indispensable commodity for the tourist industry.

Haole leaders were quick to instrumentalize hula for their own purposes. As the territory began to promote tourism, Hawaiians became necessary to convey aloha and advertise the territory's cash commodities to American markets. At world's fairs in Seattle in 1909 and San Francisco in 1915, the Hawaii Pineapple Growers' Association brought "attractive" hapa haole (part-white, part-Hawaiian) women to serve pineapple to visitors at the official Hawaiian buildings. Over a five-month period in Seattle, these "native girls" had served more than 200,000 plates of pineapple and were credited for giving visitors a favorable impression of Hawai'i and the islands' delicious fruit.[8]

In San Francisco, some of the young women not only served pineapple, but danced hula. Attractions in their own right in the territorial exhibits, Hawaiian women were in the process of becoming the ripe "fruit" of the territory, superseding even the exotic pineapple. The icon of the "hula girl" at first helped to sell commodities, but Hawaiian women would soon be marketed as commodities themselves, providing gendered labor for the territory in the form of hula.

Hula also emerged as entertainment for the developing tourist trade in the islands.[9] Haole-operated newspapers and journals saw hula and Hawaiian music as potential attractions, and public discourse began to shift in favor of hula. Hawaiian culture marked Hawai'i as unique and hula dancers provided the territory with its "destination image."[10] The reverend John T. Gulick argued in favor of the hula in 1911: "Under the right kind of supervision they [Hawaiian dances] can be made so interesting and free from objectionable features that they will be of inestimable value as a source of amusement and interest to thousands of tourists and residents of Honolulu."[11]

By the 1920s, editorials in *Paradise of the Pacific*, a Honolulu-based magazine, called for hula dancers and musicians to go on tour.[12] Yet a conflicted attitude between salvation and destruction persisted. *Paradise of the Pacific* agreed that this potential tour of "real hula dancers" in the United States might publicize Hawai'i and restore hula from its "present disgusting and degraded condition." However, it also issued this blunt directive: "It [hula] should either be restored to its pristine elegance or abolished by law."[13] By the end of the decade, kama'aina haole—particularly those who had invested capital in the tourist infrastructure—anointed themselves the guardians of authentic Hawaiian practices. They would protect Hawaiian culture from Hawaiians themselves, who crudely reduced hula to its market value without regard for public standards and authenticity. Lorrin A. Thurston, the grandson of American missionaries, had helped to orchestrate the overthrow of the Hawaiian Kingdom in 1893 and later served as the Republic of Hawai'i's annexation commissioner in Washington. In 1922 Thurston felt strongly enough about the "fake" hula skirts used in films—he wanted only Hawaiian-made skirts shown—that he tried to establish a Hawaiian board of review to censor any films that exaggerated "hula effects."[14]

Even the once scathing *Paradise of the Pacific* resurrected the hula in the 1930s, opining, "Never . . . was she [hula] an abandoned profligate. Always she was beautiful, consistently full of charm and, certainly, never boring. . . . Hula is Hawaii and Hawaii is hula."[15] Some haole considered Hawaiian cultural practices their own patrimony and, by extension, their property. This is not to say they did not feel genuinely attached to Hawai'i and Hawaiians. Yet this eulogizing of a purer hula was a form of "imperialist nostalgia," the mourning of colonizers for what they have transformed.[16] This nostalgia discursively erased the complicity of those who contributed to that change.

Po'e hula were caught in this contradictory logic. For Hawaiian cultural practices to be perceived authentic, they could not be tainted by market relations, but were in turn eagerly appropriated and commodified by the tourist industry. In the 1930s and 1940s, the tourist bureau and Big Five businesses focused on developing hula and Hawaiian music as the islands' principal resources. Hawaiians found themselves trying to ensure cultural reproduction while participating in capitalist markets. Who would mine Hawaiian culture as tourism and imperial performance circuits expanded? Native practitioners, the territorial government, Big Five businessmen, or American promoters? The stakes for selling Hawai'i's cultural resources would be raised even higher, as the United States expanded its consolidation over Hawai'i and career opportunities outside the islands grew.

Native Entrepreneurs

A young Hawaiian woman named Pualani Mossman thrilled Waikīkī tourists in the early 1930s with a "volcano hula." As Pualani danced on a raised platform, a man blew kerosene from his mouth and lit a large replica of a volcano. The volcano dance was the nightly pièce de résistance at the Lalani Hawaiian Village, a family-run Hawaiian cultural center in Waikīkī. However, the "volcano hula" was only one of a number of attractions at the village. Tourists could learn the hula from Pualani and her two sisters, eat freshly pounded poi, and sit down at a luau.[17] Pualani described the village experience: "People from all the hotels would come down so happy to see our beautiful show, the imu, taste real Hawaiian food, see the boys climbing the coconut trees, perform the knife and fire dances. All for $1 or $2."[18]

In 1932 Pualani's father, George Paele Mossman, had opened the Lalani Hawaiian Village on a large parcel of land in Waikīkī fronting the beach (see figure 33).[19] Located on the site of a former Hawaiian estate near Diamond Head, the village encouraged the learning of Native Hawaiian arts, hula, and the Hawaiian language. George Mossman sought to recreate the experience of traditional Hawai'i for both islanders and tourists, which was not easily available in an increasingly urbanized Honolulu at the time. Next to his modern house with a shingled roof, porch, and stone walkway, George reconstructed a Hawaiian village. Built by a master Hawaiian hut-maker, the village included seven hale pili (grass huts) for sleeping, cooking, eating, worshipping, kapa (bark cloth) weaving, and storing wa'a (canoes). Tall coconut palm trees grew between the huts and a large ki'i (wooden carving of a god) stood in one corner. He may well have been inspired by Johnny Wilson's Hawaiian villages erected in the midway sections of the expositions in Omaha and Buffalo at the turn of

Fig. 33 Sailors watching a hula show at Lalani Hawaiian Village.
COURTESY OF HAWAI'I STATE ARCHIVES.

the century. Like Johnny, George funded his activist interests through tourist performance.

Lalani Hawaiian Village promised the best of disappearing Hawai'i all in one site. One advertisement featured a photograph of 'ukulele players and hula dancers in lā'ī (ti leaf) skirts: "In this idyllic setting, you will thrill to the romance of Island yesterdays. Delicious foods of the Luau (native feast) will please the most discriminating. Ancient Hulas . . . native maids . . . weird chanting . . . thumping gourds . . . strumming ukuleles . . . plaintive Island melodies . . . majestic palms . . . quaint grass huts. Enjoy a never to be forgotten experience."[20] George attempted to re-create Hawaiian practices prior to Western contact. At tourist luaus, the Mossman family dressed up as ali'i in Hawaiian regalia. Resurrecting royal pageantry, George wore a chiefly 'ahu'ula (feather cape) and malo (loincloth), while his daughters stood above him holding the sign of royalty, the feathered kāhili (staff). His Hawaiian wife, Emma, sat as his consort.[21]

Despite George Mossman's seeming insistence on traditional Hawaiian experiences, Hawaiians freely mixed Hawaiian and Western performance vocabularies as they had over the last century of Euro-American

Fig. 34 Pualani Mossman at Lalani Hawaiian Village, ca. 1934.
COURTESY OF GILLIOM FAMILY.

contact. In addition to the ipu (gourd), Lalani Village musicians played the ʻukulele, an instrument that the Portuguese had introduced to the islands in the 1870s. Pualani, the eldest daughter, performed "For You a Lei," a jazz-influenced hula with English-language lyrics that maintained a Hawaiian style of poetic phrasing (see figure 34).[22]

As they mediated Hawaiian and Western cultural forms, the Mossmans were also comfortable combining Hawaiian cultural activism with capitalist savoir faire. They played up their soft primitivism for tourists, but also planned to educate other Hawaiians at the Lalani Village and resuscitate the Hawaiian culture that seemed to be disappearing.[23] One newspaper article explained the revival: "It is through these [tourist] activities [luaus and dancing] that the village is financed and that has become best known to the public, but its main purpose . . . is not merely to be an entertainment center, but to preserve the Hawaiian lore that is fast vanishing."[24]

At Lalani Hawaiian Village, the grass huts did not just provide ethno-graphic authenticity for tourists. The Mossmans housed residents from rural districts—elderly experts in Hawaiian chant and hula, and their pupils. The noted hula teacher Akoni Mika, at the age of sixty-eight, came from Keaukaha, Hilo, on the island of Hawai'i. His pupil Kekuewa joined him. Mika's hula repertoire had rarely been seen in public since Christ-ian missionaries had proscribed it in the mid-nineteenth century. He performed hula pahu (sacred drum hula) and hula ki'i (pantomime hula). Nuuhiwa Kiaaina, a cowboy and dancer from the island of Kaua'i, also lived in the village, as did the famed Kuluwaimaka, who was once a court chanter for King David Kalākaua. Kuluwaimaka was eighty-seven or eighty-eight years old in 1934; he could perform genealogical oli (chants) that stretched back centuries.[25]

These men were to perform for tourists but also pass their knowledge on to Hawaiians. George Mossman held auditions for promising young Hawaiians who were to work with tourists and learn from the resident experts. In 1934, he had only accepted two girls out of a large group. In addition to being able to sing, dance, speak Hawaiian, and cook Hawaiian food, the youngsters had to explain Hawaiian life and offer a specialized skill, such as weaving or quilt making. Said George, "The old people with the knowledge of the old Hawaiian customs are dying rapidly and their knowledge is dying with them. Our task now is to preserve everything we can."[26] Many urban Hawaiians had been born in a postoverthrow colony and were being educated in American-oriented, English-language-only schools. George Mossman employed a discourse of the Native's impending extinction that had similarly animated Kalākaua's "Ho'oulu Lāhui" (grow the nation) program, which revived ancient genealogical knowledge. But lacking kingdom or territorial sponsorship, Hawaiians like the Mossmans had to rely on private enterprise to support this opportunity structure.

The kūpuna (elders) taught hula pahu and oli to their Native students, while hapa haole hula, acculturated forms of hula that used Western instrumentation such as 'ukulele and guitars, were performed for haole tourists and soldiers. George's younger daughters, Piilani and Leilani, were often photographed dancing for tourists in cellophane hula skirts—costumes reserved for hapa haole hula.[27] Hula repertoire and costum-ing had changed to accommodate the tastes of the tourists: preferences for briefer costumes, fewer verses, and English-language lyrics. It is more likely that older sacred repertoire—if it was performed for an audience at all—was used for private recitals.

George Mossman's discourse of cultural preservation echoed that of haole proponents of tourism. It also suggests the objectification of Hawaiian culture often produced within tourist and museum regimes. In the process of "cultural objectification"—a phenomenon whereby a person sees culture as a thing outside of herself or himself—culture is something to be used and displayed, even preserved.[28] Hawai'i's tourist industry objectified Hawaiian culture by removing cultural practices from their wider social, political, and community context and creating a market value for them. Yet Hawaiians like the Mossman family also self-consciously objectified cultural practices by exhibiting themselves according to Western ideologies of primitivism that imagined Natives, and Native women in particular, as guileless, carefree, unsophisticated, and sexually expressive.

While George Mossman rightly feared the demise of Hawaiian cultural practices, hula pahu reappeared publicly by the 1930s for the first time in nearly a century. Many teachers began spreading their knowledge of traditional hula.[29] Tourist development and American interest in Hawai'i partially account for hula's resurfacing in the islands and on the U.S. continent in the 1930s. George himself had benefited from this hula revival, due to his Mormon background.[30] He began learning from hula master Samuel Pua Ha'aheo in the 1930s.[31] Ha'aheo was a Mormon elder who started teaching hula under the aegis of the Mormon Mutual Improvement Association in 1931. Forty-four years old at the time, Ha'aheo also worked as a policeman. The church encouraged Ha'aheo and other Mormon teachers, such as Keaka Kanahele, to teach and pass on their knowledge, in contrast with the earlier Protestant condemnation of hula. Ha'aheo agreed to teach hula at the Kalihi Gymnasium in Honolulu; for him hula was likely a secular practice. Indigenous dance could be benign and even beneficial for Mormon Hawaiians, so long as it was divorced from religious rituals, like those involving the kuahu (hula altar) dedicated to the goddess Laka.[32] Teachers like Ha'aheo modified hula to the constraints of the church by excising Hawaiian religious practices and repertoire. Nonetheless, Ha'aheo may have exposed his non-Mormon hula students to some Hawaiian religious protocol, such as chants to hula gods.[33]

Lalani Hawaiian Village, where cultural preservation met commerce, became popular with tourists. Even Americans who did not make it in person to Waikīkī could experience the village through Hollywood movies such as *The Kamaaina* (1929) and the promotional film *Song of the*

Islands (1934), which were filmed there. Lalani Hawaiian Village was a family operation that included every member of George Mossman's immediate family: his wife Emma, several sons, and three daughters Piilani, Leilani, and Pualani. Pualani, the oldest daughter, began to work at the age of six in her father's various Hawaiian ventures, which included ʻukulele manufacturing and a Hawaiian language school. In Waikīkī the Mossmans danced, instructed tourists, cooked pigs in the imu (underground pit), and served food at "Lalani's Poi Inn." This self-supporting enterprise resembles the small-scale family-based agricultural practices that preceded the incorporation of large tracts of land into industrial sugarcane and pineapple plantations in the late nineteenth century. Hula and music performance enabled Hawaiians to reinsert themselves into local economies.

With fewer than a dozen hotels in Waikīkī in the 1930s, the Mossmans could fill a niche tourist market with a piece of Waikīkī property and their own labor. American and transnational capital had not yet invested extensively in Hawaiʻi's tourist industry; this would happen after World War II and statehood in 1959. Lalani Hawaiian Village was a compelling example of small-scale entrepreneurship that contended with Waikīkī hotels and tourist businesses funded by haole capital. While hula did not rival the sugarcane or pineapple industries, it had its "place in the Hawaiian scene and quite a large place at that," observed a Honolulu writer in 1937.[34]

Tourism and cultural activism—the self-conscious deployment of culture for political ends—were not contradictions for many Hawaiians. The Mossmans placed themselves on display, but they were also cultural activists who pursued a range of personal and political aspirations through profitable ventures.[35] The Mossman family simultaneously fulfilled American models of economic success and stimulated the recovery of previously defamed Hawaiian cultural practices. Hula's compromised engagement with capitalism encouraged practitioners to pass on knowledge that was once taught furtively. In effect, the prospect of profit encouraged the training of more hula dancers in Hawaiʻi.

Within the restrictions of a U.S.-oriented consumer culture, Hawaiians were able to play music, dance hula, and make a decent wage. Hawaiians who left the islands as entertainers later employed similar strategies. The Mossmans' small-business prototype appears to have succeeded for their daughters Pualani and Piilani after they moved to New York City to dance. Growing up in the tourist village under the tutelage of their father and visiting hula masters, they were to parlay their knowledge into businesses of their own, such as hula studios and Polynesian catering in the continental United States.

On the one hand, Hawaiian culture was a commodity. Tourists paid a fee to experience traditional Hawai'i in the form of live dance. Yet hula was more than an object; it was also an "inalienable possession."[36] The hula genealogy descended from hula masters Kuluwaimaka and Pua Ha'aheo could neither be bought nor sold, but was passed on to those deemed worthy of a repertoire of chants and movements. After dancers received rigorous training and the ritual blessing of their teachers, they may have performed some of this repertoire for tourists, though likely not all of it, at the Lalani Hawaiian Village. The Mossmans sold luau dinners and tourist performances, but profit was not the sole aim of their cultural revival. Capitalism never disappeared but a hula economy based on reciprocity and noneconomic exchange operated within it.

Hula Queens on Tour

In 1938, a multi-island hula competition sponsored by Hollywood's Metro-Goldwyn-Mayer Studios (MGM) and the Hawai'i-based Consolidated Amusement Company sought to crown a "hula queen." In the "greatest hula contest ever staged in the Islands," nearly 500 young Hawaiian women vied for the title for over a month, going through several rounds of competition.[37] Each hoped to win the grand prize: a trip to Hollywood and a chance at stardom in the United States.

On almost every island, local audiences followed the competition with great enthusiasm, buying tickets for preliminary rounds held at movie theaters and rooting for their favorites. On Friday nights on O'ahu, islanders attended elimination rounds at the Hawaii Theater and indicated by applause their choices. In September 1938, five finalists from five different islands gathered in Honolulu for "a grand Hula-nui Nite (Big Hula Nite)." Before an overflowing theater, a board of judges crowned the contestant from Kaua'i, Alice Kealoha Pauole Holt (see figure 35). Holt subsequently passed her MGM screen test in Hollywood and spent three months there, touring as an "ambassador of good will" and dancing in the American stage and film productions of *Honolulu*.[38]

Hollywood came calling for other Hawaiian women in the 1930s. The island tourist industry had developed an infrastructure of performance sites and a pool of trained entertainers, which paved the way for Hawaiian entertainment ventures in the continental United States.[39] Performers left

Fig. 35 "Hula Queen" Alice Kealoha Pauole Holt.
COURTESY OF HAWAI'I STATE ARCHIVES.

the islands and joined the ranks of the petite bourgeoisie. One unnamed hula entrepreneur met with this enviable success: "Did you know that one hula teacher has raised her whole family to be hula artists and has a family hula troop? She has also made enough of an income from hula to build her own home and studio, and keep the family equipped with new and good looking cars. Several years ago she took the family to Hollywood for pictures and recently took another trip with some of her family back to the same place where they are reported as packing them in at the film colony's biggest night club."[40] Another "very charming" hula teacher had returned from Hollywood where she directed hula scenes for a new studio film. Her hula classes kept her going from 8 AM till 6 PM, and "if she [had] had any more it would [have been] the death of her." These profiles could have described a number of Hawaiian women from the 1930s to the 1950s.

If Hawaiians had not been self-employed entertainers, they may have been employed as plantation laborers in the two largest industries in Hawai'i—sugarcane and pineapple—or another industry controlled by the Big Five, such as shipping and warehouses.[41] Working-class Hawaiians and immigrants had few opportunities for upward mobility. Plantation labor was segregated according to a racial hierarchy: Portuguese luna (foremen) at the top; followed by Puerto Ricans, then Japanese, then Filipinos.[42] Japanese and Filipino plantation labor forces had gained only modest concessions from owners in the previous decade of strikes. Organized labor was still emerging in the 1930s, although collective bargaining was aided by the passage of the National Labor Relations Board Act. In response, big business formed the Industrial Association of Hawaii to combat "racial unions" and federal labor laws like the Wagner Act of 1936.[43] In 1937, when the first hearings of the National Labor Relations Board were held in Honolulu, there were still no minimum wage and child-labor laws in the territory and women workers were not protected in any industry. As late as 1938, striking longshoremen and clerks were crushed brutally by police.[44]

For those who left the plantations, a racialized labor and wage system awaited them. The cleaner clerical and government jobs were reserved for haole and hapa haole workers. Some Chinese and Japanese immigrant laborers started small businesses; Japanese also worked as small farmers, tradesmen, and domestics.[45] In tourist-related industries, workers sometimes worked six-day weeks and seventeen-hour days and were paid according to their race. Filipinos who worked in the kitchen or in cleaning earned $50 a month, compared with Japanese housekeepers who earned $56, and haole desk clerks who earned $102.[46]

Some Hawaiians belonged to a wealthy stratum of lawyers, doctors, and professionals, but the majority were working class, confined to low-level government, civil service, construction, or stevedore employment.[47] Hawaiian women could plot their futures as cannery workers, waitresses, or domestics; or if they were college-educated and more affluent, housewives, schoolteachers, or secretaries. Many entertainers saw themselves as wage laborers and made an effort to regulate their own labor practices. In 1939, for the first time in Hawai'i, hula teachers formed a hula teachers' hui (association), having been influenced by union organizing in the islands. Representatives of fifteen hula troupes chose George Mossman as their general chairman. The hui sought to "control the fixing of fees, rotate assignments, and generally act as a central 'casting agency' for hula performers."[48] It is understandable that performers would organize to avoid exploitation, especially since Hollywood studios had begun to shoot many films on location in Hawai'i in the 1920s and 1930s. The films *Bird of Paradise* (1932) and *Honolulu* (1939), for instance, relied heavily on the labor of local dancers and musicians.[49]

How did the "hula queens" fare after they left the islands? To find out, we are led from Hawai'i to New York City through the movements of George Mossman's oldest daughter. In 1938, the Hotel Lexington's Hawaiian Room recruited Pualani Mossman to dance hula in New York City.[50] Located on the corner of Forty-Ninth Street and Lexington Avenue in New York City, the Hawaiian Room was opened in 1937 by Charles E. Rochester, the president and managing director of the Hotel Lexington.

The Hawaiian Room was the first major showroom for live Hawaiian entertainment in the United States, and the most renowned.[51] Although a temporary experiment, the Hawaiian Room operated until 1966, and was the longest-lasting commercial venue for Hawaiian entertainment on the continent. In its first two years, the popular showroom grossed over a million dollars—a 22 percent increase over its previous incarnation— and served a half million patrons.[52] The Lexington's Hawaiian Room was but one site along U.S. hula circuits that included showrooms in California, Ohio, and Florida. While numerous American showrooms featured live Hawaiian entertainment, the Hawaiian Room served as the industry standard to beat. In many cases, performers in other American showrooms appeared at the Hawaiian Room sometime during their careers.

Located in the basement of the hotel, the Hawaiian Room was a supper club for dining, dancing, and live performance (see figure 36). Walking into the large circular room decorated with tropical palms and murals of Diamond Head and Waikīkī Beach, patrons were greeted with a flower lei, albeit it a paper one, by the Hawaiian hostess.[53] One restaurant reviewer in New York wrote in 1938:

> The Hawaiian Room . . . has all the tricks even down to swinging the Island's music for dancing. They have native dancers as part of the show and native dishes are on the menu. It's become very popular and well worth a visit, if you like to be taken out of yourself and transported, by the aid of a few drinks, to the dreamy romantic beach at Waikiki. I can't vouch for the authenticity of the food and drinks, but their names are sweet to the ear: Okolehau Punch, (60¢), Kara Bowl, served with Champagne for four persons ($4.50), Honolulu Collins . . . Io Kamanu Pulehu Pakaai, Uwala Lilii (really grilled salmon steak, parsley potatoes and poi 95¢), Moa Oma Me Leko Me Palaoa, Poached Boned Young Chicken, Hawaiian manner.[54]

Fig. 36 Hawaiian Room, Hotel Lexington, New York City. COURTESY OF AKAU FAMILY.

The key to the Hawaiian's Room's success was the "liveness" of the experience. Palm trees and tropical rainstorms set the mood, while imported Hawaiian musicians and dancers supplied the "true Island atmosphere."[55] The talent scout of Hotel Lexington president Charles Rochester signed the Hawaiian and Irish tenor Ray Kinney of Honolulu as the Hawaiian Room's orchestra leader in 1937 (see figure 37). Hotel management also contracted steel guitarist Andy Iona and composer-singer Lani McIntire. In 1938 Kinney also brought his cousin, the baritone George Kainapau, as well as the steel guitar player Sam Kamuela Makia Chung from Honolulu. The Hawaiian Room and other venues enshrined the island-born-and-bred Native Hawaiian as an ideal; Rochester himself insisted on Hawaiian musicians, preferably direct from the islands.

Yet most Hawaiian entertainers claimed racially mixed backgrounds with their names or by personal admission. Throughout his career, Ray Kinney referred to himself as the "Irish Hawaiian," but because "McIntire and Kinney" sounded too Irish, the opening billing of the Hawaiian Room originally read "Andy Iona and His Twelve Hawaiians."[56] Chinese-Hawaiian Sam Chung began using one of his Hawaiian middle names professionally when he came to New York because "Makia" sounded more Hawaiian than his Chinese surname "Chung."[57]

Fig. 37 Ray Kinney. COURTESY OF AKAU FAMILY.

Reproducing a gendered pattern from late nineteenth-century Hawaiian entertainment, the band orchestra members were invariably men, and the hula dancers women. As the principal orchestra leader, Kinney was responsible for casting Hawaiian hula dancers. Kinney assembled the "Aloha Maids" troupe in Honolulu: the solo dancer Meymo Ululani Holt plus Pualani Mossman, Mapuana Mossman Bishaw, and Jennie Napua Woodd. All four original Aloha Maids were hapa haole. "Hapa haole" literally means part-white, but in its colloquial usage in the early twentieth century it was usually used to refer to someone who was part white, part Hawaiian.[58] Commercial Hawaiian entertainment enshrined the colonial preference for lighter-skinned, mixed-race Hawaiian women, while simultaneously billing them as authentic Natives. A *New York Times* night club reviewer praised the Native Hawaiian women of the Hawaiian Room: "Instead of pawning a batch of brunettes coated with shoe polish as native dancers, as is often the case, Mr. Rochester employs the real articles. Currently it is the three Aloha Maids who are executing that hula as-

Fig. 38 Meymo
Ululani Holt.
COURTESY OF
AKAU FAMILY.

signment."[59] The majority of the dancers who performed in the Hawaiian
Room or in other U.S. showrooms in the 1930s and 1940s had hapa haole
backgrounds, but even if they did not, they fulfilled the favored phenotype with brunette hair, slim figures, and fair skin. This idealized look for
hula dancers began in the early twentieth century and persisted in 1938
when judges selected the hapa haole Kealoha Holt and other hula queen
finalists.[60]

In 1937 twenty-two-year-old Meymo Ululani Holt arrived in New
York City and became the solo dancer, or "leading lady," at the Hawaiian Room (see figure 38). Ray Kinney was married to Meymo Holt's older
sister Dawn. Meymo hailed from a wealthy and prominent hapa haole
family. Her mother's family, the Lemons, once owned the large Waikīkī
estate upon which George Mossman built the Lalani Hawaiian Village.
Her socialite grandmother was a close friend of the Hawaiian royalty, and
Holt had graduated from Punahou School, a private missionary-founded
school in Honolulu.

Fig. 39 Aloha Maids, New York City, ca. 1939. Left to right: Jennie Napua Woodd, Pualani Mossman, Mapuana Mossman Bishaw. COURTESY OF GILLIOM FAMILY.

Kinney found three other Aloha Maids in Hawai'i through kinship networks and friends (see figure 39). Pualani Mossman of Lalani Hawaiian Village was already a recognized hula dancer and model. Selected for Matson Navigation Line's national advertising campaign in 1937, Mossman became known as the "Matson Girl" and "the most photographed girl in the islands" for her pictures in *Time* and *Life* magazines.[61] Pualani ventured to New York with her cousin Mapuana Mossman Bishaw in 1938. Jennie Napua Woodd, a friend of theirs who danced hula at the Royal Hawaiian Hotel in Waikīkī, completed Kinney's dancing line. These Aloha Maids became the faces of Hawai'i in New York.

Called "Hawaiian Cinderellas" by the Honolulu press, three young high school graduates won auditions in 1940 to join a later hula line at the Hotel Lexington's Hawaiian Room.[62] Ray Kinney picked Edna Leinaala Kihoi of Waimea, Peggy Nani Todd of Hilo, and Lehua Paulson of Honolulu to join fourteen other dancers and musicians in New York City (see figures 40 and 41). Kihoi had been a finalist in the Inter-Island Hula Contest sponsored by MGM in 1938. Kinney had spotted Nani Todd at her Hilo high school dance and invited her to an audition, which she later won. In this island version of the allegory, Kinney—the veritable Prince

Fig. 40 Dancers with Ray Kinney's troupe, ca. 1944. COURTESY OF AKAU FAMILY.
Back row, left to right: Betty Puanani Makia, Lulika Ferris, Kamoa Ferris.
Front row, left to right: Edna Leinaala Kihoi, Peggy Nani Todd.

Fig. 41 Lehua
Paulson. COURTESY
OF GILLIOM FAMILY.

Charming—whisked young "Cinderellas" who fit his glass slipper off to a fairytale life in New York.[63]

For many Hawaiian women, hula presented a dream ticket out of Hawai'i, promising fame, glamour, and a middle-class status difficult to achieve in the plantation and service industries. Hula dancers could earn approximately sixty to one hundred dollars a week; this was compared to wages of four to ten dollars a week in the pineapple canneries.[64] Talent recruiters from the U.S. continent took advantage of ample labor in the islands. Orchestra leaders, Hollywood film studios, and American nightclubs periodically scouted for dancers in Hawai'i, where women often faced stiff competition for coveted hula contracts.

Upon their arrival in the United States, these women were treated as novelties and minor celebrities. As metropolitan and suburban newspapers announced their romances, marriages, and children's births in syndicated columns, Americans became intimate with the women's lives. The gossip columnist Walter Winchell gave the Aloha Maids a coveted orchid in his *Daily Mirror* column, and when the dancer Napua Woodd married the trombonist Lloyd Gilliom, Winchell reported the arrival of their first child. The appearance of a new song or performer fascinated audiences. The *New York World Telegram* profiled the leading lady Meymo Holt with five large photographs of her dancing hula in a bikini top and thigh-baring silk hula skirt.[65]

How were readers to make sense of Hawaiians and decode them? Not only were the performers' bodies exposed in close-up shots, their racial backgrounds and biographical details were scrutinized: Napua was of German, English, and Hawaiian descent. Her name, pronounced "Nap-OO-ah," meant "the flower." She was the daughter of a hula dancer, and she enjoyed sightseeing at the Washington Bridge.[66] While each dancer had distinguishing features, the women nonetheless stood in for all of Hawai'i and Hawaiian culture. "Hawaiian girls are famous for their clear, brown skins, their flashing smiles, their beautiful, dark hair, and their full yet graceful figures," read a newspaper caption below a photograph of the three Aloha Maids. Almost never photographed in contemporary Western dress for these American articles, they wore Hawaiian costumes instead. The women were framed as foreign but not too alien curiosities. Presented as sexually available, their bodies also marked Hawai'i as desirable and unthreatening. The syndicated Associated Press column by "Man about Manhattan" circulated this favorable assessment: "Pualani is grace and rhythm personified and her features are perfect for photographing. She has luxuriant black hair with a gleaming softness one hardly expects to find among those from the Pacific Islands. We have never seen more expressive eyes."[67]

Islanders back home also expected these women to properly represent Hawai'i to the United States. Hawai'i newspapers eagerly tracked their movements and published their photographs as Hawaiians took on Broadway.[68] The *Honolulu Star-Bulletin* credited hula dancers as "good will emissaries" who spread aloha spirit far and wide: "These singing and dancing islanders who invade mainland night spots provide splendid advertising for Hawaii. They take with them the charm and grace of an island paradise where two thirds of America longs to visit."[69]

Dancers also sought to humanize their island homes to the tourists they encountered. The dancer Tutasi Wilson said "the girls" saw their mission as "selling Hawai'i in a nice way."[70] She felt personally responsible for correcting images of Polynesians and Hawai'i when she met mainland Americans. She recalled, "When I got to Hollywood [in 1934], the Massie case was not too far back."[71] The infamous Thalia Massie rape case in Hawai'i, playing out in 1931—in which a navy lieutenant's wife accused five working-class islander men of rape despite evidence to the contrary—was a cause célèbre in the United States and inflamed American fears of Hawai'i's majority nonwhite population. After the trial of the five men ended with a mistrial, Massie's mother and husband kidnapped and lynched the Native Hawaiian defendant. The famed lawyer Clarence Darrow came to Honolulu to defend the Massie pair during their murder trial. They were found guilty of murder but the territorial governor commuted their sentences and freed them immediately.

During these sensational trials, American cartoonists depicted the Native Hawaiian, Japanese, and Chinese defendants as dark-skinned sexual predators in loincloths and as gorillas leering at white women. The national press declared the islands unsafe for white women and urged martial law for the islands until white women were safe again. The U.S. Navy also considered placing Hawai'i under military rule.[72] Publicity from the Massie case damaged Hawai'i's bids for statehood; a territorial delegate to Congress introduced a Hawaiian statehood bill only three days after the mistrial. The bill failed.[73]

Nearly a decade later, when Tutasi Wilson joined the Hollywood movie and hula circuit, she found that the Massie case still influenced American public opinion about Hawai'i. "In those days the 1930s and 40s, they [Americans] thought we were gorillas. When we [islanders] were on the train, they were checking to see if we were colored. You folks have it easy today."[74] Hawaiian and islander women helped to restore harmony for the territory. As women shared their aloha with Americans on tourist hula circuits, their gentle sexuality soothed the threat of hypersexualized and masculinized island men. They helped to reestablish an amicable connection between Hawai'i and the continent and legitimate a disreputable cultural practice.

Although the dancers felt a heavy burden to represent their homes properly, islanders appreciated the stature that the Hotel Lexington conferred on Hawaiians. Hawaiians had toured the United States and Europe since the late nineteenth century, performing on racialized, commercial stages such as midway sideshows, dime museums, and vaudeville theaters. In the opinion of some Hawaiians and islanders, Hawaiian performers could tarnish Hawai'i's image by participating in "cheap sideshow entertainment" that regarded them as amusing animals.[75] For example, "Prince Lei Lani and the Royal Samoans" presented a vaudeville act at the New York Hippodrome in 1928 with the hapa haole hula dancer Aggie Auld, an act that included an acrobat and "Peter the Great, Educated Ape."[76] Even dogs were made to mimic a version of hula on stage.[77] In 1934, dancers and managers at a New York burlesque theater were arrested for performing a Hawaiian dance, referred to as a "hootchy-kootchy dance." They were charged with indecency, although the charges were eventually dismissed.[78] In the Hawaiian Room, however, the white-suited Hawaiian musicians and demure Aloha Maids were respectable headliners and stars. They professionalized a suspect cultural form and transformed it into a middle-class form of leisure.

Hawaiian Fever

The clever marketing of a feminine, sensual, and uncomplicated Hawai'i put the Hawaiian Room on the map in Manhattan, and its success spawned a Hawaiian and Polynesian fever in the city and across the country: to Chicago, Cleveland, Denver, San Francisco, Buffalo, New Orleans, Minneapolis, Detroit, Ft. Lauderdale, and Hollywood. Hawaiian shows opened at the Roosevelt Hotel in Chicago, the St. Francis Hotel in San Francisco, the Statler Hotel in Buffalo, the El Dorado Club in Cleveland, and the Hotel Roosevelt in New Orleans.[79] Broadway also caught on to hula. "Hellzapoppin," a popular musical by the vaudeville veterans John Sigvard "Ole" Olsen and Harold Ogden "Chic" Johnson, featured Kinney and his Aloha Maids in one act. The dancers rushed across town to

Times Square from the Hawaiian Room and returned in time for their last show at the Lexington. In 1939, a rival Hawaiian room—the Maisonette Hawaiian—opened at the St. Regis Hotel in New York. Owned by Vincent Astor, the St. Regis hoped to cash in on the lucrative formula of Hawaiian entertainment, with the comic hula dancer Clara Inter ("Hilo Hattie") as headliner.[80] But while there were many imitators, the Hawaiian Room set the standard for Hawaiian entertainment, bringing in distinguished dancers and musicians from the islands for almost three decades.[81] Tutasi Wilson asserted, "No other clubs compared to the Hawaiian Room."[82]

Who frequented these Hawaiian rooms? Like many other nightclubs in the 1930s and 1940s, the Hawaiian Room barred African Americans as patrons.[83] According to Ray Kinney's daughter, Raylani, "At least eighty-percent of the audience was haole in the 1930s. Blacks weren't welcome at the Hawaiian Room."[84] Offering white middle-class American audiences easily digestible hula and Hawaiian music, the Hawaiian Room catered to a growing market for consumer culture and cultural commodities after the Depression and World War II. During this period, white spectators eagerly consumed other exotic performances at jazz, Cuban-themed, and "Spanish" nightclubs in New York City.[85] Jazz clubs such as the Cotton Club and the Kit Kat Club offered an "all colored . . . doggondest set of entertainers" to their white clientele.[86]

Unlike the Ritz-Carlton, the Hotel Lexington was not a luxury hotel. The Lexington was a second-tier establishment and not prohibitively expensive. Whereas a single room with bath cost seven dollars and up a night at the Ritz-Carlton, a similar room cost only four dollars at the Lexington in 1939.[87] The Hawaiian Room occupied a similar niche among hotel entertainment in the city. *Esquire's New York: A New York Guide Book for World's Fair Visitors* recommended the Hawaiian Room for its young male readers in 1939. The Room had a $1.25 cover "but reasonable prices throughout."[88] In *Where to Take Your Girl in New York on One Dollar to $20*, college men suggested the Hawaiian Room as a way "to get by on a small pocketbook."[89] Younger men and women, as well as their parents, frequented the Hawaiian Room; if one did not wish to dance to live music on the expansive floor, one might be content watching the Hawaiian show.

Much of the Hawaiian music played at the Lexington Hawaiian Room, the Maisonette, and other nightclubs on the continent was hapa haole: songs blended with American popular musical styles and usually featuring English-language lyrics and Hawaiian themes. In the 1920s and

1930s, hapa haole songs were influenced by jazz and blues.[90] Notable hits from the Lexington included Ray Kinney's compositions "Across the Sea" and "Song of Old Hawaii." The Hawaiian Room avoided Tin Pan Alley songs like "Yaaka Hula Hickey Dula" and "They're Wearing 'Em Higher in Hawaii," which had been written by New York composers with no connection to Hawai'i.[91] The Hotel Lexington's president Charles Rochester prided himself on the Hawaiian Room's authentic Hawaiian musicians and music. He protested, "Don't let Hawaiian music go modern!" and rallied for "sweet" Hawaiian music like "Ua Like No A Like" and "Song of the Islands."[92]

The dancer Betty Puanani Makia described her hula repertoire on the continent as largely limited to dances performed with English-language vocals: "We did mostly hapa haole songs. If we did one ancient number, it was an 'ōlapa, and that was 'Kawika' or 'A Kona Hema' [hula 'ōlapa in honor of King Kalākaua]. But most of it was hapa haole, because we had to introduce Hawaiian songs and dances to the haoles there. If we did it all in Hawaiian, they wouldn't understand you. So we had to do hapa haole, and that went great. We did 'Hula Hands,' '[Little] Brown Gal,' 'Grass Shack,' those old day songs."[93]

Betty remembered the hapa haole song "Little Brown Gal" as one of the most popular hula standards.[94] The song captured an outsider's thrill at encountering a "little brown gal in a little grass skirt in a little grass shack in Hawaii." Even more than the islands' beach boys, "tropical sea," or "balmy air," the little brown gal summoned the narrator to partake of the islands. Although playfully erotic and attuned to the tastes of their audiences, the dancers were careful to perform hapa haole hula in a tasteful manner. Betty insisted, "We didn't do hootch cootch. We did good Hawaiian dance. [They] might be hapa haole, but they were modest dance[s]."[95] Dancers were aware of the earlier censorious treatment of hula and viewed their hula as a form of acting or storytelling.

Twentieth-century commercial hula repertoire represented a shift from fin de siècle tours, when the hula 'āla'apapa (sacred hula performed with double gourd) and hula 'ōlapa (nonsacred hula that often honored ali'i) were performed with Hawaiian chant and instrumentation in dime-museum and vaudeville programs in the United States. However, in mid-century American showrooms, the hula 'ōlapa repertoire was limited to only a few mele, and sometimes performed with Western string instruments and only accented with 'ulī'ulī (gourd rattles) and pū'ili (bamboo rattles) for exotic effect.[96] The dancers with formal hula training likely had some knowledge of sacred dances, but did not do hula 'āla'apapa or hula pahu in tourist venues.

As revealed in a rare film of the Aloha Maids in 1938, dramatic corporeal movements became most important to illustrate the sung narrative, whether in English or Hawaiian.[97] In hapa haole mele like "Across the Sea," the dancers illustrated concepts in an indexical fashion; for example, the phrases "bidding me" and "come back" corresponded to a hand motion pointed at their chests and hands extending palm up at a forty-five-degree angle, respectively. In faster tempo songs, the women executed flowing lower-body movements that made them appear to "glide," rather than step, across the stage. An observer of hula today might be surprised to see how the dancers almost twisted their wrists when moving their hands during a basic vamp between verses, quite unlike the style of flatter, stiller hands preferred by many hula performers at present.

Dancing for American audiences necessitated other alterations in costuming and theatricality. Performers could not obtain the requisite flora and plants to make their lei and skirts, so they improvised with paper, oilcloth, and cellophane. Betty Makia explained, "We did authentic hula, but our skirts were Americanized. . . . In the beginning we wore ti leaf, but it was so expensive. Our [oilcloth] plastic skirts were so heavy, it hangs like leather. But it was nice."[98] Ray Kinney further insisted his dancers adhere to a meticulous dress code that emphasized femininity and glamour. They had to be well groomed and grow their hair long enough to curl. On stage, they were required to wear mascara and stage makeup.[99]

These changes favoring dramatic narration and theatricality over chanted or sung poetry were not only the result of tourist preferences, but because hula practitioners did not have the same degree of training in territorial Hawai'i. The transmission of hula had become more difficult to sustain in the Americanizing colony. In the monarchical period, in areas away from missionary influence, dancers had ritually graduated from pā hula (hula academies) as ho'opa'a (chanters) or 'ōlapa (dancers) and learned sacred and semisacred genres of hula and poetic chants. Some women in the circuits of the 1930s and 1940s—such as Pualani Mossman, Napua Woodd, Elinore Leilehua Becker, and Leilani Iaea—were accomplished dancers in the islands; others, such as Tutasi Wilson and Momi Kai, had had little or no dance training before being recruited for American tours and had to learn quickly from more advanced dancers.[100] Having studied to become a social worker in college, Tutasi knew almost no hula when she was hired by Ray Kinney for the Hawaiian Room line in

1939. But he told her, "Don't worry, even if you don't know how to dance. Napua will teach you."[101] The professional, social, and religious structure of dance apprenticeship had been disrupted by U.S. colonization, though its reward structure expanded through tourist commodification.

Imagined Intimacy

The Hawaiian rooms imprinted an indelible image of Hawai'i, a sunny paradise populated by "little brown gals" and jovial men. Appealing to the taste and imagination of mostly haole American audiences, male and female entertainers alike were required to perform a particular kind of Hawaiianness on stage: being docile, ever welcoming, and ever desirable. But Hawaiianness was signified primarily through the spectacle of women's eroticized bodies. Male musicians were fully clothed in white suits in the far background, while hula dancers in the front row wore bikini tops, glittering skirts, and flowers in their hair.

Hula and the young women who performed this dance served as metonyms for the Hawaiian Islands, and they made the territory intelligible to Americans. Spectators could imagine themselves transported to the islands by watching women dance to songs such as "Across the Sea" that whispered, "See the surf, comes rolling ever onwards, meets the land and melts in creamy foam."[102] Even figured as the uniting of "surf" and "land," the encounter between (male) visitor and (female) islander was represented as a sexual coupling. The islands were not so subtly coded as sexually submissive spaces, waiting to be exploited and conquered.

Live performances were intimate encounters between Hawaiian performers and American audiences, although the intimacy I refer to was not literal, but imagined. Consuming these shows, Americans came to possess Hawai'i in their dreams, imagining Hawai'i and the United States as inseparable and mutually dependent. The vast majority of Americans would never visit the islands directly, yet a fervent vision of Hawai'i—as America's exquisite escape and untouched playground—came into being through these intimate encounters. This Hawai'i was not so much an antithesis of America, but a better version of it—a respite from the harshness of urban life and industrial capitalism, yet not too foreign and different. By association with their tropical colony, Americans could believe they belonged to an optimistic, playful, and tolerant nation. This intimacy was realized best via floorshows. Women delivered an affect that radio programs, news photographs, or even movies could not produce, though this media complemented the visceral associations produced in the live shows.[103] Showrooms like the Lexington's Hawaiian Room and others around the country were crucial instruments in the circulation of Hawai'i in the American cultural imagination before World War II.

Fantasies of Hawai'i did not remain within the shows, due to mass communication, travel, and consumer markets. These showrooms were based in hotels in cities like Chicago (Hotel Roosevelt), San Francisco (St. Francis Hotel), and New Orleans (Broadmoor Hotel). As out-of-town visitors saw these shows and Hawaiians themselves circulated throughout the states, interest in the colony and Hawaiianness spread across the country. The imagined intimacy between Hawai'i and the United States continued to be amplified after spectators returned home. Americans immersed themselves in Hawaiianness by buying ukuleles, Hawaiian sheet music, and grass skirts. Syndicated newspaper columns on New York entertainment further transported hula dancers into nonmetropolitan markets. The column "Man about Manhattan," for instance, frequently rhapsodized about Hawaiian Room dancers until World War II; it was printed daily in hundreds of national and regional newspapers. Hawai'i became a larger popular cultural phenomenon, and concepts like "aloha" and the "luau" entered the American vernacular.[104]

As images and projections of Hawai'i circulated in the American cultural imagination, they produced very real material effects: the islands became feminized spaces for U.S. commercial and military domination. The dreams produced by Hawaiian floorshows helped to enable the American tourist and military penetration of Hawai'i during and after World War II. As "flesh and blood representatives" of Hawai'i, performers in the continental United States promoted Hawai'i's tourist industry in a way no advertising company could have afforded.[105] By 1938, tourists arriving in Hawai'i reached a high of 23,043, and the number continued to climb until the bombing of Pearl Harbor in 1941.[106]

U.S. militarism in the islands developed in tandem with tourism. Hawai'i's economy was increasingly supported by U.S. defense spending; between 1930 and 1940, the armed forces population had increased 61 percent from 16,291 to 26,233, and comprised over 15 percent of all employed adults.[107] Strategically positioned between the United States and Asia, the Hawaiian Islands deployed millions of American soldiers to the Pacific theater after the Pearl Harbor bombing.

In another "Pacific theater" that stretched across the U.S. continent, hula dancers like Pualani Mossman familiarized Americans with the Pacific outpost that would become the flashpoint of the war. Hawai'i was to provide safe shores and fortified military bases for the United States throughout World War II and the Cold War. Most Americans did not know about specifics of the American military presence in Hawai'i and the Pacific, but they did not need to know: the projection of Hawaiian culture and its women stood in for the entire region.

A Kiss from a Dancer

The symbolic and political value of hula in the postwar period, while not readily quantifiable, cannot be overestimated. As ambassadors of aloha on the continent, hula dancers promoted Hawai'i as a friendly American outpost in the Pacific. Their movements were critical for the colonial territory to become a state. Territorial delegates had pitched statehood bills to Congress repeatedly since 1919, and several congressional committees had held public hearings in the islands since 1935.[108]

However, even after Hawai'i had proved its military necessity during World War II, U.S. senators from Southern states argued that the island population was far too racially unassimilable, echoing objections issued during annexation debates in 1898. Recognizing that statehood would require winning the hearts and minds of ordinary and influential American citizens, the Hawaii Statehood Commission set up offices in Honolulu and Washington, D.C., and launched a publicity blitz after the war.[109] One of the weapons in its public relations campaign was the iconic hula dancer, already symbolically resonant as the embodiment of the islands. As the commission apprised Congress about the territory, Hawai'i's virtues were amplified through the bodies of its dancers.

The U.S. House of Representatives passed a statehood bill, House Resolution (HR) 49, in the spring of 1947 and forwarded it to the U.S. Senate. Hoping that the Senate would pass HR 49 and make Hawai'i the forty-ninth state, the commission premiered a short documentary film called *The 49th State*, in Washington, D.C., that had been produced as part of the documentary series "This Is America."[110] The travelogue film showcased the people, industries, and culture of the islands, but, more importantly, the commission invited a live Hawaiian to do some of this important work in person. Pualani Mossman, a strong advocate for statehood, traveled to Washington and danced hula before a cocktail-hour audience that included the secretary of the interior and other influential congressmen and senators (see figures 42 and 43). The commissioners aimed to demonstrate that Hawai'i, like Pualani, was exotic but not too foreign, and worthy of national inclusion.

Fig. 42 Pualani Mossman dancing at *The 49th State* statehood promotion, Washington, D.C., 1947. COURTESY OF HAWAI'I STATE ARCHIVES.

Fig. 43 Pualani Mossman gives a flower lei to Julius A. King, U.S. secretary of the interior, at a statehood event in Washington, D.C., 1947. Hawai'i's congressional delegate Joseph R. Farrington looks on at left.
COURTESY OF HAWAI'I STATE ARCHIVES.

Despite Pualani's charms, the bill failed to make it out of the Senate in 1947. But the issue of statehood remained visible in the halls of Congress and the popular press throughout the 1950s. Writers editorialized about Hawaiian statehood using hula dancers, as in this endorsement: "Hip-swinging girls swishing their sarongs, nostalgic music with the sound of Waikiki and Diamond Head, Island dances. . . . If that's what the Islands are like, we'll vote for statehood right now."[111] While women were interpellated into an imperial state-building project, they saw themselves making a contribution to the statehood effort that was as significant as that of politicians. Tutasi Wilson proudly said of entertainers in her generation, "We really sold Hawai'i."[112] Once considered a vulgar practice that threatened the integration of the islands, hula represented the islands on the political stage as a legitimate and valuable cultural tradition.

Many Hawaiians opposed this final political consolidation under the United States, which took on various expressions. Hawaiian tour bus drivers, for instance, exposed tourists to their antistatehood views, while the predominantly Hawaiian island of Ni'ihau voted against statehood in the plebiscite held in 1959.[113] In particular, working-class Asians in the islands stood to benefit from American statehood. The high-ranking ali'i Alice Kamokila Campbell opposed statehood on the grounds that it would hasten Americanization and grant political clout to Japanese immigrants and their descendants in Hawai'i. Hawaiian and islander performers of this generation appear to have supported statehood, at least publicly, because it offered elected representation at the state and national level.

After several years of procedural stalling in Congress, Hawai'i had its best chance for statehood in 1959, after Alaska was made a state the year prior. While it looked like the bill was assured of passing, one of the last obstacles was a House rules committee, where the bill had stalled. The territorial delegate from Hawai'i, Jack Burns, struck a bargain with the obstinate U.S. representative from Virginia, Howard "Judge" Smith, who controlled the committee. If Smith authorized a vote in the House, Burns promised him he would arrange to have a "beautiful . . . Hawaiian girl" give Smith a kiss and a flower lei. The hula dancer Kanoelani O'Connor, now living in Virginia, supported statehood and agreed to help Burns. She waited for three days with a fresh lei. When she got the call from Burns, she changed into a sarong and delivered Burns's gift. Kanoelani recalled, "He [Smith] was just delighted with his lei and a kiss."[114] Two days later, the House passed the statehood bill, making Hawai'i the fiftieth state.

While we can only speculate about the direct effect of a young woman's kiss on the passage of this bill, hula dancers like Kanoelani had brokered the larger project of state incorporation over several decades, a process that relied on the imagined sexual rapport between islander women and American men. As they circulated in congressional offices and nightclubs, hula dancers proved their usefulness in establishing an imagined intimacy between the territory and the United States. Their hula performances offered the United States a fantasy—a fantasy of intimate possession—and eventually helped to produce the fiftieth star in the American flag.

Erasing Asians

Besides binding Hawai'i to the United States, Hawaiians performing in the Pacific theater accomplished another critical function: they erased Asians from the territory. The hula circuits of Hawaiians and islanders in the United States performed the symbolic act of cleansing the territory of Asians. The Asian population of Hawai'i posed a chronic problem for the haole territorial government and the U.S. nation-state. Japanese were the largest single segment of Hawai'i's population in 1930, almost 38 percent, or 140,000 people.[115] Although the haole oligarchy in Hawai'i required Asian labor, it expressed an intense fear of being outnumbered by Asians. The alleged influence of "Orientals" in the territory damaged Hawai'i's chances for statehood and Americanization in the 1930s. Public statehood hearings in Hawai'i in 1935 concentrated on the unproven loyalty of Japanese in the territory and on their threat to U.S. national security.[116]

Furthermore, there were fears that "Oriental races" would contaminate the blood of Caucasians and Polynesians in the islands. An editor of *Paradise of the Pacific* wrote in 1924: "The Oriental races are practically all of small stature, slight physique, yellow or brown color and, in the case of the Japanese, . . . flat features, protruding teeth and short legs. We have a right to ask ourselves whether we want to incorporate such characteristics into the American body."[117] This argument about the unsuitability of Asians for American citizenship was far from unique. Asians were treated as alien and unassimilable to the U.S. national body, as demonstrated by restrictive immigration acts in 1882, 1917, 1924, and 1934 and the incarceration of 120,000 Japanese Americans on the continent and in Hawai'i during World War II. During the 1930s, the United States had begun mobilizing for a possible armed conflict with Japan. The large presence of alien—possibly enemy—Japanese in Hawai'i also had to be contained.

The Hawaiian shows domesticated Hawai'i for the approaching war by removing traces of this alien presence. On the continent, Hawai'i was packaged and presented as wholly Hawaiian, not Asian. Only Hawaiian songs were performed; no references were made to the existence of large Japanese, Chinese, and Filipino communities in Hawai'i. Listening to songs that referenced Hawaiian people, landscapes, and history, an observer would get the impression that only Native Hawaiians made their homes in Hawai'i. Yet some performers from the islands were part-Japanese, part-Chinese, or Filipino. The part-Asian or Asian dancers from Hawai'i sometimes did not reveal their Asian backgrounds to the public and were legible only as "Hawaiian," although backstage the performers knew everyone's ethnic backgrounds. Within the Hawaiian and islander entertainment community on the continent, the Japanese from the islands do not appear to have received differential treatment. Ray Kinney's troupe, for example, took pride in entertaining local Japanese men from the islands who were serving in the U.S. Army's segregated Japanese American 442nd Regimented Combat Team during World War II.[118]

Japanese hula performers from Hawai'i had to accommodate their identities in more strategic and oblique ways during the war. The hula dancer Momi Kai, who was haole and Japanese, was profiled in a New York newspaper as "a native Hawaiian now living in Flushing."[119] After the bombing of Pearl Harbor, she did not talk about her Japanese background and even participated in a "Beat-the-Jap" hula campaign to purchase a bomb. Choosing to perform publicly as a Hawaiian "hula girl," Momi Kai escaped detection as a Japanese woman (see figure 44). This performance was convincing for Americans; she was described as "the perfect Polynesian type . . . with pearl-white teeth and shoulder-length black hair." The caption below her photograph read: "Her dances help raise funds to avenge native isles." By passing as Hawaiian, at least via their public performances, Asian and part-Asian dancers escaped scrutiny and gained mobility in the continental United States. Being Hawaiian was relatively benign, while being Japanese or looking Japanese during the war could mean risking incarceration and racist castigation.

Another part-Japanese hula dancer made the decision to claim her name and racialized identity, though it was much easier to do so after the war. The hula dancer Gloria Manu Kanemura, of Hawaiian, haole, and Japanese descent, was a model who won several beauty contests in Honolulu in the late 1940s (see figure 45). While a student at the University of Hawai'i, she was encouraged to change her last name and pass as either part-haole or Hawaiian, rather than Japanese. Manu revealed:

Fig. 44 Hula dancers at the Hawaiian Room, Hotel Lexington. Left to right: Betty Puanani Makia, Tutasi Wilson, Keokeokalae Hughes, Momi Kai, Caroline Dizon, unknown. COURTESY OF MAKIA FAMILY.

"When the student body chose me to represent them [as Cosmopolitan queen], they told me, 'Why don't you change your [last] name?' It was because the yearbook was going [to be sent] to the mainland. When I heard that, I became more stubborn. My being a model made [other] Japanese feel good."[120]

Manu Kanemura refused to change her name. When she relocated to the U.S. continent to dance at the Hotel Lexington in 1950, she continued to retain her Japanese surname. Manu reported having "no problems up there," but perhaps this was because she had arrived nearly a decade after Pearl Harbor and was promoted solely by her Hawaiian moniker "Manu."

The erasure of Asians through Hawaiian shows was also critical for Hawai'i's tourist industry, which promoted Hawai'i as part of Polynesia. Hawai'i could not be too "Japanized," "Filipino," or "Chinese," if American tourists were to visit. The marketing of Hawai'i depended on an image of islands populated primarily by Hawaiians and sustained by Hawaiian practices, although Hawaiians and part-Hawaiians made up less than 15 percent of Hawai'i's population in 1930.[121] In order for Hawai'i to become the "Paradise of the Pacific," Asians had to be absent from the pic-

Fig. 45 Gloria Manu Kanemura, ca. 1970. COURTESY OF GLORIA
MANU KANEMURA BENTLEY.

ture. Indeed, an imagined intimacy was generated between Americans and those perceived as "Hawaiians," not between Americans and Asians. The circulation of indigenous Hawaiian culture in the United States—writ large as all of Hawai'i—facilitated this symbolic removal.

Behind the Curtain

Not long after her arrival in New York in 1937, dancer Napua Woodd rented an apartment that she decorated with Hawaiian dolls, lei, and kapa. She sent her father a photograph of her new apartment, noting proudly: "Notice everything in Hawaiian. Everybody open[s] their eyes when they enter my apartment because of my rare decorations. No one else has a taste of interior decoration like I have here. You know how I always liked a nicely furnished house. Well I got it."[122]

Although Americans made sense of their colony in the Pacific through live and mediated performances, Hawaiians like Napua developed their own understandings of the United States. The dancers may have been interpellated into an imperial nexus of desire, but they continued to assert their own counter-colonial desires for erotic fulfillment, fame, and financial independence. Beyond their public roles as "Cinderellas" or "hula queens," these women struggled to hold on to their own aspirations within imperial hula circuits.

Whether Hawaiian and American men recruited islander women on behalf of Hollywood studios and American nightclubs or whether other dancers asked them to join the show, they made conscious choices to leave Hawai'i and remain on the continent. They approached their departure with trepidation, but often as an adventure and opportunity. For many, hula became the means to fulfill material, educational, and professional aspirations unattainable in territorial Hawai'i. As Kini Kapahu had left Hawai'i with a dream of seeing the United States in 1892, many Hawaiian women acted on similar desires to explore a wider world, earn a living, and support their families. These dancers hailed from diverse class backgrounds, but shared an independent spirit. Nearly fifty years had passed since Kini Kapahu embarked on North American vaudeville tours, but it remained unusual for unmarried women from the islands to travel and live unaccompanied in the 1930s (see figure 46).

Newspaper reports were careful to portray the young women as genteel maidens, but the dancers flouted gendered conventions of respectability. Mary Jane Hair was an orphan raised by nuns and educated at Sacred Hearts Girls' School in Honolulu. Wanting to reinvent herself, she boldly planned an escape out of Hawai'i as an entertainer, though she had no hula experience. She worked her way across the continent into a headlining role as the leading lady "Momi Kai" at the Hawaiian Room. Meymo Ululani Holt was another rebel, quite out of step with her prominent, straitlaced Hawaiian family. Standing barely five feet tall, "she had a vocabulary that could make sailors blush," said her daughter Sherilyn Rankin Iona.[123] In 1936, at the age of twenty-one, Meymo bore Sherilyn out of wedlock. The baby was hānai (adopted Hawaiian-style) by her older sister, and the following year Meymo left for New York to become a solo dancer. Meymo was not the only dancer to have had an illegitimate child; at least three other dancers were single or divorced mothers who were separated from their children during their professional dance careers.

Fig. 46 Mapuana Mossman Bishaw and Jennie Napua Woodd leaving Hawai'i, ca. 1938. COURTESY OF GILLIOM FAMILY.

Napua Woodd and Betty Makia each had a young son whom they left behind with relatives in Hawai'i.

Others happened to fall into professional hula by a series of accidents or coincidences. Even Leilehua Becker, who hailed from a Hawaiian family of dancers, did not intend to perform hula professionally and left Hawai'i wanting to become a swing and jazz singer. Meymo Ululani Holt had dreams of her own beyond hula. An aspiring actor and writer, she saw herself more as a dramatic actress than a hula dancer. She took classes at Columbia University while in New York City and spent her spare time writing a musical comedy called "Paradise Preferred." A graduate of the University of Hawai'i in 1947, Filipina American Caroline Dizon also worked toward a master's degree at New York University while dancing on the Lexington hula line.[124] Tutasi Wilson left the islands and her prominent Samoan family to work in Hollywood before being hired by Ray Kinney. Tutasi had graduated from Kamehameha Schools, a private academy for Hawaiians, and was studying to become a social worker when she left Honolulu to work in Hollywood and Polynesian entertainment.

Before leaving for New York in 1938, Betty Makia (née Betty Puanani Kalolo Foo) worked at a pineapple cannery in Hawai'i during the day. At night, she served drinks at a bar and grill in the disreputable Hotel Street section of downtown Honolulu to support herself and her family. As Betty described, a Hawaiian band played music at the grill on the weekends and she became "smitten" with one of the musicians, a steel guitar and bass player named Sam Kamuela Makia Chung.[125] Sam, like Betty, was of Chinese and Hawaiian descent. Sam and Betty married, and not long after, Sam signed a contract with the Lexington's Hawaiian Room as part of Ray Kinney's group (see figures 47 and 48).[126] Betty decided to join her husband in Manhattan. Twenty-five years old at the time, she was a "band wife" with no intention of becoming an entertainer herself. However, she later joined the Hawaiian Room as a hula dancer and toured the United States during and after the war.

The experiences and backstage lives of these entertainers destabilize the spectacle of Hawaiianness performed under the spotlight. The women's private lives often belied their alluring on-stage personae. As Manu Kanemura recalled, when she joined the Lexington hula line as a dancer in 1951, all but ten or fifteen dollars of her salary went to pay for her apartment and union dues. Manu arrived in New York City for the first time during the cool fall. "I had nothing when I went up there . . . no warm clothes. How was I [going] to manage?" She worked at Gimbel's department store during the day to earn extra cash. To keep warm, she also wore pajamas under her pants when going to work.[127]

Leilehua "Lei" Becker made sixty-five dollars a week when she first was hired as a chorus girl in the Lexington line in 1950.[128] She was thrilled because she had been collecting unemployment for six months following a tour as a comedic hula dancer with Hawaiian bandleader Hal Aloma. But she, too, had a difficult time making ends meet and budgeting her weekly salary. She recalled, "I wore my salary on my back, spent it on furniture or clothes. I didn't save any money."[129] Whether they arrived in the 1930s or 1950s, most of the Aloha Maids had to take on side jobs to supplement their salaries.[130]

Several dancers suffered through personal sorrows like divorce and separation from their children. Lei Becker divorced her haole American

Fig. 47 Betty
Puanani Makia.
COURTESY OF
AKAU FAMILY.

Fig. 48 Sam
Kamuela Makia.
COURTESY OF
MAKIA FAMILY.

husband, who then took custody of their baby. Her ex-husband granted her visitation only once every other week. Lei remembers that during her headlining career at the Hawaiian Room, she wept whenever she saw a child who was her son's age. Her very public career at the Lexington was punctuated by the private pain of missing her young child.

In the long run, male musicians like Ray Kinney fared much better than young female hula dancers. Hawaiian men enjoyed longer careers that stretched until their sixties or seventies, while the "island girls" usually had a shelf life of several years.[131] Most of the women had never left the islands before and arrived from Hawai'i under six-month to year-long contracts. As contract laborers subject to the whims of the market, hula dancers were most popular as young adults. Gendered occupational hierarchies persisted in the workplace as Hawaiian men served as agents, middlemen, and occasional employers for women, as they had since the turn of the century. When bandleaders like Ray Kinney, Lani McIntire, and Hal Aloma were not performing at showrooms, they hired women directly for their own touring troupes. Some men received a cut of the women's pay. The father of Lexington hula dancer Napua Woodd addressed some of these charges in an interview: "Under the guidance of Mr. and Mrs. Kinney, I know that they [Napua and her sister Leimomi] are in good hands. Ray has never taken advantage of them financially, as some backbiters in town may hint. He has always insisted that the family study the girls' contracts before they are signed and has been perfectly wonderful to everyone."[132]

However, Napua herself privately grumbled that Ray was parsimonious with her salary.[133] In 1948, the American Guild of Variety Artists (AGVA), the performers' union to which dancers belonged, filed claims against Ray Kinney on behalf of two Hawaiian women he had hired for a United Service Organization (USO) tour. Ray was charged with withholding wages of $540 for six months. It is unclear whether this suit was found to be valid, but the AGVA successfully collected a second suit for $571 from Ray Kinney.[134] The dancers likely did not see themselves as free agents while working under bandleaders.

With some basic union protections like contracts and industry-wide minimum salaries, the women were far better off than the hula dancer Annie Grube, who was crippled when her manager forced her to dive off a bridge in Indiana in 1895 (see chapter 2). Yet as contracted workers, they had no medical insurance or disability benefits. Tutasi Wilson described how she was injured on the job: "When I was working for the Hawaiian

Room, there was no insurance for the girls. I got hurt; I stepped on glass and had to go to the hospital." The cut became infected and the six-week-long convalescence liquidated her savings. Tutasi later successfully fought for insurance; after that, the dancers qualified for health insurance.[135]

By the 1950s, Hawaiian women like Lei Becker and Manu Kanemura had assumed more control over their employment as "leading ladies" and were often comanaging and producing floorshows with male orchestra leaders. They had been hired by a talent agent from the General Artists Corporation who booked them for the Hawaiian Room.[136] They may have garnered slightly higher salaries and more responsibility, but they were still constrained by talent agents, upper management, and hotel owners. Nor were they valued as highly as male Hawaiian musicians and bandleaders.

After being promoted to a leading lady who sang and danced solo, Lei Becker received a hefty pay raise from $75 to $125 a week (see figure 49). Though at first she "loved the job" and "new career as a 'Hawaiian,'" being a manager was onerous and financially draining. She recounted:

[I was] always using my own money to help pay for some of the artificial flowers the show needed for the chorus. Whenever I wanted to change the show I had a battle with the powers that be. Then if they gave in, I was only allowed to spend the total of $300 for costumes . . . for the whole show! I always had to pay for my own costumes and flowers. That was understood. . . . Plus the fact that I was only allowed one, I repeat, just one full rehearsal with the band before opening a new show. I choreographed all the dances and taught the dances to the girls and the songs to the musicians in the band. Plus emceeing the show and singing. The only thing I didn't have to do was the comedy dances (and that would've been my favorite part) so it was back to being a singer and dancer who danced the solo hulas.[137]

In addition to the responsibility of producing the nightly show, Lei also had the headache of designing the costumes and hiring and firing chorus girls. Lei wanted to vary the show, but she was tightly controlled by management. She said, "I couldn't even change the songs or anything. The show stayed the same for an entire year."[138] She described feeling "bored to death" and creatively stifled during her two and a half years there.[139] Lei decided to quit the Hawaiian Room in 1953, changed her stage name to Paula Martin, and began singing with the Claude Thornhill Orchestra, a popular swing band.

Fig. 49 Leilehua Becker, 1952–53. COURTESY OF LEILEHUA BECKER FURTADO.

As multitalented as many women were, they were not unique in the eyes of American talent agents and management who treated them as interchangeable. When Momi Kai abruptly took a vacation from the Hawaiian Room, an agent hired Lei to replace her. When Momi returned two weeks later, she was out of a job. A recalcitrant hula dancer could be jettisoned in favor of another. The dancers had little negotiating room; managers did not allow dancers to behave as divas, no matter how popular. Lei replaced Momi as the newest "Cinderella" of New York's East Side, and the Hotel Lexington hung a sign outside reading "Leilehua Revue."

Believable Hawaiians

While Americans were able to indulge in a fantasy of Hawai'i, Hawaiian entertainers found themselves coping with embodied realities as racial subordinates in the United States. Many were treated as primitive savages off-stage and were conflated with other racially subjugated people.

Though they may have appeared to embrace the United States, Hawaiians could not forget that as a colonized people they did not merit equal status with whites. Philip J. Deloria has similarly described American Indian cultural actors as "co-existent but not equal" to whites.[140] Ray Kinney cut a dapper figure—he had been voted best-dressed bandleader in the United States by *Billboard*. Nevertheless, he and his family experienced the sting of American racism and segregation firsthand during their extensive travels across the continent.

Two of Ray's children, Rayner and Raylani, were still young when they accompanied their father and his troupe on tour. They did not perform with their father, but soon learned that they were racially ambiguous and objects of intense curiosity nonetheless. Rayner Kinney said, "[People from the mainland] thought we [Hawaiians] were uncivilized, savage. They would ask us questions like 'Did you drive across to get here? Do you live in grass huts? How do you get around there?'" He and his sister would retort, "We get around by swinging from tree to tree."[141] Rayner recalled, "They thought I wasn't his [Ray's] child. They thought I was Mexican or [American] Indian. Because Raylani was haole-looking, they thought Dad had kidnapped her." During tours through the Jim Crow South, Hawaiians faced the worst treatment when they were confused with African Americans; on one occasion two darker-skinned dancers were told to leave a hotel.[142]

As a preemptive move against racist whites, the entertainers developed strategies to assert their Hawaiianness and humanize themselves. "We painted a Hawaiian coat of arms on our car in New York so people would know who we were," explained Rayner. This declaration of Hawaiian identity worked well enough during World War II. The Kinneys were stopped by police on 7 December 1941 and asked how their families on the islands were faring after the Pearl Harbor bombing.[143] Their cousin Hester "Teela" Holt, a hula dancer with Ray's group in the mid-1940s, described how haole Americans could not tell which dancers in the group were Hawaiian, because of their varying complexions. She explained, "Nana [Dawn Kinney, Ray's wife] always made us wear flowers in our hair so they could tell we were Hawaiian."[144]

Hawaiian dancers could be subjected to Jim Crow treatment for their darker skin, but could also be criticized for not being "brown" enough and were therefore judged as inauthentic Natives. White audiences dismissed the light-skinned hapa haole Lei Becker for not being legibly Hawaiian. They told Lei, "If we knew you were Hawaiian we would have watched you more."[145] Lei reflected, "I had hated the 'Who's the kid from Brooklyn in the middle' kind of remarks that were tossed at me in the Hawaiian Room. I had never been a 'believable Hawaiian.'"[146] Yet at the time Lei was performing in New York, she could boast the most distinguished hula pedigree of her peers. Part of the well-regarded Beamer-Desha 'ohana of Hawaiian composers, singers, and hula dancers, Lei began her hula training almost as soon as she could walk, under the tutelage of two maternal aunts.[147] Within commercial tourist spaces, a stereotypical phenotype—light brown skin, long brown hair—communicated authentic Hawaiian-ness to Americans at the expense of an individual's wider genealogical ties and kin-based knowledge.

Lei, who had never wanted to perform professionally as a "Hawaiian," realized in her youth that hula was the entertainment pipeline available to her as a Hawaiian woman. Yet despite her skilled enactment of hula repertoire, she was unable to conform to the visual markers of a "believable Hawaiian." The constant scrutiny of her authenticity made Lei want to "get away from the Hawaiian experience," and she left the Hawaiian Room.[148] The colonial production of hospitality demanded more than the embodied knowledge of an "authentic" Hawaiian; it required a brown-skinned body to perform these acts of deference and aloha.

Ironically, other racialized women hailing from Hawai'i and other U.S. colonial sites could often pass as Hawaiian more easily than dancers who were part haole and part Hawaiian. Filipinas and Latinas were known to be cast as Hawaiian dancers with Hawaiian stage names. One of Lei's and Betty's contemporaries at the Hawaiian Room, Caroline Dizon, for instance, was a Filipina American from Hawai'i and billed under the Hawaiian name "Kalani Pua."[149] Another dancer, Loma Duke, was hired by Lei Becker to replace her as leading lady. Loma was not Hawaiian, but a Cuban who had never been to Hawai'i.[150] Two American Indian sisters, Loretta and Dolores Ferris, joined Ray Kinney's wartime troupe when it passed through their hometown of Kalamazoo, Michigan. They learned to dance hula, took on Hawaiian names, and became known professionally as "Kamoa" and "Lulika," respectively (see figure 40).[151]

Treated as outsiders and second-class colonial subjects, Hawaiians developed a racialized understanding of their difference on the continent. They could see themselves as others saw them, or to use W. E. B. Du Bois's famous phrase, they developed a "double-consciousness."[152] Even prior to their travels, they had been profoundly shaped by the American takeover of their homeland and its transformation into a tourist colony. By law and practice, English became the official language of instruction in all public and private schools in 1896, displacing ʻōlelo Hawaiʻi (Hawaiian language). Some schoolteachers punished Hawaiian children for speaking in their native tongue.[153] Hula itself was discouraged in certain island quarters as late as the 1940s, despite its cautious reemergence. Lei Becker attended Kamehameha Schools, a private school for Hawaiians, where students were not allowed to perform the "standing hula." She left the school after three years, commenting, "The fact that the hula was thought of as a 'lewd' dance was ridiculous to me."[154]

Yet, at a time when Hawaiian practices were suppressed in public life in the islands, many entertainers in the 1930s, including Ray Kinney and Napua Woodd, spoke Hawaiian freely on the continent.[155] As a form of protest, Ray Kinney's mother refused to speak English after the U.S. overthrow of the Hawaiian monarchy in 1893, so Ray and his siblings grew up speaking fluent Hawaiian.[156] Ray spoke to his hula troupe largely in Hawaiian, especially when giving the dancers directions for their performances. The troupe played hapa haole, English-language music for white tourists, but when they got together as a family and community, they performed a variety of their favorite music, including hapa haole mele and Hawaiian-language mele from the nineteenth century. His children said, "Some people criticized Dad for being too haole in his song choices. But he had to. It was his profession, and he had to cater to people on the mainland. But when he was at home, he sang Hawaiian songs."[157]

Furthermore, the hula circuit fostered creative expression and experimentation, as entertainers were inspired to write and perform new works along their tours. The mele inoa (name song), exalting aliʻi or loved ones through chant and song, became a preferred poetic medium for diasporic entertainers. Ray Kinney composed mele inoa in honor of his daughters and wife—songs like "Ululani," "Leimana," and "Orchid from Hawaii." The musician Sam Makia wrote "Puanani" (Beautiful flower) for his wife, Betty Puanani. Napua Woodd also composed in Hawaiian; her mele pana (song honoring a locale) "Haleʻiwa Hula" remains well known, thanks to the popular recording of her granddaughter Amy Hānaialiʻi Gilliom in 1997.[158]

Dance, as performed by racially subjugated groups like Plains Indians and "black" Mardi Gras Indians in New Orleans, is not reducible to opposition to white entitlements or the reoccupation of territory, Joseph Roach argues. He writes, "They also danced to possess themselves again in the spirit of their ancestors, to possess again their memories, to possess again their communities. They danced to resist their reduction to the status of commodities. In other words, they danced—and still dance—to possess again a heritage that some people would rather see buried alive."[159] On the tourist circuit, Hawaiian dancers did not frame their performances as contestation, but expressed how they felt free to take pleasure in hula. As Teela Holt put it, "I enjoyed dancing. I was always next to Betty [Makia]."[160] Teela felt most comfortable dancing in the chorus line next to her friend, whom she called "mother" while on the continent. Tourist entertainment commodified Hawaiian music and bodies, but created counter-colonial spaces where Hawaiian performers claimed their genealogies and poetic and embodied practices.

Pacific Diasporas

James Clifford notes tensions between Native communities and diasporic formations, as Fourth World ties to land come into conflict with diasporic displacement. However, he observes that contemporary tribal life is both rooted and based on circuits of travel: "For in claiming both autochthony and a specific, transregional worldliness, new tribal forms bypass an opposition between rootedness and displacement."[161] Epeli Hauʻofa's expansive vision of Oceania as a "sea of islands" also insists on both the landedness and movement of Pacific peoples.[162] Indeed, Hawaiian entertainers were simultaneously rooted and displaced.

As it was lived by islander entertainers, diaspora did not lead to an abandonment of "homeland," but an expansive and flexible notion of home. Frequently on the move, entertainers took "home" along with them as they crisscrossed the upper forty-eight states. They formed multiple identifications as New Yorkers, Californians, and Hawaiians, for example, as New York, Florida, California, and other U.S. locales became sources of attachment and affection for Hawaiian entertainers. Continuing centuries-old networks of travel, trade, and migration that Hauʻofa names as critical to the vitality of the Pacific, these new voyagers made collective homes overseas.[163] "Home" encompassed multiple locations for Hawaiian entertainers, revealing the flexibility of a hula diaspora that stretched from the island of Manhattan to the islands of Hawaiʻi.

Expanding upon older and newer kin networks and affiliations, an intimate islander community of entertainers grew in and around New York City from the 1930s to the 1950s. Far away from Hawaiʻi, these performers had to learn how to navigate new terrains of racism and cope with quotidian problems like hailing taxicabs and keeping warm during winter. Although owned and managed by Americans, the Lexington's Hawaiian Room itself served as a central gathering scene for Hawaiians and islanders. They shaped the showroom into their home away from home. Backstage, the performers were free to "talk story," cry, laugh, and argue. Raylani Kinney maintained, "Backstage was home."[164] They could relax around people who ate the same food, spoke Hawaiian or pidgin (Hawai'i Creole), and together ward off the inevitable homesickness. Betty Makia described her connection to the room: "Hawaiian Room [was] like home . . . you know, the Eastern Outpost? It was really where you would meet the people from Hawai'i. And you get homesick but when you see someone from Hawai'i, you become Native again."[165]

Betty's use of "Eastern Outpost" offers a significant inversion of a colonial model that positions the colony as the periphery. She resituated the New York metropole at the far reaches—the "outpost"—of the empire. From her vantage point, the Hawaiian Islands rested squarely at the center of the U.S. imperialist map. The entertainers came and went, were sometimes on the road for six to eight months at a time, but remained anchored around centers such as New York and Hawai'i.

When I asked Betty whether she ever wanted to return to Hawai'i after living in New York for over sixty years, she declared her attachment to both locales: "I love New York! This is home to me. I've lived here all my life, mostly . . . Hawai'i is my first love because I was born there but I only spent twenty years there. I'm like a kama'aina in New York!"[166] In everyday parlance, kama'aina (literal translation, "child of the land") refers to someone born in the islands who has strong roots in Hawai'i, regardless of ethnicity or indigeneity. A "kama'aina in New York" suggests that although Hawaiians left Hawai'i for far-off places, they did not lose their relationship to Hawai'i's 'aina (land). Sustaining their connections to their ancestral homeland, they developed deep relationships to New York and other American cities, the 'aina they had chosen as home.[167]

Philip J. Deloria has theorized the phenomenon of "Indians in unexpected places"—the incongruity of American Indians within modern landscapes.[168] Just as American Indians have been treated as strangers to modernity, as Deloria has argued, Hawaiians could also find themselves scripted as a premodern people. Yet Hawaiians, like other Native peoples, refused to remain stuck in space and time. They popped up in many unexpected places and situations—in Manhattan apartments draped with kapa and New York hotel rooms where they strung lā'ī (ti leaf) skirts and flower lei (see figure 50). In one of my favorite images of colonial hybrid-

Fig. 50 Crafting lāʻī (ti leaf) hula skirts in New York City hotel room. Left to right: Lillian Leimomi Woodd, Jennie Napua Woodd, Pualani Mossman. COURTESY OF GILLIOM FAMILY.

ity, the Aloha Maids donned wool coats over their cellophane hula skirts and hopped into a Manhattan taxicab barefoot (see figure 32). After work, Hawaiians often headed to after-hours jams in midtown and Harlem that were highly racially mixed. The Hawaiian musicians jammed with the likes of Louis Prima, the Italian American singer and trumpeter, and the African American singer Ethel Waters, and then headed to another theater to play with swing bandleader Glenn Miller.[169] The performers produced a novel sense of island modernity during their continental circuits: simultaneously island-centered, cosmopolitan, and colonial.

Many dancers became seasoned itinerant entertainers. Betty Makia, Leinaala Kihoi, Nani Todd, and Teela Holt toured most of the continental United States by bus with Ray Kinney and other musicians during the war. Teela Holt and her cousin Meymo Ululani "Billye" Kinney were teenagers when they arrived in Rochester, New York, in 1944 and traveled continuously for almost four years through thirty-six states (see figures 51 and 52). The daily rhythm was such that the troupe packed a Greyhound bus to full capacity, drove, unpacked and set up for three shows, performed, packed up again, and set out for the next booking. They literally lived out of and in the bus, removing the back seat of the bus to accom-

Fig. 51 Teela Holt, ca. 1945. COURTESY OF AKAU FAMILY.

Fig. 52 Ray Kinney's children in New York City, ca. 1938. Left to right: Meymo Ululani "Billye" Kinney, unknown, Raylani Kinney, Rayner Kinney, unknown. COURTESY OF AKAU FAMILY.

modate a poker table.[170] Teela, who had never left home before, learned how to pack their hula skirts quickly in long silk stockings and protect lei in show business bags.

Ray Kinney's daughter, Raylani Nihoa Pilialoha Kinney, spent much of her childhood on the road as her father's "mascot." Living almost continuously in buses and hotels, she remembered her difficult adjustment when she returned to Hawai'i after the war: "I didn't know what it was like to live in a house. I didn't know how to make a bed" (see figures 53 and 54). She had also picked up a Southern accent. Betty and Sam Makia used New York City as their home base in the 1940s and 1950s, doing out-of-state gigs almost every week. Betty said, "I hated to go on the road but [we] had to" in order to make ends meet.[171]

Even if their immediate families were back in the islands, Hawaiian entertainers expanded their 'ohana to include those with whom they lived and worked in buses, apartments, and hotels. Decades later when describing their community, they relied on metaphors of family and kinship. This kinship-building in diasporic contexts is a compelling example of what J. Kēhaulani Kauanui argues are the inclusive genealogical and kinship practices of Kanaka Maoli, which rely on principles of common descent, rather than blood quantum.[172] Teela Holt recalled, "I called Sam and Betty 'mother' and 'father.' They were like family while we traveled, worked together." Said Tutasi Wilson, "We all knew each other in New York. So we saw each other every day. . . . We were one big family."[173] Not everyone was married or attached; single men and women had left home and were on their own, and others were divorced. Nevertheless, this diasporic community formed gendered contours around relationships of feeding, childcare, and sisterhood.

Many women considered themselves "closer than sisters" in a place where they had few other friends and family.[174] Betty Puanani Makia described herself as a "real kua'āina" (country bumpkin), lost in the big city when she arrived at New York City's Grand Central Station for the first time in 1938.[175] But she was quickly enfolded into a group of musicians' wives, led by Dawn Holt Kinney, who met up for lunch at the Hawaiian Room at noon. At night in one of their apartments, the women would knit, crochet, and pass the time until their husbands finished work at 2 AM.[176] These friendships were further cemented because most of them had had to leave children behind in the islands.[177]

They also helped to raise children born on the continent. Young children never wanted for "calabash" aunties and uncles—the affectionate

Fig. 53 Rayner Kinney and Betty Makia in front of USO bus, ca. 1945.
COURTESY OF AKAU FAMILY.

Fig. 54 USO bus, ca. 1945. Left to right: Kamoa Ferris, Dawn Kinney, Ray Kinney.
Raylani Kinney peers out of windshield. COURTESY OF AKAU FAMILY.

island term for fictive kin—to change diapers, babysit, and take them for walks. Betty Makia went back to work as a hula dancer when her son Spike was three months old. The mother of the dancer Mealii Horio lived in the same building and took care of Spike while his parents worked. Kahala McIntire, the bandleader Lani McIntire's younger sister, was fifteen when she stowed away to come to the continent as a dancer. Still underage, Kahala stayed with Tutasi Wilson for over two years as she danced.[178] Tutasi became very protective of Kahala, describing her as "like my daughter."

The island ethos of mutual care and generosity became key to the performers' survival. They practiced Hawaiian hospitality in their everyday relations, though it was extracted from them in tourist performances. Entertainers knew they would find the door to Betty and Sam Makia's apartment on the East Side of Manhattan open to them. Within walking distance from the hotel, their apartment was located on the ground floor of the building, where several dancers also lived. The apartments in the East Side building were affordable because the Third Avenue elevated train ran right next to the apartment building every ten minutes. Several other hula dancers, including Lei Becker, lived in the walk-up building and would pop by to and from work and on their days off. The Makias became family for Kulani Purdy while he was in New York City; he had left Hawai'i at the age of eighteen to join the U.S. Army.[179]

Frequently homesick, their thoughts turned toward the most elemental component of home—Hawaiian food. Said Betty about New York: "There was this place that used to sell Hawaiian products and they sold poi in the jar. It was on Lexington [Avenue], run by [a] haole man. And we used to buy all our products there, but it was all in cans, wasn't so good. So we learned to eat flour poi. And . . . we bought fish and crab. But I really miss the food from the islands and my family."[180] An earlier generation of Hawaiians—part of an earlier settlement of vaudeville performers and stevedores—taught Betty and her friends how to ferment wheat flour to make a version of poi (Hawaiian staple of cooked taro corms).[181] For Hawaiians, the preparation and sharing of food cemented the entertainment community, as they had at fin de siècle fairs in Omaha and Buffalo. They had no taro patches or fishing ponds on the East Coast, but they insisted on feeding one another. Raylani Kinney, who toured with her parents from the ages of four to fifteen, detailed how the troupe improvised lū'au in the 1930s and '40s: "We shipped poi up to the mainland when we could. We also made laulau with fresh spinach [instead of lū'au leaves] and pork, and inamona [roasted kukui nuts] with peanut butter."[182] When Leonard "Spike" Kamuela Makia had his first birthday in 1951, his parents, Sam and Betty, and his Hawaiian Room family threw him a first-birthday lūʻau in the best Hawaiian tradition.[183]

In the early 1940s, an informal Polynesian network also formed around the home of Tutasi Wilson. Born in Samoa and raised in Honolulu, Tutasi was Samoan and haole. As a hula dancer at the Hotel Lexington from 1940 to 1953, Tutasi furnished a Polynesian-style penthouse a few doors down from the hotel, decorating it with kapa and Samoan and Hawaiian artifacts. Tutasi opened her "Polynesian Penthouse," as it became known, to aspiring entertainers and other islanders. She hosted many a struggling dancer and singer from Hawaiʻi, including the Hawaiian singers Kui Lee and Ed Kenney as they began their careers. She stocked Spam and corned beef—American canned foods so significant in the Pacific Islands that they have become central to exchange economies—in the pantry for them to eat. While keeping tabs on family and friends at home in Samoa and Hawaiʻi, Tutasi made it her mission to support other "island people" on the East Coast.

The "Hawaii House" on East Sixty-Ninth Street, between Madison and Fifth Avenue, no longer exists today, but in the 1940s islanders gathered at this renovated apartment. Former hula dancer Taneo (Taneo Kaai Blaneo), who went on to teach women to dance on Broadway, headed the Hawaii House with the help of Iwalani Helen Carino, a dancer at the Hotel Lexington.[184] The community hosted concerts, art exhibits, movies, and prepared Hawaiian lūʻau for its members. They also catered poi and laulau to students from Hawaiʻi living in university dorms. Betty Makia met one of her closest friends, Kulani Purdy, at the Hawaii House, where they would sit and "talk story."[185]

As kamaʻāina in American cities, the women became deeply involved in their new communities but never ceased missing Hawaiʻi and imagining themselves as part of the islands. Napua Woodd expressed her early hopes in a note to her father in the late 1930s: "Papa how are all my clothes are they still good keep them until I come home. I'll be there soon I know. To buy my own home too."[186] Napua was to make brief trips home to Hawaiʻi but did not return permanently until she had retired from show business in the 1970s, long after her father's death. Their emotional and kinship connections to Hawaiʻi remained intense; some women, such as Tutasi Wilson and Meymo Holt, chose to retire in Hawaiʻi after spending over half a century on the continent.

After the Show

Hula dancers did not stay more than a few years at the Hawaiian Room, often marrying or finding other entertainment or career paths. One of the original Aloha Maids, Pualani Mossman, danced for a year or two at the Lexington's Hawaiian Room and established a hula studio in the city with her sister Piilani. Pualani married the head accountant of the Hotel Lexington, a haole New Yorker named Randolph Avon, in 1939, had her first baby in 1940, and moved with her husband to Florida in 1950. There she taught hula and started a Polynesian party business with her husband.[187] Meymo Holt received her bachelor's degree in New York, married, and had a daughter. After settling in Michigan, Meymo worked in insurance and as an executive secretary for a manufacturer.[188] The nineteen-year-old Marjorie Leilani Iaea grew up in rural Makawao, Maui, and was known professionally as Leilani. Leilani was a hula queen contest contestant and appeared regularly at the Hawaiian Room after Ray Kinney recruited her. Like Meymo, she had other dreams; Leilani hoped her hula career would later allow her to attend business school on the East Coast and pursue other opportunities after school.[189] She eventually returned to Hawai'i, married, and had a family. When they left, other young women replaced them.

Te Moana Makolo was part of the last group of Lexington dancers in the early 1960s, becoming the lead choreographer of the show. She, too, had an itinerant career as a professional hula dancer. After the Hawaiian Room closed in 1966, she opened a Hawaiian room at the Emerson Hotel in Baltimore, Maryland, and continued on an overseas USO circuit with the performer Johnny Kaonohi Pineapple in the early 1970s.[190]

Of the original Aloha Maids, Napua Woodd had the longest career as a hula teacher and entertainer. She had entrusted a young son with her parents in Hawai'i in order to join the Hawaiian Room.[191] In addition to dancing in the floorshow of the Lexington's Hawaiian Room, she gave private hula lessons in New York (see figure 55). Her combined income allowed her to rent a room at the Hotel Lexington and another house in Queens. In New York Napua married her third husband, Lloyd Gilliom, a trumpet player from Indiana, and had another son. With her husband often on the road, she employed an African American woman to care for her infant son at their Lexington suite.[192] Napua eventually separated from her trumpet-player husband and raised her two sons as a single mother. A fiercely independent woman, she married six times in her lifetime, the last time in her sixties to a white American man over forty years her junior.

HAWAIIAN & POLYNESIAN Dance Instruction

Miss Napua
14 East 44th Street

Fig. 55 Advertisement for Napua Woodd's hula studio, ca. 1939. COURTESY OF GILLIOM FAMILY.

Napua opened up Hawaiian shows as a comic hula dancer in Cleveland, Reno, and Los Angeles. Her engagement at the Eldorado Club in Cleveland during World War II capitalized on her cachet as an Aloha Maid in New York City: "She's whirlwind of tropical magic/7 Years at Hotel Lexington/Star of 'HELLZAPOPPIN!'"[193] Napua eventually moved to Hollywood with her sons in the early 1950s. There she opened a hula studio, danced in nightclubs, and acted in movies (see figure 56). Working from six in the morning to midnight, Napua established herself as the social and professional center of a Polynesian diaspora in Southern California. She opened her family home to islander entertainers and arranged for them to be cast in movies and play in nightclubs. Napua also served as a director of the Polynesian-Hawaiian Society in Southern California. For the society's annual lū'au, Napua and her group provided entertainment

Fig. 56 Napua Woodd's publicity photograph, Los Angeles, ca. 1955.
COURTESY OF GILLIOM FAMILY.

and the community would kālua the pigs (a Hawaiian method of roasting food with hot rocks). She returned to Hawai'i in the 1970s and passed away on Maui at ninety years old in 2003.

Other dancers who came after Napua intended to continue their show business careers. Lei Becker, who toured with a swing band after leaving the Lexington, returned to Hawai'i in 1953, became a local television personality, and then joined a Polynesian revue in Las Vegas at thirty-nine years old. She eventually retired from show business and worked in advertising copywriting in Honolulu. Today she lives in Honolulu with her husband and occasionally entertains at senior citizens' homes. Another leading lady at the Lexington, Manu Kanemura, made appearances on national television shows in the mid-1950s, including Steve Allen's *The Tonight Show* and *The Bob Newhart Show*. After many years working in Polynesian entertainment in Florida, Nevada, and Hawaiʻi, Manu returned home and launched successful solo shows in Waikīkī from 1969 until 1973.[194]

Tutasi Wilson skillfully branched out from hula into business. After recovering from an illness, she decided to capitalize on her entertainment experience and cater Polynesian-themed parties. Polynesian Services, Inc., was born in 1953. Tutasi hired tour buses to bring corporations, unions, and trade associations to Atlantic City, New Jersey, for Hawaiian luaus. Once a year, Polynesian Services also threw a grand "South Seas Weekend." She hired Hawaiians and Samoans living in and around Washington, D.C., and along the Atlantic seaboard to provide living demonstrations of island customs in an abbreviated version of a Polynesian village. Hawaiian Room musicians and dancers like Sam Makia provided entertainment for the American guests.

Betty Makia was the sole Lexington dancer to live the rest of her days in Manhattan. Although her career as a professional dancer ended in the late 1950s, Betty found it difficult to remain in retirement. She worked in the catalog and mailing division of a department store for almost three decades. After a brief retirement and the death of her husband Sam in 1987, Betty returned to part-time work at a fast-food chicken restaurant in Greenwich Village. She retired at the age of eight-five and passed away in 2003.

Even after their careers as line dancers ended, Hawaiian and islander women formed entertainment and business networks between their homes in Florida, Hollywood, Las Vegas, Michigan, New York, and Honolulu. They introduced friends and family members to one another, facilitating social and professional relationships. Many stayed lifelong friends, keeping in touch until today. In 1989, former hula dancers and entertainers associated with the Hotel Lexington gathered in Honolulu for a reunion; more than seventy people attended. When Momi Kai (Mary Jane Hair) died in 1999, Tutasi Wilson organized a memorial service in Honolulu, gathering many women from the Lexington's Hawaiian Room.

Several dancers also reunited on the island of Hawaiʻi when orchestra leader Ray Kinney was inducted posthumously into the Hawaiian Music Foundation Hall of Fame in 2002. Betty Makia, Edna Kihoi Kwock (one of Kinney's "Cinderella" recruits), Teela Holt Hailele, Lulika Ferris Ampey, and Kamoa Ferris danced with Kinney at the Hotel Lexington and on a USO tour of military bases after World War II.[195] Kinney's daughter Raylani Kinney Akau, who resided in Waimea, Hawaiʻi, had invited all the "girls" to dance at the award ceremony.

Though elderly and residing on the continent, the former dancers flew from New York, Arizona, and California to participate. They chose one song to perform, "Little Brown Gal," an old favorite from their Lexington and military camp days. They had not performed together in over fifty years, but the choreography came back easily; as Betty said, "We did it so many times [then], you never forget." Although "Little Brown Gal" reproduces the eroticized trope of Hawaiian women whose only function is to please visitors, these women reconstituted it as their own. For them, the song was more than a tourist melody that satisfied American audiences—it reminded them of living as family on the road. Many of these hula dancers came to know each other as well as sisters while performing at over a hundred U.S. military bases on the hula circuit during and after the war.[196] Hundreds of volunteer and semiprofessional troupes like these formed a vital gendered labor force in military entertainment during and after World War II. The final chapter turns to these circuits in the Pacific theater and how the militarization of Hawai'i depended upon the aloha of hula dancers.

CHAPTER 5

THE TROUPES MEET THE TROOPS
Imperial Hospitality and Military Photography in the Pacific Theater

The Hawaiian bandleader at the Hotel Lexington, Ray Kinney, traveled to the island of Maui in 1940 to recruit new hula dancers. There he found adult dancers and a group of young children that became known affectionately as "Ray's Babies" (see figure 57). These girls performed with Kinney in Honolulu and were preparing to join his troupe in New York City, but were interrupted by the outbreak of World War II.[1] Instead, the group took on the task of entertaining U.S. troops on Maui. Led by hula teachers Elizabeth Buck and Harriet Kuuleinani Stibbard, it shifted from performing at private parties to volunteering with the United Service Organization (USO) circuit. The group entertained several hundred troops every weekend and even after the war ended continued to perform for convalescing soldiers at army hospitals.[2] In 1946 the troupe was awarded special certificates from the U.S. Marine Corps for their volunteer services.[3]

The Buck-Stibbard troupe was only one of hundreds of volunteer USO hula groups in Hawai'i (see figure 58). The Hawaiian colony was a critical node for the U.S. Armed Services and a headquarters for the entire Central Pacific command. Refiguring the martial meaning of the "Pacific theater," Hawai'i became the staging ground not only for battle, but for the leisure of millions of soldiers, defense workers, and military administrators who came to the islands.[4] The U.S. military took over tourist operations, coordinating with the USO to provide entertainment for soldiers and defense workers. En-

Fig. 57 "Ray's Babies," 1940. Left to right: Keopu Dilley, Elaine Dutro, Josephine Dutro, Carol Mae Kuuleinani Stibbard. COURTESY OF CAROL MAE KUULEINANI VANDERFORD.

Fig. 58 Buck-Stibbard hula troupe, Wailuku, Maui, ca. 1937.
COURTESY OF CAROL MAE KUULEINANI VANDERFORD.

tertainment was essential to boost the morale of soldiers and civilians during the administration of martial law in Hawai'i, officials determined. Military personnel came to the islands, instead of Hawaiians going to the continent to entertain as they had in previous decades.

Hula shows for military audiences became commonplace on land and at sea. Drawing on a half-century of experience entertaining tourists, dancers who once performed on ocean liners now danced on military vessels in the harbors. Since many soldiers were posted far from urban areas and major military bases, dancers and musicians took their shows to secluded and, sometimes, secret areas. Six to seven days a week, they traveled in military jeeps, trucks, ships, and planes—even on pack mules—to reach isolated posts.[5]

While live hula shows were ubiquitous, the military films and photographs that captured them were no less so. The visual record of wartime Hawai'i is distinguished by insistent coverage of Native Hawaiian women and cultural practices, as evidenced by the dozens of military films and photographs held by the U.S. National Archives (NA) and Hawai'i War Records Depository (HWRD), respectively. The U.S. military's extensive visual record of Hawai'i remains largely unexamined, but nearly everywhere hula dancers performed, military photographers captured them on film.[6] U.S. naval and army units staged elaborate re-creations of Hawaiian "luaus" or, on a smaller scale, took informal footage of Hawaiians dancing hula at military hospitals, airfields, and recreation camps. At the NA, I found and viewed approximately fifty such films taken from the 1930s to the 1960s.[7] While the films are concentrated on World War II, this archive also spans the French-Indochina conflict, the Korean War, and the Vietnam War.

The lūʻau is a celebratory feast incorporating lavish food preparation, hosting, and performance. As an extended elaboration of hospitality, lūʻau merged many sensory pleasures for tourists—the pleasures of eating, watching, and listening. The lūʻau emerged with the militarization of the islands in the nineteenth century, with Hawaiians hosting Euro-American military officers.[8] Increasingly described, sketched, and photographed in American tourist memoirs, political reportage, and journalistic accounts after the U.S.-backed overthrow and annexation, lūʻau became associated discursively with hula. In these visual and narrative terrains, representations of lūʻau and live performance often accompanied one other: Hawaiians were "extraordinary eaters" *and* extraordinary dancers.[9]

But it was during World War II that the lūʻau was transformed from a privileged affair for a select few tourists to one that could be shared with a mass audience beyond the islands. Military photography of Hawaiian cultural practices straddles the ethnographic and the commercial, building on earlier narratives of intimacy and hospitality that circulated through popular cultural forms. Combat cameramen in the U.S. Army Air Forces, the Army's Signal Photographic Companies, and the Navy's combat photography units documented luaus and hula extensively on film and in still photography, revealing the military's investments as an image-producer of the islands. In the militourized stagecraft of aloha, the luau was its principal scene. Like the practice of *tableaux vivants* (living pictures) that posed silent, motionless actors to stage particular scenes, the luau presented tableaux of hospitality, utilizing Hawaiian men and women. I use "tableau" here to suggest the fixity of imperial scripts that Hawaiians were expected to perform, despite the dynamism of their live, embodied performances.

In this chapter I examine this genre of wartime island entertainment, including one exemplar titled *Luau: A Native Feast*. Produced by an Army Air Forces combat photography unit in Hawai'i in 1944, this short film stages a hula pageant and feast for military officers. Offering their aloha (love and affection) to U.S. and Allied soldiers, hula dancers serve as state hostesses, while island men are relegated to the backdrop of these staged encounters. The luau was appropriated by the militarized state and made into a filmic event that allegorized the luau as a form of imperial hospitality between soldiers and islanders. Imperial hospitality—enacted and idealized performances in which islanders and soldiers play host and guest, respectively—transforms colonial possession into benign and mutually agreeable exchanges, all the while disguising the material, economic, and political conditions under which colonized islanders labored. Military photography helped to restabilize an imagined intimacy between the colony and the military during World War II—in other words, it produced Hawaii as a "pacific" space.

In my use of imperial hospitality, I am not speaking simply of the military state's instrumentalization of female or feminized bodies.[10] My interest lies beyond Hawai'i as a feminized space subject to patriarchal colonization, in how the sexuality of the indigenous population as a whole—its entire productive and reproductive capacity—commands the attention of the colonial-military state. Colonial and neocolonial state power is exercised not just through the erection of state apparatuses and policies, but also in less apparent forms, such as the gendered production of state hospitality and the discursive organization of Hawaiian sexuality. The regulation of Hawaiian sexuality was aimed at incorporating Hawaiians into a project of national survival, while waging war against Japanese who at that historical moment were considered a far more dangerous and racially othered enemy.

I draw a contrast between live hula circuits through the continental United States and hula performed on the islands during World War II: that is, the differences and continuities between *live* hula shows and hula captured on film, specifically in this genre of military films. During the war, soldiers came to Hawai'i in vastly larger numbers than Hawaiian entertainers going overseas. What happened when the "troupes" met the "troops"?

Imperial Hospitality

During the war, island tourism and the military occupation converged into a single operation that Teresia K. Teaiwa has aptly described as militourism, a "profound symbiosis between militarism and tourism."[11] The Hawaii Tourist Bureau suspended its operations in June 1942 and the U.S. military took over all travel facilities within, to, and from the islands.[12] The requirements of tourism and the military, land, a compliant local population, and entertainment overlapped significantly. The tourists, however, were now soldiers. When Pearl Harbor was bombed on December 7, 1941, nearly 43,000 soldiers were stationed on Oʻahu, but by mid-1945, there were over 250,000. This figure does not even include more than 100,000 sailors and marines, as well as Allied servicemen and civilian defense workers who were posted and passing through the islands.[13] The local population of approximately 250,000 was easily outnumbered by war-related outsiders in a short period of time.

The army created its own visitors' bureau to service officials involved in the war, but the responsibility for organizing entertainment for soldiers and defense workers largely fell to the USO.[14] The USO became a national organization in the spring of 1941, in order to better provide civilian services to soldiers.[15] While autonomous from the U.S. military, the USO coordinated its efforts with the armed services and provided crucial support for the military. The Hawaiʻi branch of the USO was uniquely positioned to service soldiers, having inherited an infrastructure and personnel directly from the tourist economy. The Hawaiʻi USO even appropriated the slogan of aloha from the tourist bureau. There was no better way to demonstrate aloha than through entertainment. An informational booklet distributed to enlisted men and women explained the USO mission: "A lot of things have changed in these lovely islands since December 7th. But not Aloha. . . . We can't take you back home, but we can give you the next best thing while you're here. . . . And most of all, we can give you Aloha."[16]

Activities sponsored by the USO were organized into numerous local clubs at YMCAs, recreation centers, schools, parks, clubs, private homes, and businesses. By the end of the war, 8,000 island residents were USO volunteers, while there were 740 paid staff members. The Hawaiʻi USO provided tours and information, and organized recreation, dances, and educational programs that were free for servicemen and war workers. The

Fig. 59 Traveling hula dancers sponsored by the Honolulu City Civic Recreation Commission, 24 March 1942. Photo 309, HWRD, University of Hawai'i, Mānoa Library. REPRINTED COURTESY OF *HONOLULU STAR-ADVERTISER*.

uso programs in Hawai'i created a camp show division a month after the war began; what distinguished this unit from its national counterpart was the sheer volume of entertainment it produced. Four hundred island performers staffed the agency, while over 27,000 entertainers performed during the first year of camp show operations.[17]

Professional hula dancers and amateurs alike joined the island uso circuit (see figure 59). Servicemen did not even need to come ashore, because hula dancers boarded ships. War workers as well as soldiers grew used to seeing "first class hula shows" offered at least once a week at uso clubs.[18] Men could even learn hula at uso clubs. While passing through the islands for a brief rendezvous, soldiers would see hula or women who passed as "real" hula girls.

Called "natural-born musicians," Hawaiians were considered critical to military success.[19] Because Hawaiians were imagined as "natural" performers and recruited for the militarized state, Hawai'i was a specific kind of militarized site that can be distinguished from other American war zones, such as the Philippines, Vietnam, or present-day Afghanistan or Iraq. Unlike Hawai'i, these places may provide gendered forms of labor, such as sex work or cultural translation, but they do not produce indigenous hospitality and entertainment for American troops. In Vietnam, entertainers like Bob Hope had to be imported for soldiers; they were not homegrown. This idea of Hawai'i as a site of hospitality was owed to the already robust cultural imaginary produced during fifty years of hula's circulation in the United States, but World War II activated this idea fully.

Hula performances organized by the USO helped to manufacture consent among islanders by installing a discourse of Hawaiian cultural participation in everyday militarized life. To apply Raymond Williams's elaboration of Antonio Gramsci's concept of hegemony, the idea that Hawaiians were important and necessary for the military cause came to be inserted into a "whole body of practices and expectations."[20] The annual Lei Day festival, celebrated annually on the first of May, was converted into "War Bond Day" with hula shows, military parades, and a "lei of dollars" woven from civilian donations for the war effort.[21] Hawaiian culture itself—whether hula, musical performance, cooking, or even lei-making—became celebrated for its military utility. Lei makers turned their talents from flowers to weaving camouflage nets for U.S. Army engineers, with the cultural authority Mary Kawena Pukui instructing them (see figure 60).[22] More than 150 Hawaiian women wove nets to hide gun emplacements and air raid warning stations on the island of O'ahu.

To be sure, Hawaiian men were also recruited for military combat; nearly 12 percent of men drafted in the Hawaiian Islands were Native Hawaiians.[23] As many as 2,000 Hawaiian men may have served in the U.S. Army during the war and a few posthumously received medals of valor for bravery on the battlefield.[24] However, their roles as soldiers were less symbolically and materially important than their roles as purveyors of leisure and musicians for white Allied servicemen.[25] Furthermore, Hawaiian soldiers were excluded from the category of soldiers requiring touristic leisure. Rather, they performed as secondary props within tableaux of luau hospitality. For this reason, the use of "soldiers" in this chapter purposely excludes Native Hawaiian men and is limited to American and Allied men.

In the unlikely event that soldiers did not see live hula, hula was still the primary signifier of an authentic island sojourn. Soldiers did not often openly report their encounters with prostitutes in red light districts, but "hula girls" were socially acceptable tourist emblems they could capture in photographs and send home.[26] Soldiers crowded photography vendors in the red light district of Hotel Street to pose with local women dressed

Fig. 60 Mary Kawena Pukui instructing Primrose Kinolau on the construction of camouflage nets for the U.S. Army, January 1942. Photo 274, HWRD, University of Hawai'i, Mānoa Library.
REPRINTED COURTESY OF *HONOLULU STAR-ADVERTISER*.

as dancers.[27] One guidebook for soldiers included a full-page advertisement for a souvenir photograph session with "Mona Lei, the only original hula girl in Waikiki."[28] Most famously, the national pictorial magazine *Life* featured a behind-the-scenes spread of thirteen sailors in its issue for December 1942. Posed in front of painted backdrops of a grass shack and Diamond Head, seamen like Carl Gaines, from Birmingham, Alabama, and Carl Massarelli, from New Philadelphia, Ohio, clasped young women in cellophane skirts and had their photographs snapped by a former cabdriver.[29] According to *Life*, some men had their pictures taken "over and over again" at seventy-five cents a shot. Those who sought a more indelible Hawaiian souvenir could have a hula girl tattooed on their bodies.[30]

Similarly, the national weekly magazine *Colliers* published a photographic feature of attractive young women dressed as hula dancers or in tropical attire.[31] This "Hawaiian Medley" of eleven girls was labeled with their racial category (e.g., "Swedish-Japanese" and "Hawaiian-Portuguese-English") and they were extolled as exemplars of interracial mixing in the islands. Men about to ship to the islands saw these pictorials in *Life* and *Colliers* and likely envisioned themselves meeting or even embracing hula girls who were as compliant as these pin-ups suspended on a magazine page. Male readers flooded *Colliers* with letters asking to contact the women and propose marriage. One letter-writer wondered: "Are they real? Are the girls in Hawaiiya' really that pretty? . . . If all the girls in the islands are as lovely . . . there should be an exodus from the states. In fact, I am broken hearted that I turned down a job at Pearl Harbor."[32]

Like Hawaiian entertainment, prostitution was another necessary wartime service requiring gendered labor in Hawai'i, but it was unofficially sanctioned by the U.S. military. The military institutionalized brothels in vice districts on the island of O'ahu in order to confine the spread of venereal disease and sexual dissolution to a professional workforce of prostitutes.[33] As indicated by their wartime classification, hula dancers and prostitutes both provided "entertainment" necessary for the morale of U.S. fighting men; the Honolulu police department even officially recognized prostitutes as "entertainers."[34]

Although the military depended on women who served as sex workers, USO volunteers, and hula dancers, the hula and the brothel represent opposite ends of the spectrum of militarized sexuality. The luau, an extended performance of hospitality in which hula played a central role, was staged in full public view and sanctioned, while the brothel was an open secret and ugly necessity. Hula promoted intimacy between Hawaiians and soldiers without actual sexual contact, encouraging them to offer aloha freely to one another. In contrast, prostitution did not and could not perform the function of diffusing tensions. Sex in a military-regulated brothel did not generate a transcendent experience between white men and eroticized racial others; in fact, prostitutes were not local women, but mostly haole women who came from the U.S. continent as sex workers. A brief encounter between a soldier and a woman in a brothel was hardly Hawaiian hospitality; it was merely a perfunctory economic and sexual exchange. Promising much more, the luau served as the innocent public surrogate for prostitution. Men indulged in a fantasy of contact without the consequences of disease and the disappointment of brief encounters on Hotel Street.

Hula's circulation and consumption in the United States during the past half century had produced a cultural imaginary and expectation of island hospitality. Live hula circuits in the 1930s conjured an imagined intimacy between Hawai'i and the continent, an eroticized fantasy encouraging the metaphoric and literal possession of the Hawaiian colony. This fantasy was anchored by an imagined relationship between American spectators and captivating islander women. The imagined intimacy produced by hula in the islands during World War II took on additional significance and value. This imagined intimacy between soldiers and "hula girls" was valuable precisely because it was imagined: it involved no sexual intimacy.

Yet this imagined intimacy between colony and colonizer was unstable; it was difficult to sustain when soldiers besieged the island by the hundreds of thousands. In situ, islanders were not simply two-dimensional magazine pin-ups, and their corporeality became a problem for military personnel. As Beth Bailey and David Farber contend, Hawai'i was "the first strange place" for newly arrived soldiers who encountered a majority population of nonwhite islanders during the war.[35] Gender and color lines did not square with those on the continent. White skin privilege was not a given here for whites; Pacific Islanders and local Asians, even Japanese Americans, enjoyed authority in civic life. Racial violence threatened to erupt, and when it did, whites did not hold the numerical advantage.

Almost as soon as American servicemen began arriving on shore, their expectations of a Hawaiian paradise faded. "Three Minnesota Lads" based in Pearl Harbor in 1942 wrote this letter to the editor of a Honolulu newspaper; their obstreperous opinions amplify those expressed by many other defense workers:

> Honolulu spells romance and adventure to people from other lands, but a sojourn of a few days educates them. This place in reality is nothing but a fifth-rate and dirty little town. It is the most foul-smelling city in the world. . . . This island propaganda is wonderful. . . . The climate isn't fit for a white person. . . . We have been wondering, though, if there are any beautiful women here. The ones we have seen all look like fourth raters. Really what have you here besides a very good chamber of commerce? It is the best in the world. . . . We'll hold an expose of this place and explode all myths and untruths—when we get back to the mainland.[36]

Instead of a rapturous seaside of sexual liberty, the main port town of Honolulu became an urban slum with recalcitrant women and resentful Native men. Soldiers and defense workers took to calling Oʻahu "the Rock" and "a camouflaged Alcatraz."[37] Contradicting the lyrics of "Hawaiian Hospitality," the song popular during the war, there were not enough "fair wahine" to make every soldier's "dream of love come true."[38] Upon arrival, soldiers received *A Pocket Guide to Honolulu* that warned: "Girls are scarce in Hawaii. When you've been off the boat for 23 minutes, you'll find that telephone numbers here carry the same classification as war plans."[39] Men outnumbered women by an estimated ratio of one woman to 100 or 1,000 men, depending on which report one believes.[40] Many islanders grew to loathe the transformation of their home into a militarized zone. Women of all ages had reason to resent military and war workers; girls as young as ten were harassed and molested.[41]

Leilehua "Lei" Becker, a dancer and singer, was a teenager during the war. She recalled, "The male to female ratio was crazy, like 250 to 1, and you couldn't go downtown without a bunch of servicemen following you."[42] Lei sang at a local nightclub with mixed civilian and military patronage during the evenings, but her American father drew the line at USO shows and refused to have her perform for soldiers. Women who lived alone listed their telephone by initials instead of names in order to deter unwanted solicitations.[43] Islander women also wrote letters to the editors of local newspapers, testifying that they did not feel safe riding the bus or walking home alone. In the worst cases, soldiers sexually assaulted them.

As the army and navy doubled their land holdings during the war to over 62,000 acres on all islands, prime beaches were either crowded with outsiders or off-limits to civilians.[44] One Hawaiian kupuna (elder) spoke of how her grandfather could not access the nearby beach, even though he had settled on a Hawaiian homestead lot in Nānākuli: "We couldn't go to the beach like we used to because there were lots of barbed wire and when Grandpa wanted to go holoholo [wander] down the beach he needed to have an ID card. Anyone wanting to go to the beach at that time needed ID cards."[45]

The cordoning off of land was accompanied by verbal insults and physical alterations. White men called Asian and Hawaiian men "gooks" and "Kanakas." Islanders retaliated by committing petty thefts and attacks against soldiers.[46] The hostility erupted in a race riot in 1945, when 500 sailors assailed a local Asian and Hawaiian neighborhood to avenge the rumored murders of two of their men, but these rumors were later proven false. However, race riots and sexual assaults became largely invisible in the islands, replaced by the ubiquity of hula.

Hula en Plein Air

The imagined intimacy between colony and continent, islanders and Americans, was most successfully realized when hula was performed on the continent, far away from its actual referent and transplanted from the lived context of the islands. Ethnographic framing devices and artifacts were necessary to impart tropical ambience in the continental United States, such as kapa (bark cloth) that hung on the walls of the Hotel Lexington's Hawaiian Room in New York City, but too much contextualization could be disruptive. Hula shows organized by the USO, although quotidian in the islands, could not be easily reconciled with the reality of wartime Hawai'i. The shows could only momentarily edit out the urbanized slums, barbed wire around the beaches, and local women who refused soldiers' advances.

Like live hula performances on the continent, USO hula shows in the islands presented mostly hapa haole music (English-language songs utilizing Hawaiian imagery and performed with Western instruments) for maximum cultural legibility. The troops could easily appreciate English-language songs like "Little Grass Shack," but some hula troupes did perform Hawaiian-language mele, such as "Alekoki," "Mi Nei," "He Nani Ka'ala."[47] Some were quick tempo mele like "Hawaiian War Chant." Others were languid love songs like "Ke Kali Nei Au," known today as the "Hawaiian Wedding Song." A typical show for one wartime USO troupe was at least an hour long. Its repertoire included solo hulas by a young female soloist, group hulas by younger girls, vocal numbers, and guitar instrumentals.[48] Hula troupes sponsored by the USO were also multiethnic, but Hawaiian or hapa haole women and girls predominated. Men did not usually dance in these troupes during the war, although men had historically been hula performers, chanters, and teachers.

The main difference between hula shows in urban American nightclubs and camp shows in the field was the degree of immersion, or how much the hula was displayed in situ. One photograph of a USO performance reveals that hula dancers performed for a transport squadron in a large tent, while men sat on the grass around them.[49] Others danced on or below the decks of ships. Dancers performed en plein air—without constructed stages and sets, and with only palm trees, the ocean, or mountains as natural backgrounds. With no proscenium and few props, these hula performances did not incorporate interpretive devices and framing artifices. The Buck-Stibbard USO hula troupe on Maui regularly performed out in the "kiawe sticks," that is, in a remote patch of kiawe

(*Prosopis pallida*) trees.[50] Carol Mae Kuuleinani Vanderford (née Stib-bard) described the show: "There were always a lot of men. A platoon of at least a hundred to several hundred men. They built a stage for us . . . you could tell it was thrown together, with little steps, and that was it."[51]

Ironically these performances seemed less "real" than Hawaiian shows that audiences experienced in American nightclubs; the latter relied on plastic palm trees in their set designs and an excess of Hawaiian signi-fiers, such as tropical rain storms and fresh pineapple. Because all of Hawai'i became a staging ground for the military, hula was presented in situ, but perhaps too much so. Hula was a less stable signifier of Hawai'i when performed in the field. Once women arrived via mule or truck at remote military camps, many had to change into costumes in makeshift tents or hangars. A tent or a grassy field provides very little backstage for a performance.

However, a backstage is necessary to preserve the distinction between the persona of a performer ("hula girl") and her nonprofessional iden-tity (civilian). To invest the performance and performer with integrity, a backstage must be kept distinct from the stage; like a set with props, the backstage frames the performance as such. With little difference between "on stage" and "backstage," the shows could not secure a convincing fan-tasy. As much as the performances attempted to produce an allegory of Hawai'i, hula was too embedded in the locale to commit necessary era-sures. What lurked outside threatened to interrupt the frame of the show, whether it was the battles the men were headed to, the smell of the hospi-tal in which they were recuperating, or perhaps the gonorrhea contracted in a downtown brothel. The monotony of the hula did not aid the soldiers' reverie either. They grew tired of hula shows, complaining of a "wearying sameness in the hula troupes," since theater actors and entertainers did not arrive from the continent until June 1943.[52]

The hula performances on stage could not keep the off-stage lives of the soldiers or the women from intruding. The imagined intimacy pro-duced by the sights and sounds of live hula, for the vast majority of men, though achieved on the continent, became unsustainable in the islands. Hula gave the soldier a glimpse of Hawaiians in a prelapsarian state, but he had also seen Hawaiians living in overcrowded urban apartments, not "grass shacks."[53] Nor did these "little brown gals" wear hula skirts while shopping or taking the bus in town. Rather than an imagined intimacy, Hawai'i in situ disrupted colonial intimacy. Thus, the fantasy of mutual aloha was short-circuited by the actual experience of living side by side in

Hawai'i. Soldiers were exposed to a much more complicated island population than the accommodating Natives they saw in live hula shows. Hula shows could not eclipse conflicts between soldiers and the local population; at most they were only temporary distractions from growing enmity.

Luau on Film

Given the limitations of live hula en plein air and live encounters, what would help to facilitate an exchange of aloha between military and locals? Military films were a more effective medium of imperial hospitality than a live hula show in Hawai'i, for they were decontextualized. Live, in situ hula shows were too close to their actual referent. But films and photographs of hula restabilized the subordinate relationship between colony and guest that a hula show could not accomplish on its own. Photography and film are more stable media that edit out the chaos of embodied interactions; photographs offer the semblance of the real but are not corporeal. Film is also an easily reproducible medium; these photographs were developed in on-island labs and published locally, but some were also widely distributed by photo bureaus to newspapers in the United States.

The militarized luau had been catering to visiting soldiers and sailors in the 1920s and 1930s, but military officials during World War II assumed the duties of a professional class of brokers that marketed and profited from Hawaiian culture by facilitating the production and dissemination of the luau. The military, working in concert with the USO, had more resources at its disposal than the Hawai'i tourist bureau, including capital, new technologies and equipment, trained cameramen, as well as a wider national distribution network and media outlets drafted for the war effort.

Combat cameramen worked in the Army Air Forces, the army's signal photographic companies, and the navy's combat photography units, documenting numerous events in Hawai'i, such as Navy Day ceremonies in Honolulu that commemorated the end of the war in 1945. *Luau: A Native Feast*, a silent 16 mm color film, was shot by the 7th Army Air Forces Combat Camera Unit in 1944.[54] Official military footage shot in Hawai'i was largely left unedited, but *Luau* was shot with multiple cameras and cameramen and edited from raw footage.[55] I focus on this film because it is typical of the military's sustained interest in hula, but exceptional in its professional production value. Military combat camera units documented luaus extensively on film and in still photographs during the war. In addition to this film, the Army Signal Corps took still photographs of luaus thrown for army personnel in the 1940s.[56] However, *Luau* may well be one of the earliest filmic representations of a luau. The twelve-minute film covers a day of feasting and pageantry enjoyed by army officers and their wives at Hickam Air Force Base on the island of Oʻahu. Hawaiian men first prepare a pig for the imu (underground oven); women kiss the officers and give them leis. Women dance hula and the Hawaiian feast is served, followed by a hula lesson for off-duty officers.

In the tradition of Robert Flaherty's *Moana: A Romance of the Golden Age*, set in Samoa, *Luau* blends documentary and entertainment.[57] Narrated with intertitles such as, "A Whole Day is in [*sic*] Spent Preparing the Feast," the film systematically explicates Hawaiian cultural practices and suggests they are best realized when generously offered to malihini (strangers). The soldier-cameramen's ethnographic impulses are revealed in the most observational section of the film: the traditional process of roasting a pig. Cultural difference unfolds step by step as Hawaiian men are filmed rubbing the pig with salt, inserting hot rocks into the pig, wrapping it in chicken wire, and lowering it into an earthen pit. Intertitles in Hawaiian, like "Hele Mai Oukou e Ai!" (Come and eat!), also convey insider knowledge.

However, the ethnographic, observational style is overwhelmed by touristic conventions. While the cooking is shot in long takes, the hula performance was not shot in such an observational style. Several hula dances are edited to a few seconds without regard to continuity or narrative flow. The cameramen seem more interested in the generic exoticism of the setting—signified by floral leis and women in aloha print dresses—than thick description. *Luau* stands in contrast to another 16 mm film, *The Hula of Old Hawaii*, shot a year earlier in Hawaiʻi by a Signal Corps photographer named George Bacon.[58] The military cameraman Bacon donated his services to the Bishop Museum in Honolulu to help preserve traditional hula on film. In *Hula*, movements by the solo dancer are revealed in long shots with no changes in camera angles.[59]

While not a combat film per se, *Luau* was produced by the Army Air Forces in a militarized zone.[60] The National Archives hold no records of the distribution and audiences of this film, but it was likely screened during training either for arriving soldiers or before arrival to boost morale. It may also have been included in propaganda newsreels shown on the continent or in the islands.[61] Some photographs taken by the Army Signal Corps circulated through the Central Pacific command to American newspapers as publicity for the war effort. World War II was the most photographed war and photography was not only useful for military intelligence and surveillance, but persuaded ordinary citizens to support the war effort.[62] As an article in *National Geographic* proclaimed in 1944, "Cameras and film have become as essential in this war as guns and bullets, on some occasions more so."[63]

During the war, camerawork became highly professionalized, due to Hollywood's involvement. Hollywood professionals helped to train camera operators in the Army Signal Corps, and one-sixth of the 240,000 workers in the production of motion pictures were in the armed services.[64] During the war, U.S. military combat camera units, such as those in Hawai'i and on the front lines, shot 16 MM film, which was considered amateur technology compared to 35 MM film. However, 16 MM film was retooled for military purposes, and its low-budget quality was resignified as authenticity and realism.[65] Thus, instead of ethnographic work like *Luau*, the visual record of the army and naval photographic units overseas included more combat scenes, like those captured by the modernist photographer Edward Steichen in his *Power in the Pacific* (1945) and *U.S. Navy War Photographs: Pearl Harbor to Tokyo Bay* (1946)— collections that brought home to Americans the Battle of Midway and the takeover of Tarawa, among many other experiences.[66] As the war progressed, photography also turned toward a realistic depiction of violence and casualties on the front lines. Military cameras in Hawai'i, however, focused their lenses insistently on the Native population and its cultural performances.

Photography and the Regulation of Peace

Foucault has argued that populations are disciplined by being forced into "compulsory visibility."[67] Drawing upon Foucault's genealogy of the new power that disciplined its subjects through surveillance and "infinite examination" in the eighteenth century and the nineteenth, John Tagg contends that the photograph contributes to this disciplinary technology. Photography, he asserts, is complicit with institutions like the asylum, hospital, and police force, which exert power and control over individual bodies.[68] Jeremy Bentham's panopticon, a metaphor for this visual technology of control, found its ideal realization in the frame of the photograph. While panoptic architecture was a disciplinary instrument in European factories, prisons, and schools, the camera became a "seeing machine" of empire—a technology that disciplined racialized bodies in colonial sites.[69] Christopher Pinney further concludes, "The surveillance of the gaze was one of the chief instruments of domination, whether of the criminal, the insane, or the subject peoples of the Empire."[70]

Pinney, following Foucault, analyzes the British colonial state's use of photography as a positivist tool in nineteenth-century India. The assumed evidentiary quality of photography helps to control and categorize Indians; photography produces indexical evidence for the state, such as hierarchies of ethnic types and castes. Pinney argues that India was a laboratory for anthropometry; for example, the photographic collection *The People of India*, published beginning in 1868, evaluated castes in terms of potential loyalty to the colonial state.[71]

In the developing American empire, the relationship between visuality, racialization, and domination is most arguably realized with American Indian subjects. The Smithsonian Institution's Bureau of American Ethnology produced more than 20,000 negatives of American Indians beginning in 1879, as removal policies and white settlement pushed Indians farther from their homes. After the massacre at Wounded Knee in 1890 marked the official end of the Indian Wars, bureau photographers continued to document the lifeways of "disappearing" Indians.[72] As the United States developed its overseas empire in the late nineteenth century, the photograph was used to discipline its newest colonial subjects, including live Filipinos who were avidly displayed and photographed at the St. Louis World's Fair in 1904.[73] Vicente L. Rafael has called these ethnological photographs "fetishes of the nation and empire" that mummified the living into the dead.[74]

What role did photography play in domesticating Hawai'i, a strategically key yet ambivalent colony, during World War II? Rather than being a colonial weapon or "seeing machine" that operates through visual supervision, the camera in military-occupied Hawai'i presents a distinct form of imperial regulation: it did not merely discipline or surveil its subjects, but was deployed by the military as a regulatory instrument of peace.[75] Foucault attentively distinguishes between disciplinary and regulatory power, discipline as a technology focused on an individual body and regulation as a technology of power centered on an entire species or population, what he terms "biopower."[76]

To be sure, both axes of power were exerted on the population of Hawai'i during the war. The colonial-military state's legal, medical, and educational apparatuses institutionalized individual bodies. Empowered by martial law that disregarded the U.S. Constitution and laws of the territory, military authorities scrutinized and managed nearly every aspect of civilian life. The territorial governor declared martial law immediately after the bombing of Pearl Harbor, under pressure from the highest-ranking army commander in the islands.[77] The U.S. Army subsequently took over all civilian courts and suspended the writ of habeas corpus. Civilians were tried in provost courts similar to courts martial, except the accused did not even have the rights and legal representation of a court martial. They faced steep fines and imprisonment in these courts.[78]

The self-appointed military governor—the lieutenant general and commanding general of the U.S. Army's Pacific Ocean areas—issued countless orders controlling wages, restaurants, bowling alleys, water chlorination, the resale of used rubber tires, even the importation of canned sardines and tomato juice.[79] Military organizations also rendered civilians highly visible. A special registration bureau performed the mass registration and fingerprinting of all civilians over the age of six, the first such procedure undertaken in the United States.[80] This was but one such exercise of "micro-power" at the level of the body—what Foucault calls "infinitesimal surveillances" and "meticulous orderings of space."[81]

However, the militarized state went beyond the disciplining of individual human bodies to biopolitical regulation, taking charge of the life and sexuality of the island population as a whole during the war. The military made a particular effort to promote the survival of the island population—and the U.S. nation in its entirety—through the sexuality of its Hawaiian hosts. Focusing on the luau, military cameras produced a sexualized rapport between the military and Hawaiian women that encouraged respectful coexistence.

Laura Wexler has advanced a theory of colonial photography called "the innocent eye." In the context of the antebellum U.S. South and the Philippine-American War, "the innocent eye" was a gendered way of seeing that developed from middle-class domestic photography.[82] This "natural" and sentimental vision could not imagine itself misrepresenting its subjects, but erased the violence of colonial encounters in the very act of portraying them. These photographs averted a viewer's gaze from race and class conflict, war, and colonization, rendering "a peace that keeps the peace."[83] Like the sentimental camera during earlier imperial moments, the military visualization of the luau restabilized the fragile fantasy of peaceful coexistence between the Hawaiian colony and the United States during martial law and occupation—a tense period of conflict between soldiers and the islander population. The military camera, as wielded by male photographers, poised hula and colonized bodies in order to render, in the words of art historian Bernard Smith, "a pacific Pacific."[84] Military photographers adopted the idioms of anthropologists and tourist promoters; they encouraged pacification by staging encounters of aloha, rather than explicit coercion.

While the U.S. military visually documented islanders and made them visible as colonial subjects during wartime, it did not subject them to a categorizing or classificatory gaze. In other words, the purpose of these films was not ethnological, that is, to categorize Natives or create a taxonomy of types. They invoked only a generic, though gendered, Native. The film participated in the regulation and integration of colonial subjects—that is, a population subject to the exercise of biopower—rather than in their containment or segregation. The military camera was not merely a tool of propaganda, but a regulatory tool of peace that sought to integrate rather than separate populations. It framed Hawai'i as a site of militouristic pleasure, editing out the war, militarization of the territory, and frequent violence that erupted between soldiers and locals.

Above all, the military camera's interest lies in visualizing an idealized metaphor: the metaphor of aloha, or love, between Natives and outsiders. These films animated a social contract upon which the military relied—of "hosts" and "guests" who each occupied distinct positions but nevertheless enjoyed each other's company. A luau, after all, is a staged encounter between locals and military—with Natives providing all the labor, and the military partaking of food, spectacle, and leisure. The military were elevated to guests of honor, and subordinate Natives served their guests in exchange for protection and security. The film encouraged hospitality to the white militourists—to see them as patrons rather than interlopers who molest their daughters on the street or overrun their beaches. It is a harmonious yet hierarchical relationship that is enacted, with Natives in the position of cheerful and cooperative supplicants, and the haole as gentlemen callers.

Not just any soldier or any islander could enact these roles; a particular kind of host and guest was needed to fulfill the imaginary of hospitality. Luaus required the essential pairing of whites and Natives to cordon off two racial menaces: blacks and Japanese. Blackness and Japaneseness were by no means racial equivalences, but their respective absences signal the discursive organizing the military state attempted through luau productions. Military luaus appear to have hosted only white men and, to a lesser extent, white women; there are no African American soldiers shown in the films or photographs.[85] Black soldiers served in segregated units and were therefore entertained separately from whites. Perhaps some of the 30,000 African American servicemen and war workers in the islands did experience luaus, but military productions did not represent them or other nonwhites being served by Hawaiians. Such depictions would have destabilized the structure of racialized subordination that placed whiteness above all others, a system on which the U.S. military depended in Hawai'i and the nation at large. In these visual texts, blackness is invisible and whiteness exalted; whiteness anchors the imaginary of eroticized cooperation with Natives.

African Americans, though denigrated as second-class citizens, were still valuable to the war effort, as were Native Hawaiians who, as the original inhabitants of the islands, could assert cultural authority over immigrants and settlers. As the United States mounted war against Japan, the loyalty of the indigenous population could help secure the broader allegiance of the occupied islands and inoculate Hawai'i against "alien" Japanese. The hosts of military luaus were invariably Hawaiian, for picturing Hawaiians as generous performers constrained other islanders, primarily the Japanese, the largest single racial group, whose mere presence was a stated danger to Hawai'i's population.[86] Their high numbers and purported resistance to assimilation inflamed the territorial and federal government's fear of "alien domination" from within.[87] The production of Hawaiian hospitality distracted from the military state's attempts to destroy the Japanese American community in Hawai'i through systematic harassment and internment, which has been analyzed extensively by Gary Y. Okihiro.[88] The continued survival of the nation depended on the biopolitical integration of loyal Hawaiians and the extermination of—or at least the exertion of disciplinary control over—a Japanese menace within and beyond the nation's borders. Thus, as Japanese became the primary targets of governmental disciplining and surveillance programs, they were kept outside the ostensibly peaceful military camera frames.

Compromising Positions

Luau accomplishes an astonishing sleight of hand by disguising military authority as island hospitality. The film suggests that Hawaiians are throwing a luau in honor of military officers, for Hawaiian women greet, kiss, and offer them leis. The Hawaiian "princess" even proffers a papaya to the luau's highest guests of honor, Lt. Gen. Robert C. Richardson Jr. and his wife. The Army Air Forces Central Film Library records held by the National Archives, however, contradict the implied relationship between host and guest with this description: "7th Air Force officers host Hawaiian pageant and party at the officers' club for combat on rest and relaxation tour." At the time of the production, Lt. Gen. Richardson was the territory's military governor, the highest-ranking army officer who had assumed power over all civil and military affairs.[89] In practical terms, Richardson was sovereign of the islands during the luau held in May 1944.

Contrary to their filmic roles as honored guests, army officers were the producers of the event: they had planned the luau and commissioned dozens of Hawaiians to perform as hosts. The Hawaiian "king" and "queen" of the pageant who welcome the soldiers were but hired hands for the real royalty of the islands: officers like Richardson who implemented the military occupation. Inverting the actual economic and social relations of the event, the film transforms militarized colonization into hospitality.

Military photography renders Hawai'i into a tranquil domestic space and Hawaiians become altruistic ethnographic objects that help keep the peace. The films' discursive function is also intertwined with their material practice—Hawaiians were recruited to labor in these military productions, while the films were ideal instructional scripts that encouraged proper encounters between islanders and soldiers. To be more precise, the films encourage imperial hospitality, a highly gendered and racialized imaginary that translates uneven relationships between Natives and outsiders into ones that appear mutually edifying and consensual. Natives, primarily Native Hawaiian women, learn to treat the military as their guests, and the soldiers to respectfully partake of Native hospitality.

Luau's military cameras linger longest not on women dancing hula *solo*, but on white men and Native women *together*, and their playful interactions (see figures 61.1, 61.2, and 61.3). The film in fact displays indifference to the women's performances. The women's hula are perfunctorily shot and edited, cut off in between verses and gestures; some are left in wide angles where their movements can hardly be seen. *Luau*, however, is most interested in showing male soldiers learning to dance hula from women on stage.

Appearing in the same frame, the "hula girls" and soldiers enjoy exchanges that appear mutual and consensual. The camera focuses tightly on the bodies of women and men standing facing each other; the women hold the men's waists to help them perform the 'ami (hip rotation) (see figure 61.3). Similar to souvenir photographs of hula girls and GIS, *Luau* implies intimacy, however brief, between island women and soldiers, and, by extension, intimacy between the colony and the militouristic state.

Fig. 61.1

Fig. 61.2

Fig. 61.3

Fig. 61.4 Stills from the U.S. Army Air Forces film *Luau* (1944). In figures 61.1–61.3, U.S. officers returned from "Down Under" pair off and learn hula from Hawaiian women. In the fourth image, the camera focuses on the backs of Hawaiian men preparing the imu.

The intimate frames depict exchanges between islanders and white arrivals as altruistic and peace-loving. On stage, the hula girls do their duty
by distracting these men from battlefield and death; the film also diverts
its viewers away from the militarization of Native land and people toward
the pleasure of leisure.

In other parts of the Pacific theater, particularly island Melanesia,
U.S. military cameras represented Native Pacific Islanders as submissive.
Lamont Lindstrom observes how war photographs position Pacific Islanders, usually men, in several "key poses," including exotic savage, servant, victim, pupil, and loyal ally. Drawing on a familiar visual vocabulary
that presented Pacific Islanders as inferior savages, the "loyal ally" was the
most frequent supporting role for Micronesians and Melanesians whose
islands were occupied by Allied forces. This image smoothed over the
colonial hierarchy by suggesting an "implicit equality."[90] Islanders from
New Guinea, Guadalcanal, and Kiribati, for example, were portrayed not
merely as servants or performers, but as fellow workers fighting the same
enemy as scouts and laborers. Despite the parity with Micronesian allies
suggested by wartime visual media, U.S. military ambitions ultimately
justified quasicolonization and nuclear testing in the region. Having
wrested Micronesia from Japan in battle, the United States seized control
of much of Micronesia after the war, administering it as a United Nations strategic trust territory. U.S. military photography as manifested
in Hawai'i, however, never aimed to ameliorate racial and colonial subordination, but amplified and normalized these conditions through the
trope of hospitality.

Furthermore, *Luau* produces a gendered regulation of Native bodies.
Unlike New Guinea or the Solomon Islands during wartime, where close
working relationships with indigenous men were emphasized, military
men in Hawai'i sought intimate relationships with Native Hawaiian
women. It is the women who are spectacularized in the film, through
closeups of their faces or kneeling poses for photographers. The camera
focuses on female dancers only, editing out the few men who dance hula
at the luau. In the film, Hawaiian men are reduced to anonymous manual
laborers and are contained visually—their shirtless backs are turned to
the cameras and their faces hardly visible (see figure 61.4).

Hawaiian men were a subordinated part of the cinematic vision of
wartime Hawai'i, eclipsed by female counterparts who performed as
volunteer dancers. Although many had enlisted as soldiers, Hawaiian
men were visually excluded from masculine categories of soldiering and

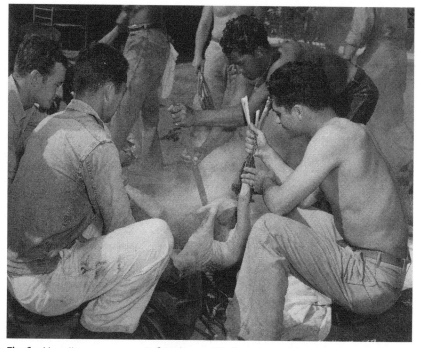

Fig. 62 Hawaiians prepare a pig for a luau, while American soldiers observe. U.S. Army Signal Corps photograph, 1942. Photo 1133, HWRD, University of Hawai'i, Mānoa Library. The original caption reads, "Under the expert guidance of a son of Hawaii, American soldiers prepare the traditional kalua pig for a luau."

defense work. Associated with leisure and the feminized labor of cook-ing, they became nonnormative, queer subjects on film. A series of luau photographs taken by the U.S. Army Signal Corps reveal that even when Hawaiian men were soldiers, as these men were, they performed domes-tic culture for American soldiers (see figure 62). On the unruly streets of Honolulu, Hawaiian men challenged the masculinity of American sol-diers through displays of physical violence and verbal threats. But they could be translated into compliant subjects within these cinematic per-formances. These displays suggest that Hawaiian men and women each have important, though different, functions to perform in the militour-istic economy—men as "backstage" performers, and women as on-stage eroticized entertainers.

With closeups and full-length shots of Hawaiian women's bodies, *Luau* and other military films of Hawai'i echo pin-up shots taken dur-ing World War II of Hollywood stars such as Jayne Mansfield, but also recycle the century-old visual icon of the eroticized Polynesian woman. The dancers are twentieth-century iterations of John Webber's painting of the Raiatean woman Poedua in 1777, although their breasts are covered. The Pacific became associated in the Euro-American imagination with the bodies of young women like Poedua (also spelled as "Poedooa" and "Poetua") during Captain James Cook's eighteenth-century explorations. Webber, the principal artist aboard the *Endeavor* on Cook's third voyage, was an early image-maker of the Pacific, creating portraits of Poedua and other Pacific Islander women for Western audiences. As Bernard Smith has argued persuasively, an important ideological function of these representations was establishing this newly encountered region as "young, feminine, desirable and vulnerable, an ocean of desire."[91] The women wait silently for men to arrive and exploit the land and ocean; nineteen-year-old Poedua gazes calmly out toward the viewer from her island abode.

These visual representations worked intertextually with published narratives extolling the ripe sexuality of Native women. Joseph Banks, the ship's botanist, wrote in 1773, "On the island of Otaheite [Tahiti] where love is the chief occupation, the favourite, nay, the sole luxury of the inhabitants, both the bodies and the souls of the women are moulded into the utmost perfection."[92] However, the portrait of Poedua disguises the violent circumstances that made her into Webber's compliant model. She was the daughter of a chief of Raiatea in the Society Islands; she had been kidnapped and held as ransom by Cook until her father returned goods stolen by other islanders.[93] She was painted on board the *Endeavor* while waiting in terror.[94]

Militouristic Patronage

Although the luau has obtained iconic status as authentic Hawaiian hospitality, the term "luau" itself is a misnomer. Rather than a feast, it in fact refers to the leaves of the taro plant that are cooked with meat. Haole visitors to Hawai'i in the early nineteenth century confused this festive dish with the parties at which it was served. The emergence of the misnamed luau is tied to the Euro-American militarization of Hawai'i, as waves of American military officers in the 1830s and 1840s were treated to feasts and entertainment by ali'i (chiefs). A British naval captain visiting the islands in 1827 described a "leuhow" party after being hosted at a royal feast by Kauikeaouli, King Kamehameha III.[95] Alternately, the authoritative modern Hawaiian language dictionary suggests that "luau" appeared as early as 1856 in the pages of the *Pacific Commercial Advertiser*, a English-language newspaper published in Honolulu, representing the interests of Euro-American settlers and businessmen.[96] In the late nineteenth century, Hawai'i's royal hospitality became renowned in the Western world, as King Kalākaua hosted luaus for foreign dignitaries such as Robert Louis Stevenson. The luau took on an official state function and was incorporated into receptions for militouristic outsiders.

In pre-Christian Hawai'i, a feast enabled man and gods to commune. Gods were invoked at the feast through highly symbolic food. The pua'a (pig), preferably a black pig, was a traditional sacrificial offering; the lau kī (ti leaves) in which meat and luau leaves were steamed were not merely decorative or functional, but entreated gods for protection.[97] Most significant for Hawaiians is the kalo (taro), from which the staple poi is made. According to Hawaiian cosmogonic genealogy, the gods Wākea and Ho'ohōkūkalani were progenitors of the kalo as well as the ali'i and all men. They gave birth to a stillborn child, who, when planted in the earth, grew into the first kalo named Hāloa. Their second-born was a boy, also named Hāloa in honor of his brother, the kalo plant. Nourished by the kalo, the boy was entrusted to care for his elder sibling. Thus kalo is not merely food, but a sacred ancestor and a living metaphor for family.[98] When Hawaiians care for kalo, they are also caring for their kūpuna.

The feast or banquet is known in 'ōlelo Hawai'i (Hawaiian language) as 'aha'aina or pā'ina, a gathering for one's family and community. On a typical weekend in the islands, one finds many backyard lū'au or 'aha'aina thrown by communities to celebrate such events as a baby's first birthday, wedding, or other rites of passage. Furthermore, the strict demarcation between "host" (those that serve) and "guest" (those who eat) does not apply to a communal feast. In Hawaiian communities, the preparation of an 'aha'aina, whether a feast after mourning or the birth of a child, requires the sharing of labor and values. The social, spiritual, and economic relations of a community are cemented not through the final act of eating, but the entire process of preparing a feast: the careful cultivation of land and sea in the form of kalo patches and fishing ponds, the rearing of pigs, and the kōkua (spirit of cooperation) and laulima (the work of many hands) that share in the labor.[99] The kupuna Louis Aila also emphasized communal endeavor when recalling the 'aha'aina of his childhood: "The Hawaiians those days [of old], they work together, they stick together. They help one another. You have a banquet, you want a preparation, whatever it is, or *kalua* the *puaa*, the pig and everything, we all go there, and participate, help. Without no pay, you know, just you help. And one night we have party at our house, you know, *ahaaina* at our house, oh the community all go in and help. That's how the Hawaiians used to live back then."[100]

During World War II, however, military authorities seized control of the luau as the new "chiefs" of the islands. They regulated the slaughtering of sows and young pigs, citing feed and meat shortages. The military banned commercial luaus outright, and private luaus were permissible only for weddings, welcome-home parties for members of the family who had been in the armed services overseas, or "some other well established racial custom."[101] Civilians were required to apply for luau permits and, even toward the end of the war, still had to abide by strict quotas of luau pigs.

These rules attempted to regulate Native customs and required Hawaiians to further depend on the military as their patron. By asserting a separation between those who served and those who feasted, the military luau disrupted the social and spiritual relations of the Hawaiian feast. A tourist board, whether civilian or military, takes on the primary function of creating a taxonomy of cultural authenticity; that is, determining what is authentic and inauthentic culture and directing resources to those that are deemed authentic. The army took over this important brokering function, defining Native authenticity as part of its exercise of state power. Arguing that monetary gift-giving practices generated unsavory profits, officials issued the Luau Defense Act, which prohibited the solicitation of money at luaus. The military director of food production argued that this practice was "quite contrary to the etiquet which was considered good form by the ancient Hawaiians."[102] This statement implies that the exchange of money tainted the ethos of aloha as generous gift-giving with no expectation of return, and that the American military, not Hawaiians, properly recognized a true luau. The maximum penalty for violating the Luau Defense Act was a $5,000 fine and one year in jail. Without military approval and patronage, Hawaiians would not have been able to hold luaus.

Yet, the fact that the military issued such harsh penalties suggests that Hawaiians were not likely to be compliant. They struggled to define the meaning and value of the lūʻau apart from patriotic military service. For as Raymond Williams reminds us, hegemony must be constantly renewed; both dominant and subaltern groups struggle to have their agendas recognized at the level of common sense and acceptance.[103] Working within the strict wartime permit system, Hawaiians continued to hold lūʻau away from the militouristic gaze. After the lifting of martial law, they returned to throwing their own unregulated lūʻau for themselves, as one young Hawaiian student at the University of Hawaiʻi described in an essay.[104]

The lūʻau (or ʻahaʻaina) nevertheless remained an important institution in Hawaiian communities. Families celebrated important occasions by hosting lūʻau, with guests of the family reciprocating with gifts of cash. Civic and religious organizations also raised funds by throwing lūʻau. The introduction of an informal cash economy notwithstanding, feasting and gift-giving allowed local communities to cement reciprocal relationships, as well as rotate turns distributing limited resources.

Wounded Warriors

War provided great publicity service for the territory, as borne out by a dramatic increase in American militourists and tourists after the war. Nearly 70 million Allied soldiers and defense workers had been entertained in wartime Hawaiʻi, and when they went back to their American homes, they took their memories of the luau and the hula with them.[105] The functions of the military and island tourist bureau—to service the military needs of the nation and publicize the islands as staunchly American but uniquely Polynesian—continued to mesh seamlessly. The accelerated postwar expansion of the tourist infrastructure and island economy also owes its thanks to U.S. military spending.

The imperial hospitality demanded of islanders during the war prepared them for postwar tourist expansion and official national incorporation in the form of statehood in 1959. Popular cinematic representations of the luau also helped to fuel this postwar tourism boom. Whereas *Luau* was the first film to formally cast Hawaiian hospitality in the form of a luau, by the 1950s the luau became a staple of Hollywood cinema, even in films set far away from Hawaiʻi.[106] The militouristic gaze continued to follow Native Hawaiians through American popular culture. In *A Place in the Sun* (1951), starring Elizabeth Taylor and Montgomery Clift, a patrician New England family and their guests assemble for a formal dinner that is a distinct interpretation of a luau: the guests wear paper leis over their suits and gowns and eat pineapple on china while a trio of Hawaiian musicians play in the background. Hawaiʻi figures nowhere in Theodore Dreiser's best-selling novel *An American Tragedy* (1925) on which the film is based, and is incidental to the developing murder plot, but the luau is entirely appropriate to authenticate the film's setting in 1950s America as well as an atmosphere of elite leisure.

The military also continued to film encounters between hula dancers and soldiers going to and from the Korean and Vietnam wars. When the first French casualties from Indochina were evacuated by U.S. naval aircraft to Paris in 1954, they stopped for some "R and R" at Hickam Air Force Base, the very location of Lt. Gen. Richardson's luau production a decade earlier. U.S. Air Force photographers recorded the men's encounters with Hawaiian women. The most severely wounded lie on gurneys while young Hawaiian girls drape leis over their heads and succor them with hula.[107] Called "Operation Wounded Warrior," the medical airlift mission and eponymous film suggest that Hawaiian women perform as both state hostesses and healers (see figures 63.1 and 63.2).

Recuperating American soldiers began camping at Fort DeRussy in Waikīkī, the islands' premiere tourist capital, during World War II. The fort housed the largest recreation center of the Mid-Pacific Command. Its ballroom seated 1,200 men, and its grounds could accommodate 10,000 soldiers and sailors.[108] Despite pleas from civilian authorities, the army refused to return Fort DeRussy to the city of Honolulu after the war and instead expanded it into a recreation center for Vietnam War personnel. It remains the most developed and popular military recreation center in the Pacific.[109] When the first American R and R troops from Vietnam arrived in 1966, they were taken to Fort DeRussy to reunite and vacation with their families, an event also filmed by the U.S. Army.[110]

The filmic scripts of Hawaiian hospitality—whether of prisoners of war from the Korean War in 1953 or U.S. soldiers from Vietnam landing at Hickam Air Force Base in 1969—are nearly identical: in every case, Hawaiian women dance on tarmacs and the soldiers partake of their performances as guests (see figures 64.1 and 64.2).[111] Over a stretch of nearly twenty years, the women and men are interchangeable in this film; what matters most is that Hawai'i provides an invaluable service to the nation—the generous reception toward its warriors—through the sexuality of island women. These films distinguish Hawai'i as a site of hospitality and healing, a role that the islands continue to fulfill as the Pacific's R and R capital.

Today, the nation's primary theater of war has shifted from Asia and the Pacific to the Middle East, but Hawai'i remains an invaluable source of leisure for U.S. armed forces. Along with its strategic location in the Pacific Ocean, what has made Hawai'i valuable to U.S. military supremacy in the twentieth century and twenty-first are these enacted and idealized performances of imperial hospitality. The U.S. Army built Hale Koa (House of the Warrior) in the 1970s in Waikīkī, a high-rise resort hotel

Fig. 63.1

Fig. 63.2 Hawaiian women wave to French soldiers (top) and dance hula in front of an ambulance carrying wounded men (bottom) at Hickam Air Force Base, Hawai'i, 29 June 1954. *Operation Wounded Warrior, 07/03/1954*, Motion picture no. 342-USAF-21595.

Fig. 64.1

Fig. 64.2 A soldier with the U.S. Army's 9th Division, 4th Battalion, 39th Infantry lands at Hickam Air Force Base, Hawai'i, on 30 July 1969, after two and a half years in Vietnam. Bottom, hula dancers greet the soldiers. *Keystone Eagle Return of 9th Division, 4th Battalion, 39th Infantry from Vietnam to Hawaii, Hickam AFB, Hawaii, 07/08–1969–08/27–1969*, Motion picture no. 342-USAF-48145.

and affordable R and R destination for military personnel. Paying rates far below market, over one million retired or enlisted members of the armed forces and their families retreat to the Waikīkī beachfront property every year. During recent U.S. wars in Iraq and Afghanistan, Hale Koa offered an "Operation Iraqi Freedom R & R Special" to all U.S. forces serving in these regions. Eligible personnel could reserve an "R & R Waikiki vacation" at a 20 percent discount that included access to the Hale Koa resort's luau. Twice a week, island women perform at the show and continue the well-worn tradition of imperial hospitality on tarmacs, ship decks, and military bases.

Counter-Colonial Volunteerism

Despite the overexposure of their bodies in military film productions of the twentieth century, the identities and experiences of USO hula performers are nearly undetectable in Hawaiian and American archives. Interchangeable and anonymous commodities, individual Hawaiian performers are almost never named in military films and photographs.[112] In contrast to chapter 4 of this book, which derives its methodological and epistemological framework from the lived experiences of Hawaiian women, this chapter has its origins in the temperature-controlled motion picture collections of the U.S. National Archives in College Park, Maryland. There I watched hours of military films that yielded little personal information about the women within.

Yet by bringing subjugated knowledges of hula performers and performance to bear on this cinematic archive, we can begin to see the contours of hidden transcripts within the dancers' wartime volunteerism. Like earlier generations of hula dancers who toured the continental United States during the colonization of the islands, performers inserted their own counter-colonial performances, desires, and tactics into militouristic scripts. They reappropriated militarized time and land according to their own interests.[113] Their participation in wartime entertainment was not directly oppositional to the state or U.S. imperial interests, but allowed them to insert individual and collective desires that were not aligned squarely with either Hawaiian nationalist or American patriotic sympathies.

The first counter-colonial scenario explored here is developed through a reading of potentially subversive eruptions within the film *Luau*. Heretofore I have concentrated on rigid and fixed aspects of the colonial script of hospitality that cast both military and indigenous participants in predetermined roles. However, there are useful contradictions and tensions to observe between colonial tableaux and living scenarios. Examining a scenario, to draw from Diana Taylor, helps to assess "embodied behaviors," such as nuanced gestures that are not reducible to language.[114] These live, dynamic contexts exceed the bounds of scripted, imperial narratives and therefore may undo their intended meaning and reception.

In the climax of the film, hula dancers teach basic hula steps to uniformed military officers on stage, making them mimic hip movements (see figures 61.1, 61.2, and 61.3). The militouristic luau encouraged cooperative partnership through this scripted dance—the white man performing hula with the Native woman—that allegorizes an idealized relationship between colonial male protector and colonized female supplicant. This humorous instruction—the "white men can't dance" element that has become canonized in every commercial luau today in the islands—is designed to provoke laughter from the audience, but produces transitory opportunities for insurgency and the testing of limits.[115]

In the film, the men cannot execute the steps; they are imperfect, awkward pupils moving clumsily on stage. Trying to execute an 'ami or kaholo, the men's uniformed bodies jerk, lose control, and suddenly appear unskilled: they have been exposed, dressed down by their own awkwardness. Momentarily, the officers have become undignified objects of ridicule, while the women take the lead and demonstrate their mastery. Laughing at the men who cannot keep up with them, they are able to mock their colonial rulers in front of an audience of military guests. As the camera pans, we also catch glimpses of other young women sitting behind the hula performers (presumably waiting for their turn on stage) unsmiling, looking off into the distance, bored. Their enthusiasm will have to resume when they dance, but for the time being, they are disengaged.

James C. Scott argues that the hidden transcript tests the limits of domination. It is "continually pressing against the limit of what is permitted on stage, much as a body of water might press against a dam."[116] The women's mockery and recalcitrance within the luau may serve as rehearsals for bigger confrontations to come, a refusal to participate in future tableaux of hospitality. Taking liberties with the script is a familiar practice and resource for those who have performed for tourists. Dancing in Waikīkī, my hula sisters and I smiled broadly when tourists snapped photographs of us, but after they'd turned their backs, we'd sometimes roll our eyes at their sunburned bodies or unwelcome questions. We played within the tourist script, exchanging impromptu winks with each other that bordered on insolence. The kaona, or veiled meanings, of a performance include those sideway glances of dancers who are observing the tourists looking at them, suggesting that concealed expressions are enacted during scenarios of insouciant deference.

From these muted critiques within imperial performances, we may also turn toward the young girls and women who volunteered for the USO and their discrepant motivations for participating. When the war broke out, Leilehua Becker was fourteen years old. Lei became a widely admired pin-up among sailors, soldiers, and civilian workers while in high school (see figure 65). Her photograph appeared in *Colliers*' "Hawaiian Medley" photograph spread of island girls, and she was later chosen as the "Sweetheart" of O'ahu's Seacoast Artillery.[117] Yet for Lei, who was "crazy about singing," the wartime invasion did not mean mollifying restless troops; it represented adventure and a chance to hone her dancing and singing talents for island and military audiences. Along with her mother and brother, Lei worked in the military governor's office as an official mimeograph operator. Late at night, the Beckers and other musician-workers, including the Hawaiian steel guitar virtuoso Merle Kekuku, interrupted the military curfew and blackouts by dancing hula and playing guitar and 'ukulele. Six nights a week during the war, Lei also sang with the well-known Don McDiarmid Orchestra and famed Hawaiian vocalist Alfred Apaka at the Kewalo Inn. Since Lei was only sixteen years old, her mother supervised her by working the inn's hatcheck counter.

Lei Becker's contemporary, Carol Mae Kuuleinani Vanderford, also has vivid recollections of dancing hula during the war (see figure 66). Born in 1929, Carol Mae was about twelve years old when she began entertaining soldiers nearly every weekend during the war. Though disappointed at not having been able to join "Uncle Ray" Kinney's hula troupe in New York City, Carol Mae had only "wonderful memories" of her experience as a USO volunteer in Hawai'i. For Hawaiian children, traveling with the USO became a thrilling adventure. She said, "A bus would pick us up, and our whole troupe would pile into the bus, and we'd sing all the way to where we'd go. [We would] put on the show, eat, and then sing all the way back." The dancers and musicians were never paid for their work—the shows were "kōkua" only (offered in the spirit of cooperation)—but the entertainers were rewarded in other ways. They ate meals provided by the army and navy, often dining in the captains' cafeteria. When they performed on naval ships, they were given special tours and allowed to descend into the galley. Carol Mae and the other children collected gold

Fig. 65 Leilehua Becker, age sixteen, 1944. COURTESY OF LEILEHUA BECKER FURTADO.

Fig. 66 Carol Mae Kuuleinani Stibbard, age twelve, 1941. COURTESY OF CAROL MAE KUULEINANI VANDERFORD.

pins handed out by the local USO director after each volunteer performance. She insisted, "I didn't think of it as work, just total fun, total, total fun. We looked forward to the weekends."

Nearly fifty years later, Carol Mae received a letter from the troupe's pianist, who remembered the Hawaiian community created through USO hula. The old friend wrote, "We always ended our shows with 'Aloha 'Oe' and the troops always cried. Your mom [Harriet Kuuleinani Stibbard] was so kind and loving to all of us. She made the maids feed us well after rehearsals. We loved her so dearly. She always said you and John [Carol Mae's brother] were her treasures."[118] The pianist's memory decenters the experience of soldiers; they become anonymous, while individual performers are cherished. Arguably the soldiers themselves were incidental, merely the excuse or occasion for local socializing and communion. Carol Mae was able to name each performer in her mother's troupe and their kin, but never knew the names or identities of the GIs or sailors.[119] She remarked, "Once we left the base or outfit, we never saw those guys again."[120]

Extending the Hawaiian practice of expressing aloha for a special locale through oli (chant) and song, the troupe celebrated and venerated their home island by singing mele pana (songs honoring a place) about Maui at USO shows. Carol Mae's mother, the hula teacher Harriet Kuuleinani Stibbard, made sure to include her own favorite love songs in the USO repertoire—the Hawaiian-language love songs "Mi Nei" and "Hoonanea."[121] Iwalani Wilson, the troupe's youngest dancer, was about six years old when she performed as the "baby" soloist of the Buck-Stibbard troupe. So tiny she had to stand on orange crates to reach the microphone, Iwalani impressed listeners with her big voice. The Maui USO circuit became the start of her successful professional singing career. Known as Iwalani Kahalewai, she sang in the famed "Hawaii Calls" radio show and became a headlining solo vocalist and dancer with Alfred Apaka's Tapa Room at the Hawaiian Village in Waikīkī in 1958.[122] That same year, Iwalani recorded her version of "Hoonanea," one of the troupe's USO standards, with a piano arrangement similar to the way she had sung for servicemen during the war.[123]

Other Hawaiian entertainers, including Sonny Kamaka, Lei Becker, and Leilani Alama, all began performing on the USO circuit and became professionals after the war.[124] Furthermore, USO entertainment, although primarily for the military, also brought pleasure and relaxation to islander performers and audiences. One USO hula troupe made use of officers'

clubs to play volleyball, dance, and drink at the bar after hours, while Hawaiians living near army and navy recreation centers attended hula shows
there.[125] Hawaiians managed to interrupt the script of the militourized
luau and introduce their own relationships of aloha that endured long
after the removal of barbed wire.

Outside the Frame

Rachel Lee has aptly identified the "excess of visibility" to which women
of color have been historically subjected.[126] Military films produced very
real material effects—conscripting Hawaiians into the service of the state
and the further militouristic development of the islands—but these media can enable inscriptions of other meanings. More than a technology of
subordination, might these photographs suggest other counter-colonial
inscriptions? How did hula performers experience their own alterity as
they were being captured on film?

Fatimah Tobing Rony has proposed that racialized people who have
been objectified by the ethnographic gaze have developed a "third eye"
as they experience themselves being looked at—an eye that enables a
critique of their objectification.[127] Entertainers from the USO, although
they were objects of militouristic photography that instrumentalized
their aloha, developed a third eye through their personal photographic
archives. At the same time Hawaiians were interpellated by the state as
hosts, they were also working as critics, archivists, and producers of their
own extensive collections. Through a reading of these alternative, if not
oppositional, archives, hula performers can be seen reappropriating the
militouristic gaze through their use and circulation of photographs.[128]

Discussing Hawaiians as image-makers demands a larger historical
context, for coming into visibility did not automatically signify abjec-
tion. Historically Hawaiians and other Native peoples have had a very
creative, intersubjective relationship with photography, appropriating
colonial technologies to assert their collective humanity or individual
celebrity. For example, King David Kalākaua and his consort Kapiʻolani
displayed large portraits of themselves as evidence of their modernity at
the Women's Industries and Centenary Fair in Sydney in 1888 and the
Exhibition Universelle in Paris in 1889 (see figure 67). Adorned in Western
regalia, Kalākaua's portrait presents him as the sovereign of a modern
nation-state.

Even Hawaiian performers consigned to the disreputable midway
sections of international expositions in the late nineteenth century and

Fig. 67 "Hawaiian Exhibits Sent by the King of the Hawaiian Islands," Women's Industries and Centenary Fair, Sydney, Australia, 1888. PPO-1.
COURTESY OF HAWAI'I STATE ARCHIVES.

the early twentieth had their portraits taken. These images were likely sold as tourist souvenirs of "hula hula girls," but these photographs also comprised part of each other's personal archives and served as a record of their cosmopolitan travels. Photographs of hula dancers, including those of Mele and Malie from the Omaha Greater America Exposition in 1899, were found in the estate of their fellow dancer Kini Kapahukulaokamāmalu, or Mrs. Jennie Kapahu Wilson, after her death in 1962 in Hawai'i at the age of ninety (see figures 18.1 and 18.2). This suggests that performers developed their own intimate relationships to ethnographic portraits beyond the imperial gaze of tourists.

Hula performers' ways of reading and circulating photographs interrupt the objectifying ethnographic gaze. To be sure, they posed themselves as "hula girls"; these pin-up photographs were a requisite casting and publicity tool from the early 1900s to the 1960s, and resembled postcards sold to soldiers. However, they circulated these photographs as "tokens of affections" among themselves with personal inscriptions like "To Hanakaulani, a great pal," or "To Mama—aloha nui" (see figure 47). These dedications disrupt the delivery of the women as mere objects; the messages embedded on the photographs hinder the easy reduction of the

Fig. 68 USO dance, Wailuku, Maui gymnasium, 1945. COURTESY OF
CAROL MAE KUULEINANI VANDERFORD.

image to that of a "hula girl." They imply a history, a set of relationships
outside the frame. Or, as Vicente L. Rafael has suggested in his readings
of colonial Filipino photographs, they imply a third viewer beyond the
intended viewer or the colonial state, perhaps even someone in the future
who may regard them.[129] Because photographs, particularly ethnographic
or tourist photographs, fix Natives in a timeless "ethnographic present,"
these particular inscriptions insist on temporality and historicity, connecting them to specific times, spaces, and relationships.

   During the time *Luau* was shot, Hawaiian performers took informal
photographs and snapshots of their time with the troops—these were
neither elaborately staged portraits nor intimate two-shots with soldiers.
Their photographs do not showcase performers as exotic figures in costume, but in groups, often backstage or in transit to the next location.
For nearly sixty years Carol Mae Kuuleinani Vanderford has maintained
her own visual record of her troupe's encounters with the troops. In a
series of photographs taken at a USO dance in a gymnasium in Wailuku,
Maui, soldiers and the local community gather (see figure 68). The men
are not paired off with the women, and there is no clear hierarchy or order
suggested. Everyone—local male entertainers, soldiers, young girls, older
women—gathers in no particular grouping. It is not immediately evident

Fig. 69 Ray Kinney's hula troupe and band at a picnic, ca. 1944.
COURTESY OF AKAU FAMILY.

who the performers are. The soldiers also become objects of curiosity, perhaps for the dancers who snapped this photograph.

Similarly, Hawaiian musician and bandleader Ray Kinney, his family, and musical troupe spent three and a half years on the USO hula circuit in the continental United States during and after the war. They traveled by bus to over 150 highly restricted army and Marine Corps bases in places like Louisville, Kentucky, and Cherry Point, North Carolina. On at least one occasion, they were flown into the Parris Island Marine Recruit Depot in South Carolina to entertain marine recruits.[130]

The Kinney family photographs rarely show their military audiences or their performances on stage, but instead focus on their travels as they went from base to base. Calling themselves "one big family," the troupe piled together in rented buses for stretches of six to seven months. While on the road the troupe—a mix of Hawaiians and haole musicians and hula dancers—stopped between bases to relax and have a picnic for themselves (see figure 69). They eat and enjoy beers together. This photograph is one family's souvenir of their time "on the road," but it could easily be any other family photograph, for it does not immediately signify "entertainment." I choose to end with this image of the picnic because it stands in stark contrast to a staged, militarized luau. "Hawaiianness" does not signify "service" or "entertainment," nor does whiteness signify the "military," for no obvious racial, class, or occupational hierarchy is implied. In fact, it was Ray Kinney, a Hawaiian man, who hired, paid, and occasionally fired the white musicians. In these photographs, war and its apparatuses are domesticated (e.g., the military bus becomes a traveling home), rather than the land and people being domesticated for militourism. Or, in other words, we can see that the military is indigenized and domesticated by Native practices of travel.

These photographs did not simply come to rest in a photo album—they traveled from Waimea, Hawai'i, to New York City over fifty years after they were shot. I came to see these photographs in both locales, as shared by two different women. Ray Kinney's daughter Raylani Kinney Akau grew up on the road with the older hula dancers; they were reunited at a ceremony honoring her father in 2002. The dancers did not remember any of the individual soldiers they entertained, but they regarded each other as a large family connected over several decades. Raylani sent an album to each of the surviving hula dancers as a living archive of their extended 'ohana during the war. These photographs were memory prompts that activated fictive kin networks.

What Rony calls the "taxidermic" quality of ethnographic media perhaps made Hawaiian entertainers uninterested in posing as acquiescent performers when they were off-stage.[131] While photographs from World War II promoted harmonious relationships in the interest of nation building, these photographs suggest affiliations outside the state, such as desires for work, celebrity, adventure, and love. They tell other stories of associations and repertoires beyond the well-worn inscriptions of "host" and "guest."

On the first afternoon of the Merrie Monarch Festival of 2006, eleven men and women boarded a rented tour bus for Edith Kanakaʻole Stadium with their kumu hula, Ed Collier, who encouraged them to "Imua Lanakila!" (Go forward to victory). Hālau o Nā Pua Kukui was one of twenty-three hālau hula invited to compete in this prestigious hula showcase. Earlier that day, the dancers performed oli and hula at the edge of Halemaʻumaʻu crater, the home of Pele, the volcano goddess (see figure 70). They threw hoʻokupu (offerings) of flower lei, beer, and gin into the crater and prayed for Pele to bless their performances. Their entreaties and efforts paid off when, on the last evening, the men won third place in the hula ʻauana (modern hula) category (see figure 71).[1]

While the dancers prepared backstage, inside the stadium hundreds of Japanese women dressed in brightly colored muʻumuʻu (Hawaiian dresses) posed for photographs and perused the wares of local vendors selling flower lei and food (see figure 72). Besides the competitors and their supporters, the largest single group of festival ticketholders are these hula aficionados between the ages of thirty and sixty who belong to hula studios in Japan. Several kumu hula who regularly compete in or judge the Merrie Monarch Festival teach at profitable "sister" studios and hālau in Japan, where there are an estimated 400,000 hula students and more than 100 hula studios.[2]

During the competition, packed buses of tourists and performers drove past a sprinkling of Hawaiian protesters demonstrating against Hawaiʻi's occupation by the United States. Standing outside the packed parking lot, they held up placards reading "Stop the Akaka Bill!" "Stop OHA [the Office of Hawaiian Affairs]!" and

Fig. 70 Hālau o Nā Pua Kukui dancing for Pele at Halemaʻumaʻu crater, Hawaiʻi. 20 April 2006. PHOTOGRAPH BY AUTHOR.

Fig. 71 Kāne of Hālau o Nā Pua Kukui, Hula ʻauana performance at Merrie Monarch Festival, 22 April 2006. Left to right: Landon Patoc, Sean Nakayama, Clint Onigama. PHOTOGRAPH BY DALTON SUE.

Fig. 72 Japanese tourist trying on floral lei at Merrie Monarch festival, 2006. PHOTOGRAPH BY AUTHOR.

"Oh Say Can You See, America is a Thief." The so-called Akaka Bill is a proposal for federal recognition of a Hawaiian governing entity that has been repeatedly sponsored by Hawai'i's U.S. senators, Daniel Akaka and Daniel Inouye, since 2000. This congressional legislation would create a nation-within-a-nation system of governance for Native Hawaiians, with limited self-determination. Although it is supported by the Office of Hawaiian Affairs, a state agency, many Hawaiian activists argue that such a federal bill would preemptively extinguish the rights of Kanaka Maoli to self-governance and undermine their inherent sovereignty.[3] Largely out of view from 3,000 hula spectators, this activism seemed marginal, if not irrelevant, to the vigorous commerce, cultural capital, and sheer devotion generated by hula.

From these particular scenes, it would seem that Merrie Monarch hula, as one crossroads of competitive hula and contemporary global capitalism, is quite literally fenced off from the concerns of Native Hawaiian sovereignty and self-determination. Activists waving upside-down

Hawaiian flags as signs of distress appear estranged from dynamic hula dancers who spend a year preparing for a seven-minute performance and the opportunity to gain recognition before an island community and a larger global audience. Dance and politics may seem like they cannot comfortably occupy the same stage. Yet this separation between the culture and politics of Kanaka Maoli does not obtain when one carefully examines everyday relations and movements of po'e hula. In fact, hula has become coterminous with Native rights activism; it is an essential part of political life in Hawai'i as it was in the 1830s and 1930s, although its praxis and tactics may appear different today. A critical opportunity structure during Hawai'i's colonization, hula constitutes an emergent structure of feeling in the islands that merges self-determination politics and pragmatic capitalism.

One familiar face at the Merrie Monarch Festival, the kumu hula Victoria "Vicky" Holt Takamine, embodies this emergence of po'e hula as political actors (see figure 73).[4] Takamine, when not sitting as a competition judge or teaching hula to her hālau, Pua Ali'i 'Ilima, may just as likely be seen holding signs for Kanaka Maoli causes in Waikīkī or at the Hawai'i state capitol. A longtime hula performer and teacher, kumu Vicky launched her career as an activist when she organized a coalition of po'e hula called 'Ilio'ulaokalani in response to a Hawai'i state legislative bill in 1997. This bill would have severely curtailed, if not terminated, the rights of the Kanaka Maoli to gather plants on land and in the ocean. Although a decision by the Hawai'i state supreme court in 1995 guaranteed the constitutional rights of Hawaiians to gather natural resources on undeveloped land, the real estate industry pushed the state legislature to introduce a law that would have required permits for traditional gathering. Takamine said: "I couldn't believe the language in that bill . . . asking Native Hawaiians to go register with the Land Use Commission for permission to gather the natural resources vital to our traditional and customary practices. They wanted me to list everything that I pick— every fern, flower and seashell—and the places that I gather them and show by a clear preponderance of the evidence that my ancestors gathered them prior to 1898."[5]

Takamine and her haumāna (students) quickly began calling other hula performers to take their pahu (sharkskin drums) to the legislature: "We just called everyone in the phone book who had a hālau listing. We didn't even know everyone. We had forty hālau—or at least forty drums there."[6] Po'e hula, for whom many of these natural resources are essential,

Fig. 73 Kumu hula Vicky Holt Takamine, 2010. PHOTOGRAPH BY REID YOKOTE.

were spurred to action. For nearly twenty-four hours straight, hundreds of teachers and students drummed, chanted, and danced in what was an explicitly political staging of a religious and cultural performance. They performed "Au'a 'ia," a hula pahu (sacred drum hula) performed at heiau (temples) in precolonial Hawai'i.[7] Hula performed that day was not meant to entertain; po'e hula decided in advance that they would not wear hula costumes or adornments.[8] Lawmakers felt the pahu vibrations in their legislative chambers and shelved the bill. For the time being, hula dancers and Native healers may enter private land to gather materials for cultural practices.

Hula performances that are self-consciously and intentionally oppositional have since been termed "hula kū'ē," or hula that resists or opposes.[9] Although the protest in 1997 was the formal beginning of the 'Īlio coalition, its work continues through hula kū'ē and other grassroots activism, as the Hawaiian community has been buffeted by numerous legal challenges by non-Hawaiian plaintiffs and the State of Hawai'i. Continuing the century-long legacy of their forebears, po'e hula have taken on a visible role in Hawai'i, publicizing Hawaiian political issues and mobilizing community members. Po'e hula exhibit hula kū'ē at numerous "Justice for Hawaiians" marches that oppose lawsuits and policies that undermine Native Hawaiian rights.[10] The kumu hula Sonny Ching explained, "The kumu hula are standing up and taking their place in the sovereignty movement. It's hard to say we're at the forefront of the movement, because so many other entities have come before us and done so much work in that direction, but the 'kumu' is more prominent and visible."[11]

Beginning in 2003, the first set of lawsuits has targeted Kamehameha Schools, a private educational institution funded by the estate of an aliʻi. Initiated by anonymous non-Hawaiian plaintiffs, the suits challenged the legality of the admissions policy of Kamehameha Schools, which grants preference to Native Hawaiian children.[12] A second critical arena of political activity by poʻe hula is their timely response to the State of Hawaiʻi's attempted sale of the misnamed "ceded lands" held in trust by the state. Although popularly known as "ceded lands," these lands are actually approximately 1.8 million acres of crown and government lands of the Hawaiian kingdom seized by the Republic of Hawaiʻi in 1894. These lands make up over 40 percent of the islands' total acreage. The republic, whose leaders had participated in the overthrow of the kingdom, "ceded" these lands to the United States upon its illegal annexation of Hawaiʻi in 1898.[13] When Hawaiʻi became the fiftieth state in 1959, the State of Hawaiʻi gained control of these lands via a public trust. Almost the entirety of the state's lands, including those on which the Honolulu International Airport, the University of Hawaiʻi, and most public buildings sit, are trust lands. As instituted by the Admissions Act of 1959 and amended by the Hawaiʻi State Constitution in 1978, revenues from the use of the public land trust must go to five purposes, one of them the benefit of Native Hawaiians. However, at least since the early 1990s, the state has attempted to sell or transfer these lands, prompting legal battles that made their way up to the U.S. Supreme Court. In early 2009, the Supreme Court heard oral arguments about the proposed sale of trust lands.[14]

The instrumentation of aloha as mutuality that developed in the late nineteenth century has been extended to assert the privileges of dominant settler populations, including entitlements to these trust lands. Frequently the ethos of aloha is interpreted as multicultural sharing that conveniently dispenses with the rights of Kanaka Maoli and their history of dispossession. "Aloha for All" is the rhetorical argument of one influential libertarian activist group headed by the attorney H. William Burgess and his wife Sandra Puanani Burgess. They, along with other non-Hawaiians and Hawaiians, insist that state and federal laws should not favor Kanaka Maoli in the spirit of "sharing" aloha with all citizens of Hawaiʻi. Beginning in 2000, William Burgess helped to organize a number of lawsuits filed by non-Hawaiian and Hawaiian residents of the state;

these lawsuits challenge the constitutionality of agencies and institutions that support Hawaiians and are funded by income from trust lands.

Kanaka Maoli have responded quickly to this usurpation of their aloha. Prior to and during the Supreme Court's deliberations over the trust lands issue, hundreds of Kanaka Maoli and their allies gathered at vigils organized by 'Īlio'ulaokalani. Holding "Seized, Not Ceded" signs and wearing red shirts at the state capitol, protesters flew Hawaiian flags upside down as an internationally understood sign of distress. They also practiced hula kū'ē, performing a set repertoire of oli and beating pahu every hour for twelve hours. The kumu hula Mapuana de Silva of Hālau Mōhala 'Ilima, Vicky Takamine's hula sister, brought about twenty-five members of her hālau to underscore the inextricable relationship between Hawaiians and land.[15] She insisted, "You take the land away and Hawaiians do not have a base."[16]

Yet because Hawaiian lands are critical to national military strategy, they are continually under threat by the U.S. military. Only four days after the annexation of Hawai'i, 1,300 U.S. troops arrived to establish the islands' first permanent garrison.[17] The annexation further opened the doors to the military expropriation of Hawaiian land. The State of Hawai'i assumed control as trustee over the crown and government lands formerly belonging to the Hawaiian kingdom after Hawai'i became a state in 1959. However, the military held on to 10 percent of these lands and leased even more back from the state for token sums. At present, the military, according to its own reports, controls almost 6 percent of the total land in Hawai'i, with its heaviest concentration of military reservations and bases on O'ahu, the most populous island.[18]

As the center of the U.S. Pacific Command, the largest unified military command in the nation, Hawai'i has taken on an important training and staging role after 9/11 for the Iraq and Afghanistan wars. The U.S. Army has based Stryker Brigade mobile units, nineteen-ton armored vehicles that are the lynchpin of its new, flexible combat strategy, in the Hawaiian Islands. After training in Hawai'i, these 4,000 soldier brigades are able to rapidly deploy to the Middle East, where they patrol insurgent areas. Hawaiian groups and environmentalists, including 'Īlio'ulaokalani, filed lawsuits and protested the U.S. Army's expropriation of land for Stryker training, citing the release of toxic contaminants and damage to sacred Hawaiian religious sites, among other consequences.[19]

In addition to land rights, 'Īlio has coordinated community meetings about related issues of biopiracy and bioprospecting in Hawai'i, with particular attention to genetic modification of kalo (taro), the spiritual ancestor of Hawaiians. When the University of Hawaiʻi, Mānoa, took out patents of kalo in 2006, Hawaiians launched protests that included hula performance.[20] Although these varieties of kalo were hybridized, not genetically modified, Kanaka Maoli assert that no one has the right to own their ancestor, whether a public university or a corporation like Monsanto. This resistance to biopiracy underscores the continued vital role of kalo in Hawaiian life, which far exceeds kalo's utility in militourized luau performances.

Given the attempted alienation of the former kingdom's land base by military, state, and corporate interests and Hawaiian vigilance against the incursions of global capital, one may conclude that Kanaka Maoli revile state-sponsored commercial tourism. Yet as I have traced in this book, hula performance and its global circulation can be read neither as wholly complicit with a colonial or neocolonial system nor unproblematically resistant to it. Hula performers continually made their living through tourism while mobilizing anticolonial and counter-colonial interests among Hawaiians. Performers on vaudeville and world's fair circuits, for instance, practiced strategic commodification, discerning which forms of hula were appropriate for alienation and which were inalienable. They also instrumentalized tourist venues as platforms for critiques of empire. Noncommodified hula practice and knowledge continued during the past century of colonization, but tourist circuits, far from hastening the demise of hula, also helped to keep hula alive during the past century of colonization. "Deep knowledge of esoteric traditions has been passed into the present by women," Amy Kuʻuleialoha Stillman contends.[21] Today's hula activism can be seen emerging from this genealogy of tourist performers who fostered deep knowledge, creative innovations, and counter-colonial tactics, despite the manipulation of their aloha and American imperial maneuvering.

Hula remains an extremely adaptive and resilient practice; poʻe hula often operate within the constraints of the tourist industry and against it selectively. Rather than altogether rejecting tourism, these performers savvily negotiate the seeming contradiction between Native self-determination and their participation in a market-oriented economy that has commodified their land, bodies, and cultural practices. Hula is rarely a self-supporting profession. As in precontact and postcontact Hawaiʻi, hālau hula are the formal institutions responsible for the cultural reproduction of hula. There are perhaps as many as 300 hālau hula active in

Hawai'i today, but state support is inconsistent and elusive. Takamine observes, "We [hālau hula] are the largest arts organization in the state and we get the least funding. Ballet dancers get more funding [from the state] than hula, though the state needs us to survive."[22] Some kumu hula may enjoy lucrative careers in the islands and through their overseas sister hālau, but few hula practitioners can make a living teaching hula full-time. Most dancers support themselves by charging tuition for hula classes, working in state-sponsored tourism, or in other professions altogether.

Vicky Holt Takamine, among many other hula practitioners, personifies this expansive approach to commodification and tourism.[23] Rather than regard political activism and tourism as contrary, she embraces tourism and acculturated hula as part of her heritage and hula genealogy. Like many other Hawaiian women performers, Takamine's professional career as a dancer began in tourist showrooms. She remarked: "I don't think people realize that most of us kumu hula got our start in hapa haole [acculturated performance]. My teacher, kumu hula Aunty Maiki [Aiu], put me in a hula show in Waikīkī when I was seventeen years old. I did the Queen's Surf luau. I danced for International Market Place—I must've danced in every show in Waikīkī."[24]

As a kumu hula, Takamine has been associated with the resurgence of the genre of hula kahiko, or "ancient hula," during the Hawaiian Renaissance in the 1970s. She trained in a contemporary version of Kini Kapahukulaokamāmalu's late nineteenth-century hālau hula, receiving 'ūniki (graduate) status upon completion of her training with the kumu hula Maiki Aiu. Takamine's foundation, she asserts, is "kahiko." Literally translated as "the old," the genre of hula kahiko has become shorthand for "traditional" hula of varying degrees of transformation, from European contact to the present.[25] Hālau hula must compete in hula kahiko during the first of two days at the Merrie Monarch Festival; this genre is usually what is performed at rallies and on solemn anniversaries of the U.S. overthrow and annexation. It is perceived as more authentically Hawaiian, compared to the genre of "hapa haole" hula associated with Western costuming, musical scales, and English-language lyrics. Yet Takamine values hapa haole hula, saying, "I think because of the Hawaiian renaissance and the movement to uphold kahiko, hapa haole has been neglected. But my kumu hula, the late Auntie Maiki Aiu Lake, always said to support and know everything."[26]

Cellophane skirts and other so-called artificial costuming are explicitly prohibited at most hula competitions; they are generally eschewed by contemporary hula performers, except in performances meant to self-consciously evoke "nostalgia" of the early twentieth century.[27] Aiming to support tourist-oriented hula as an important Hawaiian innovation, Takamine asserts the hapa-haole cellophane skirt as her heritage as much as the ancient pahu: "Aunty Maiki danced in a cellophane skirt, I danced in a cellophane skirt, my mother danced in a cellophane skirt, and we all did hapa haole music."[28] Dancers from the height of the midcentury hapa haole hula era also express their affection for acculturated skirts. Betty Puanani Makia enthusiastically recalled her costume worn on the U.S. continent, "We had to use cellophane as a second costume [when ti leaves weren't available], but it was just glamorous."[29] Carol Mae Kuuleinani Vanderford, a generation younger than Aunty Betty, recognizes the current antipathy to acculturated hula repertoire and style. She insists, "I love cellophane. I don't care what they say today."[30]

Takamine's twenty-year entertainment career reveals how po'e hula negotiate the Native revivalist goals of hālau hula with the dictates of the commercial tourism: "I ran the Paradise Cove luau show for ten years. When we initially started it, it was . . . my hālau [Pua 'Alii 'Ilima] and O'Brian Eselu and Thaddius's [Wilson's] hālau [Nā Wai 'Ehā o Puna]. The two hālaus started that luau show and ran it as hālau performances for ten years. We did do Tahitian and Maori [dance] which the industry required. But all the hula we did, it was hula we did in hālau. Hula was not geared for, contrived for the tastes of the tourist."[31]

Paradise Cove Luau is a popular tourist attraction featuring luau dinner shows on the West side of O'ahu. The kumu hula O'Brian Eselu continues to produce and emcee this Polynesian luau revue where he is known for his lovely falsetto voice and comedic flair. Despite performing for tourists, Eselu and his hālau, Ke Kai o Kahiki, seem to have lost little cultural capital among judges and local audiences; their professional experience has even made them a more polished "competition hālau," as hālau appearing on the competition circuit are known. Ke Kai o Kahiki recently won top honors at the Merrie Monarch Festival in 2010.

Many other hula practitioners traffic frequently between competition and tourist sites. Kamele Collier noted that her experience in her father's hālau, Hālau o Nā Pua Kukui, enabled her to become a better professional dancer.[32] The discipline she acquired from hālau practice helped her to perfect and train her fellow dancers as a "line captain" of a Polynesian show in Waikīkī. Another kumu hula, April Chock, works as a tour escort for Germaine's Luau, singing and playing 'ukulele on the tour bus.[33] One of my hula brothers, Blaine Ikaika Dutro, competitively danced for Johnny Lum Ho's hālau hula, but also danced at the local restaurant Billy's, in Hilo, and on tourist boats. He now teaches Hawaiian studies and hula at a high school on O'ahu and leads a small hālau hula.

While organizing political vigils and protests, Takamine has concentrated her energies on two projects that merge hula activism with tourist performance. The first is a cultural entertainment program, "Ho'okipa Aloha" (Welcome Aloha), for Norwegian Cruise Line's Hawai'i cruise ships.[34] Takamine coordinates an on-board hula program for large, 2,000-passenger ships. Her hālau, along with two respected troupes led by female kumu hula Mapuana de Silva and Malia Loebenstein Carter, greet tourists with traditional and contemporary hula on the ship's pool deck. Takamine has been criticized by some Kanaka Maoli for performing hula on cruises, particularly given her opposition to cruise ship traffic and pollution in Hawaiian waters. She is founder and president of KAHEA, a community-based environmental justice alliance of Kanaka Maoli and environmental activists that monitors natural and cultural resources on the islands. Avoiding a purist philosophy, Takamine has argued that kumu hula are better equipped to educate visitors about Hawaiian culture than the tourist industry; for kumu hula have the kuleana (privilege and responsibility) to protect and promote hula. The cruise ship program is one opportunity for Kanaka Maoli to control their message and receive compensation.

The second cultural engagement is the Hapa Haole Hula and Music Festival. Debuting in Waikīkī in 2003, the festival features contests for hula soloists, groups, and a lead vocalist.[35] The festival's goal is to jumpstart the reopening of Hawaiian showrooms that capture the high style of the hapa haole era. Despite the glamour of Waikīkī and showrooms in the continental United States, venues in Hawai'i for acculturated Hawaiian performance shuttered in the 1980s and 1990s. Providing much-needed employment for Hawaiians, these venues would showcase headlining Hawaiian entertainers, comic hula dancers, and "leading ladies" along the lines of erstwhile stars Meymo Ululani Holt, Jennie Napua Woodd, Lei Becker, and Ray Kinney. Takamine and Meymo Holt share a history in hapa haole performance, as well as haole and Hawaiian kūpuna (ancestors). Rather than hastening the demise of Hawaiian cultural practices, as is commonly assumed, "The hapa haole period served a real purpose," argues Takamine. "It kept Hawaiian culture alive."[36] The festival has received a small grant from the Hawai'i Tourist Authority, the state agency responsible for planning and managing Hawai'i's tourist industry.[37] In 2006, the group also launched the Hapa Haole festival at Bally's Resort in Las Vegas, an important nightlife capital and the center of a large Hawaiian diasporic community.

Despite their involvement in state-sponsored tourism, po'e hula remain cognizant of the way the state and multinational capital commodify Native Hawaiian bodies and labor without regard to economic need, cultural dictates, and protocols. Hawaiian women, who have had a particularly vexed relationship with tourism, remain especially vulnerable as they are conflated with compliant hula maidens in the fantasy of imperial hospitality. They struggle with the public unveiling of their bodies as they try to define their terms of engagement. An early pioneer on the vaudeville circuit, Kini Kapahu was expected to dance for Americans with her breasts exposed, but refused. At one point during her career, Takamine walked away from tourist entertainment: "I loved the tourist industry until they decided to dictate to me what they wanted me to wear. They wanted coconut bras. Hawaiians never put their boobs into coconut shells. We served 'awa [drink made of kava root] and did 'awa ceremony rituals with those [coconuts]! They're not for boobs. When they started to dictate what they wanted to see on stage, I said forget it."[38]

Furthermore, hula has historically been a customary and necessary component of official state and military ceremonies (see chapter 5). Hawaiian performance and blessings sanction state projects and symbolize the hospitality and cooperation of Kanaka Maoli. When the State of Hawai'i's new Hawai'i Convention Center opened in 1997, costing $350 million, it asked hālau hula to perform in the opening ceremonies. Takamine elaborated: "The state spent over one million dollars on art [for the Convention Center], but not one Native Hawaiian artist was commissioned.... They wanted the kumus, the drums [at the opening]. But I said no. You only want us for decoration. I said, I want to know what you're going to do to protect our culture and the cultural practitioners.... They come to ask me to dance for free. But I want to make a living off of my job. I want to make a living off of my art."[39]

Several hālau hula affiliated with 'Īlio'ulaokalani refused to contribute their blessing and boycotted the convention center, citing the state's convenient and free use of Hawaiian labor whenever it needed Hawaiian support for tourist projects. Takamine critiques the instrumentalization of the hospitality of Kanaka Maoli: "You [the state] sell us, you sell our culture, you use our dancers, you use our aloha spirit as a marketing tool. You use our music, our images . . . but you don't support the essence of that. You only support things that are geared for tourists."[40]

This opinion is widely shared among Kanaka Maoli. According to a survey commissioned by the Hawai'i Tourism Authority (HTA) and released in 2010, Native Hawaiians are less favorable toward the tourism industry than all other racial and ethnic groups in the islands. Nearly 60 percent disagreed with the statement that the tourism industry "helps to preserve Native Hawaiian language and culture."[41] While state funding has been elusive, the state tourist agency, the HTA, recognizes that it requires the participation of Hawaiians to survive. It recently established "Kūkulu Ola—Living Hawaiian Culture Program" to "honor and preserve the Hawaiian culture."[42] The HTA distributed $600,000 to Hawaiian groups, funding several programs for the preservation or performance of hula.[43]

The simultaneous accommodation and antipathy of Hawaiian performers to tourism suggests their tremendous flexibility; po'e hula work within the constraints of the multinational tourist industry and selectively mobilize against its detrimental aspects. Merging political and cultural praxes with entrepreneurship, hula remains an important cultural and economic opportunity structure in the islands and may provide a path for decolonization. The seeds of today's self-determination and nationalist revival are also found within the century-old tourist hula circuit that simultaneously commodified and transmitted cultural knowledge. Faced by the loss of their kingdom, performers on the tourist circuit sang songs in honor of their deposed queen and produced veiled critiques of empire, while performing Hawaiianness for paying tourists. Po'e hula will continue to create and transform cultural and political institutions that support themselves, their communities, and their environment. While aloha has been Hawai'i's most exploited asset, commodity, and cultural value, it is not for sale by po'e hula, or at least it is not free for the taking. Hula practitioners insist on deciding how they will display and perform their aloha. Determined to represent themselves, they are voicing and performing their critiques on stage, at public protests, and in legislative testimony. In other words, they are restaging imperial performances of aloha.

CHRONOLOGY

Hawai'i Exhibits at International Expositions, 1894–1915

Provisional Government and Republic of Hawai'i

1894   Midwinter International Exposition, San Francisco*

1898   Trans-Mississippi Exposition, Omaha

1899   Greater America Exposition, Omaha*

Territory of Hawai'i

1900   Exposition Universelle de Paris

1901   Pan-American Exposition, Buffalo, N.Y.*

1903   National Industrial Exposition, Osaka, Japan

1904   Louisiana Purchase Exposition, St. Louis

1907   Jamestown Tri-Centennial Exposition, Norfolk, Va.

1909   Alaska-Yukon-Pacific Exposition, Seattle*

1915   Panama-Pacific International Exposition, San Francisco*

* Hawaiian performers present

ABBREVIATIONS OF COLLECTIONS, LIBRARIES, AND ARCHIVES

BK: John H. Wilson Research Papers of Bob Krauss, U-163, Hawai'i State Archives

BM: Bishop Museum

CKV: Carol Mae Kuuleinani Vanderford, personal collection

GMB: Gloria Manu Kanemura Bentley, personal collection

HK: Henry Kekahuna collection, M-445, Hawai'i State Archives

HSA: Hawai'i State Archives

HWRD: Hawai'i War Records Depository, University of Hawai'i, Mānoa

JHW: John H. Wilson Papers, M-182, Hawai'i State Archives

JNW: Jennie Napua Woodd, personal collection

LBF: Leilehua Becker Furtado, personal collection

NA: U.S. National Archives at College Park, College Park, Md.

NYPL: New York Public Library

RKA: Raylani Kinney Akau, personal collection

TK: Theodore Kelsey Collection, M-86, Hawai'i State Archives

WC: Warshaw Collection of Business Americana, Collection 60, Smithsonian National Museum of American History, Archives Center

ZWF: Zim World's Fair Collection, Collection 519, Smithsonian National Museum of American History, Archives Center

NOTES

Introduction

1. Hālau hula must be invited to participate in the Merrie Monarch Hula Festival. In turn, kumu hula (master teachers) select their best dancers to represent the group. It is the highest honor to dance in and win a trophy at the competition.

2. Kamele Collier Marquez, interviewed by the author, 14 July 2007. Kamele's professional positions in hula included dancing and choreographing for Tihati Productions, a Polynesian dance company, and "John Hirokawa's Magic of Polynesia," a Las Vegas–like show in Waikīkī featuring an illusionist. She also performed as a hula soloist at the Kahala Mandarin Hotel (now the Kahala Hotel and Resort).

3. The nomenclature "hula sister" and "hula brother" refer to fictive kin, dancers taught by the same kumu hula in the same hālau.

4. The hālau also dances in the exhibition portion of the Hula Ho'olauna Aloha, a hula competition held in Honolulu for Japanese hālau and judged by Hawaiian kumu. One of its principal sponsors is JALPAK, a division of Japan Airlines that sells overseas package tours. The company wishes to encourage more travel to Hawai'i through "cultural exchange." See Eloise Aguiar, "Japan Hooked on Hula and the 'Ukulele," *Honolulu Advertiser*, 11 July 2005.

5. In my use, "Native Hawaiian" and "islander" are distinct and not interchangeable terms. "Native Hawaiian" and "Hawaiian" refers to the indigenous people of the Hawaiian archipelago, not residents of Hawai'i. Instead, I use "islander" to refer to someone from the Hawaiian Islands, regardless of ethnic or indigenous background. Thus the term "islander" includes Hawaiians, Japanese, Filipinos, Chinese, even haole (Caucasians) hailing from the islands.

6. Hawaiian men also perform hula, but women practitioners and teachers far outnumber men for reasons I discuss throughout the book.

7. Despite the tourist industry's dependence on hula to "brand" Hawai'i, there are few professional full-time hula dancers in Hawai'i today. Instead, dancers may be mail carriers, students, engineers, clerks, housewives, bartenders, waitresses, secretaries, former army intelligence officers, and retirees. Most dancers pursue hula as a serious avocation that requires time, dedication, and their unpaid labor.

8. United Airlines, 30 March 2010, Internet offer, "United Offers and Announcements."

9. Hawaiian entertainers also toured Asia and the Pacific, but to a lesser degree. For instance, Kent Ghirard, a haole musician and entertainer, brought his "Hula Nani Girls" troupe from Hawai'i to Japan in 1955. The Samoan-Hawaiian Moe family also toured East Asia, South Asia, Southeast Asia, and the Middle East extensively from the late 1920s to the 1960s.

10. Today Guam and American Samoa are unincorporated territories and Puerto Rico is a commonwealth of the United States.

11. In 1898 the United States annexed Hawai'i by the Newlands Resolution, a joint resolution of U.S. Congress, rather than by treaty. The resolution required a simple majority vote, whereas a two-thirds vote in each house was necessary to ratify a treaty. Two previous attempts at passing an annexation treaty failed: the first after President Cleveland withdrew the treaty in 1893, and the second in 1897, after massive Kanaka Maoli organized resistance. See N. K. Silva, *Aloha Betrayed*, 131–63. Hawai'i remained a territory until 1959, when Congress passed a bill making the territory the fiftieth state of the union and Hawai'i's population approved statehood via plebiscite. However, this plebiscite offered only two choices on the ballot: statehood or continued territorial status. Furthermore, military personnel and non-Hawaiians who outnumbered Kanaka Maoli were allowed to vote. Trask, *From a Native Daughter*, 30, 235; and Kauanui, "Colonialism in Equality," 643.

12. "The Annexation Question," *Daily Inter-Ocean*, 31 January 1893.

13. Daws, *Shoal of Time*, 388.

14. Whitney, *Hawaiian America*, 7.

15. Scholars have largely discussed the emergence of the United States as a colonial power in the late nineteenth century in terms of political economy and trade. William Appleman Williams (*The Tragedy of American Diplomacy*) and Walter LaFeber (*The New Empire*) offer economic explanations for American expansion, such as the China trade. LaFeber, for instance, maintains that the rapid industrialization of the last half of the nineteenth century stimulated a need for new markets, as opposed to a previous agrarian need for land. American politicians like William McKinley turned to Pacific colonies—Hawai'i,

Samoa, and the Philippines—for access to new markets and the China trade. Scholarly accounts of American expansion in Hawai'i by political scientists and historians investigate economic and political motivations, rather than the influence of cultural phenomena. See, for example, Tate, *The United States and the Hawaiian Kingdom*; Kent, *Hawaii*; Dudden, *The American Pacific*; Johnson, *The United States in the Pacific*. Amy Kaplan and Donald Pease, however, have asserted the importance of reinserting cultural frameworks into analyses of U.S. empire and imperial frameworks into cultural analyses. See Kaplan, "'Left Alone with America,'" and Pease, "New Perspectives on U.S. Culture and Imperialism."

16. Thomas, *Colonialism's Culture*, 2.

17. *Morning Edition*, National Public Radio, 11 August 2008.

18. For example, Cokie Roberts's comments about Hawai'i were voted "most inane punditry" of the U.S. presidential election in 2008 in a poll sponsored by the progressive media watchdog website *Media Matters for America*, http://mediamatters.org, 22 December 2008.

19. In 2008, ForbesTraveler.com ranked Waikiki Beach nineteenth out of the top twenty-five U.S. tourist attractions; it and the Metropolitan Museum of Art had four and a half million visitors apiece. In 2009, 4,280,286 visitors arrived by air from the continental United States. This figure does not include visitors arriving by cruise ships. Hawai'i Tourism Authority, *2009 Annual Visitor Research Report*, 11.

20. In a more recent articulation of Hawai'i as predictable leisure and conventional taste, the extended clan on the ABC sitcom *Modern Family* travel from Los Angeles to a Maui resort, where two characters ultimately renew their marriage vows. This episode from the first season of *Modern Family*, titled "Hawaii," was originally broadcast on 12 May 2010.

21. In 1887 King David Kalākaua was forced by a white settler militia to adopt a revised constitution that became known as the Bayonet Constitution. The constitution limited the king's authority. The same year, the weakened king relinquished Pearl Harbor to the United States in exchange for the renewal of the Reciprocity Treaty.

22. The queen yielded her crown while appealing to the U.S. executive in 1893. She abdicated in 1895 after she was arrested and threatened with the execution of her supporters. However, she renounced that abdication upon her release. Liliuokalani, *Hawaii's Story by Hawaii's Queen*.

23. While there was no live Hawaiian performance at an exposition until 1893, ali'i (chiefs) did display such sacred objects as feather lei, kapa, and capes at world expositions. Imada, "The Hawaiian Kingdom on the World Stage, 1855–1889."

24. Pukui and Elbert, *Hawaiian Dictionary*, 21.

25. Reverend Akaiko Akaka frequently preached about aloha in Kawaiahaʻo Church sermons until 1932. Quoted by Kanahele in *Kū Kanaka*, 478. Hawaiian educator and scholar George Kanahele argued that while aloha is a core value in contemporary Hawaiʻi, there is not enough evidence to demonstrate that it was the most important in precontact Hawaiian society. He believes aloha was one of many values that ordered Hawaiian life, among them loyalty, obedience, and generosity. See Kanahele, *Kū Kanaka*, 478–80.

26. Landgraf, *E Nā Hulu Kūpuna Nā Puna Ola Maoli Nō*, 12–13.

27. Meyer, *Hoʻoulu*, ix. Meyer quotes Ai: "Aloha is the intelligence with which we meet life."

28. Ibid., 9.

29. These imperial works were published between 1898 and 1914. William S. Bryan's *Our Islands and Their People* (1899) was one of the most popular, selling 400,000 copies. Thompson, "Representation and Rule in the Imperial Archipelago," 3–4.

30. Bryan, *Our Islands and Their People as Seen with Camera and Pencil*, 425.

31. These quotations are taken respectively from Abbie Fisher, "Native Hawaiians," *Los Angeles Times*, 19 November 1899, and Stevens and Olesen, *Picturesque Hawaii*, 21. John L. Stevens was the former U.S. minister who collaborated with white settlers to overthrow the monarchy. W. B. Olesen was a white settler and teacher who helped draft the Bayonet Constitution of 1887 that constrained King Kalākaua's authority.

32. For example, writer Casper Whitney opined in his Hawaiʻi guidebook of 1899 that, from his personal vantage point in Hawaiʻi, Hawaiians did not seem to care much about the fallen monarchy and were unwilling to fight for restoration. He wrote, "The natives' view of the changed political condition is purely lackadaisical." Whitney, *Hawaiian America*, 21.

33. This armed "counterrevolution" by royalists in 1895, called Kaua Kuloko in Hawaiian, attempted to restore Liliʻuokalani to the throne, but was a military failure that resulted in Liliʻuokalani's abdicating her crown to the republican government of Hawaiʻi. She was later tried for treason and imprisoned. Amy K. Stillman provides a concise summary of these events in "History Reinterpreted in Song," 3–5.

34. See, for instance, Kuykendall, *The Hawaiian Kingdom, Volume III, 1874–1893*, and Daws, *Shoal of Time*, on statehood. Chapter 9 of *Shoal of Time* is titled, "Now We Are All Haoles," implying that U.S. statehood was largely uncontested by the local population. Noenoe K. Silva, however, has analyzed the resistance of Kanaka Maoli who mounted anticolonial struggles in Hawaiʻi. N. K. Silva, *Aloha Betrayed*.

35. W. A. Williams, *Empire as a Way of Life*; Teresia K. Teaiwa offers a valuable theoretical framework for "militourism" in two pieces: "Reading

Paul Gauguin's Noa Noa with Epeli Hau'ofa's *Kisses in the Nederends*" and "Militarism, Tourism and the Native."

36. Teaiwa, "Reading Paul Gauguin's Noa Noa with Epeli Hau'ofa's *Kisses in the Nederends*," 251.

37. Tourism in Hawai'i accounts for at least a quarter of the state's gross domestic product and about one-third of its jobs, according to Leroy Laney, a Hawai'i economist (quoted in Allison Schaefers, "State Tourism in 'Crisis Mode,'" *Honolulu Star-Bulletin*, 2 April 2009). In 2005, Hawai'i's tourist industry accounted for approximately 23 percent of the state's $55 billion gross state domestic product, or GSP (about $12.6 billion), compared with approximately 13 percent in direct federal government spending (about $7.12 billion). Military spending is the largest segment of direct federal spending, or over 60 percent, at $4.4 billion; it is at least 8 percent of the state's total GSP. However, the actual contribution of federal and Department of Defense spending to the state's economy is much higher than these figures indicate, as GSP calculations are limited to federal monies spent on employee wages and procurement contracts; they do not include other substantial contributions such as retirement, disability, medical benefits, and state and local contracts. In 2004, these non-GSP contributions amounted to an extra $5.3 billion. Hawai'i State Department of Business, Economic Development, and Tourism, Research and Economic Analysis Division, *Federal Economic Activities in Hawai'i*, 1–2, 11, 21.

38. See, for instance, Hawai'i Visitors and Convention Bureau, *Hawaii: The Islands of Aloha, Official Visitors' Guide, 2009*. The Hawai'i tourist bureau decided the word "aloha" could singularly communicate the islands' attractions in the period of accelerated tourist growth after World War II. See Daws, *Shoal of Time*, 394.

39. See, for instance, Hawai'i Visitors and Convention Bureau, *Islands of Hawai'i Visitors' Guide, 2010–11*, 8. One study of the island hotel industry succinctly referred to the latter as the "Aloha Trade." Stern, *The Aloha Trade*.

40. Quoted from Hawai'i Visitors and Convention Bureau, *Hawaii: The Islands of Aloha, Official Visitors' Guide, 2009*. "Perhaps more than any of its incomparable natural wonders and diversions, the Aloha Spirit is what truly makes Hawaii unique." Hawaiians have resisted this commodification of their cultural values in myriad ways. Bumper stickers and placards reading "No Hawaiians, No Aloha" began appearing in the late 1990s in Hawai'i, protesting the use of Hawai'i's "host culture," while entitlements for Hawaiians were being systematically dismantled by state and federal policies. See this book's epilogue for a discussion of these developments and Hawaiian responses to them.

41. Schaefers, "State Tourism in 'Crisis Mode'"; Robbie Dingeman, "Hawaii

Tourists Down 12.5%, Spending Drops by $149.7 Million," *Honolulu Advertiser*, 26 February 2009; and Robbie Dingeman, "Hotels Continue Occupancy Drop," *Honolulu Advertiser*, 1 June 2009.

42. Hawai'i Tourism Authority press release, "HTA Awards $600,000 to Organizations that Perpetuated Hawaiian Culture," 16 February 2010.

43. Scholars of empire have taken up "intimacy" as a productive keyword and framework for analyses of imperial relations and formations. Ann Stoler, for instance, investigates how colonial authority in Java intruded into intimate zones of the body and mind, whether the management of reproduction, child rearing, sexual relations, and racialized and gendered colonial categories. She argues that these intimate affairs are at the "heart of colonial politics" (*Carnal Knowledge and Imperial Power*, 8). Contributors to Stoler's edited collection, *Haunted by Empire*, similarly discuss colonial intimacies in relationships as diverse as "Hindu" marriages in the Pacific Northwest and a leprosy colony in the colonial Philippines. Although I examine how colonial processes of rule in Hawai'i depended upon and intruded into everyday intimate spaces like scenarios of feasting and the affective labor of hospitality and hosting— what Stoler calls the "microphysics of colonial rule"—my theoretical emphasis in "imagined intimacy" is the production of intimacy between the United States and Hawai'i on a macro, transnational scale.

44. "Hawaii Passion Dance," *Washington Post*, 27 November 1893; *Brooklyn Eagle*, 23 January 1893.

45. See B. Smith, *Imagining the Pacific*.

46. Ibid., 210.

47. Babcock, "A New Mexican Rebecca," 403; and Babcock, "First Families," 207, 217.

48. Kauanui and Han have discussed the sexualized dimensions of "primitivism" that distinguish Pacific Islander racialization and sexualization from that of Asians. Kauanui and Han, "'Asian Pacific Islander,'" 378.

49. See Sahlins, *Islands of History*, 1–7, and Ralston, "Ordinary Women in Early Post-Contact Hawaii," 46–47. Both rely on writings by Captain James Cook and his officers published in Beaglehole, *The Journals of Captain Cook, Vol. III, the Voyage of the Resolution and Discovery, 1776–1780*, including part 1, 265–66, 486, 559, and part 2, 1083, 1085, 1154, 1159.

50. Thompson, "Representation and Rule in the Imperial Archipelago," 15, 31. These representations of beautiful Hawaiian women contrasted to those of the Philippines, whose tribal women were considered "unattractive and hateful" (33).

51. Chatterjee, *The Nation and Its Fragments*, 120–21.

52. *Pacific Commercial Advertiser*, 10 July 1856.

53. Noenoe K. Silva discusses the legal regulation of hula that resulted in its near disappearance from the public sphere. "He Kānāwai E Hoʻopau I Na Hula Kuolo Hawaiʻi," 41.

54. *Honolulu Star-Bulletin*, 16 August 1913; 16 September 1913; 6 October 1913; 9 October 1913.

55. Nathaniel B. Emerson's *Unwritten Literature of Hawaii* was published by the Smithsonian Institution's Bureau of American Ethnology in 1909.

56. Emerson, *Unwritten Literature of Hawaii*, 7–8.

57. Jennie Kapahukulaokamamalu Wilson, interviewed by Joann Kealiinohomoku, 1962 July, tape HAW 59.7.1, BM.

58. Hester "Teela" Holt Hailele, interviewed by the author, 24 April 2004.

59. Wanda Adams, "Making Hula Pono," *Honolulu Advertiser*, 6 November 2007.

60. Trask, *From a Native Daughter*, 145.

61. McGregor-Alegado, "Hawaiians: Organizing in the 1970s," 42, 51–52; Trask, "The Birth of the Modern Hawaiian Movement."

62. Morales, *Hoʻihoʻi Hou*. See also McGregor, *Nā Kuaʻāina*, 249–85.

63. Roach, *Cities of the Dead*, 26.

64. Said, quoting Marx early in *Orientalism*.

65. "Sweet Mionomai," *Atchison Daily Globe*, 27 January 1899, reprinted from *New York Journal*.

66. Teaiwa, "bikinis and other s/pacific n/oceans"; Jolly, "From Point Venus to Bali Haʻi," 99–122.

67. Althusser, *Lenin and Philosophy*, 170. "Ideology interpellates individuals as subjects," states his central thesis.

68. Moorehead, *The Fatal Impact*. Fatal contact refers to, in Moorehead's words, "that fateful moment when a social capsule is broken open, when primitive creatures, beasts as well as men, are confronted for the first time with civilization" (xiii). In this paradigm, Native peoples could do nothing to resist or alter their fates; the "impact" doomed them to death, cultural loss, and environmental degradation.

69. Diaz, "Repositioning the Missionary," 9, and *Repositioning the Missionary: Rewriting the Histories of Colonialism, Native Catholicism, and Indigeneity in Guam*, 23.

70. R. Williams, *Problems in Materialism and Culture*, 39–40.

71. N. K. Silva, *Aloha Betrayed*, 123–63.

72. R. Williams, *Marxism and Literature*, 94.

73. Osorio, *Dismembering Lāhui*, 225; N. K. Silva, *Aloha Betrayed*, 89.

74. Scott, *Domination and the Arts of Resistance*.

75. This definition is derived from Pukui and Elbert, *Hawaiian Dictionary*, 130.

76. Scott, *Domination and the Arts of Resistance*, 183.

77. Clifford, *Routes*, 17–46.

78. P. J. Deloria, *Indians in Unexpected Places*.

79. "Only Members of the Polynesian Family Who Are Citizens of the United States," *New York Times*, 6 May 1906.

80. Raylani Kinney Akau, interviewed by the author, 24 April 2004.

81. Elizabeth Buck, for example, focuses on the transformation of hula and Hawaiian chant under Western imperialism and the contemporary reappropriation of commodified entertainment by Hawaiian activists. See Buck, *Paradise Remade*.

82. The Smithsonian Institution's National Museum of American History holds guidebooks and travelogues on world's fairs, while the Hawaiʻi State Archives and Bishop Museum are important repositories for photographs, manuscripts, and a few personal collections.

83. Stoler, "Colonial Archives and the Arts of Governance," 87–109. Some individual dancers began to be identified by name in the 1930s in American newspaper gossip columns but were still discussed within descriptive categories of "envoys," "hula girls," "maids," and "hularinas."

84. Ironically, despite the predominance of women in hula, there is a gendered erasure of Hawaiian women from archives. As I discuss later in the book, male Hawaiian performers have garnered more archival and historical attention than their female counterparts.

85. Whether in ʻōlelo Hawaiʻi (Hawaiian language) or ʻōlelo haole (English language), newspapers tended to discuss performance venues like "Hoikeike," or international expositions, in generalities.

86. I am grateful to Robert R. Alvarez Jr., who proposed "lived observation," as opposed to "participant observation," as a method and model of ethnographic research. Here I adapt his concept to "lived participation," which involves deep, continuous engagement through lifelong trust and social bonds, rather than entering and exiting a fieldsite. These relationships exceed "rapport" with informants.

87. Foucault, *Power/Knowledge*, 81.

88. Ibid., 82.

89. Taylor, *The Archive and the Repertoire*, 19, 24.

90. Ibid., 28–29.

91. Roach, *Cities of the Dead*, 26–27.

92. *Aunty Betty* (2000) is about Betty Puanani Makia, who at the time of filming was eighty-five years old.

93. Scott, *Domination and the Arts of Resistance*.

94. Hartman, *Scenes of Subjection*, 11.

95. For example, see Said, *Orientalism*; Alloula, *The Colonial Harem*; Guha, *A Subaltern Studies Reader*; Clifford and Marcus, *Writing Culture*; L. T. Smith, *Decolonizing Methodologies*.

96. See Kaeppler, *Hula Pahu*, on the chant and movement repertoires preserved by kumu hula and practitioners of what she terms the "classical," "composite," and "generative" hula traditions.

97. Kumu hula Kaui Zuttermeister, for instance, objected to having nonauthorized practitioners "borrow" her hula repertoire or movements. Kaeppler, *Hula Pahu*, 114. Mary Kawena Pukui, according to her daughter Pat Bacon, also strictly preserved the hula kahiko (old hula) in "the way it was taught to her by her kumu." W. Silva and Suemori, *Nānā i Nā Lōea Hula*, 122. As for performance shifts, one of the most drastic examples is a kumu hula like Patrick Makuakane, whose San Francisco–based hālau Nā Lei Hula i ka Wēkiu has created a "hula mua" (futuristic hula) that incorporates hip hop, pop, and techno music and movements.

98. I draw from Philip J. Deloria's concept of "playing Indian," the American performance of fantasies about Indians. These fantasies were usually staged by non-Indians, but I suggest that Hawaiians also "played Hawaiian" for their own discrepant purposes. P. J. Deloria, *Playing Indian*.

1. Lady Jane at the Boathouse

1. N. K. Silva, *Aloha Betrayed*, 108–10.

2. The founding date of Hui Lei Mamo in 1886 was specified by Kini Kapahu in Jennie Kapahukulaokamamalu Wilson, interviewed by Joann Kealiinohomoku, 1962 July, tape HAW 59.8.2, BM. In interviews conducted by Theodore Kelsey, Kini referred to the Hui Lei Mamo as a "glee club" of "girls." She also identified "Iolani" as the all-male glee club of singers that "belonged to King Kalakaua." Kelsey, "Mrs. Jennie Wilson."

3. Stevenson, *The Letters of Robert Louis Stevenson*, 243.

4. While there is no record of the specific repertoire, the women may have performed mele in honor of Kalākaua similar to that at his coronation in 1883 and his fiftieth birthday jubilee in 1886, songs like "Eia no Davida ka Heke o na Pua" (Here is David, the most glorious of all flowers). See appendix B, "Papa Kuhikuhi o na Hula Poni Moi, Feb. 12, 1883," reproduced in Stillman, *Sacred Hula*, 70–83.

5. Young, *The Boston at Hawaii*, 12; Whitney, *Hawaiian America*, 294.

6. Kini confirmed during an interview in 1962 that she had joined Kalākaua's court at the age of fourteen. Jennie Kapahukulaokamamalu Wilson, interviewed by Joann Kealiinohomoku, tape HAW 59.12.2, BM. This information is corroborated in "Last Living Court Dancer," *Honolulu Star-Bulletin*, 29 May 1960. However, another secondary source offers a slightly different account. Although Kalākaua had asked Kini to join the troupe earlier, Kini's mother Kapahukulaokamāmalu refused. Only when her mother's friend Queen Kapiʻolani intervened after Kini's sixteenth

birthday was she permitted to dance hula with the group. Clarice B. Taylor, "Tales about Hawaii," *Honolulu Star-Bulletin*, 14 April 1952.

7. See Kaeppler, *Hula Pahu*, 23. Hula pahu is the most traditional remnant of ha'a and hula surviving today, but only a select few individuals were taught these pahu dances.

8. John Kaha'i Topolinski, a noted kumu hula writes, "Without [the chant] there was no dance." Topolinski, "The Hula," 150.

9. Barrère, "The Hula in Retrospect," 22.

10. Dorothy B. Barrère suggests that hula groups may have been "permanently attached" to chiefly households. However, "most late 18th and early 19th century hula dancers seem to have been mainly self-supporting," occasionally providing entertainment for chiefs. Ibid., 13.

11. Pukui, "The Hula, Hawaii's Own Dance," 70. Mary Abigail Kawena'ula-okalanihi'iakaikapoliopelekawahine'aihonua Wiggin Pukui (1895–1986), along with her hānai daughter Patience Namakauahoaokawena'ula-okalaniikiikikalaninui Wiggin Bacon, graduated as ho'opa'a (chanters) from kumu hula Keahi Luahine, following a traditional hu'elepo ritual graduation ceremony in 1936. Kaeppler, *Hula Pahu*, 149. In addition to her extensive knowledge of sacred hula pahu (sharkskin drum hula) and oli (chant), Pukui was the most esteemed Hawaiian scholar of the twentieth century, having authored or coauthored nearly all Hawaiian reference books of language and culture until the 1970s. She appears both as an important historical subject and a knowledge-producer in this book.

12. Barrère, "The Hula in Retrospect," 22.

13. Appendix A, "Interview with Mrs. Mary Pukui," in Costa, "Dance in the Society and Hawaiian Islands as Presented by the Early Writers, 1767–1842."

14. Ellis, *A Narrative of a Tour thru Hawaii, or Owhyee*, 86. The incident in Kailua took place on 14 July 1823.

15. Noenoe K. Silva reveals how the missionary-led interdiction of hula helped to discipline Hawaiians into wage laborers who would be useful for colonial capitalism. N. K. Silva, "He Kānāwai E Ho'opau I Na Hula Kuolo Hawai'i," 29–48.

16. Barrère, "The Hula in Retrospect," 21.

17. Bingham, *A Residence of Twenty-One Years in the Sandwich Islands*, 124–25.

18. Barrère, "The Hula in Retrospect," 40.

19. Violators were subject to a $500 fine or imprisonment for six months with hard labor. By the 1870s the legislature reduced these penalties to $100 or three months' hard labor, and performances were no longer restricted to Honolulu. N. K. Silva, "He Kānāwai E Ho'opau I Na Hula Kuolo Hawai'i," 41, and Barrère, "The Hula in Retrospect," 41.

20. "Interview with Pukui," in Costa, "Dance in the Society and Hawaiian Islands as Presented by the Early Writers."

21. "Pau ole no hoi ka hana kahiko o Hawaii nei," *Nupepa Kuokoa*, 7 July 1866, Hawaiian Ethnological Notes Newspapers, BM.

22. See Barrère, "The Hula in Retrospect," 43–46, for additional examples of Hawaiian critiques of hula.

23. Osorio, *Dismembering Lāhui*, 224.

24. N. K. Silva, *Aloha Betrayed*, 89–90.

25. In 1887, membership rolls in the Hawaiian League numbered 405. See Thurston, *Memoirs of the Hawaiian Revolution*, 135–36.

26. Kuykendall, *The Hawaiian Kingdom, Volume II, 1854–1874*, 248. The U.S. secretary of war sent an army major general and a brigadier general to Hawai'i in 1873 under secret orders to assess the "defensive capabilities of the different ports and their commercial facilities." On this trip, the general set his sights on the natural harbor, the only one in the north Pacific, for a naval and commercial port.

27. N. K. Silva, *Aloha Betrayed*, 92.

28. Ibid., 108–20.

29. Stillman, "The Hula Ku'i," 58. Many hula ku'i (modern hula) were composed especially for the coronation, including "Poni ia oe e kalani" (You are crowned, O Heavenly One), a mele about Kalākaua's crowning. "Au'a 'ia" and "Kaulilua" were two hula pahu performed at the coronation.

30. Folder 142, TK, Theodore Kelsey Collection, M-86, folder 142, HSA. It appears Kelsey took these notes by hand from Nathaniel B. Emerson's fieldnotes for his manuscript of *Unwritten Literature of Hawaii*. The Kelsey Collection in the Hawai'i State Archives indicates that Emerson's informant was Frederick William Kahapula Beckley. Beckley was an ali'i who served as chamberlain to King Kalākaua. He was also governor of Kaua'i from 1880 until his death in 1881.

31. Pukui, "The Hula, Hawaii's Own Dance," 70.

32. N. K. Silva, *Aloha Betrayed*, 92.

33. Ibid., 89.

34. "King Kalakaua's Coronation," *St. Louis Globe-Democrat*, 13 March 1883, reprinted from *The New York Sun*.

35. N. K. Silva, *Aloha Betrayed*, 108.

36. Stillman, "The Hula Ku'i," 37; Jennie Kapahukulaokamamalu Wilson, interviewed by Joann Kealiinohomoku, tape HAW 59.4.1, BM.

37. These students included Robert William Kalanihiapo Wilcox (also known as Wilikoki), who led rebellions against the "Reform Government" of sugar planters and missionary sons in 1889 and against the U.S.-backed Republic of Hawai'i in 1895. The program was funded by the legislature beginning in 1882, with an appropriation of $15,000. However, in 1887, the king was forced to dismiss his cabinet and accept a new constitution ("Bayonet Constitution") that greatly curtailed his authority. The new "Reform Cabinet" proceeded to cut the king's expenditures and recalled

the students to Hawai'i. The total amount spent on the program between 1880 and 1892 was $86,883. See Quigg, "Kalakaua's Hawaiian Studies Abroad Program," 171–72.

38. Ibid., 183.

39. Besides the women dancers of Hui Lei Mamo, my research also suggests these individual practitioners were affiliated with Kalākaua's court: Kuluwaimaka (male), Emalia Kaihumua, Kauhai Likua, Annie Grube (or Ani Gurube), Malie Kaleikoa, Aiala, and Namakokahai (these six all women). The grandmother of Eddie Kamae, a contemporary musician and filmmaker, was Kauhai Likua (1868–1938). Houston, *Hawaiian Son*, 16.

40. Nathaniel B. Emerson also wrote *The Unwritten Literature of Hawaii: The Sacred Songs of the Hula*, which was published by the Smithsonian Institution's Bureau of American Ethnology in 1909. Copies of some of Emerson's fieldnotes are in the TK collection, M-86, HSA. The Emerson collection at the Huntington Library in San Marino, California, also holds some of Emerson's original notes.

41. There were ali'i women in Hale Nāua and Ka Papa Kū'auhau, but no maka'āinana women.

42. Barrère, "The Hula in Retrospect," 13.

43. For example, in the late nineteenth century Mary Kawena Pukui's kumu hula, Keahi Luahine, had a kumu hula from Waimea who was māhū. Pukui describes a māhū as "a hermaphrodite, having qualities of both sexes." Pukui, "Ancient Hulas of Kauai," 76. Contemporary hula's association with gay and queer members and sensibilities has intensified, as many kumu hula and haumāna are self-identified māhū.

44. Pukui, "The Hula, Hawaii's Own Dance," 73.

45. Pukui, "Ancient Hulas of Kauai," 77. Pukui's kumu hula, Kapua, "felt that a woman had no business to learn a man's part in the hula" (i.e., the role of ho'opa'a). She writes, "His disgust was freely expressed, but what could he do with a determined woman?"

46. Ibid., 76.

47. For more on the biographies and hula training of these women, see Kaeppler, *Hula Pahu*, 147–54. The orphaned infant daughter of Japanese immigrants, Patience Nāmaka Wiggin was adopted by Mary Kawena Pukui's parents but was raised by Pukui.

48. Pukui, "Ancient Hulas of Kauai," 75.

49. Stillman, "Passed into the Present: Women in Hawaiian Entertainment," 216.

50. As the wife of John H. Wilson, the first Democratic mayor of Honolulu, Kini Kapahu (also known as Mrs. Jennie Wilson) assumed the unofficial role of "first lady" of Hawai'i in 1920, when her husband was

elected mayor, and served as such until her death in 1962. She wielded tremendous authority in political and cultural circles in Hawaiʻi and was respected as a hula expert later in her life. She served as a delegate to the Democratic National Convention in New York City in 1924 and cast one of Hawaiʻi's first three presidential electoral ballots in 1960. In 1959, the Hawaiʻi state legislature designated her the honorary first lady of the state. She was president of the elite Hawaiian women's society ʻAhahui Kaʻahumanu. Presiding over protocol at Aloha Week festivals, she often vocalized harsh judgments on Hawaiian tourist entertainment. See Sereno, "Images of the Hula Dancer," 155; "Last Living Court Dancer," *Honolulu Star-Bulletin*, 29 May 1960; "Wary Tourism Officials Skirt Issue of Aunt Jennie's Aloha Week Blast," *Honolulu Star-Bulletin*, 22 October 1958.

51. Jennie Kapahukulaokamamalu Wilson, interviewed by Joann Kealiinohomoku, tape HAW 59.5.1, BM.

52. Ibid., tape HAW 59.8.1, BM. In the fieldnotes of the folklorist Dr. Nathaniel B. Emerson (folder 52, M-445, HK), this kumu hula is identified as "Na-make-ʻelua." In 1898, Namakeʻelua told Emerson that he was the head kumu hula during the jubilee.

53. According to Kini, Annie Grube, transliterated into Hawaiian as "Ani Gurube," was Hawaiian and German but was raised by Hawaiians. Pauahi Pinao was Hawaiian and had been named in remembrance of her aunt who had perished in a schoolhouse fire, hence her name "Pau-ahi" (dead by fire). Jennie Kapahukulaokamamalu Wilson, interviewed by Joann Kealiinohomoku, tape HAW 59.3.1, BM. Because Kini referred to her peers by their first names or, in some cases, by a single Hawaiian name, I have chosen to abide by her preference.

54. Ibid. A search for Nakai's name in Hawaiian and English-language newspapers has not yielded any information.

55. Stillman, *Sacred Hula*, 23. Barrère, however, does not interpret hula in nineteenth-century "Christianized" Hawaiʻi as a sacred or religious performance; rather, she contends that it retained a spiritual aspect. "The Hula in Retrospect," 63.

56. For more on traditional hula training, see Emerson, *Unwritten Literature of Hawaii*, 28–37, and Pukui, "The Hula, Hawaii's Own Dance," 70–73.

57. Pukui, "The Hula, Hawaii's Own Dance," 71.

58. Jennie Kapahukulaokamamalu Wilson, interviewed by Joann Kealiinohomoku, tape 59.3.1, BM.

59. Ibid., tape 59.5.2, BM.

60. Pukui, "The Hula," 8.

61. Jennie Kapahukulaokamamalu Wilson, interviewed by Joann Kealiinohomoku, tape 59.8.2, BM.

62. Stillman, *Sacred Hula*, 16. According to Stillman, the hula ālaʻapapa,

unlike the hula ʻōlapa, has neither standardized length of text nor phrasing. It is also more closely associated with hula kuahu, or hula performed under the protection of Laka, "hula whose creation and transmission are bound by the observance of altar rituals honoring Laka" (23). Kini, however, tended to gloss over the difference between these genres; she claimed that ʻōlapa and ālaʻapapa are the same thing, with ʻōlapa being the shortened version of ālaʻapapa. Jennie Kapahukulaokamamalu Wilson, interviewed by Joann Kealiinohomoku, tape HAW 59.8.1, BM.

63. Jennie Kapahukulaokamamalu Wilson, interviewed by Joann Kealiinohomoku, tape HAW 59.12.2, BM.

64. Kameʻeleihiwa, *Native Land and Foreign Desires*, 19–20. For instance, some of the mele would have celebrated a sovereign's genealogy back to the gods; others like "Auʻa ʻia," the genealogy of the gods and the formation of the islands.

65. This is not to say that all hula was meant to be creative and improvisational. Hula pahu, derived from haʻa, ancient temple ritual movements and performed with the sharkskin drum, were meant to be transmitted as taught.

66. Different hālau claim different genealogies (i.e., different origins); they may offer different interpretations of a mele.

67. Kameʻeleihiwa, *Native Land and Foreign Desires*, 19–20.

68. Malie Kaleikoa, one of the Hui Lei Mamo members, and Hana [Hannah] Lilikalani, the sister of the dancer Pauahi Pinao, were two active members of this mourning group. "Hoalohaloha alii," *Ka Makaainana*, 28 October 1895.

69. Stillman, "Of the People Who Love the Land," 92.

70. In Honolulu on 1 June 1825, for instance, Governor Boki's poʻe hula, who were young female dancers, performed a "hura-hura, or national dance" in honor of Lord George Anson Byron. Barrère, "The Hula in Retrospect," 34.

71. Coronation dinner, 1883, program reprinted in Stillman, "The Hula Kuʻi," 36.

72. Jennie Kapahukulaokamamalu Wilson, interviewed by Joann Kealiinohomoku, tape HAW 59.12.2, BM. During this interview in 1962, Kini could not remember the other two women's names.

73. Jennie Kapahukulaokamamalu Wilson, interviewed by Joann Kealiinohomoku, tape HAW 59.5.1, BM.

74. Pukui and Elbert, *Hawaiian Dictionary*, 174.

75. Stillman, "History Reinterpreted in Song," 20.

76. Jennie Kapahukulaokamamalu Wilson, interviewed by Joann Kealiinohomoku, tape HAW 59.5.1, BM.

77. According to Silva, hula practitioners invented the new genre of hula kuʻi at Kalākaua's poni mōʻī (coronation) in 1883. N. K. Silva, *Aloha Betrayed*, 108. However, Stillman more broadly credits the emergence of hula kuʻi to Kalākaua's cultural revival. Stillman, "History Reinterpreted in Song," 20.

78. Daws, *Shoal of Time*, 165.

79. Bushnell, *The Gifts of Civilization*, 182.

80. Stevenson, *The Letters of Robert Louis Stevenson*, 248.

81. Stevenson, *Travels in Hawaii*, 102.

82. Whitney, *Hawaiian America*, 295.

83. Dening, *Islands and Beaches*, 2, 20.

84. Partlow, "The Merry Monarch of Hawaii," 73.

85. "An Actor's Experience with the King of the Cannibal Islands," *Daily Picayune*, 7 December 1890.

86. Bakhtin, *Rabelais and His World*, 10.

87. "An Actor's Experience with the King of the Cannibal Islands."

88. Beckwith, *The Kumulipo*, 12.

89. Malo, *Ka Moolelo Hawaii*, 30, 173. The English-language translation from this edition is by Malcolm Naea Chun.

90. Kamakau, *Na Poe Kahiko*, 4. As Kamakau explains, men were occasionally able to ascend in rank by skill. "Sometimes the hereditary chief lost his land, and the kingdom was taken by force and snatched away by a warrior, and the name of 'chief' given to him because of his prowess. He then attached himself to the chiefly genealogies, even though his father may have been of no great rank (noanoa), and his mother a chiefess."

91. Lorch and Schweizer, "Royal Hawaiian Band," 336, 339.

92. Kalākaua not only played the ʻukulele, his favorite instrument, but designed and made his own. He patronized Portuguese ʻukulele manufacturer Augusto Dias and granted him special permission to stamp the royal crown on Dias's creations. Kanahele, "David Kalakaua," 202.

93. It was not unusual for Kalākaua to produce musical performances. His Hui Lei Mamo competed with glee clubs headed by his two sisters— the princesses Miriam Likelike and Liliʻuokalani—and brother, Prince Leleiohoku. The four siblings, known as "Nalani Eha," or "The Four Chiefs," were all exceptional composers and musicians.

94. "Boston Gossip," *St. Louis Globe-Democrat*, 15 May 1887.

95. Daws, *Shoal of Time*, 165.

96. While there is little doubt of the disreputable nature of the harbor, common Hawaiian women who bartered sex are not reducible to "prostitutes." What Westerners interpreted as aggressive sexuality enabled these women to gain some rewards, whether those rewards were access to new foreign goods, increased status, or affection. Chappell, "Shipboard Relations between Pacific Island Women and EuroAmerican

Men, 1767–1887," 135–39; see also Ralston, "Ordinary Women in Early Post-Contact Hawaii," 45–64.

97. Chappell, "Shipboard Relations," 137.

98. "Boston Gossip," *St. Louis Globe-Democrat*, 15 May 1887; "Dancing the Hula Hula," *Rocky Mountain News*, 2 February 1888 (reprinted from *San Francisco Examiner*).

99. "An Actor's Experience with the King of the Cannibal Islands." This group of dancers may not have been the Hui Lei Mamo but another that performed hula āla'apapa and 'ōlapa, older precontact forms of dance.

100. Jennie Kapahukulaokamamalu Wilson, interviewed by Joann Kealiinohomoku, tape HAW 59.7.1, BM.

101. Pukui, "The Hula, Hawaii's Own Dance," 70. Also in Pukui, "The Hula."

102. W. Silva and Suemori, *Nānā i Nā Lōea Hula*, 129.

103. Jennie Kapahukulaokamamalu Wilson, interviewed by Joann Kealiinohomoku, tape HAW 59.13.3, BM.

104. Ibid., tape HAW 59.14.1, BM.

105. Ibid.

106. Betty Patterson, "Aunt Jennie at 90 Recalls Her Teens," *Honolulu Star-Bulletin*, 4 March 1962.

107. See photograph of hula ku'i in Emerson, *Unwritten Literature of Hawaii*, 251.

108. MacCannell, *Empty Meeting Grounds*, 27–35.

109. Quoted in Bederman, *Manliness and Civilization*, 201.

110. Jacobson, *Whiteness of a Different Color*, 227–33.

111. Ibid., 228.

112. See Dominguez, "Exporting U.S. Concepts of Race," 369–70, for a discussion of nineteenth-century racial classification of Hawaiians.

113. Kamakau, *Ruling Chiefs of Hawaii*, 420. The original text is reprinted in Kamakau, *Ke Aupuni Mō'ī*, 312, and appeared in the Hawaiian-language newspaper *Ke Au Okoa* on 23 September 1869.

114. "Kalākaua Rex," *North American and United States Gazette*, 19 March 1874.

115. See, for instance, "Kalakaua," *Daily Inter-Ocean*, 13 January 1875, and "How the King of the Sandwich Islands Spent His Second Day in Chicago," *Daily Inter-Ocean*, 14 January 1875; "Curiosities of Literature," *St. Louis Globe-Democrat*, 6 January 1876; *Daily Rocky Mountain News*, 1 December 1874; *Daily Inter-Ocean*, 12 December 1874 and 23 December 1874.

116. "On a Royal Drunk," *Georgia Weekly Telegraph and Georgia Journal and Messenger* (Macon), 2 February 1875; *Los Angeles Times*, 5 December 1890.

117. See, for example, cartoons of Lili'uokalani on the covers of *Puck*, 28 February 1894, and *Judge*, 17 February 1894.

118. Printed respectively in *North American* (Philadelphia), 18 May 1895; *Morning Oregonian* (Portland, Oregon), 15 January 1894; and *Irish World and American Industrial Liberator* (New York, N.Y.), 10 February 1894, reprinted from *New York Evening World*.

119. The Kingdom of Hawai'i had also restricted Chinese immigration by passing laws in 1887, 1888, 1890, and 1892. See Kuykendall, *The Hawaiian Kingdom, Volume III, 1874–1893*, 177–85.

120. *Honolulu Star-Bulletin*, 1 December 1956.

121. Kauanui, *Hawaiian Blood*. Congress instituted the 50 percent blood quantum criterion in the federal Hawaiian Homes Commission Act (HHCA) of 1921. Proposing to "rehabilitate" and return urban Hawaiians to the land in the form of homesteads, the HHCA replaced collective Hawaiian entitlements to land and positioned Hawaiians as "beneficiaries" and wards of the territorial and federal governments. Furthermore, only "native Hawaiians" who could prove 50 percent blood quantum were eligible for Hawaiian homestead lands. Ultimately this act effectively secured Hawaiian lands for corporate sugar and ranching interests.

122. Kauanui, *Hawaiian Blood*, 13, 173.

123. Jennie Kapahukulaokamamalu Wilson, interviewed by Joann Kealiinohomoku, tape HAW 59.4.1, BM.

124. Napua Stevens, transcribed interview by Bob Krauss, 3 June 1989, Bob Krauss Workbook "Wilson Tapes Transcribed," BK.

125. Certeau, *The Practice of Everyday Life*, 31. He writes, "They metaphorized the dominant order: they made it function in another register. They remained other within the system which they assimilated and which assimilated them externally. They diverted it without leaving it."

2. Modern Desires

1. Jennie Kapahukulaokamamalu Wilson, interviewed by Joann Kealiinohomoku, 1962 July, tape HAW 59.3.1, BM.

2. "Jennie Wilson," typescript, Bob Krauss Workbook 3 (September 1891–June 1893), HSA.

3. Jennie Kapahukulaokamamalu Wilson, interviewed by Joann Kealiinohomoku, tape HAW 59.3.1, BM. A similar account was published in Betty Patterson, "Aunt Jennie at 90 Recalls Her Teens," *Honolulu Star-Bulletin*, 4 March 1962.

4. Jennie Kapahukulaokamamalu Wilson, interviewed by Joann Kealiinohomoku, tape HAW 59.3.1, BM.

5. 'Ōlapa was the dancer, distinct from the ho'opa'a (chanter and drummer). See Kaeppler, *Hula Pahu*, 4.

6. Kanuku and Kamuku may have been associated with Kalākaua's court as well, although Kini did not specify how she knew them.

7. According to "Hula Hula Dancer Is in Hard Luck," *Chicago Daily Tribune*, 24 August 1895, at the time of his death, Kalākaua had been preparing twelve dancers to represent the country at the Chicago fair. However, Harry Foster's troupe was a private venture that had no relationship with the Hawaiian monarchy or the provisional government that had overthrown the monarchy in 1893.

8. Jennie Kapahukulaokamamalu Wilson, interviewed by Joann Kealiinohomoku, tapes HAW 59.8.2 and 59.12.2, BM.

9. The troupe left Honolulu in April 1892. Honolulu newspapers, however, reported that the troupe left in May 1893. *Daily Bulletin*, 23 May 1893; *Pacific Commercial Advertiser*, 25 May 1893.

10. "Last Living Court Dancer," *Honolulu Star-Bulletin*, 29 May 1960. Since this photograph was in Kini Kapahu's collection at the time the article was written, she would have been the most likely source of this information. A photograph of the troupe at the Hawai'i State Archives also identifies the location as San Francisco.

11. Jennie Kapahukulaokamamalu Wilson, interviewed by Joann Kealiinohomoku, tape HAW 59.3.1, BM. I have found no American or Canadian newspaper coverage of the troupe prior to its arrival at the Chicago World's Columbian Exposition.

12. The hula troupe appeared with the following performers at these venues on these dates: *The Creole Show* (Madison Opera House, Chicago, 1893), Bedouin Arabs (Gilmore's Auditorium, Philadelphia, 1895), bearded ladies and mind readers (Ninth and Arch dime museum, Philadelphia, 1895), and the boxing kangaroos (Folies-Bergère, Paris, ca. 1894). For a detailed chronology of these fin de siècle hula tours, see Imada, "Transnational *Hula* as Colonial Culture." Jayna Brown discusses African American female performances at *The Creole Show* staged outside of the Chicago fairgrounds in 1893 (*Babylon Girls*, 100–110).

13. Hawaiians had performed hula in coastal locales like California and Maine as early as the late eighteenth century and the early nineteenth. Carr, "In the Wake of John Kanaka."

14. Kent discusses these hegemonic economic structures in *Hawaii: Islands under the Influence*, while Osorio provides an excellent treatment of Western interventions in ali'i and monarchical autonomy in *Dismembering Lāhui*.

15. Among the major changes of this proposed constitution were the abolition of race and language restrictions for voting, the reduction or elimination of property requirements for enfranchisement, and the restoration of the queen's executive powers. N. K. Silva, *Aloha Betrayed*, 167, and Kuykendall, *The Hawaiian Kingdom, Volume III, 1874–1893*, 586.

16. See United States Congress, *100th Anniversary of the Overthrow of the*

Hawaiian Kingdom, Public Law 103–50, 103d Congress, 1st Session, 107 Stat. 1510, S.J. Res. 19, 23 November 1993. This joint resolution of Congress, also signed by President Clinton, records the American involvement in the illegal overthrow of the Hawaiian kingdom in 1893.

17. Mellen, "Honolulu's First Lady," 38.

18. Certeau, *The Practice of Everyday Life*, xvii.

19. Ibid., xii, xiii, xiv.

20. Ibid., 31, 36–37.

21. Diaz, *Repositioning the Missionary*, 23.

22. N. K. Silva, *Aloha Betrayed*, 123–63.

23. Ibid., 88.

24. Kelley, *Race Rebels*, 9.

25. Thomas, *Colonialism's Culture*, 2.

26. David A. Chappell has cautioned against confusing agency with overt action. In "Active Agents vs. Passive Victims," he argues for more subtle, flexible analyses of resistance and protest that "combine various degrees of action, passivity, and victimization" (313).

27. For a detailed, reconstructed chronology of these hula tours through North America and Europe, interested readers may consult my article "Transnational *Hula* as Colonial Culture."

28. Some biographical sketches of Kini Kapahu are available in national and regional newspapers published in the United States. Kini's collection at the Hawai'i State Archives (HSA), catalogued under the name Jennie Wilson, consists only of a handful of photographs and letters, whereas a sizable government archive is retained for her husband, John H. Wilson, who served as Honolulu mayor. The most extensive primary source on nineteenth-century tourist hula is approximately fifteen hours of audiotaped oral histories of Kini Kapahukulaokamāmalu conducted by ethnomusicologist Joann Kealiinohomoku in 1962, when Kini was eighty-nine years old. Aeko Sereno utilized these tapes for her dissertation, "Images of the Hula Dancer and 'Hula Girl': 1778–1970," which is also a helpful source. I have also relied on mid-twentieth-century articles on Kini in Hawai'i periodicals and newspapers; Hawaiian and English-language newspapers from the late nineteenth century mention only a few po'e hula by name. Newspaper columnist and reporter Bob Krauss's fieldnotes and interviews at the HSA and his biography of John H. Wilson are also valuable sources on Kini Kapahu and her hula experiences. Krauss, *Johnny Wilson.*

29. Jennie Kapahukulaokamamalu Wilson, interviewed by Joann Kealiinohomoku, tape HAW 59.12.2, BM.

30. See, for instance, Nathaniel B. Emerson's foundational ethnography of hula, *Unwritten Literature of Hawaii*, and anthropologist Helen H. Roberts's audio recordings and manuscript collection of chants and mele

held by the Bishop Museum. Their respective archives remain valuable today for practicing poʻe hula.

31. Scott, *Domination and the Arts of Resistance.*

32. Certeau, *The Practice of Everyday Life*, xv.

33. For examples of this methodology in subaltern studies, see Guha, "In Defense of the Fragment"; Chakrabarty, "Postcoloniality and the Artifice of History," in *Provincializing Europe*; and Chatterjee, *The Nation and Its Fragments*. Kamala Visweswaran also argues for strategic uses of partial knowledge and the fragment in feminist ethnographic praxis. See *Fictions of Feminist Ethnography*, 48–50.

34. "Dark-Eyed Beauties," *Daily Inter-Ocean*, 13 February 1893; also printed in *Milwaukee Sentinel*, 14 February 1893.

35. "The Women of Hawaii: The Most Beautiful of All the Dark Skinned Races," *Fayetteville Observer*, 13 April 1893.

36. "Calls the Hula Dancers Beautiful," *Chicago Daily Tribune*, 3 March 1893.

37. Barbara Kirshenblatt-Gimblett describes the process of people and things becoming "ethnographic," through detachment from their original use and conversion into objects of study or scrutiny. *Destination Culture*, 18.

38. Chappell, *Double Ghosts*, 32, 122–23.

39. Thompson, "Representation and Rule in the Imperial Archipelago."

40. Here I expand on Thompson's claim to suggest that a managerial form of territorial rule is applied to Hawaiʻi and advanced by imperial hula performances. Ibid., 30.

41. McClintock, *Imperial Leather*, 21.

42. Foucault, *Discipline and Punish*, 27.

43. "Theatrical Gossip," *Chicago Daily Inter-Ocean*, 30 July 1893.

44. Balme, "New Compatriots," 332.

45. "Hawaii Passion Dance," *Washington Post*, 27 November 1893.

46. "Is Gone Dance Crazy," *Chicago Daily Tribune*, 6 August 1893.

47. R. Adams, *Sideshow U.S.A.*; *The North American*, 26 March 1895. Adams cites the display of the African Ota Benga at the St. Louis Fair and the Bronx zoo and the promotion of microcephalic twin sisters as freaks from the Yucatan. *Sideshow U.S.A.*, 30–32.

48. Nasaw, *Going Out*, 71. Though exposition attendance figures were inflated, Nasaw suggests that even dividing these figures in half would mean Chicago had nearly 14 million fairgoers, still a huge audience for a nation of 62 million.

49. The Paris Exposition Universelle of 1889 introduced the ethnographic model of "human showcases," as described by Paul Greenhalgh in *Ephemeral Vistas*. Raymond Corbey has also analyzed the midway sections of imperial fairs as "ethnographic showcases" in "Ethnographic Showcases, 1870–1930."

50. Buffalo Bill's Wild West show featured performances by American Indians and was also attached to the Chicago exposition.

51. The organizer of the Chicago Midway, Sol Broom, had been influenced by living villages of French colonies on display at the Paris world's fair in 1899.

52. See Rydell, *All the World's a Fair*, 64–65.

53. Mitchell, *Colonising Egypt*, 6.

54. Ibid., 9.

55. Hawthorne, "Foreign Folk at the Fair," 568.

56. Jennie Kapahukulaokamamalu Wilson, interviewed by Joann Kealiinohomoku, tape HAW 59.3.1, BM. Kini did not write this poem herself; a haole man who had seen her troupe's hula show returned the following day and offered his composition. In this interview from 1962, Kini still remembered the words to this ballyhoo.

57. Napua Stevens, transcribed interview by Bob Krauss, 3 June 1989, Bob Krauss Workbook "Wilson Tapes Transcribed," BK. Kini fought American promoters to dance clothed, as Hawaiian women had from at least the mid-nineteenth century. Dancers did not dance with their breasts bared; they wore a hybrid costume of cotton blouse, cotton underskirt or pantaloons, and dried grass skirts, as revealed in a photograph of Pauahi and Kini taken at a Chicago photography studio in 1893. As Kini explained, missionaries had mandated that women wear impractical muʻumuʻu (long dresses) when swimming in the ocean.

58. Marx, *Capital*, 164–65.

59. For example, during Kalākaua's coronation and jubilee, hula performances proceeded from morning till night for two weeks.

60. Jennie Kapahukulaokamamalu Wilson, interviewed by Joann Kealiinohomoku, tape 59.3.1, BM. Kini did not name specific mele. However, in another interview on tape HAW 59.8.2, she said they performed hula ʻālaʻapapa instead of hula ʻōlapa. Kini tended to use these terms interchangeably, although Amy Kuʻuleialoha Stillman makes a clear argument for their structural and spiritual differences in *Sacred Hula*, 16.

61. Since the terms "hula ʻuliʻuli" and "hula pūʻili" do not specify genre, but simply indicate the kind of instrumentation used, they could refer to hula kuʻi performed with these instruments.

62. Hula kuʻi is the "modern sung form" of hula ʻōlapa performed with guitars and ʻukulele. Stillman, *Sacred Hula*, 3.

63. Both hula ʻōlapa and hula ʻālaʻapapa are performed with the ipu heke (double gourd). However, hula ʻālaʻapapa is distinguished by having an unstandardized length of text and uneven phrasing. Stillman, *Sacred Hula*, 16, 23. Two extant examples of hula ʻālaʻapapa are the mele "No luna i ka halekai" and "Hole Waimea i ka ihe a ka makani."

64. Jennie Kapahukulaokamamalu Wilson, interviewed by Joann Kealiinohomoku, tapes HAW 59.8.2 and 59.5.1, BM.

65. Ibid., tape HAW 59.7.1, BM.

66. David Blanchard discusses Mohawk entertainers from Kahnawake who performed on remarkable pageantry and dance circuits in the United States and Europe from the mid-nineteenth century through the early twentieth century. These tours brought important revenue to Kahnawake communities while enabling them to "maintain a spirit of material independence" from Great Britain and Canada. Blanchard, "Entertainment, Dance and Northern Mohawk Showmanship." John W. Troutman, in his study *Indian Blues*, tracks Native musicians who also performed their "Indianness" on wide-ranging tours. Gaining new audiences, fame, and financial success through entertainment, they intervened in federal Indian policy and resisted assimilation. *Indian Blues*, 208–9.

67. Shea Murphy, *The People Have Never Stopped Dancing*, 23.

68. V. Deloria, "The Indians," 52, 54.

69. Shea Murphy, *The People Have Never Stopped Dancing*, 69.

70. Osorio, *Dismembering Lāhui*, 203.

71. Malie Kaleikoa, one of the Hui Lei Mamo dancers, was active in proroyalist causes after the overthrow. "Hoalohaloha alii," *Ka Makaainana*, 28 October 1895.

72. *Chicago Inter-Ocean*, 30 July 1893.

73. Noenoe K. Silva argues that foreigners watching hula at Kalākaua's fiftieth-birthday jubilee celebration could not interpret the true meanings of the parades and hula, nor identify the types of hula being performed. N. K. Silva, *Aloha Betrayed*, 113, 116. Even today, anticolonial, nationalist mele such as "Kaulana Nā Pua" are performed for unsuspecting tourists.

74. Jennie Kapahukulaokamamalu Wilson, interviewed by Joann Kealiinohomoku, tape HAW 59.14.1, BM.

75. *Daily Bulletin*, 24 May 1893.

76. Dennett, *Weird and Wonderful*, 68.

77. Plantation workers laboring in fields under often brutal conditions made about three dollars a week. The basic pay scale is from the Honokaa Sugar Plantation on the island of Hawai'i. Beechert, *Working in Hawaii*, 109.

78. "Hula Hula Dancer Is in Hard Luck," *Chicago Daily Tribune*, 24 August 1895.

79. "Unfortunate Hula Girls," *Hawaiian Gazette*, 6 September 1895.

80. Thompson, *The Making of the English Working Class*.

81. Brown, *Babylon Girls*, 7.

82. Jennie Kapahukulaokamamalu Wilson, interviewed by Napua Stevens Poire and Kenneth Emory, 6 June 1956, tape HAW 58.4, BM.

83. Topolinski, "The Hula," 147. Jennie Kapahukulaokamamalu Wilson, interviewed by Joann Kealiinohomoku, tape HAW 59.8.2, BM.

84. Weiner, *Inalienable Possessions*.

85. W. Silva and Suemori, *Nānā i Nā Loea Hula*, 110.

86. Tagg, *The Burden of Representation*, 66.

87. Alloula, *The Colonial Harem*, 4.

88. Rafael, *White Love and Other Events in Filipino History*, 77.

89. Thompson, "Representation and Rule in the Imperial Archipelago," 30.

90. Musick was a journalist and lawyer who wrote popular histories related to U.S. national expansion.

91. Young, *The Boston at Hawaii*, 76–77. Another memoir and travelogue, *Hawaii Nei*, by Mabel Craft reveals what she calls "modern hula dancers" who do not wear blouses. Leis are draped over their chests to conceal, but also draw attention to, their breasts.

92. R. Adams, *Sideshow U.S.A.*, 33.

93. J. K. Brown, *Contesting Images*, 79.

94. Although hula dancers became known as "hula girls" in the United States, they were not called "hula girls" by Native Hawaiians but "'ōlapa," or "po'e hula." "Hula girl" is a gendered and sexualized term that emerged from missionary and tourist discourse in Hawai'i and during American tours of hula performers in the late nineteenth century. For more on the emergence of the iconography of the "hula girl" in American popular culture, see Sereno, "Images of the Hula Dancer and 'Hula Girl.'"

95. Kini's collection from the Omaha Greater America Exposition in 1899 include photographs of the female hula dancers Mele and Malie, suggesting that po'e hula continued to sell photographs of themselves.

96. Bogdan, *Freak Show*, 11.

97. J. K. Brown, *Contesting Images*, 110.

98. "Hula Girls in Hard Luck," *Hawaiian Gazette*, 13 August 1895. The *Pacific Commercial Advertiser* of Honolulu also reported a similar story, "Hula Girls Stuck in Logansport, Indiana," 13 August 1895.

99. Mellen, "Honolulu's First Lady," 38.

100. Patterson, "Aunt Jennie at 90 Recalls Her Teens."

101. hooks, *Black Looks*, 115–31. The oppositional gaze provides "spaces of agency . . . for black people, wherein we can both interrogate the gaze of the Other but also look back, and at one another, naming what we see," 116.

102. See S. M. Smith, *Photography on the Color Line*.

103. These Hawaiian examples are provided in Chappell, "Shipboard Relations between Pacific Island Women and EuroAmerican Men," 139; and they are derived from V. M. Golovnin, *Around the World in the Kamchatk, 1817–1819* (Honolulu: University of Hawaii Press, 1979), 175, 181; and William F.

Wilson, *With Lord Byron at the Sandwich Islands: Being Extracts from the MS Diary of James Macrae, Scottish Botanist* (Honolulu, 1922), 28.

104. *Nupepa Kuokoa*, 1 January 1876. Author's translation.

105. Ibid., 5 April 1876, 1 March 1879, 19 April 1879, 3 May 1888.

106. *Chicago Daily Inter-Ocean*, 2 August 1893.

107. Jennie Kapahukulaokamamalu Wilson, interviewed by Joann Kealiinohomoku, tape HAW 59.4.1, BM. As Kini explained, they posed in dried lā'ī (ti leaf) skirts for a photograph at a San Francisco studio after they disembarked from the steamship. Their skirts had dried during the ocean voyage. Hula dancers posed for photographs wearing fresh lā'ī skirts in 1880s Honolulu; see, for example, photographs in HSA's PP–32–8, "Photos: Hula Dancers, Musicians, Groups."

108. White vaudeville producer Sam T. Jack revised the familiar minstrel show formula by bringing sixteen light-skinned African American women to *The Creole Show*. Until this point, black women had been a rare sight on the vaudeville stage. Krasner, *Resistance, Parody and Double Consciousness*, 18; J. Brown, *Babylon Girls*, 92–97.

109. The J. B. Wilson studio took portraits of middle-class Chicago residents and vaudeville performers from the late nineteenth century.

110. Severa, *Dressed for the Photographer*, and Schorman, *Selling Style*.

111. Severa, *Dressed for the Photographer*, 458.

112. Schorman, *Selling Style*, 47.

113. McRobbie, *In the Culture Society*, 39.

114. Krauss, *Johnny Wilson*, 66.

115. Stevens, transcribed interview by Bob Krauss, 3 June 1989, Bob Krauss Workbook "Wilson Tapes Transcribed," BK.

116. Peiss, *Cheap Amusements*, 64.

117. Schorman, *Selling Style*, 47.

118. "Hula Girls in Hard Luck," *Hawaiian Gazette*, 13 August 1895.

119. Liliuokalani, *Hawaii's Story by Hawaii's Queen*.

120. N. K. Silva, *Aloha Betrayed*, 150.

121. Rafael, *White Love and Other Events in Filipino History*, 100.

122. Hebdige, *Subculture*, 16.

123. Ibid., 17, 90, 104–5.

124. McRobbie, *In the Culture Society*, and McRobbie, *Feminism and Youth Culture*.

125. Kelley, *Race Rebels*, 58.

126. Krauss, *Johnny Wilson*, 181.

127. Certeau, *The Practice of Everyday Life*, 38.

128. In *Photography on the Color Line*, Shawn Michelle Smith develops this concept of an archive that contests dominant representations, 7–10.

129. Jennie Kapahukulaokamamalu Wilson, interviewed by Joann Kealiinohomoku, tape HAW 59.8.2, BM.

130. Teaiwa, "Militarism, Tourism and the Native," 159.

131. P. J. Deloria, *Indians in Unexpected Places*, 68, 136, and 177.

132. Coe and Gates, *The Snapshot Photograph*, 8. In the 1890s, other innovations made photography more responsive to amateur use. For example, in 1891 Eastman issued the Daylight Kodak, a new type of handheld camera that allowed film to be loaded and unloaded in daylight, and in 1895 the popular Pocket Kodak camera, a compact daylight-loading design. *The Snapshot Photograph*, 19.

133. Jennie Kapahukulaokamamalu Wilson, interviewed by Joann Kealiinohomoku, tape HAW 59.7.1, BM. Kini referred to the troupe's female members as "girls" but was using "girls" in a colloquial sense to refer to young women, as her photograph reveals teenage and young women in the troupe.

134. Te Awekotuku, *Mana Wahine Maori*, 79–81.

135. Teaiwa, "Militourism, Tourism and the Native," 161.

136. Between 1806 and 1872, an annual average of 560 men registered with the Hawaiian government before going abroad, as required by kingdom law. The fur trade consolidated in 1821 under Hudson's Bay Company, which opened up a recruiting office in Honolulu. In the 1820s, ships in the fur trade stopped in Hawai'i between the Pacific Northwest, where they picked up pelts, and China, where the pelts were sold. Hawai'i also became the center of a global whaling economy in the 1840s and '50s, employing thousands of Hawaiian men. In a three-year period from 1845 to 1847, for example, almost 2,000 Hawaiians enlisted as sailors on foreign vessels. Beechert, *Working in Hawaii*, 76; Barman and Watson, *Leaving Paradise*, 2, 7; Kuykendall, *The Hawaiian Kingdom, Volume II, 1854–1874*, 138; and Kuykendall, *The Hawaiian Kingdom, Volume I, 1778–1854*, 312–13.

137. Barman and Watson, *Leaving Paradise*, 17–33.

138. Chappell, "Shipboard Relations between Pacific Island Women and EuroAmerican Men, 1767–1887," 144.

139. Ibid., 144–45.

140. Harriet Ne, transcribed interview by Bob Krauss, Bob Krauss Workbook 4 (July 1893–December 1896), BK.

141. Patterson, "Aunt Jennie at 90 Recalls Her Teens."

142. Jennie Kapahukulaokamamalu Wilson, interviewed by Joann Kealiinohomoku, tape HAW 59.1.1, BM.

143. "Last Living Court Dancer," *Honolulu Star-Bulletin*, 29 May 1960.

144. Peiss, *Cheap Amusements*, 7.

145. Matthews, *The Rise of the New Woman*.

146. Ngai, "Transnationalism and the Transformation of the 'Other,'" 61.

147. The literature on world's fair performances has focused on the contribution of fairs to empire-building, the colonial desires of Euro-

Americans, and the exoticization of colonial subjects on display. For example, see Rydell, *All the World's a Fair*, and Rydell, Findling, and Pelle, *Fair America*.

148. Tagg, *The Burden of Representation*, 85.

149. Jennie Kapahukulaokamamalu Wilson, interviewed by Joann Kealiinohomoku, tape HAW 59.3.1, BM.

150. *Pacific Commercial Advertiser*, 7 April 1893. The merchant H. J. Moors arranged this private exhibition after the Samoan government declined an invitation to the Chicago exposition. Although this village was supposed to be called "Polynesian," exposition guidebooks refer to it as a "Samoan village." Photographs and drawings of Samoans were published in fair guidebooks and periodicals, such as the *Illustrated American*, but none of the Hawaiians appeared.

151. Jennie Kapahukulaokamamalu Wilson, interviewed by Joann Kealiinohomoku, tape HAW 59.14.1, BM.

152. There is some evidence that Pacific Islander performers appropriated imperial exhibitions for their own edification and cultural exchanges with their Pacific cousins. Maori, Cook Islander, and Fijian performers exchanged gifts and ceremonial greetings at the New Zealand International Exhibition of Arts and Industries held in Christchurch in 1906–7. Johnston, "Reinventing Fiji at 19th-Century and Early 20th-Century Exhibitions," 36–37.

153. "Belly dance" refers to all solo dance forms with origins in North Africa, the Middle East, and Central Asia. Although the belly dance was billed as Egyptian at the Chicago Exposition and Kini herself referred to her friends as "Egyptian," the women may have hailed from anywhere in North Africa or the Middle East. Shay and Sellers-Young, *Belly Dance*, 1. For example, the famous Chicago Midway performer "Little Egypt" played a dancer from Armenia. J. Brown, *Babylon Girls*, 101.

154. The *Morning Oregonian* (Portland), for instance, reported that the danse du ventre, nautch dance, and hula-hula "all symbolize the supreme vital function in a manner shocking to Western ideas of decorous reticence." *Morning Oregonian*, 11 August 1894.

155. Jennie Kapahukulaokamamalu Wilson, interviewed by Joann Kealiinohomoku, tape HAW 59.14.1, BM.

156. Ibid., tape HAW 59.14.2, BM.

157. Thomas, *Entangled Objects*, 101.

158. Hackler, "My Dear Friend," 112. The bracelet is on display at the Queen Emma Summer Palace, Hānaiakamalama, in Nuʻuanu Valley on Oʻahu.

159. In this photograph, Queen Emma stands next to the silver christening cup given by Queen Victoria to her son, Prince Albert Edward Kauikeaouli Leiopapa a Kamehameha. Victoria had agreed to be Albert's godmother, but the cup has never been used since he died in 1862.

160. Emma ran for sovereign in 1874, but lost to Kalākaua.

161. Stillman, "The Hula Ku'i," 58.

162. Ali'i nui and other members of the royal family went abroad to be educated and develop diplomatic relationships. In 1823, Kamehameha II and Queen Kamamalu sailed to England to negotiate a treaty of alliance between Hawai'i and Britain, but they contracted measles and died there. Prince Alexander Liholiho and his brother Prince Lot Kapuāiwa, the future sovereigns Kamehameha IV and Kamehameha V, respectively, traveled to the United States and Europe in 1849–50. Queen Emma, the consort of Kamehameha IV, traveled to England, France, Italy, and Germany in 1865–66. Besides his world tour in 1881, Kalākaua toured the United States in 1876. He was recuperating from an illness in San Francisco when he died there in 1891. Kalākaua's and Lili'uokalani's niece, Princess Victoria Ka'iulani, was educated in England from 1889 until 1897.

163. The dates referring to Germany on Kini's charm bracelet are from April 1894 to August 1894. She stated that her group toured for one year, but it is also conceivable that she returned to the United States after six months and joined the vaudeville circuit. The troupe members who went to Europe were the three dancers Kini, Annie Grube, Pauahi, and the ho'opa'a Kamuku; the dancer Nakai and ho'opa'a Kanuku had decided to go to Samoa after the Chicago Exposition with performers from the Samoan village. See Imada, "Transnational *Hula* as Colonial Culture."

164. Mellen, "Honolulu's First Lady," 38.

165. Rydell and Kroes, *Buffalo Bill in Bologna*.

166. Mellen, "Honolulu's First Lady," 38; Patterson, "Aunt Jennie at 90 Recalls Her Teens"; and Hopkins, "Kini Wilson."

167. Emerson, *Unwritten Literature of Hawaii*, 98. Kini, though not identified by name, was one of Emerson's informants. She found the European puppet show similar to the Hawaiian hula ki'i (puppet hula).

168. Jennie Kapahukulaokamamalu Wilson, interviewed by Joann Kealiinohomoku, tape HAW 59.3.1, BM.

169. P. J. Deloria, *Indians in Unexpected Places*, 69.

170. Stevens, transcribed interview by Bob Krauss, 3 June 1989, Bob Krauss Workbook "Wilson Tapes Transcribed," BK. Krauss, "Jennie Wilson's Charm Bracelet." Bob Krauss provides a detailed description of Kini's charm bracelet. When Krauss examined the bracelet around 1989, it was in the possession of Don Medcalf, owner of Hawaiian Islands Stamp and Coin, Honolulu, Hawai'i. Her charm bracelet includes these dates and cities: 28 April 1894 (Hamburg), 10 May 1894 (München), 6 June 1894 (Chemnitz), 26 June 1894 (German coin), and 1 August 1894 (Berlin).

171. In the late nineteenth century, Queen Victoria of England gave then-princess Lili'uokalani a bracelet engraved with the queen's name. The bracelets, known today as "Hawaiian heirloom" bracelets, became much-

imitated keepsakes in the islands. The charm bracelet is a precursor to these bracelets collected and worn by islander women. Made of precious metals, they are inalienable objects and gifts, bearing the names of ancestors, children, and other loved ones. New bracelets are given to relatives and namesakes on special occasions and older bracelets are inherited after an owner's passing.

172. Stewart, *On Longing*, 137–38.

173. Marx, *Capital*, 165.

174. Weiner, *Inalienable Possessions*.

175. Stevens, transcribed interview by Bob Krauss, 3 June 1989, Bob Krauss Workbook "Wilson Tapes Transcribed," BK.

176. "Unfortunate Hula Girls," *Hawaiian Gazette*, 6 September 1895. The women were trying to make their way west and eventually return to the islands. Three of the dancers stopped once again in Chicago in the summer of 1895. They had been left destitute after their manager caused compatriot Annie Grube serious injury and fired them. While Annie was hospitalized with a broken leg, Kini and Pauahi tried to earn enough for a return passage to Hawai'i by performing hula.

177. Jennie Kapahukulaokamamalu Wilson, interviewed by Joann Kealiinohomoku, tape HAW 59.4.1, BM.

178. Ibid.; Mellen, "Honolulu's First Lady," 38. The Bana Lahui comprised multinational musicians (e.g., Hawaiians, Filipinos, Portuguese) formerly employed in the kingdom's Royal Hawaiian Band, which had refused to sign an oath of loyalty to the pro-American provisional government after the overthrow. "Puali Puhiohe Lahui" is the nineteenth-century transliteration without diacritical marks; it is transliterated "Pū'ali Puhi'ohe Lāhui" in modern Hawaiian orthography.

179. "Hawaii Passion Dance," *Washington Post*, 27 November 1893.

180. Hawaiian performers also sang the queen's songs along their tours to the Buffalo and Omaha expositions in 1899 and 1901.

3. Impresarios on the Midway

1. "Mayor Awakened by Band Music on His Birthday," *Honolulu Star-Bulletin*, 15 December 1923.

2. John H. Wilson first toured the United States from 1895 to 1896 as manager of the Bana Lahui or Puali Puhiohe Lahui (Hawaiian National Band), which publicized Hawaiian opposition to the Republic of Hawai'i and support for the restoration of Queen Lili'uokalani.

3. See this book's introduction, note 11, on the Newlands Resolution. Noenoe K. Silva details the petition campaigns that defeated a treaty of annexation in *Aloha Betrayed*, 131–63.

4. Everyday practices of resistance also preceded annexation, including

wearing pins of the Hawaiian national flag and the composing of mele lāhui (national songs). Some started petition campaigns, while others took up arms. Amy K. Stillman discusses these mele in "History Reinterpreted in Song," 1–30.

5. While a hidden transcript is a "discourse that is ordinarily excluded from the public transcripts of subordinates by the exercise of power," I would venture to add performance to this productive formulation. Scott, *Domination and the Art of Resistance*, 27.

6. The Hawaiian lyrics and English translation of the song "Aloha 'Āina" (Love of the land), are printed in Elbert and Mahoe's *Nā Mele o Hawai'i Nei*, 62–64. Known popularly today as "Kaulana Nā Pua" (Famous are the flowers), this mele was composed in 1893 after the overthrow by Ellen Kekoaohiwaikalani Wright Prendergrast, a lady-in-waiting to Queen Lili'uokalani. Members of the Royal Hawaiian Band refused to sign an oath of loyalty to the provisional government and resigned. They begged Prendergrast to write them a song of protest. This royalist band became known as the Bana Lahui and played this song during their tours of the United States in 1895–96. See Nordyke and Noyes, "Kaulana Nā Pua," 27–42; and Stillman, "'Aloha Aina,'" 83–99. This band was managed by John H. Wilson and some of its musicians may have joined his troupes at the Omaha and Buffalo expositions.

7. Go, "The Chains of Empire," 1–42, 208.

8. Kama'āina translates to "child of the land," which implies having been Hawai'i-born and raised. The Big Five companies were Castle & Cooke, C. Brewer, Amfac, Alexander & Baldwin, and Theo Davies.

9. Kent, *Hawaii*, 69.

10. Quoted in Kuykendall, *The Hawaiian Kingdom, Volume III, 1874–1893*, 635.

11. Kent, *Hawaii*, 69.

12. Fuchs, *Hawaii Pono*, 154. The most powerful political position in the islands belonged to the governor, who could not be impeached; he made numerous appointments and had veto power over the legislature. The elected delegate to Congress was also important to sugar interests, because while he was a nonvoting member, he could lobby for favorable trade tariffs, immigration policies, and improvement of harbors. On a local level, the elected legislature and board of supervisors levied taxes and instituted some land policies.

13. Ibid., 174.

14. Rowland, "The Establishment of the Republic of Hawaii, 1893–1894," 214–15.

15. Fuchs, *Hawaii Pono*, 155. Haole made up less than 22 percent of the population in the 1890s.

16. Japanese and Chinese were essentially barred from achieving citizenship

in the republic. No alien could attain citizenship unless he or she was from a country that had arranged naturalization policies by treaty with the Republic of Hawai'i. Rowland, "The Establishment of the Republic of Hawaii, 1893–1894," 216.

17. The United States purchased the Philippines from Spain for $22 million, and Filipino leaders were not present at the treaty's signing in Paris.

18. These fairs included the Greater America Exposition in Omaha, Nebraska (1899), Exposition Universelle de Paris (1900), the Pan-American Exposition in Buffalo, New York (1901), and the Louisiana Purchase Exposition in St. Louis, Missouri (1904). The territorial displays ranged in size and scope, depending on legislative allocation. The territory of Hawai'i did not allocate any monies for the Buffalo exposition of 1901 and mounted only a small educational exhibit.

19. Thrum, *Hawaiian Almanac and Annual*, 162.

20. *Pacific Commercial Advertiser*, 14 August 1899.

21. "Some Interesting Sights," *Omaha World-Herald*, 2 August 1899.

22. *Omaha World-Herald*, 18 August 1899.

23. *Pacific Commercial Advertiser*, 3 August 1899.

24. *Pacific Commercial Advertiser*, 12 September 1899.

25. Sanford B. Dole, Correspondence from Governor's Office. 10 November 1900, GOV 1, vol. 2 (letterbook—24 June 1900–19 September 1901), HSA.

26. "Logan at Omaha," *Hawaiian Gazette* and *Pacific Commercial Advertiser*, 18 August 1899.

27. The commissioner of the Greater American Exposition (GAE) wrote directly to President Sanford Dole of the Republic, wanting to engage the (Royal) Hawaiian Band for the exposition, but did not express an interest in having hula. The GAE was willing to pay $1,800 a week for four weeks for thirty-six people, including bandleader Henry Berger and two female soloists. Ultimately the band did not play music at the exposition, although the reason remains unknown. W. W. Umsted to Sanford Dole, 9 May 1899, FO and EX 1899 (folder: 1899, Misc., Foreign, January–June), HSA.

28. Rydell, *All the World's a Fair*, 139.

29. Ibid., 143–49.

30. Barry, *Snap Shots on the Midway of the Pan-Am Expo*, 146.

31. In Omaha, there were forty Hawaiians, according to "They Made a Hit," *Pacific Commercial Advertiser*, 11 August 1899, reprinted from *Omaha World-Herald*. Kini Kapahu said there were twenty-six Hawaiians in Omaha. Eighteen young women and twenty-six young men performed in Buffalo, per Johnny Wilson's notes. Wilson to Abel Green, 4 August 1952, JHW.

32. Four million people attended the Buffalo exposition, while the Omaha fair drew fewer than one million.

33. *Omaha World-Herald*, 6 August 1899, and 12 August 1899.

34. *Omaha World-Herald*, 27 August 1899. Attendance at the GAE was 843,217, of which about half were paid attendees. However, the majority paid only twenty-five cents admission. *Omaha Bee*, 31 October 1899.

35. "Midway and Its Many Shows," *Buffalo Courier*, 30 June 1901.

36. *Pacific Commercial Advertiser*, 6 March 1902.

37. Beechert, *Working in Hawaii*, 109

38. Troutman, *Indian Blues*, 208–9.

39. Wilson to E. W. McConnell, 31 March 1938, Bob Krauss Workbook 26 (January 1938–June 1939), BK.

40. The Omaha troupe from the islands included the Quintette Club (Mekia Kealakai, Tom Silva, Tom Hennessey, W. H. Sea, James Shaw, J. Edwards, East [Kahulu], Ben Jones); hula dancers Kalani, Kaluna, Mele Kaulana, Api, and Kaleo; male hoʻopaʻa Kaai; male chanters and dancers Kualii and Inana; and female chanter Pioe. In addition there was a man expert in canoeing named Sam Kamakee and a woman identified as Miss Leilehua. Some of the musicians traveled as families: J. Edwards came with his wife and daughter; James Shaw with his wife and two children; Ernest Kaai with his wife; and Sam Kamakee with his son. Ed Towse, letter dated 29 August 1899, printed in *Pacific Commercial Advertiser*, 12 September 1899.

41. A photograph of the Hawaiian hula troupe in Buffalo reveals that there were at least two young children who performed hula and one older man who was a hoʻopaʻa. Barry, *Snap Shots on the Midway of the Pan-Am Expo*, 18. The dancer Mele, who had performed in Omaha, was another member of the troupe. Kimokeo and Opu were swimmers who were to participate in international swimming matches. *Pacific Commercial Advertiser*, 3 April 1901.

42. This photograph of musicians is also printed with names in Kanahele, *Hawaiian Music and Musicians*, 275. Johnny Wilson's show diary, covering the years 1901–2, records musicians' names as well. John H. Wilson, *Diary, 1901 Buffalo Fair*, Bob Krauss Workbook 6 (June 1899– September 1902), BK.

43. Kanahele, "Mekia Kealakai," 209. Kanahele dates this encounter between Sousa and Kealakai to the Hawaiian National Band's tour in 1895 of the continental United States. However, Sousa probably met Kealakai and Wilson's band at the Pan-American Exposition of 1901 in Buffalo, New York, instead, which is suggested by photographic evidence. See photograph captioned "Mr. Sousa Stopping by to Chat with the Hawaiian Band," *Cosmopolitan* 31, no. 5 (September 1901): 504.

44. Keoni Wilsona was the Hawaiian transliteration of "John Wilson."

45. These family names and genealogies are taken from Queen Liliʻuokalani's

"crazy quilt," which was sewn by Lili'uokalani and John Wilson's mother, Eveline Townsend Wilson, during Lili'uokalani's palace imprisonment in 1895. One square of the quilt relays the Townsend-Blanchard-Wilson family tree, with its Hawaiian, Tahitian, and American members. Hackler and Woodard, *The Queen's Quilt.*

46. According to the family tree embroidered on the queen's quilt, John's maternal great-grandmother was an ali'i named Kahola Kamokuiki. Bob Krauss writes that Harriet Ne, one of his informants and a family friend of the Wilsons', identified John's Hawaiian great-grandmother as "Koloa," an ali'i from Moloka'i. Krauss, *Johnny Wilson,* 7.

47. The Scottish trader and captain Charles Burnette Wilson was born in Tahiti and was the son of a London Missionary Society missionary. Ibid., 9–10.

48. Ibid., 45–46.

49. George Monewa Townsend was not sentenced to hard labor like other participants in the rebellion, in exchange for providing evidence of the plot. Ibid.

50. Paige Raibon discusses Kwakwaka'wakw George Hunt and other mixed-race cultural brokers at the turn of the century who participated in the Chicago World's Columbian Exposition in 1893. Similarly, Johnny Wilson enjoyed access to white American institutions and training and brokered Hawaiian culture to elite and middlebrow Americans. Raibon, *Authentic Indians,* 62–73.

51. Claus Spreckels had expanded into Hawaiian sugar plantations in the 1870s, with land and water rights leased from the Hawaiian government. He had become extremely powerful during King Kalākaua's reign, holding over half of the kingdom's debt and controlling most of the islands' sugar crop. Daws, *Shoal of Time,* 229, 231.

52. For this reason, Johnny and many other politically active Hawaiians—regardless of party affiliation—supported statehood because it would mean the power of the oligarchy would be kept in check by Washington.

53. Krauss, *Johnny Wilson,* 64, 65, 69.

54. In 1897, Coelho was accused of embezzling $140 while working as a district court clerk of Honolulu, Republic of Hawai'i. A public trial ensued. He vigorously denied guilt and his defense counsel argued that there was no proof Coelho had taken the money since the court maintained no account ledgers. Nevertheless, Coelho was indicted and sentenced to two years and court costs in May 1897. He filed for a new trial that month, and in November 1897 the indictment was dismissed and a retrial was ordered by the Hawai'i Supreme Court because one of the jurors, a Hawaiian man, had refused to take an oath supporting the Republic of Hawai'i. *Hawaiian Gazette,* 12 February, 26 March, 4 May, 5 May, 11 May, 14 May, 2 November 1897.

55. Coelho was a volunteer inspector for the Citizens Sanitary and Relief Committee of the Board of Health and served in this capacity from 1895 at least through the plague crisis on Oʻahu in 1899. *Hawaiian Gazette*, 27 September 1895, 29 December 1899, 27 September 1895.

56. The issue of *Hawaiian Gazette* from 29 December 1899 announced Coelho's nomination for notary public. Mookini, *The Hawaiian Newspapers*, 49. Noenoe K. Silva describes *Nupepa Kuokoa* as an "establishment" paper representing dominant and prevailing interests. *Aloha Betrayed*, 56.

57. The Young Hawaiians Institute and its concerts were covered in *Hawaiian Gazette*, 2 August 1895, 18 October 1895, and 25 October 1895.

58. Fuchs, *Hawaii Pono*, 156–58. Some Hawaiians chose the Republican Party, while others were affiliated with the Home Rule party after 1900.

59. Ibid., 168.

60. "Mr. Hanna Encounters Several Incidents," *Buffalo Courier*, 22 May 1901.

61. "Cleopatra and the Hula-Hula," *Buffalo Courier*, 7 May 1901.

62. A bass viol (or viola da gamba) was a bowed six-string instrument with frets, usually played on the lap or between one's legs. Developed during the Renaissance, the viol was played as a solo instrument until the middle of the eighteenth century. Today the guitar and the ʻukulele are customary lead instruments for Hawaiian vocal music, but at the turn of the century it was the violin.

63. "Midway Gleanings," *Omaha World-Herald*, 13 August 1899.

64. James C. Scott has argued that forms of dissent exercised against the dominant order are not simply "harmless catharsis" that serve as a safety valve. Scott, *Domination and the Arts of Resistance*, 187.

65. Lipsitz, *Time Passages*, 100.

66. Roach, *Cities of the Dead*, 26.

67. Ibid. "Counter-memories," as Joseph Roach writes, are "the disparities between history as it is discursively transmitted and memory as it is publicly enacted by the bodies that bear its consequences."

68. Hartman, *Scenes of Subjection*, 62.

69. Pukui, "Songs (Meles) of Old Kaʻu, Hawaii," 247.

70. Noelani Arista suggests that the interpretation and practice of kaona has shifted from a strategy that targets particular listeners to one that sees it as multiple meanings that exclude listeners. "Navigating Uncharted Oceans of Meaning," 665–66.

71. Pukui, "Songs (Meles) of Old Kaʻu, Hawaii," 248.

72. Wilson recorded sales of this sheet music in his tour diary for the Buffalo fair of 1901. Wilson, *Diary, 1901 Buffalo Fair*. The other songs they performed were "Aloha ʻOe," "Moanalua," "[Kuʻu Pua i] Paoakalani," "Liko no a Hiki," "Ahi Wela," "Sweet Lei Lehua," "[Ua] Like no a Like," and "Lei Poni Moi."

73. Liliuokalani, *The Queen's Songbook*, 226–27. Composed a few years after the overthrow, "Lei Poni Moi" was first published in 1899.

74. "Some Good Things on the Midway," *Buffalo Courier*, 16 June 1901. On this occasion in Buffalo, the village hosted special guests and chose to perform "Akahi Hoi," a love song composed by King David Kalākaua for his wife Kapiʻolani.

75. The Wilson family appears to have assumed conflicting roles in this domestic and political drama. Johnny's father and Kitty's husband Charles B. Wilson was the sheriff who inspected the queen's reading materials, deliveries, and gifts. At one point, Kitty Wilson revealed to her husband that she thought the queen had received newspapers furtively, and C. B. Wilson berated Kitty after discovering that news had been brought in the guise of wrapping paper. Liliuokalani, *Hawaii's Story by Hawaii's Queen*, 291–92.

76. See Elbert and Mahoe, *Nā Mele o Hawaiʻi Nei*, 72. The queen herself wrote without identifying Johnny Wilson by name, "I used to find great comfort in the bits of newspaper that were wrapped around my bouquets which were brought to me from my own garden at Uluhaimalama." Ibid., 290–91.

77. Ibid., 291.

78. Typical of Hawaiian poetic forms at this time, the lyrics were put either into couplets with no chorus that were adapted from traditional chant or a Western-influenced structure that alternated verse-chorus-verse. Nogelmeier and Stillman, introduction to *Buke Mele Lāhui*, xvii.

79. Lipsitz, *Time Passages*, 16.

80. English translation by Mary Kawena Pukui; see also the English-language translation in Elbert, *Nā Mele o Hawaiʻi Nei*, 28.

81. "Midway Gleanings," *Omaha World-Herald*, 23 August 1899.

82. "Midway Gleanings," *Omaha World-Herald*, 20 August 1899.

83. "Feast in Honor of Queen Lil," *Omaha World-Herald*, 26 August 1899. The lūʻau did not appear to have materialized in Washington, D.C., for reasons unknown, but Johnny traveled from Omaha to visit the queen and brought gifts of poi and fish.

84. "Midway Gleanings," *Omaha World-Herald*, 20 August 1899.

85. Rydell, *All the World's a Fair*, 194–98.

86. *Buffalo Express*, 30 June 1901, photographs; *Buffalo Courier*, 8 June 1901, and 11 August 1901, respectively.

87. *Around the "Pan" with Uncle Hank*, 82.

88. Ibid., 32–33. The other midway attraction that fascinated Uncle Hank was the Oriental Theater, which featured a belly dance with hip movements that appeared to be similar to the hula: to the "Hooche Cooche" music, a "voluptuous little muscle-dancer swayed her form in undulating and rhythmical contortions" (36).

89. *Pacific Commercial Advertiser*, 24 June 1901. According to Richard Hayes Barry, W. Maurice Tobin was also "the only American spieler at the Late Paris Exposition" (i.e., the Paris Exposition Universelle in 1900). *Snap Shots on the Midway of the Pan-Am Expo*, 82.

90. *Buffalo Courier*, 2 June 1901.

91. *Pacific Commercial Advertiser*, 5 December 1901.

92. A description on the back of Mele's photograph identifies her as "Miss Mele" with a partially legible surname of "Nawianu," "Kaniana," or possibly "Kaulana." The handwritten note continues, "Hula Dancer, 19 yrs., John H. Wilson, Manager." The caption was likely written either by Johnny Wilson or Kini Kapahu. PP–33–3, Photos, Hula Dancers, Musicians, Groups (Portraits, Early Period), HSA.

93. Winona Beamer, a famed hula teacher and composer, was only a small child when her grandmother brought her and other family members to learn from Kini. This is her recollection quoted in Krauss, *Johnny Wilson*, 198–99.

94. "Aunt Jennie's Views of Aloha Week: Artificiality, Misuse, Exploitation," *Honolulu Star-Bulletin*, 21 October 1958, and "Wary Tourism Officials Skirt Issue of Aunt Jennie's Aloha Week Blast," *Honolulu Star-Bulletin*, 22 October 1958.

95. *Buffalo Morning Express*, 28 April 1901.

96. Barry, *Snap Shots on the Midway of the Pan-Am Expo*, 18.

97. Ibid., 20.

98. By 1893, Lorrin Thurston was used to freely mixing his private business and annexationist politics. Not only was he a budding concessionaire in Chicago, but he was also appointed the provisional government's annexation commissioner in Washington in 1893. In the spring of 1893, Thurston traveled to Washington to lobby for annexation. He later moved the volcano cyclorama to the Mid-Winter Exposition in San Francisco in 1894, generating profits for investors. Thurston reported that the cyclorama "scored a success financially" in San Francisco. Thurston, *Writings of Lorrin A. Thurston*, 83. Exposition showman E. W. McConnell then purchased the concession from Thurston's Cyclorama Company and brought it to the Pan-American Exposition in Buffalo in 1901.

99. Malo, *Ka Moolelo Hawaii*, 194.

100. *Rand McNally & Co.'s a Week at the Fair*, 233. Chicago World's Fair, Box 4, WC.

101. *World's Columbian Exposition Illustrated*, Box 60, Newsprint, ZWF.

102. *Rand McNally & Co.'s a Week at the Fair*, 233.

103. *The Daily Inter-Ocean* 22, no. 220 (1 November 1893): 25–32. Map Case 2, Drawer 12, Folder 5, WC.

104. "Meaning in the Hawaiian Ceremony," *Buffalo Courier*, 27 June 1901.

William Ellis, a London Society missionary, observed the chant during mourning for the Maui chief Keeaumoku and published it in *The Narrative of a Tour through Hawaii, or Owhyhee.* A similar oli was printed in *Ka Lama,* 14 February 1834.

105. The ʻōlelo noʻeau or proverb goes, "I ka ʻōlelo nō ke ola, I ka ʻōlelo nō ka make" (In speech there is life, in speech death).

106. Pukui, "Songs (Meles) of Old Kaʻu, Hawaii," 249.

107. See Pukui, *Nā Mele Welo,* 108–10 and Emerson, *Unwritten Literature of Hawaii,* 186–201, for chant and hula performed for Pele. Oli and hula in honor of Pele and her feats were a part of standard hula repertoire; Hawaiians also continue to appease and honor Pele with oli and hula at Kīlauea crater on the island of Hawaiʻi.

108. P. J. Deloria, *Indians in Unexpected Places,* 28.

109. Sereno Bishop had written hyperbolic editorials published in the American press defaming the hula and Queen Liliʻuokalani after the overthrow. He impugned Liliʻuokalani's morality and Christian faith by accusing her of paying a hula troupe six dollars for a "very vile" performance. Pratt, *Expansionists of 1898,* 164. Bishop also opined in the *Rocky Mountain News,* 4 February 1894, reprinted from the *Independent:* "[The hula dances] are pantomimes of the unspeakable. . . . The hula, with its obscene chanting accompaniments, simply constitutes the drama of heathen lewdness and the loathsome liturgy of idolatrous worship. In no other function of the old savage life of Hawaii is the essence of heathen vileness so completely embodied as in the hula." In marked contrast, in 1891 the same Reverend Bishop had praised Liliʻuokalani for her cultivation, Christian charity, and "influence against drunkenness, the hula dancers, and the kahunas [priests]" in the *Review of Reviews* after her accession to the throne. Quoted in Pratt, *Expansionists of 1898,* 168.

110. *Hawaiian Gazette,* 12 December 1899.

111. "Something in Addition to a Midway Exhibit," *Buffalo Courier,* 2 May 1901.

112. *Pacific Commercial Advertiser,* 14 May 1901.

113. *Pacific Commercial Advertiser,* 22 April 1901. The Kamehameha Girls' School sent fine lace work, the Kamehameha Boys' School manual work, and Kawaiahaʻo Seminary written educational samples.

114. Ibid.

115. *Pacific Commercial Advertiser,* 23 April 1901.

116. *Pacific Commercial Advertiser,* 4 June 1901.

117. Manifest Destiny in the United States persisted until the formal acquisition of overseas territories in the late nineteenth century. Only Indians choosing to become "civilized" individual landowners were

allowed to remain. If a tribe rebelled, President Thomas Jefferson warned that the federal government would seize their land and drive them across the Mississippi.

118. "Will Talk of Display," *Pacific Commercial Advertiser*, 1 May 1902.

119. Ibid.

120. *Pacific Commercial Advertiser*, 2 May 1902.

121. *Pacific Commercial Advertiser*, 24 October 1902.

122. *Honolulu Advertiser*, 6 September 1945.

123. "Cut Out Hula Hula," *Los Angeles Times*, 18 July 1903.

124. R. Williams, *Marxism and Literature*, 112.

125. Denning, *The Cultural Front*, 63.

126. R. Williams, *Marxism and Literature*, 128–35.

127. P. J. Deloria, *Indians in Unexpected Places*, 104–5.

128. Troutman, *Indian Blues*, 208–9.

129. "The Fall Festival," *Hawaiian Gazette*, 27 October 1899.

130. Wilson to Harriet Magoon, 30 October 1938, JHW.

131. *Honolulu Star-Bulletin*, 17 June 1921.

132. Krauss, *Johnny Wilson*, 116.

133. "Mr. Hanna Encounters Several Incidents," *Buffalo Courier*, 22 May 1901.

134. *Pacific Commercial Advertiser*, 10 June 1901.

135. "Mr. Hanna Encounters Several Incidents," *Buffalo Courier*, 22 May 1901.

136. "Playing Indian," the phenomenon of non-Indians' performing fantasies about Indians, enact important cultural myths for Euro-Americans, including the mythical founding of America. Like Indians who were scripted into "playing Indian" in commercial entertainment, Hawaiians "played Hawaiian" on show circuits. These imperial tableaux cast Euro-Americans as benevolent guests and Hawaiians as submissive hosts. P. J. Deloria, *Playing Indian*; and Rayna Green, "The Tribe Called Wannabee."

137. Scott, *Domination and the Arts of Resistance*, 20.

138. *Buffalo Courier*, 13 May 1901.

139. Scott, *Domination and the Arts of Resistance*, 6.

140. "Hawaiians of the Midway at Church," *Buffalo Courier*, 13 May 1901.

141. "Cold Keeps Crowd Away, but Exposition Work Advances," *Buffalo Courier*, 6 May 1901.

142. "Hawaiians of the Midway at Church," *Buffalo Courier*, 13 May 1901.

143. Ibid.

144. William J. Coelho to Jonah Kūhiō Kalanianaʻole, 10 March 1910, quoted in Fuchs, *Hawaii Pono*, 168.

145. Felix and Senecal, *The Portuguese in Hawaii*, 1978.

146. Kamins and Potter, *Mālamalama*, 3. The objections of the haole plantation owners to a public college were quite clear and racialized: nonwhites leaving the plantations would threaten the feudal system.

147. Pukui, Elbert, and Mookini, *Place Names of Hawaii*, 22. Although I grew up a few miles from Coelho Way in this neighborhood, I only learned of Coelho's significance in the course of researching Hawaiian entertainment circuits.

148. *Pacific Commercial Advertiser*, 20 September 1899.

149. *Buffalo Courier*, 2 May, 4 May, and 12 May 1901.

150. Rydell, *All the World's a Fair*, 150. There was an outbreak of tuberculosis in the Filipino Village and Indian Congress, as well as eleven recorded cases of measles in the Eskimo Village.

151. Jennie Kapahukulaokamamalu Wilson, interviewed by Joann Kealiinohomoku, tape HAW 59.7.1, BM.

152. Jennie Kapahukulaokamamalu Wilson, interviewed by Joann Kealiinohomoku, tapes HAW 59.14.1 and HAW 59.7.1, BM.

153. Jennie Kapahukulaokamamalu Wilson, interviewed by Joann Kealiinohomoku, tape HAW 59.1.1, BM.

154. Mele, one of the Omaha dancers, married the bandleader Mekia Kealakai, and toured Europe and the United States with her husband until 1920, when they returned home.

155. K. Silva, *He Aloha Moku o Keawe*, 1–3.

156. *Ka Makaainana*, 5 April 1897.

157. *Pacific Commercial Advertiser*, 4 January 1902.

158. The territorial government assumed control of Hawaiian music concessions at the Alaska-Yukon-Pacific Exposition in Seattle in 1909, the Pan-Pacific International Exposition in San Francisco in 1915, and Paris Coloniale Exposition in 1931.

159. All but one Japanese concessionaire at the Buffalo exposition appeared to be Euro-American, according to a list of names in the *Buffalo Courier*, 8 May 1901.

160. "No More Ear-Splitting Bally-Hoo," *Buffalo Courier*, 1 July 1901.

161. "Midway Men Say They Will Fight," *Buffalo Courier*, 24 June 1901.

162. *Buffalo Courier*, 14 July 1901.

163. Mellen, "Honolulu's First Lady," 38.

164. A divorce suit from Wilson's wife in 1900 accused John and an unidentified woman, presumably Kini Kapahu, of having committed adultery in Omaha in 1899 and in San Francisco.

165. "Mayor Awakened by Band Music on His Birthday."

166. Elbert and Mahoe, *Nā Mele o Hawai'i Nei*, 73.

167. Kanahele, "Lei 'Awapuhi ('Ginger Lei')," 224.

168. After the Buffalo fair closed in November 1901, fourteen members of the troupe went back to Hawai'i; Ben Waiwaiole, W. Keawe, and H. Kauhane were some of those who returned. Twelve of the men and women, however, went to another fair, the South Carolina Interstate and

West Indian Exposition, which opened in Charleston in December 1901. Lead by a man named Joe Puai, the Charleston group started a Hawaiian show of their own, with hula dancers Lily Wert and Abbie Clark. *Pacific Commercial Advertiser*, 5 December 1901.

169. In the early twentieth century, the showmen Benjamin Franklin Keith and Edward F. Albee revolutionized the vaudeville business. They established a national show business empire through a centralized booking agency that handled all their theaters. Keith and Albee determined who would perform and how much they would be paid in their theaters. Johnny would have had to negotiate with Keith and Albee agents to secure bookings for his Hawaiian troupe. Snyder, *The Voice of the City*, 34.

170. Wilson to Abel Green, 4 August 1952; *Brooklyn Eagle*, 1 December, 3 December, 4 December, 6 December 1901.

171. The male musicians were "a great hit" in San Francisco, playing songs like "Aloha 'Oe" and "Tomi Tomi," with 'ukulele, guitars, and a flute. *Pacific Commercial Advertiser*, 6 March 1902.

172. Kanahele, "Mekia Kealakai," 210.

173. Kanahele, "Toots Paka's Hawaiians," 388–89.

174. Kanahele, "Alfred Unauna Alohikea," 14.

175. Wilson to Edward G. Cooke, 4 July 1937, JHW.

4. "Hula Queens" and "Cinderellas"

1. "Leis Worn at Fair as Crowds Join in Honoring Hawaii," *New York Times*, 9 August 1939.

2. "Table 22. Selected Employment Statistics: 1878–1960," in *Historical Statistics of Hawaii, 1778–1962* (Honolulu: Department of Planning and Research, State of Hawaii, 1962), 17.

3. Yost, "Hawaii's Leading Crop of the Future," 27.

4. "Telling the World," *Paradise of the Pacific* 47, no. 7 (July 1935): 3.

5. By the late 1930s, Matson had shut down all of its rivals and had direct corporate "interlocks" with fifty-eight Big Five–controlled corporations. Kent, *Hawaii*, 81.

6. Hibbard and Franzen, *The View from Diamond Head*, 125.

7. Although generally experiencing growth in the twentieth century, tourism suffered a setback after the stock market crash in 1929. During the Great Depression, visitors dropped from 22,190 in 1929 to 18,651 in 1930; by 1932, only 10,370 tourists visited. The industry took until 1935 to return to pre-Depression levels. "Table 20. Visitor Arrivals, Visitors Present, and Visitor Expenditures: 1922–1961," in *Historical Statistics of Hawaii, 1778–1962*, 15.

8. *Participation in the Alaska-Yukon-Pacific Exposition*, 87.

9. Barrère, "The Hula in Retrospect," 64. Though hula had been utilized as

tourist entertainment since the early nineteenth century, it began to gain
a more favorable reputation in the 1910s.

10. Desmond, *Staging Tourism*, 13.

11. "Folk Dances of Polynesia," *Honolulu Advertiser*, 24 September 1911.

12. "Are We Ready for the Tourist," *Paradise of the Pacific* 33, no. 9
(September 1920): 21; and "Hawaiian Music as Publicity," *Paradise of the
Pacific* 34, no. 3 (March 1921): 1.

13. "Hawaiian Music as Publicity," *Paradise of the Pacific* 34, no. 3 (March
1921): 1.

14. "'Ware the Hula!," *Paradise of the Pacific* 35, no. 11 (November 1922): 16.

15. "Hula of Hawaii," *Paradise of the Pacific* 49, no. 12 (December 1937): 53.

16. Rosaldo, *Culture and Truth*, 69. While Rosaldo uses "imperialist
nostalgia" to analyze postcards from the colonial Philippines, this
concept also informs a colonial Hawaiian context.

17. The fin de siècle Hawaiian villages at U.S. expositions and the Lalani
Hawaiian Village were precursors to contemporary ethnographic tourist
displays, such as the Polynesian Cultural Center (PCC) in Lā'ie, O'ahu,
which is operated by the Church of Latter-Day Saints. At the PCC,
tourists wander through re-created Pacific Island "villages" and observe
live cultural activities.

18. Tim Ryan, "Face of Hawaii," *Honolulu Star-Bulletin*, 29 March 1999.

19. George Mossman's father was Scottish and his mother Native Hawaiian.
Coffin, "Hawaiian Village, 1936," 15.

20. Photograph, N. R. Farbman Photograph Collection, Folder, Tourists and
Tourism, BM.

21. Ibid.

22. See *Photograph No. CP 74612* (Tai Sing Loo, photographer); "Hula Dancer
with Lei at Mossman's Hawaiian Village with Song 'For You a Lei,'" BM.
Composed by the "Hawaiian King of Jazz," the hapa haole musician
Johnny Noble, the song "For You a Lei" became a hit in Hawai'i in 1929.

23. See B. Smith, *European Vision and the South Pacific*, for a discussion of
the construction of Pacific Islanders as soft and hard primitives during
European voyages.

24. "Hula of Old Hawaii Being Revived Here," *Honolulu Star-Bulletin*, 23
February 1934.

25. Kenneth Emory, Bishop Museum anthropologist, recorded many of
Kuluwaimaka's genealogical oli in 1933.

26. "Hula of Old Hawaii Being Revived Here," *Honolulu Star-Bulletin*, 23
February 1934. Mossman had reason to fear Hawaiian extinction, for
the Native Hawaiian population was decimated by Western-introduced
syphilis, smallpox, cholera, and measles. While figures vary, the Hawaiian
population is estimated to have fallen from as much as 800,000 to 40,000

after a century of Euro-American encounters, which began in 1778. See
Stannard, *Before the Horror.*

27. *Photograph CP 121, 265 (N.R. Farbman)*; "Hula Show at Lalani Hawaiian
    Village, Waikiki, ca. 1935"; folder (Social and Personal Activity: Tourists
    and Tourism), Lalani Hawaiian Village, BM. See also photographs in N. R.
    Farbman Collection, folder, Tourists and Tourism, BM; and Photographs,
    Hula, 1900, folder no. 5, BM.

28. Handler, "On Sociocultural Discontinuity," 55–71.

29. By using the term "traditional hula," I refer to hula performed with Native
    instrumentation and associated with precontact dance performances,
    like the hula pahu (sacred drum dance that originated in temple ritual)
    or hula ʻālaʻapapa (dance performed with the gourd that honored rulers
    and gods or relayed historical epics). See Topolinski, "The Hula,"
    149. Although ethnomusicologist Adrienne L. Kaeppler documents
    this renaissance of hula pahu in the 1930s, she does not account for
    its appearance at that particular historical moment. She writes, "[A]
    fortuitous combination of the right people at the right time occurred on
    the island of Oʻahu in the 1920s. . . . After nearly a century of obscurity,
    the tradition re-emerged with renewed vigor as hula pahu." Kaeppler,
    Hula Pahu, 28.

30. In 1913, Latter-Day Saints missionaries estimated that 22 percent of
    Hawaiians were Mormons. See Britsch, *Moramona*, 119.

31. Kaeppler, *Hula Pahu*, 106. Besides Mossman, Haʻaheoʻs other notable
    students included David "Daddy" Bray, an influential kahuna (priest) and
    entertainer; his wife Lydia "Mama" Bray; and Kaui Zuttermeister, a hula
    teacher on Oʻahu.

32. Believing Polynesians were a lost tribe of the House of Israel, the
    Church of Latter-Day Saints had developed deep ties in the Pacific
    Islands since the mid-nineteenth century. Mormons took a particular
    interest in Polynesian cultural practices and made deeper inroads than
    the Protestant missionaries who preceded them. Mormon interest in
    genealogy matched well with Polynesian genealogical traditions; Mormon
    prohibitions against coffee, tea, and alcohol also meshed with the kapu
    system that Hawaiians had lived under until 1820.

33. Kaeppler, *Hula Pahu*, 107–8.

34. Bonnie Beach, "Teaching Hula Dancing Becomes a Big Business in
    Hawaii," *Honolulu Star-Bulletin*, 24 July 1937.

35. The Mossmans were not the only Hawaiian family to merge commercial
    culture and hula practice. The Bray family debuted as the Bray Troupe
    at the opening of the Royal Hawaiian Hotel in Waikīkī in 1927. David
    "Daddy" Bray and Lydia "Mama" Bray performed with their children
    David, Michael, Odetta, Kahala, Helen, and Lono. Daughters Odetta and

Kahala Bray later danced and toured with orchestra leader Harry Owens and the Royal Hawaiians for four years in Colorado Springs, Los Angeles, and New Orleans. Both daughters remained on the U.S. continent and danced in Hollywood films. Todaro, "Island Personalities."

36. See Weiner, *Inalienable Possessions*. As Weiner discusses, these "inalienable possessions" were cultural objects primarily made by women. Given as gifts, they facilitated cultural reproduction and exchange networks in the Pacific.

37. "Hawaii's Hula Queens Vie for Hollywood Trip: Inter-Isle Hula Contestants Prepare for Honolulu Final," *Honolulu Advertiser*, 11 September 1938.

38. "Hula Queen Back Today: Kealoha Holt Completes Work in Musical 'Honolulu,'" *Honolulu Advertiser*, 28 December 1938.

39. In addition to the Lalani Hawaiian Village, the Kodak Hula Show and Royal Hawaiian Girls Glee Club, which began entertaining visitors in 1937 and 1927, respectively, catered to growing tourist traffic. Desmond, *Staging Tourism*, 16, 105–6.

40. Beach, "Teaching Hula Dancing Becomes a Big Business in Hawaii."

41. Tourism would remain a distant third until after World War II, when local corporations aggressively built a tourist infrastructure with American, and later multinational, capital. Fuchs, *Hawaii Pono*, 378.

42. In Milton Murayama's fictional account of Hawaiian plantation life in the 1930s, *All I Asking for Is My Body*, the young local Japanese American narrator makes this astute comment on the racial hierarchy of the plantation camp: "Shit too was organized according to the plantation pyramid. Mr. Nelson [the owner] was top shit on the highest slope, then there were the Portuguese, Spanish, and *nisei lunas* [second-generation Japanese American foremen] with their indoor toilets which flushed into the same ditches, then Japanese camp, and Filipino Camp" (96).

43. Fuchs, *Hawaii Pono*, 236.

44. Plantation owners colluded with the local police to suppress strikes. During the bloody "Hilo Massacre" shipping strike in 1938, fifty men and women were wounded. Daws, *Shoal of Time*, 359–60, and Beechert, *Working in Hawaii*, 265–66.

45. Chinese immigrants were recruited as plantation laborers in the 1850s, but Kingdom of Hawai'i passed acts in 1887, 1888, 1890, and 1892 that restricted Chinese immigration. See Kuykendall, *The Hawaiian Kingdom, Volume III, 1874–1893*, 142–85. Japanese immigration began in the 1880s and continued sporadically until the Gentlemen's Agreement of 1907 between the United States and Japan. Portuguese and Puerto Ricans arrived in the islands in the 1870s, followed by Koreans and Filipinos in the early 1900s.

46. Beechert, *Working in Hawaii*, 251.

47. Kent, *Hawaii*, 83.

48. "Hula Teachers Join to Standardize Craft," *Honolulu Advertiser*, 19 January 1939.

49. The Musicians' Association of Hawaii, a local affiliate of the American Federation of Musicians, was formed in 1923.

50. Piilani Mossman does not seem to have performed regularly at the Hotel Lexington, although she joined Pualani in New York City. By 1939 the two sisters had started their own hula studio in the city.

51. Kanahele, "Hawaiian Room (Hotel Lexington)," 120–21.

52. As of 1953, the formula was still successful: the Hawaiian Room had entertained almost 4 million patrons, given out 2 million paper leis, and used 400,000 coconuts. "Hawaiiana in New York: Authentic Polynesian Entertainment Is Basis for Success Story," *Paradise of the Pacific* 65, no. 4 (April 1953): 32–33.

53. Kanahele, "Hawaiian Room (Hotel Lexington)," 120. Former Hawaiian Room dancers and employees whom I interviewed spoke fondly of Mrs. Tita Andrade, who worked as the hostess and lei greeter at the Hawaiian Room for many years.

54. Middleton, *Dining, Wining and Dancing in New York*, 119.

55. Noble, *Hula Blues*, 101.

56. Ibid., 102.

57. "Makia" was one of Sam's legal and given middle names. Sam and his family also made a legal name change to "Makia." Betty Puanani Makia, interviews by the author, 2001.

58. While "hapa haole" signified mixed white and Hawaiian ancestry in the twentieth century, the use of "hapa haole" in Hawai'i today has a less fixed meaning and can refer to someone of mixed Asian and white ancestry. In Asian American contexts on the continent, "hapa" has been appropriated as an affirming term of self-identification by mixed-race Asian Americans and has been problematically decoupled from its Hawaiian meaning.

59. "Views of the Night Clubs," *New York Times*, 24 April 1938.

60. See Desmond, *Staging Tourism*, 66, 103–4, for analysis of the racialization of hula dancers like Tootsie Notley.

61. The quotation is from George Tucker, "Man about Manhattan," 21 June 1938, Associated Press, JNW. This column was also printed in the *Times Mirror* (Warren, Penn.), 14 June 1938, RKA.

62. "Island Girls Win Chance for Fame in New York," *Honolulu Advertiser*, 21 March 1940.

63. On Maui in 1940, Ray Kinney found a new addition, Marjorie Leilani Iaea, at Harriet Kuuleinani Stibbard's hula studio. The same year Kinney asked

his wife's friend Tutasi Wilson to join the dancing line. Tutasi, a former Honolulu resident, had been working in Hollywood films as an actress. She went to the Hawaiian Room, learned hula from fellow dancer Napua Woodd, but returned frequently to Hollywood when a Polynesian was needed for a film. Carol Mae Kuuleinani Vanderford, interviews by the author, 1999; Tutasi Wilson, interviews by the author, 1999.

64. In "Our Envoys of the Hula" (*Honolulu Star-Bulletin*, 30 September 1939), Betty MacDonald reported dancers' earning salaries of $75 to $100 a week, but $60 was closer to the figures other dancers later remembered earning only a decade later. Leilehua Becker Furtado, interviews by the author, 2000. As of 1948, and perhaps even earlier, the union that represented many hula dancers, American Guild of Variety Actors, mandated minimum weekly salaries of $60 for hula dancers.

65. William D. O'Brien, "Meymo Holt Dances an Authentic Hula Mostly with her Weaving Hands," *New York World-Telegram*, 16 October 1937, JNW.

66. Douglas Gilbert, "Those Hula Dancers Don't Mean What You Think; At Least, Some of Them Don't, Declares Napua," *New York World-Telegram*, n.d., JNW. This article provided an inaccurate pronunciation and translation of Napua's name. It means "the flowers."

67. George Tucker, Associated Press, "Man about Manhattan," n.d., JNW.

68. See, for example, among many other newspaper sources, *Honolulu Advertiser*, 16 June 1940; *Honolulu Star-Bulletin*, 1 March 1941. "Broadway Goes Hawaiian," read one caption of a photograph of the Hotel Lexington hula dancers.

69. MacDonald, "Our Envoys of the Hula."

70. Tutasi Wilson, interviewed by the author, 23 August 1999.

71. Ibid.

72. Fuchs, *Hawaii Pono*, 189.

73. See Daws, *Shoal of Time*, 317–27, 333–38; Rosa, "Local Story," 93–116; and Stannard, *Honor Killing*.

74. Tutasi Wilson, interviewed by the author, 28 August 1999.

75. MacDonald, "Our Envoys of the Hula." It is likely that some Hawaiians remained critical of commercial Hawaiian performances in the United States in the 1930s, although published accounts of the touring performers were highly flattering. Some hula teachers disliked commercial hula because of its emphasis on creativity and departure from traditional forms. Hula offended some strict Christians, including Hawaiians, for whom hula was still associated with Hawaiian religious worship. Furthermore, the American emphasis on Hawaiian women's sexuality and semiclothed bodies in the performances may have offended some islanders and resulted in the refusal of some families to allow their daughters to participate in the auditions and accept the jobs themselves.

76. Epstein, *The New York Hippodrome.*

77. "The Playhouses," *Los Angeles Times,* 28 February 1899.

78. "Policeman Dances for Court in Vain," *New York Times,* 27 December 1934. It is not clear from the article whether the dancers were Hawaiian.

79. "Lexington Hotel Onetime Mecca for Island Sound," *Ha'ilono Mele* 5, no. 1 (January 1979): 4.

80. Clara Inter ("Hilo Hattie") appeared on stage with dancers Leo Lani, a Ho'olaule'a (festival) pageant princess, and Lily Padeken, a former dancer with the Royal Hawaiian Girls Glee Club. Inter had learned how to dance hula at the Lalani Hawaiian Village in the early 1930s. Mapuana Mossman Bishaw, previously at the Lexington, later joined the line.

81. The production of the Hawaiian Room show passed in this approximate order: Ray Kinney, Hal Aloma, Johnny Coco, Lani McIntire, Sam Makia, Momi Kai, Lei Becker, Gloria Manu Kanemura, Keola Beamer, to Te Moana Makolo, when the room closed in 1966. Betty Puanani Makia, interviews by the author, 2000, and Marcie Te Moana Makolo, interviewed by the author, 18 July 2002.

82. Tutasi Wilson, interviewed by the author, 14 January 2000. New York showrooms like the Hawaii Kai and Luau 400 continued to compete with the Hawaiian Room formula as late as the 1950s and 1960s.

83. After 1919, many newly opened nightclubs in Harlem catered to whites and some explicitly barred African Americans. One of the most prominent, the Cotton Club, which opened in 1923, upheld a whites-only policy. Haskins, *The Cotton Club,* 23–26.

84. Raylani Kinney Akau, interviewed by the author, 24 April 2004. "Haole" here serves as a shorthand for "Caucasian."

85. The Havana-Madrid Club offered jazz, mambo, and salsa by Latin American and Caribbean musicians.

86. Middleton, *Dining, Wining and Dancing in New York,* 109.

87. *Souvenir Guide Book of New York City* (New York, 1939).

88. *Esquire's New York: A New York Guide Book for World's Fair Visitors.*

89. Davidson, *Where to Take Your Girl in New York on One Dollar to $20.*

90. See Tatar, *Strains of Change,* 5, for a description of historical and contemporary categories of Hawaiian music, including hapa haole.

91. Tin Pan Alley refers to the popular American sheet music industry that emerged in Manhattan in the early twentieth century. After around 1915, non-Hawaiian composers and lyricists began writing humorous songs that presented the islands as paradisiacal escapes. Tatar, *Strains of Change,* 11–12.

92. Quoted in Kanahele, "Hawaiian Room (Hotel Lexington)," 122.

93. Betty Puanani Makia, interviewed by the author, 27 February 2000.

94. Betty Puanani Makia, interviews by the author, 2003. The song was popular with haole audiences, Makia said, because of its simple, English-

language lyrics. "Little Brown Gal" was composed in 1935 by Don McDiarmid and Lee Wood and was first recorded by Ray Kinney that year. See Kanahele, "Little Brown Gal," 232.

95. Betty Puanani Makia, interviewed by the author, 20 November 1999.

96. Betty Puanani Makia, interviewed by the author, 27 November 2000.

97. *Ray Kinney and his Royal Hawaiian Orchestra and the Aloha Maids* (1938).

98. Betty Puanani Makia, interviewed by the author, 27 February 2000.

99. Raylani Kinney Akau, interviewed by the author, 23 April 2004.

100. Before leaving for the continent, Manu Kanemura learned hula from Rose Joshua and Eleanor Hiram, notable kumu hula. Lei Becker came from a family of dancers and started dancing at an early age. Napua Woodd also seems to have had formal training—she was a Royal Hawaiian Glee Club dancer before going to New York—but her kumu hula are not known.

101. Tutasi Wilson, interviewed by the author, 23 August 1999.

102. The song "Across the Sea" was composed by Ernest Kaai, Ray Kinney, and John Noble in 1919 but was performed at the Hawaiian Room in the 1930s.

103. Hawaiian music was broadcast nationally once a week from the Hawaiian Room in the late 1930s. Beginning in 1935, the radio show "Hawaii Calls" was broadcast nationwide from the Moana Hotel in Waikīkī.

104. Schoolchildren at summer camp performed plays about Hawai'i and pretended to eat poi in the 1930s. For example, the Orchard Hill Camp in Illinois had a popular Hawaiian program in 1933. PP 20–6, Photographs, folder (Exposition: Chicago, 1933), HSA.

105. MacDonald, "Our Envoys of the Hula."

106. "Table 20. Visitor Arrivals, Visitors Present, and Visitor Expenditures: 1922–1961," in *Historical Statistics of Hawaii, 1778–1962* (Honolulu: Department of Planning and Research, State of Hawaii, 1962), 15.

107. "Table 22. Selected Employment Statistics: 1878–1960," in *Historical Statistics of Hawaii, 1778–1962*, 17.

108. Not all of the haole oligarchy favored statehood; some prominent members, such as Lorrin P. Thurston, publisher of the *Honolulu Advertiser*, opposed statehood until early postwar years.

109. This national "Statehood for Hawaii" publicity campaign was heavily funded by territorial appropriations. McLane, "Hawai'i—49th State by '49?," 341. The historian Gavan Daws writes, "The Hawaii Statehood Commission did its best to keep the territory's qualifications before the notice of Congress, and as Senator Guy Cordon of Oregon said, far more was known about Hawaii than about any territory previously admitted to the union of states." Daws, *Shoal of Time*, 385.

110. "Hawaii Statehood Group Gives Cocktail Party," *Washington Post*, 8 October 1947.

111. Martin Burden, "Going out Tonight?," *New York Post*, n.d., ca. 1951, GMB.

112. Tutasi Wilson, interviewed by the author, 23 August 1999.

113. Daws, *Shoal of Time*, 390; taken from *Honolulu Star-Bulletin*, 1 November 1955. In 1946, Hawai'i was on the United Nations' list of non-self-governing territories. When the United States initiated a statehood plebiscite in 1959, it offered only two choices on the ballot: statehood or continued territorial status. U.S. military personnel and non-Hawaiians who outnumbered Kanaka Maoli were allowed to participate, further ensuring statehood would pass. After Hawai'i's population voted for statehood, the United States reported to the UN that Hawai'i was the fiftieth state. Hawai'i was subsequently removed from the list of non-self-governing territories. Trask, *From a Native Daughter*, 30, 235; and Kauanui, "Colonialism in Equality," 643. Kauanui writes, "The statehood vote worked as a preemptive move [by the United States] to solidify Hawai'i's status" (643).

114. Krauss, "The Day Statehood Hung by a Lei."

115. Schmitt, "Table 26. Ethnic Stock: 1900–1960," 120.

116. Daws, *Shoal of Time*, 333–38. A subcommittee of the House of Representatives Committee on Territories came to Hawai'i to investigate Hawai'i's statehood potential and heard public testimony in 1935, but the subcommittee did not make a recommendation for or against statehood. The testimony pointed to Japanese in Hawai'i as aliens and potential conspirators with imperial Japan.

117. Irwin, "Ed Irwin More Than Suggests That We Should Not Try to 'Americanize' Orientals in Hawaii, Even If We Can," 54–56.

118. Raylani Kinney Akau, interviewed by the author, 24 April 2004.

119. "Pearl Harbor Inspires Hawaiian to Dance for Beat-the-Jap Funds," *Long Island Star-Journal*, 23 April 1942, JNW.

120. Gloria Manu Kanemura Bentley, interviewed by the author, 9 August 1999. In 1949, Manu won the title of "queen" of the St. Louis College carnival, of the University of Hawai'i yearbook, and of the University of Hawai'i baseball congress. *Honolulu Star Bulletin*, 26 September 1951. The "Cosmopolitan Queen" of the University of Hawai'i was for contestants of mixed racial background. Manu's father was Japanese and her mother Hawaiian and haole.

121. Schmitt, "Table 26. Ethnic Stock: 1900–1960," 120.

122. Photograph, JNW.

123. Sherilyn Rankin Iona, interviewed by the author, 18 July 1999.

124. Ann Koga, "Honoluluan in Hula Troupe at Lexington Hotel," *Honolulu Star-Bulletin*, 19 January 1949.

125. Betty Puanani Makia, interviews by the author, 2001.

126. Betty Puanani Makia, interviewed by the author, 27 February 2000.

127. Gloria Manu Kanemura Bentley, interviewed by the author, 9 August 1999.

128. Lei Becker replaced Lehua Florence Dang in the Honolulu Maids line. The other Maids were Tutasi Wilson of Samoa and Honolulu; Kalani Pua Caroline Dizon of Manoa Valley; and Mealii Virginia Horio of Kapahulu. Betty Puanani Makia, wife of guitarist Sam Makia, was "swing girl." Ann Koga, "Islanders Were Busy in New York," *Honolulu Star-Bulletin*, 23 February 1951.

129. Leilehua Becker Furtado, unpublished manuscript, LBF.

130. According to Tutasi Wilson, "Mapuana [Bishaw] had no money. It was a small contract they were on for about six months, from about 1938. [They] had to have other jobs to make extra money." Tutasi Wilson, interviewed by the author, 28 August 1999.

131. There are a few exceptions. Female Hawaiian entertainers such as Jennie Napua Woodd and Clara Inter ("Hilo Hattie"), for example, could perform as comedic hula dancers when they were middle-aged. The comedic dancer role, which accommodated older, heavyset women, was distinct from that of the young, slender "hula maids" in the chorus line and the headlining "leading lady."

132. MacDonald, "Our Envoys of the Hula."

133. Lloyd Gilliom, interviews by the author, August 1999.

134. Ann Koga, "Ray Kinney Named in Complaint Filed by Hawai'i Dancer," *Honolulu Star-Bulletin*, 28 October 1948.

135. Tutasi Wilson, interviews by the author, 23 August 1999 and 14 January 2000.

136. Furtado, unpublished manuscript, LBF.

137. Ibid.

138. Leilehua Becker Furtado, interviewed by the author, 12 January 2000.

139. Furtado, unpublished manuscript, LBF.

140. P. J. Deloria, *Indians in Unexpected Places*, 28.

141. Raylani Kinney Akau, interviewed by the author, 24 April 2004.

142. Hester "Teela" Holt Hailele, interviewed by the author, 24 April 2004.

143. "Kinneys, Told of Attack, Said It Couldn't Happen," *Honolulu Advertiser*, 22 December 1941.

144. Hester "Teela" Holt Hailele, interviewed by the author, 24 April 2004.

145. Robert M. Dana, "Hula Queen Masters a New Step," *New York World-Telegram and Sun*, 26 March 1952, LBF.

146. Furtado, unpublished manuscript, LBF.

147. As a child, Lei Becker was already a semiprofessional dancer, dancing on the weekends at Lau Yee Chai restaurant. Lei's maternal grandmother, Isabella Kalili Miller Desha (1864–1949), lived and trained in a hālau hula from the age of seven until seventeen and began to teach hula

openly in 1899. Isabella trained daughter Helen Desha Kapuailohia Siemson Beamer (1881–1952), who became Lei's first hula teacher. Helen was also the composer of well-known mele like "Kawohikūkapulani." Lei later learned from another aunt, Louise Walker Beamer, the wife of her maternal uncle who owned a hula studio. Leilehua Becker Furtado, interviews by the author, 2000; Furtado, unpublished manuscript, LBF.

148. Furtado, unpublished manuscript, LBF.

149. Lee Mortimer, "South Sea Magic in the Mysterious East (Side)," *Sunday Mirror Magazine*, 29 June 1951.

150. Lei Becker only hired girls from Hawai'i until she broke her "code" by selecting her replacement, Loma Duke, "a girl who had never even been to Hawai'i." Furtado, unpublished manuscript, LBF.

151. Lulika and Kamoa Ferris had professional careers as hula dancers and hula teachers in Michigan. According to Betty Makia, they were Native American high school students from Michigan who met Ray Kinney and his traveling hula troupe, became enamored with the hula, and asked Kinney if they could join the tour after they graduated. They learned to dance hula from Makia and her colleagues and passed easily as Native Hawaiians. After leaving the Hotel Lexington and the USO tour, they continued to teach hula in Michigan.

152. Du Bois, *The Souls of Black Folk*, 5.

153. Lucas, "E Ola Mau Kākou I Ka 'Ōlelo Makuahine," 8–9.

154. Furtado, unpublished manuscript, LBF.

155. Many of the 1930s and 1940s entertainment groups in New York spoke Hawaiian; Napua Woodd was a fluent Hawaiian speaker. However, many of the later Hawaiian arrivals were not fluent speakers.

156. Raylani Kinney Akau, interviewed by the author, 24 April 2004.

157. Raylani Kinney Akau and Rayner Kinney, interviewed by the author, 24 April 2004.

158. Amy Hānaiali'i Gilliom recorded "Hale'iwa Hula" on her first album, *Hawaiian Tradition* (1997).

159. Roach, *Cities of the Dead*, 210–11.

160. Hester "Teela" Holt Hailele, interviewed by the author, 24 April 2004.

161. Clifford, *Routes*, 254.

162. Hau'ofa, "Our Sea of Islands."

163. Ibid., 154.

164. Raylani Kinney Akau, interviewed by the author, 24 April 2004.

165. *Aunty Betty* (2000).

166. Ibid.

167. Betty Makia's memories of the changing landscape of Manhattan—the building of the World Trade Center, Verrazano Bridge, and other New York landmarks—suggest her deep associations with New York lands. She

became so attached to her apartment on the East Side of Manhattan that she needed to be cajoled by her husband to move just three avenues west.

168. P. J. Deloria, *Indians in Unexpected Places*.

169. Raylani Kinney Akau, interviewed by the author, 24 April 2004.

170. Rayner Kinney joined the tour after graduating from high school and was part of the moving crew. Rayner Kinney, interviewed by the author, 24 April 2004.

171. Betty Puanani Makia, interviewed by the author, 27 February 2000.

172. Kauanui, *Hawaiian Blood*, 38.

173. Tutasi Wilson, interviewed by the author, 23 August 1999.

174. Tutasi Wilson, interviews by the author, 1999–2000.

175. Betty Puanani Makia, interviewed by the author, 27 February 2000.

176. Betty Puanani Makia, interviewed by the author, 20 February 2000.

177. Raylani Kinney Akau, interviewed by the author, 24 April 2004. Raylani's mother, Dawn Kinney, had left Raylani behind with family in Hawai'i in order to join her husband in New York.

178. Tutasi Wilson, interviewed by the author, 24 October 1999.

179. Kulani Purdy, interviews by the author, 2000.

180. Betty Puanani Makia, interviewed by the author, 6 February 2000.

181. Some of these Hawaiians had been performers on vaudeville circuits or stevedores on mid-Atlantic ports. Betty Puanani Makia, interviews by the author, 2000.

182. Raylani Kinney Akau, interviewed by the author, 23 April 2004.

183. Ann Koga Mortimer, "Leilehua Becker Top Attraction at Hawaiian Room," *Honolulu Star-Bulletin*, 24 May 1951.

184. Ann Koga, "Hawaiian Show Featured in NY Nightclub," *Honolulu Star-Bulletin*, 19 January 1949.

185. Betty Puanani Makia and Kulani Purdy, interviewed by the author, 6 February 2000. While no longer extant, the Hawaiian Society, also known as Na Oiwi o Hawaii (The Natives of Hawaii), headed by Fred C. Allen, may also have been a formal social organization serving Hawaiians in New York. Fred C. Allen—who may have been Hawaiian or from Hawai'i—managed the Hawaiian village at the New York World's Fair of 1939. The village employed Hawaiian musicians and hula dancers. Some of these performers were Hawaiians living on the East Coast, such as Lulu Keliiholokai of Hartford, Connecticut, and Anna Kaniho, whose husband played with Ray Kinney at the Lexington.

186. Napua Woodd to her father, n.d., JNW.

187. Pualani Mossman Avon died in Florida in 2006 at the age of eighty-nine. Christie Wilson, "Pualani Mossman Avon, Face of Hawai'i in 1930s," *Honolulu Advertiser*, 9 May 2006.

188. Sherilyn Rankin Iona, interviewed by the author, 18 July 1999. Meymo

Ululani Holt returned to Oʻahu in the early 1990s and died of lung cancer in 1995 at the age of eighty.

189. MacDonald, "Our Envoys of the Hula."

190. Marcie Te Moana Makolo, interviewed by the author, 18 July 2002. The niece of the long-standing hula teachers Puanani and Leilani Alama, Te Moana Makolo began dancing as a child.

191. Born in 1912, Jennie Napua Woodd was from Honolulu, where her haole father worked at the Mutual Telephone Company. Her Hawaiian mother was from Molokaʻi. Napua had married at a young age in Honolulu and separated from her husband. Lloyd Gilliom, interviews by the author, 1999.

192. Ibid.

193. Misc. clippings, JNW.

194. Gloria Manu Kanemura Bentley, interviewed by the author, 9 August 1999; Wayne Harada, "Talented Cast Says 'Iorana Hawaiiki," *Honolulu Advertiser*, 5 April 1972.

195. Sisters Lulika Ferris Ampey and Kamoa Ferris are still known to their friends by their Hawaiian stage names.

196. Raylani Kinney Akau, interviewed by the author, 24 April 2004.

5. The Troupes Meet the Troops

1. "Maui Children to Appear with Kinney Troupe," *Maui News*, 9 March 1940; Carol Mae Kuuleinani Vanderford, interviewed by the author, 21 July 1999.

2. Carol Mae Kuuleinani Vanderford, interviewed by the author, 13 July 2002.

3. "443 Maui Volunteer Workers Receive Special Citations," *Honolulu Advertiser*, 10 January 1946.

4. Nearly 7 million servicemen and war workers were entertained in Hawaiʻi in 1942, the USO's first year of operation. Hawaii United Service Organization, *United Service Organizations of the Territory of Hawaii*, 6.

5. Hawaii United Service Organization, *First Annual Report of the Hawaii United Service Organization, 1942*, 18; W. C. Brown, "The Show Goes On—in Hawaii," 24.

6. A few works have critically examined tourist and commercial photography of Hawaiʻi and the Pacific Islands. Davis, *Photography in Hawaiʻi*; Feeser and Chan, *Waikīkī*.

7. The motion pictures are held by U.S. National Archives (NA)'s Motion Picture, Sound, and Video Division in College Park, Maryland, and the still photographs by the Hawaiʻi War Records Depository (HWRD) at the University of Hawaiʻi, Mānoa, in Honolulu, Hawaiʻi. The films are filed separately by either subject matter (e.g., "World War II, Hawaii, Recreation") or by the producing unit (e.g., Army Air Forces). There are

no fewer than twenty-five military films produced by the army and navy featuring hula or Hawaiian cultural performances during the 1940s, as well as about thirteen in the 1950s and fifteen in the 1960s.

8. I use the Hawaiian "lūʻau" to refer to the local celebratory feast and to distinguish it from the English-language idiom "luau" (without diacritical marks) that signifies a practice produced for tourist consumption. (The plural form of the Hawaiian "lūʻau" is the same; the plural of "luau," as an English word, is "luaus.") I rely on this rough demarcation between island and tourist practices, although there is traffic between the two realms. I maintain, however, that there can be no "authentic" or "pure" lūʻau, since its formation in Hawaiʻi was always already hybrid, having developed in response to outsiders.

9. Among many examples from the turn of the century is in *Brooklyn Eagle*, 23 January 1898. This merging of dance and food has become the standard formula of today's commercial tourist luau, where tourists enjoy a live hula show while they eat Hawaiian foods.

10. Kathy E. Ferguson and Phyllis Turnbull have usefully observed how waves of settlers and sojourners, from missionaries to soldiers, gendered Hawaiʻi's land and its people as excessively female. In a related vein, Haunani-Kay Trask has likened Hawaiʻi under the yoke of state-sponsored corporate tourism to a sexually exploited Native woman (*From a Native Daughter*, 143). Ferguson and Turnbull, *Oh, Say, Can You See?*, 6, 91.

11. Teaiwa, "Militarism, Tourism and the Native," 5.

12. Armitage, "Tourist Bureau Says Aloha," 73–74.

13. Allen, *Hawaii's War Years, 1941–1945*, 219.

14. Ibid., 221.

15. The USO became an umbrella organization for six other organizations—the YMCA, YWCA, National Catholic Community Service, the National Jewish Welfare Board, the Travelers Aid Association, and the Salvation Army. The USO was autonomous from the U.S. military, accepting contributions from private donors. Yellin, *Our Mothers' War*, 86.

16. *Aloha to the Men and Women of the Armed Forces from the USO in Hawaii.*

17. Allen, *Hawaii's War Years, 1941–1945*, 255, and Hawaii United Service Organization, *First Annual Report of the Hawaii United Service Organization, 1942.*

18. Central YMCA USO program, call no. 58.02, HWRD.

19. Allen, *Hawaii's War Years, 1941–1945*, 218.

20. R. Williams, *Marxism and Literature*, 110.

21. *Honolulu Star-Bulletin*, 29 April 1943, 30 April 1943; "Lei Day, 1943," *Paradise of the Pacific* 55, no. 5 (May 1943): 5.

22. See photographs 274, 275, 276, HWRD. Photograph 274, "On Camouflage Detail," was published in the *Honolulu Star-Bulletin*, 31 January 1942.

23. Allen, *Hawaii's War Years, 1941–1945*, 264.

24. The figure of 2,000 Hawaiian soldiers in World War II is quoted from McNaughton, "Hawaiians in World War II."

25. The participation of Hawaiian men in combat during World War II has also been eclipsed narratively and historically by that of "Americans of Japanese Ancestry" (AJAS) from Hawai'i who volunteered in record numbers to prove their patriotism. Although Japanese were enemies of the state and were interned on the continent and in Hawai'i, these men served in segregated combat units, including the U.S. Army's 442nd Regimented Combat Team, the most decorated unit in U.S. military history. Allen, *Hawaii's War Years, 1941–1945*, 268.

26. Prostitutes were often absent from men's oral histories, although Bailey and Farber's study *The First Strange Place* reveals the widespread dependence of the occupying military on prostitution.

27. These women were most likely not hula dancers—dancers would have been performing for soldiers, not posing for photographs.

28. *To Do Today in Honolulu and on Oahu for the Week of July 21–27, 1945*, call no. 18.04, HWRD.

29. "Speaking of Pictures," *Life*, 28 December 1942, 4–5, 7.

30. Other militarized colonial zones depended on gendered tourist representations. French colonial soldiers sent postcards of Algerian women to France as souvenirs. See Alloula, *The Colonial Harem*.

31. "Hawaiian Medley," *Colliers*, 11 December 1943, 16–17. In 1945 a book of these photographs called *Hawaiian Types* was published with a foreword by Andrew Lind, a University of Hawai'i sociologist. The photographs were taken by Henry Inn, a local Chinese American photographer. See Inn, *Hawaiian Types*. The conflation of mixed-race hula dancers and mixed-race women is suggested by the appearance of Leilehua Becker and Mealii Horio in the *Hawaiian Types* spread; Becker and Horio later became hula dancers at the Hawaiian Room in New York.

32. Letters to the editor, *Colliers*, n.d., LBF.

33. Bailey and Farber, *The First Strange Place*, 99. Men lined up at brothels in downtown Honolulu and Chinatown for hours. It is important to note that the vast majority of prostitutes in wartime Honolulu were working-class white women who arrived from the continent. As long as sex workers were discreet and confined their residences to certain neighborhoods, they were not harassed. However, sex workers could be criminalized easily; one Irish American prostitute named Jean O'Hara was harassed by vice police and eventually prosecuted in a provost court for disregarding vice rules. The regulated brothels thrived until

the territorial governor shut them down in September 1944. Bailey and Farber, *The First Strange Place*, 113–19, 130.

34. Ibid., 98.

35. Ibid. While there were some African American soldiers posted in the islands, they were in the minority.

36. *Honolulu Star-Bulletin*, 16 December 1942.

37. "He's a Nonchalant Non-whistler," *Honolulu Star-Bulletin*, 11 December 1942.

38. "Hawaiian Hospitality" was recorded by Ray Kinney in 1944.

39. "A Pocket Guide to Honolulu," *Paradise of the Pacific* 57, no. 3 (March 1945): 30.

40. The U.S. military refused to issue a definitive figure for fear of alerting the enemy to the size of its armed personnel. Allen, *Hawaii's War Years, 1941–1945*, 246.

41. Bailey and Farber, *The First Strange Place*, 184.

42. Leilehua Becker Furtado, unpublished manuscript, LBF.

43. Allen, *Hawaii's War Years, 1941–1945*, 352.

44. Ibid., 241.

45. Keala, *Ka Poʻe Kahiko o Waiʻanae*, 71. See Kauanui, *Hawaiian Blood*, for an analysis of the creation of Hawaiian homesteads through the federal Hawaiian Homes Commission Act of 1921. Homesteads were made available only to those "native Hawaiians" who could prove 50 percent blood quantum.

46. Grier, "Stationed in Paradise, 101.

47. Patience Namaka Wiggins, the adopted daughter of Mary Kawena Pukui, says in an interview in the film *The Hula of Old Hawaii* that traditional Hawaiian language mele were not popular with GIs and tourists and therefore were not performed. Zimmerman, *Reel Families*, 102–3. Carol Mae Kuuleinani Vanderford recalls that she and other dancers performed hapa haole songs and a few "old Hawaiian songs." Carol Mae Kuuleinani Vanderford, interviewed by the author, 13 July 2002.

48. Carol Mae Kuuleinani Vanderford, interviewed by the author, 13 July 2002.

49. Photograph 18 in Hawaii United Service Organization, *First Annual Report of the Hawaii United Service Organization*, 1942.

50. Carol Mae Kuuleinani Vanderford, interviewed by the author, 13 July 2002.

51. Ibid.

52. Alexander, "Hula Was Not Enough," 26.

53. The popular hapa haole hit "Little Grass Shack" was composed by the Hawaiian songwriter and bandleader Johnny Noble in 1933. Its chorus goes, "I want to go back to my little grass shack in Kealakekua, Hawaiʻi."

54. The Army Signal Corps was founded on 10 June 1861 by Major Albert Myer to deal with army communications. Brownlow, *War, West, and Wilderness*, 119. Though photography was used during the Civil War, it played no significant part in Signal Corps activities, but in 1917 the corps was given the task of recording every stage of the American involvement in the war. This responsibility continued through World War II, but it became much more professionalized.

55. *LUAU, 05/06/1944* (Motion picture no. 18-CS-1705) is the edited, 16 mm version of *Luau: A Native Feast*, shot in color. *LAUA (I.E., LUAU) Hickam Field, Oahu, Hawaiian Islands* (Motion picture no. 18-CS-1299) is 35 mm black-and-white unedited footage.

56. The Naval Photographic Center, Department of the Navy, also filmed hula at Pearl Harbor.

57. Robert Flaherty's *Moana: A Romance of the Golden Age* (1926) also relies on intertitles to explain the gathering of food in Samoa.

58. What is not immediately apparent from watching the film is that George Bacon later married the young dancer from the film, Patience Namaka Wiggins (the daughter of Mary Kawena Pukui), and settled in Hawai'i.

59. Patricia R. Zimmerman argues that this film was intended to leave a "usable ethnographic record" of these dances. Zimmerman, *Reel Families*, 104.

60. Hawai'i was designated a military area by Executive Order 9066 in October 1942.

61. A lieutenant Kerr is the cameraman and credited in raw footage. The NA holds no records of the distribution and intended audiences of this film.

62. Maslowski, *Armed with Cameras*, 6. World War II may have been the most photographed war during the age of analog photography, but the advent of digital photography and other technologies such as camera phones and webcams have arguably broadened the visualization and broadcast of twenty-first-century warfare, particularly by combatants.

63. Colton, "How We Fight with Photographs," 257.

64. Zimmerman, *Reel Families*, 91.

65. Ibid., 90–91.

66. Prominent art photographer Edward Steichen was in charge of photography in the U.S. Army during World War I. He received a special commission to become the officer heading the U.S. Naval Combat Photography Unit during World War II, although he was too old for induction into active duty collection. Six million copies of *U.S. Navy War Photographs* were sold at cost and sold out within a year of their printing in 1945. Steichen, *U.S. Navy War Photographs*. Photographs from *Power in the Pacific* were exhibited at the Museum of Modern Art in 1945.

67. Foucault, *Discipline and Punish*, 187.

68. Tagg, *The Burden of Representation*, 77.
69. Foucault, *Discipline and Punish*, 207.
70. Pinney, "Classification and Fantasy in the Photographic Construction of Caste and Tribe," 260.
71. Pinney, *Camera Indica*, 35.
72. Marien, *Photography*, 130 and 144, on the Modoc Wars and Bureau of American Ethnology, respectively. See also Truettner, *The West as America*. Edward S. Curtis's twenty-volume *The North American Indian*, issued between 1907 and 1930, did much cultural work by circulating romanticized images of the disappearing Indian; these volumes consisted of more than 2,000 photographs of eighty tribes.
73. Filipinos were organized by tribe at this fair. See also the photographs of Jesse Bartox Beals at the St. Louis World's Fair in 1904. About 2,000 indigenous ethnographic subjects were displayed in St. Louis. Marien, *Photography*, 236.
74. Rafael, *White Love and Other Events in Filipino History*, 81.
75. Foucault, *Discipline and Punish*, 207.
76. Foucault, *The History of Sexuality*, 139–40.
77. While these military orders were ostensibly directed at the entire population of Hawai'i, Gary Y. Okihiro has demonstrated that the Japanese, alien and citizen alike, were the primary targets of these controls. Okihiro, *Cane Fires*, 226–27. Military rule had been planned long before Pearl Harbor, at least since the 1930s, for the purpose of containing and controlling the large Japanese population in the islands. *Cane Fires*, 209.
78. Anthony, *Hawaii under Army Rule*, 9–10.
79. Ibid., 13.
80. Allen, *Hawaii's War Years, 1941–1945*, 120.
81. Foucault, *The History of Sexuality*, 145.
82. Wexler, *Tender Violence*, 6.
83. Ibid., 33. Wexler's reading is of Frances Benjamin Johnston's domestic photographs of the U.S.S. *Olympia* during the Spanish-American War.
84. B. Smith, *Imagining the Pacific*, 210.
85. The military audience in *LUAU, 05/06/1944* (Motion picture no. 18-cs-1705; 1944), for instance, includes some white women civilian guests and uniformed white women who may have been members of the Women's Army Corps (WACs). However, these female guests are far outnumbered by the primary audience of male soldiers. The former are shown eating and drinking, but do not learn hula from Hawaiian women. The USO did hold luaus for female army, navy, and Red Cross nurses; at least one of these events was photographed by the U.S. Army Signal Corps in 1942. See photographs 1181 Army and 1182 Army, HWRD.

86. Schmitt, "Table 26. Ethnic Stock: 1900–1960," 120.

87. Quoted in Okihiro, *Cane Fires*, 97.

88. Okihiro, *Cane Fires*.

89. Lt. Gen. Richardson relinquished this title only on 30 June 1944, and Hawai'i was not reinstated to civilian authority until October 1944.

90. Lindstrom, "Images of Islanders in Pacific War Photographs," 116.

91. B. Smith, *Imagining the Pacific*, 210.

92. Banks, "Thoughts on the Manners of Otaheite," 330.

93. B. Smith, *Imagining the Pacific*, 210.

94. John Webber also painted Cook peacefully greeting Pacific peoples—extending a hand to greet Natives or observing dances—never as the man who cut off ears in Tonga.

95. McClellen, "Ahaaina or Luau in Old Hawaii," 10.

96. Pukui and Elbert, *Hawaiian Dictionary*, 214.

97. Pukui, Haertig, and Lee, *Nānā i Ke Kumu (Look to the Source), Volume I,* 2–3.

98. Ritte and Freese, "Haloa," 11–14; Handy and Pukui, *Polynesian System in Ka'u, Hawai'i*, 3–4. Hawaiians protested against patents of hybridized kalo by the University of Hawai'i, Mānoa, in 2006. This activism against biopiracy, in the interest of protecting Hāloa, underscores the continued resonance of the spiritual relationship between Hawaiians and kalo. The university responded by withdrawing its patents in June 2006.

99. Pukui, Haertig, and Lee, *Nānā i Ke Kumu*, 3.

100. Louis Aila was interviewed in Mākaha, O'ahu, on June 9, 1977, by June Gutmanis. The interview was published in *Life Histories of Native Hawaiians*, 73–101.

101. Allen, *Hawaii's War Years, 1941–1945*, 163; "Baby Luau Gift Money Out for the Duration," *Honolulu Star-Bulletin*, 14 June 1945.

102. "Reduced Quotas for Luau Pigs Are Set by OFP," *Honolulu Star-Bulletin*, 20 June 1945.

103. R. Williams, *Marxism and Literature*, 112.

104. Alana, "Luau and War."

105. Total attendance for USO shows during the war reached 67 million. Hawaii United Service Organization, *United Service Organizations of the Territory of Hawaii, USA*. Although this figure likely includes individuals who attended multiple times, it nevertheless suggests that the islands accommodated an overwhelming number of outsiders, a number many times the size of its prewar population.

106. *Bird of Paradise* (1932), although filmed in Hawai'i with Hawaiian extras as "natives," is set on a generic "South Seas" island. The film does not have a luau per se, but a feast with pigs and goats roasted over a fire. The animated Disney film *Lilo and Stitch* (2002) also features a luau. Luaus

figure prominently in postwar Hollywood films set in Hawai'i and those set far from the islands, such as *Gidget* (1959), and *Blue Hawaii* (1961).

107. *Operation Wounded Warrior, 07/03/1954* (Motion picture no. 342-USAF-21595).

108. Allen, *Hawaii's War Years, 1941–1945*, 259.

109. Ferguson and Turnbull, *Oh, Say, Can You See?*, 98.

110. *Arrival First R and R Troops from Vietnam, Honolulu, Hawaii, 3 August 1966* (Motion picture no. 50441).

111. See ibid., and *Keystone Eagle Return of 9th Division, 4th Battalion, 39th Infantry from Vietnam to Hawaii, Hickam AFB, Hawaii, 07/08–1969–08/27–1969* (Motion picture no. 342-USAF-48145).

112. I have not been able to identify the female civilian volunteers in photographs taken by the Army Signal Corps, with one exception—Maenette Ah Nee-Benham, the dean of Hawai'inuiākea, the School of Hawaiian Knowledge at the University of Hawai'i, Mānoa, happened to recognize her mother as one of the performers in the civic entertainers photograph (see figure 59), after an earlier version of this chapter was published in article form.

113. Here I borrow from Certeau, *The Practice of Everyday Life*, xii, xiii, xiv.

114. Taylor, *The Archive and the Repertoire*, 28.

115. Scott, *Domination and the Acts of Resistance*, 197.

116. Ibid., 196.

117. Furtado, unpublished manuscript, LBF; Leilehua Becker Furtado, interviewed by the author, 12 January 2000.

118. Dolly Murray to Carol Mae Vanderford, n.d., CKV.

119. For example, Carol Mae Kuuleinani Vanderford named Edna and Rogers Aki, Mabel Nakea, the Kalawehi sisters, and Harry Murray as the troupe's singers. The young Dutro girls (Elaine Kaiwa Keopulani Dilley, Josephine Kealoha) were Carol Mae's fellow hula sisters and close friends, and were selected by Ray Kinney to perform in New York City. The troupe's youngest dancer, Iwalani Wilson, was about five years old and performed as the "baby" solo vocalist. Eighteen- or nineteen-year-old Blanche "Sweetie" Wilson, Iwalani's older sister, was the female solo dancer.

120. Carol Mae Kuuleinani Vanderford, interviewed by the author, 13 July 2002.

121. The mele "Hoonanea" celebrates lovemaking; it was composed by Hawaiian vocalist Lena Machado in 1933.

122. Kahalewai died in 2009. Todaro, *The Golden Years of Hawaiian Entertainment*, 163.

123. Kahalewai, *An Hawaiian Happening*.

124. Before graduating from high school in 1943, eighteen-year-old Leilani Alama performed for USO shows with the Moana entertainers. Leilani

Alama and her sister Puanani became hula soloists and teachers; they both continue to teach hula in Honolulu today. Sonny Kamaka was another singer who frequently joined the Buck-Stibbard troupe during its Maui USO performances; he later became a well-known entertainer with the group The Invitations on Oʻahu. Carol Mae Kuuleinani Vanderford fondly remembers Sonny's beautiful falsetto voice.

125. Sarah Kawailima, 64; June Lily Cerney Keala, 71; Ellen McEnroe and Sybil Lynch, 116, in *Ka Poʻe Kahiko o Waiʻanae.*

126. Lee, "Notes from the (non)Field."

127. Rony, *The Third Eye,* 4–6.

128. Interestingly, scholars have noted that photographs of wartime encounters made by Pacific Islanders cannot be located. Lamont Lindstrom and Geoffrey White state that Islanders were not "photograph-makers," particularly in the case of the Solomon Islands, Papua New Guinea, New Hebrides (Vanuatu), Guam, Palau (Belau), and other parts of the Pacific where battles did take place. Lindstrom and White, *Island Encounters,* 7. However, Hawaiians were active image-makers as they were being made objects of images. While not deposited in national or state archives, private collections in Hawaiʻi suggest that this historical record does exist and therefore may on other Pacific Islands.

129. Rafael, *White Love,* 96–98.

130. Raylani Kinney Akau and Rayner Kinney, interviewed by the author, 24 April 2004.

131. Rony, *The Third Eye,* 101, 116.

Epilogue

1. The men of Hālau o Nā Pua Kukui performed a hula of "Mahaiʻula."

2. Kumu hula Aloha Dalire, Derek Kiaʻaina Nuʻuhiwa, Kekaimoku Yoshikawa, Michael Canopin, and Rich Pedrina have hālau or studios in Japan, while Olana Ai, Noelani Chang, Johnny Lum Ho, Ray Fonseca, Sonny Ching, and Frank Kawaikapuokalani Hewett teach workshops there. See also Eloise Aguiar, "Japan Hooked on Hula and the ʻUkulele," *Honolulu Advertiser,* 11 July 2005; Rod Staton, "Japanese Flock to Merrie Monarch Fest," *Honolulu Advertiser,* 19 April 2004. There are an estimated 400,000 hula students and more than 100 hula studios in Japan.

3. The protesters held signs identifying themselves as members of the "Reinstated Hawaiian Kingdom." For a detailed discussion of the Akaka Bill, see Kauanui, "Precarious Positions," 1–27, and Kauanui, *Hawaiian Blood,* 172, 184–86. As of July 2011, the federal Akaka Bill is awaiting scheduling for a U.S. Senate floor vote. On 7 July 2011 the Hawaiʻi governor Neil Abercrombie signed Hawaiʻi Senate Bill 1520 into law,

which is a state-level version of the Akaka Bill that is intended to help advance federal recognition legislation. Regardless of whether the Akaka Bill passes, SB 1520 begins a process of creating a "Native Hawaiian governing entity" and a registry of qualified Kanaka Maoli members. Hawaiian activists continue to resist this process, which they see as usurping Hawaiian sovereignty and subordinating Hawaiian nationhood to the United States. Kauanui, "The Stolen Sovereignty of Hawai'i's Indigenous People"; B. J. Reyes, "New Law Upholds Hawaiian Identity," *Honolulu Star-Advertiser*, 7 July 2011.

4. Vicky Holt Takamine was one of the judges at the Merrie Monarch festival in 2006.

5. Durbin, "Hula Power," 68.

6. Vicky Holt Takamine, interviewed by the author, 13 April 2006.

7. Momiala Kamahele, who coorganized the coalition's first legislative protest with Takamine, provides an insightful analysis of this bill and kumu hula organizing strategies in "'Ilio'ulaokalani: Defending Native Hawaiian Culture."

8. Ibid., 53.

9. Ibid., 56.

10. In 2000, the U.S. Supreme Court ruled the state's Hawaiians-only voting for the Office of Hawaiian Affairs (OHA) violated the Constitution's Fifteenth Amendment. In the wake of the Court's decision, lawsuits have challenged the constitutionality of agencies and institutions supporting Hawaiians, including OHA and the Department of Hawaiian Home Lands. The last of these lawsuits was rejected in 2006 by the Supreme Court. For an excellent summary of this litigation, see Losch, "Hawaiian Issues," 222–23. In September 2003, for instance, Takamine and the coalition organized a March for Justice through Waikīkī in response to these lawsuits and a court order that admitted a non-Hawaiian student into Kamehameha Schools. Wade Kilohana Shirkey, "Red T-shirts Reflect Spirit of Hawaiian Solidarity," *Honolulu Advertiser*, 26 September 2003; Vicki Viotti, "Hawaiians Hope to Stir Community Support," *Honolulu Advertiser*, 1 September 2003.

11. Kekoa Catherine Enomoto, "Kumu Hula: Taking a Stand in Hawai'i's Politics," *Honolulu Star-Bulletin*, 16 April 1998.

12. After numerous legal challenges by non-Hawaiian plaintiffs and their attorneys over the past seven years, the Kamehameha Schools' preferential admissions policy remains intact for the time being. A federal district judge upheld the private schools' admissions policy in 2003, but an anonymous plaintiff appealed the decision to the U.S. Ninth Circuit Court of Appeals and in August 2005, the ruling was overturned in a 2 to 1 decision. Kamehameha Schools then petitioned

for an en banc panel convened from fifteen judges; the en banc panel upheld the legality of Kamehameha Schools' preference policy with an 8 to 7 ruling. See Losch, "Hawaiian Issues," 225, and "Kamehameha Schools Admissions Challenge: Legal Summary and Documents," Kamehameha Schools, www.ksbe.edu/lawsuit/summary.php, accessed 15 June 2010. The John Doe plaintiff and his attorneys petitioned the U.S. Supreme Court to review the Ninth Circuit Court's ruling upholding Kamehameha's admissions policy; the plaintiff withdrew the petition in 2007 after reaching a confidential monetary settlement with Kamehameha Schools' trustees. Jim Dooley, "Kamehameha Schools settled lawsuit for $7M," *Honolulu Advertiser*, 8 February 2008; Thomas Yoshida, "Kamehameha Schools and 'John Doe' Settle Admissions Lawsuit," 14 May 2007, Kamehameha Schools, http://www.ksbe.edu/article.php?story=20070514073144797.

13. The near entirety of the State of Hawai'i's lands are these former kingdom lands; they were seized by the new Republic of Hawai'i, whose leaders had overthrown the monarchy. The new republic later ceded these lands to the United States when the United States illegally annexed Hawai'i in 1898. Kauanui, "Colonialism in Equality," 642; Kauanui, *Hawaiian Blood*, 28–30.

14. In 1994 the Office of Hawaiian Affairs and four individual Native Hawaiian plaintiffs sued to prevent the state from selling 1,500 acres of ceded lands in Lāhaina, Maui, and Kona, Hawai'i. The Hawai'i State Circuit Court ruled in 2002 that the state could sell these lands; in 2008 the state supreme court reversed the lower court ruling and blocked the sale of lands; in March 2009, the U.S. Supreme Court unanimously overturned the state supreme court's ruling. In turn, in July 2009, as a compromise between three of the four plaintiffs, the governor, and OHA, the Hawai'i state legislature passed Act 176, which requires two-thirds approval by both houses for the sale of any ceded lands. The Hawai'i supreme court dismissed the claims of the one remaining plaintiff, Jonathan Kamakawiwo'ole Osorio, who had rejected the legislative compromise. T. Ilihia Gionson, "Native Hawaiians Protest State's U.S. Supreme Appeal over Ceded Land Sales," *Ka Wai Ola*, 12 December 2008; Helen Altonn and Gregg K. Kakesako, "Ceded Lands Case Sent Home," *Honolulu Star-Bulletin*, 31 March 2009; and "Ceded Lands Suit to Be Dismissed," *Honolulu Advertiser*, 28 October 2009.

15. Mapuana de Silva and Vicky Holt Takamine are "hula sisters," having graduated, or 'ūniki, in the same cohort under kumu hula Maiki Aiu Lake.

16. Gordon Y. K. Pang, "'Hawaiians Only' Issue Not Raised at Hearing by Supreme Court," *Honolulu Advertiser*, 26 February 2009.

17. "History of the Services in Hawaii," *Paradise of the Pacific* 62, no. 7 (July 1950): 7.

18. Department of Defense, Office of the Deputy Undersecretary of Defense, Installations and Environment, *Base Structure Report: Fiscal Year 2009 Baseline.*

19. As of this writing, the legal challenges to the Stryker Brigade have run their course, and the U.S. Army has based the Stryker Brigade in Hawaiʻi. For more on grassroots organizing and legal challenges to the Stryker Brigades, see Kelly, *Noho Hewa* (2009); William Cole, "Lawsuit Opposes Stryker Brigade," *Honolulu Advertiser*, 18 August 2004; and William Cole, "Army EIS Picks Hawaiʻi as Stryker First Choice," *Honolulu Advertiser*, 16 February 2008.

20. Jan TenBruggencate, "Many Questioning Why UH Should Own Hybrids," *Honolulu Advertiser*, 2 May 2006.

21. Stillman, "Passed into the Present," 216.

22. Vicky Holt Takamine, interviewed by the author, 13 April 2006.

23. Indeed, many kumu hula and their haumāna (students) perform for tourists, including Robert Cazimero and Ed Collier. ʻIlio member Sonny Ching and his Hālau Nā Mamo O Puʻuanahulu, for instance, have performed at state-sponsored Waikīkī Beach tourist shows and at one point were "adopted" by the Hyatt Regency Waikīkī Hotel.

24. Vicky Holt Takamine, interviewed by the author, 13 April 2006.

25. As the ethnomusicologist Amy Kuʻuleialoha Stillman has pointed out, "ancient hula kahiko," as presented in hula competitions, includes several kinds of hula genres of varying degrees of transformation from European contact to the present. It is more important that the category of "kahiko," or traditional hula, "invoke perceived conventions of ancientness." Stillman, "Hawaiian Hula Competitions," 367–69.

26. Wayne Harada, "Festival Fetes Hapa-Haole Music's Legacy," *Honolulu Advertiser*, 1 August 2003.

27. Amy Kuʻuleialoha Stillman argues that these competition rules prohibiting artificial flowers and cellophane assert a particular "interpretation of traditionality" by "explicitly eschewing key visual components of hula associated with tourist entertainment of the World War II years and since." Stillman, "Hawaiian Hula Competitions," 371.

28. Kurt Matthews, "Festival Hopes to Bring Back Past," 21 March 2006, KHON2, http://khon.com.

29. Betty Puanani Makia, interviewed by the author, 27 February 2000.

30. Carol Mae Kuuleinani Vanderford, interviewed by the author, 13 July 2002.

31. Vicky Holt Takamine, interviewed by the author, 13 April 2006.

32. Kamele Collier Marquez, interviewed by the author, 14 July 2007.

33. International Waikiki Hula Conference program, Kumu Hula biographies, International Waikiki Hula Conference, http://www.waikiki hulaconference.com/Home/Kumu—Teachers/Kumu-Profiles.aspx, accessed 22 June 2010.

34. This "Hoʻokipa Aloha" program debuted in 2007. Norwegian Cruise Line withdrew two passenger cruise ships from Hawaiʻi (its *Pride of Hawaiʻi* and *Pride of Aloha*); currently *Pride of America* is its sole ship cruising in Hawaiʻi.

35. Harada, "Festival Fetes Hapa-Haole Music's Legacy."

36. Kathryn Drury, "It Lives!," *Honolulu Weekly*, 13 August 2003.

37. The Hapa Haole Hula and Music Festival first received a grant in 2006. Prior to this, the Hawaiʻi Tourism Authority (HTA) did not support cultural practitioners. Takamine lobbied the state legislature for four years for some of this money to reach Hawaiian cultural practitioners. The HTA now supports Hawaiian culture with $600,000 annually.

38. Vicky Holt Takamine, interviewed by the author, 13 April 2006.

39. Ibid.

40. Ibid.

41. OmniTrak Group, "Resident Sentiment Survey Prepared for Hawaiʻi Tourism Authority," 12 February 2010, Hawaiʻi Tourism Authority, http://www.hawaiitourismauthority.org/research-reports/reports/ evaluation-performance-measures/.

42. Hawaiʻi Tourism Authority, "HTA Awards $600,000 to Organizations That Perpetuate Hawaiian Culture," 16 February 2010, press release.

43. Some of the awardees include the PAʻI Foundation, another organization led by Takamine; a hula festival for Japanese tourists, Hula Hoʻolauna Aloha; and a Maui hula competition.

GLOSSARY

'aha'aina—feast, banquet

ali'i—chiefs

ali'i nui—high-ranking chiefs; in the nineteenth century, monarchs

aloha—love, affection, compassion; a greeting, for example, hello, good-bye

hālau hula—hula school or troupe

haole—foreigner; in the nineteenth century, a white person

hapa haole hula—acculturated forms of hula performed to music with Western instrumentation like 'ukulele and guitars. Although the song lyrics were in English, they often utilized Hawaiian poetic devices and imagery, particularly if composed by someone with fluency in Hawaiian language.

ho'opa'a—chanters and musicians who receive further training and advance to kumu hula

hula 'āla'apapa—hula performed with an ipu heke (double gourd) and often dedicated to the gods. This genre does not have the standardized poetic phrasing of hula 'ōlapa and is of greater antiquity.

hula 'auana—genre of "modern" hula

hula kahiko—genre of "ancient" hula that emerged with the advent of late twentieth-century hula competitions

hula ku'i—hybrid hula incorporating indigenous and Western performance vocabularies that emerged during King David Kalākaua's reign

hula 'ōlapa—a nonsacred genre of hula performed with ipu heke (double gourd) that often honors ali'i. It has a standardized poetic pattern, often phrased in couplets, and a concluding line, "Haina 'ia mai ana kapuana" (Let the story be told).

hula pahu—sacred genre of hula performed with the sharkskin drum and associated with ancient temple rituals ipu—gourd instrument used in hula

kalo—taro; principal Hawaiian staple

kamaʻāina—lit., child of the land; native born. Usually refers to someone born and raised in Hawaiʻi

kamaʻāina haole—a white person born in Hawaiʻi

Kanaka Maoli—real person; that is, a Native Hawaiian

kaona—hidden meaning, veiled reference

kapa—tapa, bark cloth

kapu—sacred, consecrated

kuahu—altar dedicated to the goddess Laka, patron of the hula

kumu hula—hula master or teacher

kupuna—elder, ancestor

lāhui—nation

lāʻī—ti leaves

makaʻāinana—ordinary people or commoners

mana—divine or sacred power

mele—song, chant, poem

mōʻī—monarch, sovereign

ʻohana—family, kin group

ʻōlapa—dancer

ʻōlelo Hawaiʻi—Hawaiian language

oli—chant not accompanied by dance

ʻōlohe hula—hula master

pā hula—hula school

pāʻū kapa—bark-cloth skirts

poʻe hula—hula practitioners

poi—mashed, cooked taro corms

pūʻili—bamboo rattle used in hula

ʻulīʻulī—gourd rattle used in hula

ʻūniki—ritual graduation exercise

BIBLIOGRAPHY

Newspapers and Periodicals

Atchison Daily Globe
Brooklyn Eagle
Buffalo Courier
Buffalo Morning Express
Chicago Daily Tribune
Chicago Inter Ocean
Daily Bulletin (Honolulu)
Daily Inter-Ocean
Daily Rocky Mountain News
Fayetteville Observer
Georgia Weekly Telegraph and Georgia Journal and Messenger
Hawaiian Gazette
Honolulu Advertiser
Honolulu Star-Advertiser
Honolulu Star-Bulletin
Illustrated American
Irish World and American Industrial Liberator
Judge
Ka Lama
Ka Makaainana
Ke Au Okoa
Los Angeles Times
Maui News
Milwaukee Sentinel
Morning Oregonian (Portland)
New York Times
North American

North American and United States Gazette
Nupepa Kuokoa
Omaha Bee
Omaha World-Herald
Pacific Commercial Advertiser
Paradise of the Pacific
Puck
Rocky Mountain News
St. Louis Globe-Democrat
Washington Post

Archival Sources

Alana, Glenn. "Luau and War." 1947. Folder 24.01. HWRD.
Aloha to the Men and Women of the Armed Forces from the USO in Hawaii.
    Call no. 58.02. HWRD.
Dole, Sanford B. Correspondence from Governor's Office. 10 November 1900.
    GOV 1, vol. 2 (Letterbook—24 June 1900–19 September 1901), HSA.
Hawaii United Service Organization. *First Annual Report of the Hawaii United
    Service Organization, 1942.* HWRD, 1943.
———. *United Service Organizations of the Territory of Hawaii, USA. Reports
    on Its Final Year of War.* HWRD, 1945.
Kelsey, Theodore. "Mrs. Jennie Wilson." Folder 397, TK.
Krauss, Bob. "Jennie Wilson." Typescript. Bob Krauss Workbook 3 (September
    1891–June 1893), BK.
———. "Jennie Wilson's Charm Bracelet." Bob Krauss Workbook 3 (September
    1891–June 1893), BK.
Photograph 309. "Civic Recreation Entertainers." 24 March 1942. HWRD.
Photograph 1133. "Under the Expert Guidance of a Son of Hawaii, American
    Soldiers Prepare the Traditional Kalua Pig for a Luau." 1942. U.S. Army
    Signal Corps, HWRD.
Photograph CP 121, 265 (N. R. Farbman). "Hula Show at Lalani Hawaiian
    Village, Waikiki, ca. 1935." Folder, Social and Personal Activity: Tourists
    and Tourism, Lalani Hawaiian Village, BM.
Photograph CP 74612 (Photographer Tai Sing Loo). "Hula Dancer with Lei at
    Mossman's Hawaiian Village with Song 'For You a Lei.'" Folder, Social and
    Personal Activity: Tourists and Tourism, Lalani Hawaiian Village, BM.
Photographs. Folder, Exposition: Chicago, 1933, PP–20–6. HSA.
Photographs. Hula, 1900. Folder no. 5, BM.
Photographs. "Hula Dancers, Musicians, Groups." PP–32–8. HSA.
Photographs. "Hula Dancers, Musicians, Groups (Portraits, Early Period)."
    PP–33–3 and PP–33–4, HSA.
Photographs. N. R. Farbman Collection, Folder, Tourists and Tourism, BM.

Photographs 274, 275, 276. "On Camouflage Detail," "Camouflage Worker," and "Camouflage Workers Observing First Anniversary." 1942. HWRD.

Photographs 1181 and 1182. "The USO Luau in Honor of Army, Navy, and Red Cross Nurses, Given at Hindrichsen Estate, Wahiawa, T.H." 11 October 1942. U.S. Army Signal Corps, HWRD.

Pukui, Mary Kawena. "The Hula." Typescript in Folder 51, HK.

"The Story of Midway Plaisance." In *The Daily Inter-Ocean* 22, no. 220 (1 November 1893): 25–32. Map case 2, drawer 12, folder 5, WC.

To Do Today in Honolulu and on Oahu for the Week of July 21–27, 1945. Call no. 18.04, HWRD.

Wilson, Jennie Kapahukulaokamamalu. Interviewed by Joann Kealiinohomoku. 1962. BM, Honolulu, Hawai'i. Tapes HAW 59.1.1, HAW 59.3.1, HAW 59.4.1, HAW 59.5.1, HAW 59.5.2, HAW 59.7.1, HAW 59.8.1, HAW 59.8.2, HAW 59.12.2, HAW 59.13.3, HAW 59.14.1.

Wilson, John H. *Diary, 1901 Buffalo Fair.* Bob Krauss Workbook 6 (June 1899– September 1902), BK.

Films

Arrival First R and R Troops from Vietnam, Honolulu, Hawaii, 3 August 1966. Motion picture no. 50441. Records of the U.S. Army, Office of the Chief Signal Officer, Series LC, Record Group 111, NA.

Aunty Betty. Dir. Adria L. Imada. 2000.

Bird of Paradise. Dir. King Vidor. RKO Radio Pictures, 1932.

Blue Hawaii. Dir. Norman Taurog. Paramount Pictures, 1961.

Gidget. Dir. Paul Wendkos. Columbia Pictures, 1959.

Keystone Eagle Return of 9th Division, 4th Battalion, 39th Infantry from Vietnam to Hawaii, Hickam AFB, Hawaii, 07/08–1969–08/27–1969. Motion picture no. 342-USAF-48145. Records of U.S. Air Force Commands, Activities, and Organizations, *1900–2003,* Record Group 342, NA.

LAUA (I.E., LUAU), Hickam Field, Oahu, Hawaiian Islands. Motion picture no. 18-CS-1299. Records of the Army Air Forces, ca. 1902–1964, Record Group 18, NA.

Lilo and Stitch. Dir. Dean DeBlois and Chris Sanders. Buena Vista Pictures, 2000.

Luau, 05/06/1944. Motion picture no. 18-CS-1705. Records of the Army Air Forces, ca. 1902–1964, Record Group 18, NA.

Moana: A Romance of the Golden Age. Dir. Robert J. Flaherty. Paramount Pictures, 1926.

Noho Hewa: The Wrongful Occupation of Hawai'i. Dir. Anne Keala Kelly. Kuleana Works, 2009.

Operation Wounded Warrior, 07/03/1954. Motion picture no. 342-USAF-21595.

Records of U.S. Air Force Commands, Activities, and Organizations, *1900–2003*, Record Group 342, NA.

A Place in the Sun. Dir. George Stevens. Paramount Pictures, 1951.

Ray Kinney and His Royal Hawaiian Orchestra and the Aloha Maids. Dir. Roy Mack. Vitaphone Melody Master, 1938.

Books and Articles

Adams, Rachel. *Sideshow U.S.A.: Freaks and the American Cultural Imagination.* Chicago: University of Chicago Press, 2001.

Alexander, Daniel A. "Hula Was Not Enough." *Paradise of the Pacific* 55, no. 11 (November 1943): 26–27, 31.

Allen, Gwenfread. *Hawaii's War Years, 1941–1945.* Honolulu: University of Hawaii Press, 1950.

Alloula, Malek. *The Colonial Harem.* Minneapolis: University of Minnesota Press, 1986.

Althusser, Louis. *Lenin and Philosophy.* New York: Monthly Review, 1972.

Anthony, J. Garner. *Hawaii under Army Rule.* Stanford: Stanford University Press, 1955.

Arista, Noelani. "Navigating Uncharted Oceans of Meaning: *Kaona* as Historical and Interpretive Method." *PMLA* 125, no. 3 (2010): 663–69.

Armitage, George T. "Tourist Bureau Says Aloha." *Paradise of the Pacific* 54, no. 12 (holiday 1942): 73–74.

Around the "Pan" with Uncle Hank; His Trip through the Pan-American Exposition. New York: Nut Shell, 1901.

Babcock, Barbara A. "First Families: Gender, Reproduction, and the Mythic Southwest." In *The Great Southwest of the Fred Harvey Company and the Santa Fe Railway.* Ed. Marta Weigle and Barbara A. Babcock, 207–17. Phoenix: Heard Museum, 1996.

———. "A New Mexican Rebecca." *Journal of the Southwest* 32 (1990): 400–437.

Bailey, Beth, and David Farber. *The First Strange Place: Race and Sex in World War II Hawaii.* Baltimore: Johns Hopkins University Press, 1994.

Bakhtin, Mikhail. *Rabelais and His World.* Trans. Hélène Iswolsky. Bloomington: Indiana University Press, 2009.

Balme, Christopher. "New Compatriots: Samoans on Display in Wilhelminian Germany." *Journal of Pacific History* 42, no. 3 (2007): 331–44.

Banks, Joseph. "Thoughts on the Manners of Otaheite." In *The Endeavour Journal of Joseph Banks, 1768–1771.* Vol 2. Ed. John Cawte Beaglehole. Sydney, Australia: Trustees of the Public Library of New South Wales in association with Angus and Robertson, 1962.

Barman, Jean, and Bruce Watson. *Leaving Paradise: Indigenous Hawaiians in the Pacific Northwest, 1787–1898.* Honolulu: University of Hawai'i Press, 2006.

Barrère, Dorothy B. "The Hula in Retrospect." In Dorothy B. Barrère, Mary

Kawena Pukui, and Marion Kelly, *Hula: Historical Perspectives*, 1–66. Honolulu: Bishop Museum, 1980.

Barrère, Dorothy B., Mary Kawena Pukui, and Marion Kelly. *Hula: Historical Perspectives*. Honolulu: Bishop Museum, 1980.

Barry, Richard Hayes. *Snap Shots on the Midway of the Pan-Am Expo*. Buffalo, N.Y.: Robert Allan Reid, 1901.

Beaglehole, J. C. *The Journals of Captain Cook, Vol. III, the Voyage of the Resolution and Discovery, 1776–1780, Parts I and II*. Cambridge: Cambridge University Press, 1967.

Beckwith, Martha. *The Kumulipo: A Hawaiian Creation Chant*. Chicago: University of Chicago Press, 1951.

Bederman, Gail. *Manliness and Civilization: A Cultural History of Gender and Race in the United States, 1880–1917*. Chicago: University of Chicago Press, 1995.

Beechert, Edward D. *Working in Hawaii: A Labor History*. Honolulu: University of Hawaii Press, 1985.

Bingham, Hiram. *A Residence of Twenty-One Years in the Sandwich Islands*. Hartford: Hezekiah Huntington, 1848.

Blanchard, David. "Entertainment, Dance and Northern Mohawk Showmanship." *American Indian Quarterly* 7 (1983): 2–26.

Bogdan, Robert. *Freak Show: Presenting Human Oddities for Amusement and Profit*. Chicago: University of Chicago Press, 1988.

Britsch, R. Lanier. *Moramona: The Mormons in Hawaii*. Lāʻie, Hawaiʻi: Institute for Polynesian Studies, Brigham Young University, Hawaii, 1989.

Brown, Jayna. *Babylon Girls: Black Women Performers and the Shaping of the Modern*. Durham: Duke University Press, 2008.

Brown, Julie K. *Contesting Images: Photography and the World's Columbian Exposition*. Tucson: University of Arizona Press, 1994.

Brown, Willard C. "The Show Goes on—in Hawaii." *Paradise of the Pacific* 54, no. 12 (holiday 1942): 23–25.

Brownlow, Kevin. *War, West, and Wilderness*. New York: Knopf, 1979.

Bryan, William S., ed. *Our Islands and Their People as Seen with Camera and Pencil*. Vol. 2. New York: Thompson, 1899.

Buck, Elizabeth. *Paradise Remade: The Politics of Culture and History in Hawaiʻi*. Philadelphia: Temple University Press, 1993.

Bushnell, O. A. *The Gifts of Civilization: Germs and Genocide in Hawaiʻi*. Honolulu: University of Hawaiʻi Press, 1993.

Carr, James Revell. "In the Wake of John Kanaka: Musical Interactions between Euro-American Sailors and Pacific Islanders, 1600–1900." Ph.D. diss., University of California, Santa Barbara, 2006.

Certeau, Michel de. *The Practice of Everyday Life*. Berkeley: University of California Press, 2002.

Chakrabarty, Dipesh. *Provincializing Europe: Postcolonial Thought and Historical Difference*. Princeton: Princeton University Press, 2000.

Chappell, David A. "Active Agents vs. Passive Victims: Decolonized Historiography or Problematic Paradigm?" *Contemporary Pacific* 7, no. 2 (fall 1995): 303–26.

———. *Double Ghosts: Oceanian Voyagers on Euroamerican Ships*. London: M. E. Sharpe, 1997.

———. "Shipboard Relations between Pacific Island Women and EuroAmerican Men, 1767–1887." *Journal of Pacific History* 27, no. 2 (1992): 131–49.

Chatterjee, Partha. *The Nation and Its Fragments: Colonial and Postcolonial Histories*. Princeton: Princeton University Press, 1993.

Clifford, James. *Routes: Travel and Translation in the Late Twentieth Century*. Cambridge: Harvard University Press, 1997.

Clifford, James, and George E. Marcus, eds. *Writing Culture: The Poetics and Politics of Ethnography*. Berkeley: University of California Press, 1986.

Coe, Brian, and Paul Gates. *The Snapshot Photograph: The Rise of Popular Photography, 1888–1939*. London: Ash and Grant, 1977.

Coffin, Harold. "Hawaiian Village, 1936." *Paradise of the Pacific* 48, no. 9 (September 1936): 15, 32.

Colton, F. Barrows. "How We Fight with Photographs." *National Geographic* 56 (September 1944): 257–80.

Corbey, Raymond. "Ethnographic Showcases, 1870–1930." *Cultural Anthropology* 8, no. 3 (August 1993): 338–69.

Costa, Mazeppa King. "Dance in the Society and Hawaiian Islands as Presented by the Early Writers, 1767–1842. " M.A. thesis, University of Hawaii, 1951.

Craft, Mabel. *Hawaii Nei*. San Francisco: William Doxey, 1899.

Davidson, Frank C. *Where to Take Your Girl in New York on One Dollar to $20*. New York: Robley Service, 1940.

Davis, Lynn Ann, ed. *Photography in Hawai'i*. Special issue, *History of Photography* 25 (autumn 2001).

Daws, Gavan. *Shoal of Time: A History of the Hawaiian Islands*. Honolulu: University of Hawaii Press, 1968.

Deloria, Philip J. *Indians in Unexpected Places*. Lawrence: University Press of Kansas, 2004.

———. *Playing Indian*. New Haven: Yale University Press, 1998.

Deloria, Vine, Jr. "The Indians." In *Buffalo Bill and the Wild West*, 45–56. Brooklyn, N.Y.: Brooklyn Museum, 1981.

Dening, Greg. *Islands and Beaches: Discourse on a Silent Land, Marquesas, 1774–1880*. Honolulu: University Press of Hawaii, 1980.

Dennett, Andrea Stulman. *Weird and Wonderful: The Dime Museum in America*. New York: New York University Press, 1997.

Denning, Michael. *The Cultural Front: The Laboring of American Culture in the Twentieth Century*. New York: Verso, 1996.

Department of Defense, Office of the Deputy Undersecretary of Defense, Installations and Environment. *Base Structure Report: Fiscal Year 2009 Baseline*. Washington, 2009.

Desmond, Jane. *Staging Tourism: Bodies on Display from Waikiki to Sea World*. Chicago: University of Chicago Press, 1999.

Diaz, Vicente M. *Repositioning the Missionary: Rewriting the Histories of Colonialism, Native Catholicism, and Indigeneity in Guam*. Honolulu: University of Hawai'i Press, 2010.

———. "Repositioning the Missionary: The Beatification of Blessed Diego Luis de Sanvitores and Chamorro Cultural History." Ph.D. diss., University of California, Santa Cruz, 1992.

Dominguez, Virginia R. "Exporting U.S. Concepts of Race: Are There Limits to the U.S. Model?" *Social Research* 65, no. 2 (summer 1998): 369–99.

Du Bois, W. E. B. *The Souls of Black Folk*. New York: Penguin, 1989.

Dudden, Arthur Power. *The American Pacific: From the Old China Trade to the Present*. New York: Oxford University Press, 1992.

Durbin, Paula. "Hula Power: Using Dance to Make a Difference." *Dance Teacher* 22, no. 9 (November 2000): 66, 68, 70.

Elbert, Samuel H., and Noelani Mahoe. *Nā Mele o Hawai'i Nei: 101 Hawaiian Songs*. Honolulu: University of Hawaii Press, 1970.

Ellis, William. *A Narrative of a Tour thru Hawaii, or Owhyee; With Remarks on the History, Traditions, Manners, Customs and Language of the Inhabitants of the Sandwich Islands*. London: H. Fisher Son and P. Jackson, 1827.

Emerson, Nathaniel B. *Unwritten Literature of Hawaii: The Sacred Songs of the Hula*. Honolulu: 'Ai Pōhaku, 1997.

Epstein, Milton. *The New York Hippodrome: A Complete Chronology of Performance, from 1905–1939*. New York: Theater Library Association, 1993.

Esquire's New York: A New York Guide Book for World's Fair Visitors. New York: Esquire-Coronet, 1939.

Feeser, Andrea, and Gaye Chan. *Waikīkī: A History of Forgetting and Remembering*. Honolulu: University of Hawai'i Press, 2006.

Felix, John Henry, and Peter F. Senecal. *The Portuguese in Hawaii*. Honolulu: Felix, 1978.

Ferguson, Kathy E., and Phyllis Turnbull. *Oh, Say, Can You See? The Semiotics of the Military in Hawai'i*. Minneapolis: University of Minnesota Press, 1999.

Foucault, Michel. *Discipline and Punish*. New York: Vintage, 1995.

———. *The History of Sexuality: An Introduction, Volume I*. 1978. New York: Vintage, 1990.

——. *Power/Knowledge: Selected Interviews and Other Writings, 1972–1977.* New York: Vintage, 1980.

Fuchs, Lawrence H. *Hawaii Pono: An Ethnic and Political History.* Honolulu: Bess Press, 1961.

Gilliom, Amy Hānaiali'i, with Willie K. *Hawaiian Tradition.* Honolulu: Mountain Apple, 1997.

Go, Julian. "The Chains of Empire: State Building and 'Political Education' in Puerto Rico and the Philippines." In *The American Colonial State in the Philippines: Global Perspectives.* Ed. Julian Go and Anne L. Foster, 1–42. Durham: Duke University Press, 2003.

Green, Rayna. "The Tribe Called Wannabee: Playing Indian in America and Europe." *Folklore* 99, no. i (1998): 30–55.

Greenhalgh, Paul. *Ephemeral Vistas: The Expositions Universelles, Great Exhibitions and World's Fairs, 1851–1939.* Manchester: Manchester University Press, 1988.

Grier, Edward F. "Stationed in Paradise." *General Magazine and Historical Chronicle of the General Alumni Society of the University of Pennsylvania* (winter 1946): 93–102.

Guha, Ranajit. "In Defense of the Fragment: Writing about Hindu-Muslim Riots in India Today." In *A Subaltern Studies Reader: 1986–1995.* Ed. Ranajit Guha, 1–33. Minneapolis: University of Minnesota Press, 1997.

——, ed. *A Subaltern Studies Reader.* Minneapolis: University of Minnesota Press, 1997.

Hackler, Rhoda E. A. "My Dear Friend: Letters of Queen Victoria and Queen Emma." *Hawaiian Journal of History* 22 (1988): 101–30.

Hackler, Rhoda E. A., and Loretta G. H. Woodard. *The Queen's Quilt.* Honolulu: Friends of 'Iolani Palace, 2004.

Handler, Richard. "On Sociocultural Discontinuity: Nationalism and Cultural Objectification in Quebec." *Current Anthropology* 25, no. 1 (February 1984): 55–71.

Handy, E. S. Craighill, and Mary Kawena Pukui. *Polynesian System in Ka'u, Hawai'i.* 1972. Honolulu: Mutual, 1998.

Hartman, Saidiya. *Scenes of Subjection: Terror, Slavery, and Self-Making in Nineteenth-Century America.* New York: Oxford University Press, 1997.

Haskins, Jim. *The Cotton Club.* New York: Random House, 1977.

Hau'ofa, Epeli. "Our Sea of Islands. " *Contemporary Pacific* 6, no. 1 (spring 1994): 147–61.

Hawai'i State Department of Business, Economic Development, and Tourism, Research and Economic Analysis Division. *Federal Economic Activities in Hawai'i.* Honolulu: June 2007.

Hawai'i Tourism Authority. *2009 Annual Visitor Research Report.*

Hawai'i Visitors and Convention Bureau. *Hawaii: The Islands of Aloha, Official Visitors' Guide, 2009.*

———. *Islands of Hawai'i Visitors' Guide, 2010–11.*

Hawthorne, Julian. "Foreign Folk at the Fair." *Cosmopolitan* 15, no. 5 (September 1893): 567–76.

Hebdige, Dick. *Subculture: The Meaning of Style.* New York: Routledge, 1988.

Hibbard, Don, and David Franzen. *The View from Diamond Head: Royal Residence to Urban Resort.* Honolulu: Editions Limited, 1986.

hooks, bell. *Black Looks: Race and Representation.* Boston: South End, 1992.

Hopkins, Jerry. "Kini Wilson." In *Notable Women of Hawaii.* Ed. Barbara Bennett Peterson, 406–8. Honolulu: University of Hawaii Press, 1984.

Houston, James D. *Hawaiian Son: The Life and Music of Eddie Kamae.* With Eddie Kamae. Honolulu: 'Ai Pōhaku, 2004.

Imada, Adria L. "The Hawaiian Kingdom on the World Stage, 1855–1889." In *Coast to Coast: Case Histories of Modern Pacific Crossings.* Ed. Prue Ahrens and Chris Dixon, 21–42. Newcastle upon Tyne: Cambridge Scholars, 2010.

———. "Transnational *Hula* as Colonial Culture." *Journal of Pacific History* 46, no. 3 (September 2011): 149–76.

Inn, Henry. *Hawaiian Types.* New York: Hasting House, 1945.

Irwin, Edward P. "Ed Irwin More Than Suggests That We Should Not Try to 'Americanize' Orientals in Hawaii, Even If We Can." *Paradise of the Pacific* 37, no. 12 (December 1924): 54–56.

Jacobson, Matthew Frye. *Whiteness of a Different Color: European Immigrants and the Alchemy of Race.* Cambridge: Harvard University Press, 1999.

Johnson, Donald D. *The United States in the Pacific: Private Interests and Public Policies, 1784–1889.* Westport: Praeger, 1995.

Johnston, Ewan. "Reinventing Fiji at 19th-Century and Early 20th-Century Exhibitions." *Journal of Pacific History* 40, no. 1 (2005): 23–44.

Jolly, Margaret. "From Point Venus to Bali Ha'i: Eroticism and Exoticism in Representations of the Pacific." In *Sites of Desire, Economies of Pleasure: Sexualities in Asia and the Pacific.* Ed. Lenore Manderson and Margaret Jolly, 99–122. Chicago: University of Chicago Press, 1997.

Kaeppler, Adrienne L. *Hula Pahu: Hawaiian Drum Dances.* Vol. 1, *Ha'a and Hula Pahu: Sacred Movements.* Honolulu: Bishop Museum, 1993.

Kahalewai, Iwalani. *An Hawaiian Happening.* 1958. Honolulu: Lehua Records, 2008.

Kamahele, Momiala. " 'Īlio'ulaokalani: Defending Native Hawaiian Culture." *Amerasia Journal* 26, no. 2 (2000): 38–65.

Kamakau, Samuel Mānaiakalani. *Ke Aupuni Mō'ī: Ka Mo'olelo no Kauikeaouli, Keiki Ho'oilina a Kamehameha a Me Ke Aupuni Āna i Noho Mō'ī Ai.* Honolulu: Kamehameha Schools, 2001.

———. *Na Poe Kahiko: The People of Old.* Trans. Mary Kawena Pukui. Ed. Dorothy B. Barrère. Honolulu: Bishop Museum, 1968.

———. *Ruling Chiefs of Hawaii.* Honolulu: Kamehameha Schools, 1961.

Kame'eleihiwa, Lilikalā. *Native Land and Foreign Desires: Pehea lā e Pono ai?* Honolulu: Bishop Museum, 1992.

Kamins, Robert M., and Robert E. Potter. *Mālamalama: A History of the University of Hawai'i.* Honolulu: University of Hawai'i Press, 1998.

Kanahele, George Hu'eu Sanford. *Kū Kanaka (Stand Tall): A Search for Hawaiian Values.* Honolulu: University of Hawaii Press, 1986.

Kanahele, George S. "Alfred Unauna Alohikea." In *Hawaiian Music and Musicians: An Illustrated History.* Ed. George S. Kanahele, 13–16. Honolulu: University Press of Hawaii, 1979.

———. "David Kalakaua." In *Hawaiian Music and Musicians: An Illustrated History.* Ed. George S. Kanahele, 200–203. Honolulu: University Press of Hawaii, 1979.

———, ed. *Hawaiian Music and Musicians: An Illustrated History.* Honolulu: University Press of Hawaii, 1979.

———. "Hawaiian Room (Hotel Lexington)." In *Hawaiian Music and Musicians: An Illustrated History.* Ed. George S. Kanahele, 120–22. Honolulu: University Press of Hawaii, 1979.

———. "Lei 'Awapuhi ('Ginger Lei')." In *Hawaiian Music and Musicians: An Illustrated History.* Ed. George S. Kanahele, 223–24. Honolulu: University Press of Hawaii, 1979.

———. "Little Brown Gal." In *Hawaiian Music and Musicians: An Illustrated History.* Ed. George S. Kanahele, 232. Honolulu: University Press of Hawaii, 1979.

———. "Mekia Kealakai." In *Hawaiian Music and Musicians: An Illustrated History.* Ed. George S. Kanahele, 209–10. Honolulu: University Press of Hawaii, 1979.

———. "Toots Paka's Hawaiians." In *Hawaiian Music and Musicians: An Illustrated History.* Ed. George S. Kanahele, 388–90. Honolulu: University Press of Hawaii, 1979.

Kaplan, Amy. "'Left Alone with America': The Absence of Empire in the Study of American Culture." In *Cultures of United States Imperialism.* Ed. Amy Kaplan and Donald E. Pease, 3–21. Durham: Duke University Press, 1993.

Ka Po'e Kahiko o Wai'anae: Oral Histories of the Wai'anae Coast of O'ahu. Honolulu: Wai'anae Coast Culture and Arts Society and Topgallant, 1986.

Kauanui, J. Kēhaulani. "Colonialism in Equality: Hawaiian Sovereignty and the Question of U.S. Civil Rights." *South Atlantic Quarterly* 107, no. 4 (2008): 635–50.

———. *Hawaiian Blood: Colonialism and the Politics of Sovereignty and Indigeneity.* Durham: Duke University Press, 2008.

———. "Precarious Positions: Native Hawaiians and U.S. Federal Recognition." *Contemporary Pacific* 17, no. 1 (2005): 1–27.

———. "The Stolen Sovereignty of Hawai'i's Indigenous People." *Guardian,* 6 July 2011.

Kauanui, J. Kēhaulani, and Ju Hui "Judy" Han. "'Asian Pacific Islander': Issues of Representation and Responsibility." In *The Very Inside: An Anthology of Writing by Asian and Pacific Islander Lesbian and Bisexual Women.* Ed. Sharon Lim-Hing, 376–79. Toronto: Sister Vision, 1994.

Kelley, Robin D. G. *Race Rebels: Culture, Politics, and the Black Working Class.* New York: Free Press, 1994.

Kent, Noel J. *Hawaii: Islands under the Influence.* Honolulu: University of Hawaii Press, 1993.

Kirshenblatt-Gimblett, Barbara. *Destination Culture: Tourism, Museums, and Heritage.* Berkeley: University of California Press, 1998.

Krasner, David. *Resistance, Parody and Double Consciousness in African American Theatre, 1895–1919.* New York: St. Martin's, 1997.

Krauss, Bob. *Johnny Wilson: First Hawaiian Democrat.* Honolulu: University of Hawaii Press, 1994.

Kuykendall, Ralph S. *The Hawaiian Kingdom, Volume I, 1778–1854, Foundation and Transformation.* 1938. Honolulu: University of Hawaii Press, 1991.

———. *The Hawaiian Kingdom, Volume II, 1854–1874, Twenty Critical Years.* Honolulu: University of Hawaii Press, 1953.

———. *The Hawaiian Kingdom, Volume III, 1874–1893, The Kalakaua Dynasty.* Honolulu: University of Hawaii Press, 1967.

LaFeber, Walter. *The New Empire: An Interpretation of American Expansion.* Ithaca: Cornell University Press, 1963.

Landgraf, Anne Kapulani. *E Nā Hulu Kūpuna Nā Puna Ola Maoli Nō.* Kaneohe, s.n., 1987.

Lee, Rachel. "Notes from the (non)Field: Theorizing and Teaching 'Women of Color.'" *Meridians* 1, no. 1 (fall 2001): 85–109.

Life Histories of Native Hawaiians. Honolulu: Ethnic Studies Oral History Project, Ethnic Studies Program, University of Hawaii, Manoa, 1978.

Liliuokalani. *Hawaii's Story by Hawaii's Queen.* 1898. Tokyo: Charles E. Tuttle, 1964.

———. *The Queen's Songbook: Her Majesty Queen Lili'uokalani.* Ed. Barbara Barnard Smith. Honolulu: Hui Hānai, 1999.

Lindstrom, Lamont. "Images of Islanders in Pacific War Photographs." In *Perilous Memories: The Asia-Pacific War(s).* Ed. T. Fujitani, Geoffrey M. White, and Lisa Yoneyama, 107–28. Durham: Duke University Press, 2001.

Lindstrom, Lamont, and Geoffrey M. White. *Island Encounters: Black and White Memories of the Pacific War.* Washington: Smithsonian Institution, 1990.

Lipsitz, George. *Time Passages: Collective Memory and American Popular Culture.* Minneapolis: University of Minnesota Press, 1990.

Lorch, Allie, and Niklaus Schweizer. "Royal Hawaiian Band." In *Hawaiian*

Music and Musicians: An Illustrated History. Ed. George S. Kanahele, 335–44. Honolulu: University Press of Hawaii, 1979.

Losch, Tracie Ku'uipo Cummings. "Hawaiian Issues." *Contemporary Pacific* 19, no. 1 (2007): 222–31.

Lucas, Paul F. Nakoa. "E Ola Mau Kākou I Ka 'Ōlelo Makuahine: Hawaiian Language Policy and the Courts." *Hawaiian Journal of History* 34 (2000): 1–28.

MacCannell, Dean. *Empty Meeting Grounds: The Tourist Papers.* London: Routledge, 1992.

Malo, Davida. *Ka Mooolelo Hawaii: Hawaiian Traditions.* Trans. and ed. Malcolm Naea Chun. Honolulu: First People's Productions, 1996.

Marien, Mary Warner. *Photography: A Cultural History.* New Jersey: Prentice Hall, 2003.

Marx, Karl. *Capital: A Critique of Political Economy.* Vol. 1. Trans. Ben Fowkes. 1976. London: Penguin Books, 1990.

Maslowski, Peter. *Armed with Cameras: The American Military Photographers of World War II.* New York: Free Press, 1993.

Matthews, Jean V. *The Rise of the New Woman: The Women's Movement in America, 1875–1930.* Chicago: Ivan R. Dee, 2003.

McClellen, Edwin North. "Ahaaina or Luau in Old Hawaii." *Paradise of the Pacific* 52, no. 1 (January 1940): 9–12, 25.

McClintock, Anne. *Imperial Leather: Race, Gender, and Sexuality in the Colonial Context.* New York: Routledge, 1995.

McGregor, Davianna Pōmaika'i. *Nā Kua'āina: Living Hawaiian Culture.* Honolulu: University of Hawai'i Press, 2007.

McGregor-Alegado, Davianna. "Hawaiians: Organizing in the 1970s." *Amerasia Journal* 7 (1980): 29–55.

McLane, George H. "Hawai'i—49th State by '49?" In *Hawai'i Chronicles III: World War Two in Hawai'i, from the Pages of Paradise of the Pacific.* Ed. Bob Dye, 337–41. Honolulu: University of Hawai'i Press, 2000.

McNaughton, James C. "Hawaiians in World War II." Command Historian, Defense Language Institute, Foreign Language Center, Presidio of Monterey, 25 May 2000.

McRobbie, Angela. *Feminism and Youth Culture.* London: Routledge, 2000.

———. *In the Culture Society: Art, Fashion, and Popular Music.* London: Routledge, 1999.

Mellen, Kathleen Dickenson. "Honolulu's First Lady." *Paradise of the Pacific* 63, no. 12 (December 1952): 36–38, 119.

Meyer, Manulani Aluli. *Ho'oulu: Our Time of Becoming.* Honolulu: 'Ai Pōhaku, 2003.

Middleton, Scudder. *Dining, Wining and Dancing in New York.* New York: Dodge, 1938.

Mitchell, Timothy. *Colonising Egypt*. Berkeley: University of California Press, 1991.

Mookini, Esther K. *The Hawaiian Newspapers*. Honolulu: Topgallant, 1974.

Moorehead, Alan. *The Fatal Impact: An Account of the Invasion of the South Pacific, 1767–1840*. London: H. Hamilton, 1966.

Morales, Rodney, ed. *Hoʻihoʻi Hou: A Tribute to George Helm and Kimo Mitchell*. Honolulu: Bamboo Ridge, 1984.

Moses, L. G. *Wild West Shows and the Images of American Indians, 1883–1933*. Albuquerque: University of New Mexico Press, 1996.

Murayama, Milton. *All I Asking for Is My Body*. Honolulu: University of Hawaii Press, 1988.

Musick, John R. *Hawaii: Our New Possessions, an Account of Travels and Adventure, with . . . an Appendix Containing the Treaty of Annexation to the United States*. New York: Funk and Wagnalls, 1898.

Nasaw, Paul. *Going Out: The Rise and Fall of Public Amusements*. Cambridge: Harvard University Press, 1999.

Ngai, Mae M. "Transnationalism and the Transformation of the 'Other': Response to the Presidential Address." *American Quarterly* 57, no. 1 (2005): 59–65.

Noble, Gurre Ploner. *Hula Blues: The Story of Johnny Noble, Hawaii, Its Music and Musicians*. Honolulu: Tongg, 1948.

Nogelmeier, M. Puakea, and Amy Kuʻuleialoha Stillman. Introduction to *Buke Mele Lāhui: Book of National Songs*, xiii–xvii. Honolulu: University of Hawaiʻi Press, 2003.

Nordyke, Eleanor C., and Martha H. Noyes. "Kaulana Nā Pua: A Voice for Sovereignty." *Hawaiian Journal of History* 27 (1993): 27–42.

Okihiro, Gary Y. *Cane Fires: The Anti-Japanese Movement in Hawaii, 1865–1945*. Philadelphia: Temple University Press, 1991.

Osorio, Jonathan Kay Kamakawiwoʻole. *Dismembering Lāhui: A History of the Hawaiian Nation to 1887*. Honolulu: University of Hawaiʻi Press, 2002.

Participation in the Alaska-Yukon-Pacific Exposition. Washington: Government Printing Office, 1911.

Partlow, Leo L. "The Merry Monarch of Hawaii." *Asia: The Journal of the American Asiatic Association* 32 (1932): 73–79, 131–32.

Pease, Donald E. "New Perspectives on U.S. Culture and Imperialism." In *Cultures of United States Imperialism*. Ed. Amy Kaplan and Donald E. Pease, 22–37. Durham: Duke University Press, 1993.

Peiss, Kathy Lee. *Cheap Amusements: Working Women and Leisure in New York City, 1880 to 1920*. Philadelphia: Temple University Press, 1985.

Pinney, Christopher. *Camera Indica: The Social Life of Indian Photographs*. Chicago: University of Chicago Press, 1997.

———. "Classification and Fantasy in the Photographic Construction of Caste and Tribe." *Visual Anthropology* 3, no. 2 and 3 (1990): 259–88.

Pratt, Julius W. *Expansionists of 1898: The Acquisition of Hawaii and the Spanish Islands*. Baltimore: Johns Hopkins University Press, 1936.

Pukui, Mary Kawena. "Ancient Hulas of Kauai." In *Hula: Historical Perspectives*. Ed. Dorothy B. Barrère, Mary Kawena Pukui, and Marion Kelly, 74–89. Honolulu: Bishop Museum, 1980.

———. "The Hula, Hawaii's Own Dance." In *Hula: Historical Perspectives*. Ed. Dorothy B. Barrère, Mary Kawena Pukui, and Marion Kelly, 70–73. Honolulu: Bishop Museum, 1980.

———, trans. *Nā Mele Welo: Songs of Our Heritage*. Honolulu: Bishop Museum, 1995.

———. "Songs (Meles) of Old Ka'u, Hawaii." *Journal of American Folkore* 62, no. 245 (1949): 247–58.

Pukui, Mary Kawena, and Samuel H. Elbert. *Hawaiian Dictionary: Revised and Enlarged Edition*. Honolulu: University of Hawaii Press, 1986.

Pukui, Mary Kawena, Samuel H. Elbert, and Esther T. Mookini. *Place Names of Hawaii*. Rev. ed. Honolulu: University Press of Hawaii, 1974.

Pukui, Mary Kawena, E. W. Haertig, and Catherine A. Lee. *Nānā i Ke Kumu (Look to the Source)*. Vol. 1. 1979. Honolulu: Queen Lili'uokalani Children's Center, 2001.

Quigg, Agnes. "Kalakaua's Hawaiian Studies Abroad Program." *Hawaiian Journal of History* 22 (1988): 170–208.

Rafael, Vicente L. *White Love and Other Events in Filipino History*. Durham: Duke University Press, 2000.

Raibmon, Paige. *Authentic Indians: Episodes of Encounter from the Late-Nineteenth-Century Northwest Coast*. Durham: Duke University Press, 2005.

Ralston, Caroline. "Ordinary Women in Early Post-Contact Hawaii." In *Family and Gender in the Pacific: Domestic Contradictions and the Colonial Impact*. Ed. Margaret Jolly and Martha MacIntyre, 45–64. Cambridge: Cambridge University Press, 1989.

Ritte, Walter, and Bill Freese. "Haloa." *Seedling* (October 2006): 11–14.

Roach, Joseph. *Cities of the Dead: Circum-Atlantic Performance*. New York: Columbia University Press, 1996.

Rony, Fatimah Tobing. *The Third Eye: Race, Cinema, and Ethnographic Spectacle*. Durham: Duke University Press, 1996.

Rosa, John P. "Local Story: The Massie Case Narrative and the Cultural Production of Local Identity in Hawai'i." *Amerasia Journal* 26, no. 2 (2000): 93–116.

Rosaldo, Renalto. *Culture and Truth*. Boston: Beacon, 1989.

Rowland, Donald. "The Establishment of the Republic of Hawaii, 1893–1894." *Pacific Historical Review* 4, no. 3 (September 1935): 201–20.

Rydell, Robert W. *All the World's a Fair: Visions of Empire at American*

International Expositions, 1876–1916. Chicago: University of Chicago Press, 1984.

Rydell, Robert W., John E. Findling, and Kimberly D. Pelle. *Fair America: World's Fairs in America.* Washington: Smithsonian Institution, 2000.

Rydell, Robert W., and Rob Kroes. *Buffalo Bill in Bologna: The Americanization of the World, 1869–1922.* Chicago: University of Chicago Press, 2005.

Sahlins, Marshall. *Islands of History.* Chicago: University of Chicago Press, 1985.

Said, Edward. *Orientalism.* New York: Vintage, 1978.

Schmitt, Robert C. *Demographic Statistics of Hawaii: 1778–1965.* Honolulu: University of Hawaii Press, 1968.

———. "Table 26. Ethnic Stock: 1900–1960." In *Demographic Statistics of Hawaii: 1778–1965,* 120. Honolulu: University of Hawaii Press, 1968.

Schorman, Rob. *Selling Style: Clothing and Social Change at the Turn of the Century.* Philadelphia: University of Pennsylvania Press, 2003.

Scott, James C. *Domination and the Arts of Resistance: Hidden Transcripts.* New Haven: Yale University Press, 1990.

Sereno, Aeko. "Images of the Hula Dancer and 'Hula Girl': 1778–1960." Ph.D. diss., University of Hawai'i, 1990.

Severa, Joan L. *Dressed for the Photographer: Ordinary Americans and Fashion, 1840–1900.* Kent, Ohio: Kent State University Press, 1995.

Shay, Anthony, and Barbara Sellers-Young, eds. *Belly Dance: Orientalism, Transnationalism and Harem Fantasy.* Costa Mesa: Mazda, 2005.

Shea Murphy, Jacqueline. *The People Have Never Stopped Dancing: Native American Modern Dance Histories.* Minneapolis: University of Minnesota Press, 2007.

Silva, Kīhei de. *He Aloha Moku o Keawe: A Collection of Songs for Hawai'i, Island of Keawe.* Kailua: Kīhei de Silva, 1999.

Silva, Noenoe K. *Aloha Betrayed: Native Hawaiian Resistance to American Colonialism.* Durham: Duke University Press, 2004.

———. "He Kānāwai E Ho'opau I Na Hula Kuolo Hawai'i: The Political Economy of Banning the Hula." *Hawaiian Journal of History* 34 (2000): 29–48.

Silva, Wendell, and Alan Suemori, eds. *Nānā i Nā Loea Hula: Look to the Hula Resources.* Honolulu: Kalihi-Palama Culture and Arts Society, 1984.

Smith, Bernard. *European Vision and the South Pacific: 1768–1850.* Oxford: Clarendon, 1960.

———. *Imagining the Pacific: In the Wake of the Cook Voyages.* New Haven: Yale University Press, 1992.

Smith, Linda Tuhiwai. *Decolonizing Methodologies: Research and Indigenous Peoples.* Dunedin: University of Otago Press, 1999.

Smith, Shawn Michelle. *Photography on the Color Line: W. E. B. Du Bois, Race, and Visual Culture*. Durham: Duke University Press, 2004.

Snyder, Robert W. *The Voice of the City: Vaudeville and Popular Culture in New York*. New York: Oxford University Press, 1989.

Stannard, David E. *Before the Horror: The Population of Hawai'i on the Eve of Western Contact*. Honolulu: Social Science Research Institute, University of Hawaii, 1989.

———. *Honor Killing: Race, Rape, and Clarence Darrow's Spectacular Last Case*. New York: Penguin, 2006.

Steichen, Edward. *Power in the Pacific: A Navy Picture Record Compiled by Capt. Edward Steichen, USNR*. New York: Museum of Modern Art, 1945.

———. *U.S. Navy War Photographs: Pearl Harbor to Tokyo Bay*. New York: U.S. Camera, 1946.

Stern, Bernard W. *The Aloha Trade: Labor Relations in Hawaii's Hotel Industry, 1941–1987*. Honolulu: University of Hawaii, College of Continuing Education and Community Service, Center for Labor Education and Research, 1988.

Stevens, John Leavitt, and W. B. Olesen. *Picturesque Hawaii: A Charming Description of Her Unique History, Strange People, Exquisite Climate, Wondrous Volcanoes, Luxurious Productions, Beautiful Cities, Corrupt Monarchy, Recent Revolution and Provisional Government*. Philadelphia: Hubbard, 1894.

Stevenson, Robert Louis. *The Letters of Robert Louis Stevenson: Volume 6, August 1887–September 1890*. Ed. Bradford A. Booth and Ernest Mehew. New Haven: Yale University Press, 1994.

———. *Travels in Hawaii*. Honolulu: University Press of Hawaii, 1973.

Stewart, Susan. *On Longing: Narratives of the Miniature, the Gigantic, the Souvenir, the Collection*. Durham: Duke University Press, 1993.

Stillman, Amy K. "History Reinterpreted in Song: The Case of the Hawaiian Counterrevolution." *Hawaiian Journal of History* 23 (1989): 1–30.

Stillman, Amy Kuʻuleialoha. "'Aloha Aina': New Perspectives on 'Kaulana Nā Pua.'" *Hawaiian Journal of History* 33 (1999): 83–99.

———. "Hawaiian Hula Competitions." *Journal of American Folklore* 109, no. 434 (autumn 1996): 357–80.

———. "The Hula Kuʻi: A Tradition in Hawaiian Music and Dance." M.A. thesis, University of Hawaii, 1982.

———. "Of the People Who Love the Land: Vernacular History in the Poetry of Modern Hawaiian Hula." *Amerasia Journal* 28, no. 3 (2002): 85–108.

———. "Passed into the Present: Women in Hawaiian Entertainment." In *Asian/Pacific Islander American Women: A Historical Anthology*. Ed. Shirley Hune and Gail M. Nomura, 205–20. New York: New York University Press, 2003.

———. *Sacred Hula: The Historical Hula 'Āla'apapa*. Honolulu: Bishop Museum, 1998.

Stoler, Ann Laura. *Carnal Knowledge and Imperial Power: Race and the Intimate in Colonial Rule*. Berkeley: University of California Press, 2010.

———. "Colonial Archives and the Arts of Governance." *Archival Science* 2 (2002): 87–109.

———, ed. *Haunted by Empire: Geographies of Intimacy in North American History*. Durham: Duke University Press, 2006.

Tagg, John. *The Burden of Representation: Essays on Photographies and Histories*. 1988. Minneapolis: University of Minnesota Press, 1993.

Tatar, Elizabeth. *Strains of Change: The Impact of Tourism on Hawaiian Music*. Honolulu: Bishop Museum, 1987.

Tate, Merze. *The United States and the Hawaiian Kingdom: A Political History*. New Haven: Yale University Press, 1965.

Taylor, Diana. *The Archive and the Repertoire: Performing Cultural Memory in the Americas*. Durham: Duke University Press, 2003.

Teaiwa, Teresia K. "bikinis and other s/pacific n/oceans." *Contemporary Pacific* 6, no. 1 (1994): 87–109.

———. "Militarism, Tourism and the Native: Articulations in Oceania." Ph.D. diss., University of California, Santa Cruz, 2001.

———. "Reading Paul Gauguin's Noa Noa with Epeli Hau'ofa's *Kisses in the Nederends*: Militourism, Feminism, and The 'Polynesian Body.'" In *Inside Out: Literature, Cultural Politics, and Identity in the New Pacific*. Ed. Vilsoni Hereniko and Rob Wilson, 249–63. Oxford: Rowman and Littlefield, 1999.

Te Awekotuku, Ngahuia. *Mana Wahine Maori: Selected Writings on Maori Women's Art, Culture, and Politics*. Auckland: New Women's, 1991.

Thomas, Nicholas. *Colonialism's Culture: Anthropology, Travel, and Government*. Princeton: Princeton University Press, 1994.

———. *Entangled Objects: Exchange, Material Culture, and Colonialism in the Pacific*. Cambridge: Harvard University Press, 1991.

Thompson, E. P. *The Making of the English Working Class*. New York: Vintage Books, 1963.

Thompson, Lanny. "Representation and Rule in the Imperial Archipelago: Cuba, Puerto Rico, Hawai'i, and the Philippines under U.S. Dominion after 1898." *American Studies Asia* 1 (2002): 3–39.

Thrum, Thomas G. *Hawaiian Almanac and Annual*. Honolulu: Black and Auld, 1900.

Thurston, Lorrin A. *Memoirs of the Hawaiian Revolution*. Ed. Andrew Farrell. Honolulu: Advertising Publishing, 1936.

———. *Writings of Lorrin A. Thurston*. Ed. Andrew Farrell. Honolulu: Advertising Publishing, 1936.

Todaro, Tony. *The Golden Years of Hawaiian Entertainment.* Honolulu: Tony Todaro, 1974.

———. "Island Personalities: Mama and Daddy Bray." *Paradise of the Pacific* 66 (holiday 1954): 114–16.

Topolinski, John Kaha'i. "The Hula." In *Hawaiian Music and Musicians: An Illustrated History.* Ed. George S. Kanahele, 146–53. Honolulu: University Press of Hawaii, 1979.

Trask, Haunani-Kay. "The Birth of the Modern Hawaiian Movement: Kalama Valley, O'ahu." *Hawaiian Journal of History* 21 (1987): 126–53.

———. *From a Native Daughter: Colonialism and Sovereignty in Hawai'i.* 1993. Honolulu: University of Hawai'i Press, 1999.

Troutman, John W. *Indian Blues: American Indians and the Politics of Music, 1879–1934.* Norman: University of Oklahoma Press, 2009.

Truettner, William, ed. *The West as America: Reinterpreting Images of the Frontier, 1820–1920.* Washington: Smithsonian Institution, 1991.

Visweswaran, Kamala. *Fictions of Feminist Ethnography.* Minneapolis: University of Minnesota Press, 1994.

Weiner, Annette. *Inalienable Possessions: The Paradox of Keeping-While-Giving.* Berkeley: University of California Press, 1992.

Wexler, Laura. *Tender Violence: Domestic Visions in an Age of U.S. Imperialism.* Chapel Hill: University of North Carolina Press, 2000.

Whitney, Caspar. *Hawaiian America: Something of Its History, Resources, and Prospects.* New York: Harper and Brothers, 1899.

Williams, Raymond. *Marxism and Literature.* Oxford: Oxford University Press, 1977.

———. *Problems in Materialism and Culture: Selected Essays.* London: Verso, 1980.

Williams, William Appleman. *Empire as a Way of Life: An Essay on the Causes and Character of America's Present Predicament, along with a Few Thoughts about an Alternative.* New York: Oxford University Press, 1980.

———. *The Tragedy of American Diplomacy.* 1959. New York: W. W. Norton, 1988.

Yellin, Emil. *Our Mothers' War: American Women at Home and at the Front during World War II.* New York: Free Press, 2004.

Yost, Harold H. "Hawaii's Leading Crop of the Future." *Paradise of the Pacific* 34, no. 4 (April 1921): 27.

Young, Lucien. *The Boston at Hawaii; Or, the Observations and Impressions of a Naval Officer during a Stay of Fourteen Months in Those Islands on a Man-of-War.* Washington: Gibson Bros., 1898.

Zimmerman, Patricia R. *Reel Families: A Social History of Amateur Film.* Bloomington: Indiana University Press, 1995.

INDEX

"Across the Sea," 178, 180, 318n102
activism. *See* political activism
Admissions Act of 1959, 260
Afghanistan War, 218, 245, 261
African American soldiers, 231–32,
     326n35
aha'aina, 239–41
"Ahi Wela," 125, 305n72
Ahutoru, 67
Ai, Olana, 9, 331n2
"Aia i Hilo One," 145
Aiala (dancer), 44, 45f, 79, 284n39
Aila, Louis, 239–40
Aiu, Maiki, 263–64
"Akahi Hoi," 124, 306n74
Akaka, Akaiko, 8, 276n25
Akaka, Daniel, 257
Akaka Bill, 255–57, 331n3
Alama, Leilani, 249, 330n124
Alapa'i, Ralph Ka'ōnohiokalā, 8
Alaska, 184
Alaska-Yukon-Pacific Exposition of
     Seattle, 126, 269, 310n158
"Alekoki," 224
Alfred, Duke of Edinburgh, 97
ali'i. *See* chiefs
Allen, Steve, 209
Alloula, Malek, 78
"Aloha 'Āina," 301n6
"aloha" (as term), 8–9; as hospitality,

9–12, 276nn38–40, 278n43; as
     mutuality, 260–61
Aloha Betrayed (Silva), 64, 300n4
Aloha Maids, 153–54, 155f, 170–80,
     191; private lives of, 188, 190, 193,
     201; wages of, 174, 191, 193, 316n64,
     320n130
"Aloha 'Oe," 101–2, 123, 249, 300n180,
     305n72
Alohikea, William, 114, 115f, 151
Aloma, Hal, 191, 193, 317n81
alternative politics. *See* counter-colonial
     tactics of hula
Althusser, Louis, 17
American Guild of Variety Artists
     (AGVA), 193
American Indians: assimilation of,
     131, 308n117; dance performances
     of, 74, 294n66; European tours of,
     99; imagemaking of, 138, 300n136;
     musical performance of, 114;
     photographic records of, 229, 328n72
American Tragedy, An (Dreiser), 241
Ampey, Lulika Ferris. *See* Ferris, Lulika
Annexation Club, 62
Apaka, Alfred, 247, 249
Army Signal Corps, 226–28, 237, 327n54
Asians in Hawai'i, 5, 10, 27, 108–10,
     185–88, 222–23
Astor, Vincent, 177

Adria L. Imada is associate professor of ethnic studies
at the University of California, San Diego.

Library of Congress Cataloging-in-Publication Data
Imada, Adria L. (Adria Lyn)
Aloha America : hula circuits through the U.S.
empire / Adria L. Imada.
p. cm.
Includes bibliographical references and index.
ISBN 978-0-8223-5196-2 (cloth : alk. paper)
ISBN 978-0-8223-5207-5 (pbk. : alk. paper)
1. Hula (Dance)—Social aspects. 2. Hula (Dance)—
Political aspects. 3. Hawaii—Relations—United
States. 4. United States—Relations—Hawaii. I. Title.
GV1796.H8I43 2012
784.18'87—dc23   2011053299

Made in the USA
San Bernardino, CA
28 January 2020